The imperial premiership

Manchester University Press

The imperial premiership

The role of the modern Prime Minister in foreign policy making, 1964–2015

Sam Goodman

Manchester University Press

Copyright © Sam Goodman 2016

The right of Sam Goodman to be identified as the author of this work has been asserted by him in accordance with the Copyright, Designs and Patents Act 1988.

Published by Manchester University Press
Altrincham Street, Manchester M1 7JA

www.manchesteruniversitypress.co.uk

British Library Cataloguing-in-Publication Data
A catalogue record for this book is available from the British Library

Library of Congress Cataloging-in-Publication Data applied for

ISBN   978 1 5261 0901 9 paperback

First published 2016

The publisher has no responsibility for the persistence or accuracy of URLs for any external or third-party internet websites referred to in this book, and does not guarantee that any content on such websites is, or will remain, accurate or appropriate.

Typeset
by Toppan Best-set Premedia Limited
Printed in Great Britain
by Bell and Bain Ltd, Glasgow

Contents

Foreword by the Rt Hon. Lord Owen	vi
Acknowledgements	xiii
Timeline	xv
Introduction	1
Prologue	5
1 Harold Wilson, 1964–70	35
2 Ted Heath, 1970–74	61
3 Harold Wilson, 1974–76	85
4 James Callaghan, 1976–79	103
5 Margaret Thatcher, 1979–90	113
6 John Major, 1990–97	147
7 Tony Blair, 1997–2007	173
8 Gordon Brown, 2007–10	231
9 David Cameron, 2010–15	261
Conclusion	309
Epilogue	315
Bibliography	325
Index	349

Foreword

In terms of reversing the trend towards an imperial premiership there is no greater action that can be taken than for Members of Parliament to use their power to remove the leader of their party when that leader is also Prime Minister.

On four occasions over the last century Members of Parliament have removed British Prime Ministers from power. In all four cases the seeds of their downfall lay in foreign policy: Lloyd George in 1922 following the Treaty of Paris; Neville Chamberlain in 1939 after appeasement of Hitler; Margaret Thatcher in 1990 after the three 'no's on the EU; and Tony Blair in 2007, over Lebanon after the Israeli attack. All four Prime Ministers, after an initial period of good governance, had put an ever increasing emphasis on the centralisation of power within 10 Downing Street, on the diminution of the power of Cabinet colleagues and developing a contemptuous attitude to their own MPs. These three characteristics, as this book credibly demonstrates, are all aspects of an imperial premiership. They are also part of the fourteen signs and symptoms of Hubris Syndrome.[1]

What of removing or censuring Prime Ministers whose conduct is such that the House of Commons as a whole wishes to register their disapproval? A vote of censure through a nominal reduction in salary is an existing sanction, but of no effect when the individual has left Parliament. Should we retain the present mechanism, perhaps modified, of impeachment which has been left on the shelf still capable of being revived? Or can there be in its place a mechanism to deter lying built on contempt of Parliament? Just as lying is contempt of court and a very serious offence, should not contempt of Parliament likewise be a very serious offence?

It is a sad fact that Anthony Eden's lie to the House of Commons on 20 December 1956 when winding up the debate still stands uncorrected in Hansard where he said 'I want to say this on the question of foreknowledge, and to say it quite bluntly to the House that there was not foreknowledge that Israel would attack Egypt'. Eden never returned to the House of Commons. His Cabinet knew he had lied. His Chief Whip, Edward Heath, wrote in his book, 'I felt like burying my head in my hands' as the man he admired maintained this 'fiction'.[2]

Eden resigned from the House of Commons in early January 1957 and there was a genuine feeling that his conduct in large part was due to ill health. The Suez invasion, however, left lasting damage to Parliament's credibility in failing to bring the Cabinet's decision-making, judged illegal by its own law officers, to account. For many years very few people even knew that Parliament had been lied to. There was a total refusal to establish an official inquiry. When the Cabinet minutes of 23 October were eventually revealed, under the thirty-year rule, it was discovered in an annexe that the Cabinet were told about the collusion with Israel by the Prime Minister. 'From secret conversations which had been held in Paris with representatives of the Israeli Government, it now appeared that the Israelis would not alone launch a full scale attack against Egypt. The United Kingdom and French Governments were thus confronted with the choice between an early military operation or a relatively prolonged operation.'

It was a huge error of judgement that the Conservative Government of Harold Macmillan, who replaced Eden, refused Parliament's request on a cross-party basis for an inquiry into Suez. My own individual protest to the Suez crisis came when Selwyn Lloyd was voted in as Speaker in 1971. Selwyn Lloyd had been Foreign Secretary throughout the Suez crisis. The fact that he turned out to be a good Speaker was irrelevant. As a fairly new MP I voted against him because he had been complicit in Eden lying to the House of Commons and I felt then and still feel today that fact should have excluded him from being Speaker.

Whether or not Tony Blair committed an impeachable offence in 2002 and 2003 before the military invasion of Iraq can only be determined by a Select Committee of senior parliamentarians taking into account, but not governed by, the Chilcot Report. A Select Committee, perhaps the body consisting of all the chairmen of the Select Committees rather than just the Procedure Committee, will have before it the long overdue Chilcot Report published on 6 July 2016. But more documents may become available from the USA by September/October, the earliest time they can be expected to reach a verdict. In October 2015, for example, a cache of emails held on a private server by Hillary Clinton, the former US Secretary of State, were released on orders from the US courts and one of these was written by Colin L. Powell, then US Secretary of State, in March 2002 to President Bush. This internal US document would never have been expected to have been available to the Chilcot Inquiry who were only promised all UK documents, summaries of meetings and telephone conversations. This is an unexpected and important insight, therefore, into Blair's thinking. It is what the Americans call a 'heads up' on the 'Subject. Your Meeting with United Kingdom Prime Minister Tony Blair, April 5–7 at Crawford'. The key paragraph is the opening one:

> Blair continues to stand by you and the US as we move forward on the war on terrorism and on Iraq. He will present to you the strategic, tactical and public affairs lines that he believes will strengthen global support for our common cause.

As long ago as 2 February 1906 Lord Sanderson, just retired as the senior diplomat in charge of the Foreign Office, wrote an internal memorandum that touched on impeachment in circumstances that have many parallels. Describing his call on the French Ambassador M. Cambon, which he had undertaken on the instructions of the Foreign Secretary, Sir Edward Grey, after taking with him a copy of Sir Edward's own account of the meeting the previous day, the two men compared notes. Sanderson wrote

> as I was no longer an official, I might speak to him quite freely...on my own personal views....I told him that I thought that if the Cabinet were to give a pledge which would morally bind the country to go to war in certain circumstances, and were not to mention this pledge to Parliament, and if at the expiration of some months the country suddenly found itself pledged to war in consequence of this assurance, the case would be one which would justify impeachment, and which might even result in that course unless at the time the feeling of the country were very strongly in favour of the course to which the Government was pledged.[3]

Over the centuries the Civil Service has had to face the dilemma of ministers lying to Parliament and there is no easy answer. Selwyn Lloyd's Private Secretary, Donald Logan, who had been present at both meetings at Sevres, where collusion with Israel and France was planned, was asked by Peter Hennessy what he thought of Eden's statement to the House of Commons on collusion.

> Hennessy: You don't regard lying in the House of Commons as a cardinal sin on the part of an elected politician?
> Logan: Whatever I may think it is I think for ministers to decide their own conduct in the House of Commons and the public to judge ministers on their performance.[4]

Sanderson's criteria of an impeachable offence should be the text for assessing Blair's conduct.

It is almost farcical that Parliament will only have been allowed to see such limited quotes in the Chilcot Report from Blair to Bush which the British Cabinet Secretary, Sir Jeremy Heywood – a person who served in Blair's private office in No. 10 during the period of the Iraq War under scrutiny – gave Chilcot permission to publish, not necessarily what the Inquiry may have wished to publish. The Cabinet Secretary assumed a power to censor as if the Inquiry had not been vested with the power to decide by the Prime Minister Gordon Brown when he established the Iraq Inquiry that Parliament had repeatedly demanded. There was no doubt that all British statements would be available to the Inquiry, but obviously not American.

'Disingenuous' was the word used to describe Blair's conduct by the former Cabinet Secretary, Lord Butler, in his speech in the House of Lords.[5] What should Parliament do? Blair, though no longer in Parliament, can still be ordered by the Speaker to stand before him at the bar of the House of Commons to hear the Speaker read out a statement defining the charge which needs to relate to conduct bringing the House into disrepute. Then Blair would have to read out a formal apology agreed with the Speaker beforehand. If that procedure for any reason is not used then a modified form of impeachment may have to be considered. This is irrespective of any action taken by relatives of soldiers in the civil courts or by the International Criminal Court.

The Chilcot verdict had clearly been deliberately delayed in the hope that time alone would defuse the issues. But the verdict had, to a considerable extent, already been delivered in the published oral evidence to Chilcot. Blair's Foreword to the document published on 24 September 2002 had been examined for its veracity. The Foreword had been established as being Blair's own document and different to the document itself, *Iraq's Weapons of Mass Destruction: The Assessment of the British Government*, which was the responsibility of the government as a whole. John Scarlett, then Chairman of the Joint Intelligence Committee, in his evidence disowned responsibility for the content and language of the Foreword. In the document Blair's Foreword stated 'What I believe the assessed intelligence has established beyond doubt is that Saddam has continued to produce chemical and biological weapons, that he continues in his efforts to develop nuclear weapons and that he has been able to extend the range of his ballistic missile programme…' Any fair-minded reading of the questioning by Sir Roderic Lyne, a member of the Iraq Inquiry, of Major General Michael Laurie, a senior member of the Defence Intelligence Staff, confirms that Blair's Foreword was not a justifiable encapsulation.

It is a sound judgement of the author of this fascinating and important book to highlight in his Prologue the debate of 29 August 2013 when David Cameron became the first Prime Minister in 150 years to lose a vote in the House of Commons on an issue of military deployment.

That vote, against bombing President Assad's forces in Syria without UN legal authority, will have done much to check the growth of an imperial premiership. The author's description of the political to-ing and fro-ing at Westminster as MPs were recalled from their summer holiday is excellent. It may be correct that the decision was to some extent inadvertent, but the vote happened and it needed to happen. President Obama looked less than enthusiastic about the planned military action, which never appeared to have the necessary strategic underpinning. Rather it appeared as reaction from a President self-impaled on the rhetorical use of the words 'red line' in relation to chemical weapons. Despite protestations to the contrary, MPs on a cross-party basis sensed that UK action was being lined up without Security Council authority so that UK forces could be seen to strike at exactly the same time as the US, for presentational rather than operational reasons. The doubts expressed by the then Leader of the Official Opposition, Ed Miliband, were prescient and he deserves praise not criticism. Nor were they unprecedented. The Suez crisis, as it gathered momentum through the summer of 1956, was a time in recent history when Hugh Gaitskell, the Labour Party leader in opposition, grew ever more critical about supporting Prime Minister Eden's ill-fated and illegal adventure.

In 2010 the developing situation in and around Benghazi in Libya had appeared to be a clear case for a humanitarian military intervention and I was one of the first to call for the imposition of a NATO no-fly zone. Ed Miliband, as Leader of the Opposition, talked to me at the time and I mentioned that Hugh Gaitskell had been damaged by initially supporting and then appearing to pull back and that the Leader of the Opposition had little room for manoeuvre after initially supporting. So support should only be given if it was pretty certain it could be maintained. The Libyan intervention turned out an abysmal failure because there was no readiness to put NATO troops on the ground on which NATO in the air could rely. Yet the bombing continued with little recognition that the damage being done to infrastructure in particular was such as to bring chaos when Gaddafi's authority collapsed. There was too little regard for the tribal history of Libya and insufficient negotiation and pausing of the bombing. Russia and China, who had reluctantly decided to abstain in the Security Council, found themselves aligned with regime change. It was foolish for the USA, UK and France not to call together the Russian/NATO Council as I argued for at the time. In that body military to military exchanges could have explained why Gaddafi could not be ring-fenced to survive as leader when he fought to maintain total control.

The situation in Syria by 2013 was redolent with memories of Libya and bedevilled by the number of separate Sunni military forces, to some of whom it was very hard to justify giving weapons. It had been known for some time that the more acceptable elements to whom one could have supplied arms had links with more undesirable elements. With arms passing to and fro the ineffectiveness of bombing just for retaliation purposes relating to Assad's use of chemical weapons was very hard to justify. Also there was the potential problem of the so-called Islamic State building up in Iraq, but with aims to spread into Syria and the Levant. Abu Musab al-Zarqwi, the founder of ISIL, had begun to build his insurgency operation in Iraq in 2003. He was killed in 2006 by a US air strike, but ISIL continued and by the time the USA had pulled back from Iraq in 2011, ISIL, under its new leader Abu Bakr al-Baghdadi, was starting to quietly expand into Syria.

If President Obama had gone ahead with the limited bombing in late August 2013 on Assad in Syria it would have been a bombing campaign that would likely have weakened Assad but without toppling him. That intervention would also have been blamed for the later build-up of ISIL forces. In June 2014 ISIL made world news headlines by taking Mosul in Iraq and capturing US weaponry in large numbers. ISIL having built up their strength even further in Iraq then took Palmyra in Syria in 2015.

It was not foolish for the House of Commons to initially make a distinction between Iraq, where RAF bombers from Cyprus had been invited by the recognised government to bomb ISIL forces, and Syria where military action was not invited, and was based on retaliation against Assad but not removing him. A far better course was on hand, namely for chemical weapons to be negotiated out of Syria which was begun within days of the House of Commons vote under an initial Russian/American agreement. Deplorably, despite this, Assad was still using chlorine in 2015, though not as lethal as sarin gas. Russia should have called Assad to account for this.

Having supported military interventions in Iraq, in Afghanistan and Libya, all of which failed, many MPs were not ready to support another failure over Syria in 2013. The House of Commons on a cross-party basis made the correct decision, and President Obama, within days, put the same question to the US Congress and they backed off endorsing military action, it appears also predominantly because of the absence of a real strategic policy to settle the Syrian conflict.

The attack by ISIL in Paris made a much stronger case for judging the threat from ISIL as justifying action in self-defence under Article 51 of the UN Charter. The French-drafted UN Resolution, as amended by Russia, was unanimously agreed on 20 November 2015 and the way was cleared for Parliament to agree the UK should bomb Syria. The traditional right of the UK Prime Minister with the power to declare war will never be the same again. It has become, in effect, a qualified power. There is now a political imperative to involve Parliament wherever possible. There will be democratic debate and Parliament in all but the most urgent and dire circumstances will vote before the UK goes to war. That is a major curtailment of the imperial premiership, inevitable after the 2003 Iraq War which had full authorisation by the House of Commons.

The individual chapters of this book, from Harold Wilson to David Cameron, show very clearly why the imperial premiership had to be checked. There are many valuable insights and they help bring out inescapable lessons from the past which help reinforce the case for never returning to an unqualified right to declare war. The lessons are not ones that can be easily enshrined in an Act of Parliament but they are the product of a cumulative wisdom which the electorate as a whole senses and which MPs will be determined to uphold in all but the most exceptional circumstances.

Rt Hon Lord Owen
June 2016

Notes

1 David Owen, *In Sickness and In Power: Illness in Heads of Government, Military and Business Since 1900* (London: Methuen, 2016), pp. xix–xxviii.
2 Edward Heath, *The Course of My Life* (London: Hodder & Stoughton, 1998) p. 176.
3 David Owen, *The Hidden Perspective. The Military Conversations 1906–1914* (London: Haus Publishing, 2014).
4 Peter Hennessy, *Having It So Good* (London: Allen Lane, 2006), pp. 431–453.
5 *Hansard* (HL Deb, 22 February 2007, col. 1230).

Acknowledgements

When I started my research in January 2012 I had no idea where it would lead. Over four years I have had the privilege of meeting and interviewing some of the most important people in British foreign policy from the last fifty years. It has been an education like no other. I am so grateful to everyone I interviewed, who generously gave up time from their busy schedules to talk about issues of such importance. Their thoughts, reminiscences and stories will stay with me for ever and for that I would like to thank:

Lord Robert Armstrong, Rt. Hon. Dame Margaret Beckett MP, Admiral Lord Mike Boyce, Rt. Hon. Alistair Burt MP, Lord Robin Butler, Lord Menzies Campbell, Rt. Hon. Lord Peter Carrington, Rt. Hon. Charles Clarke, General Lord Richard Dannatt, Lord Bernard Donoughue, Michael Dugher MP, Rt. Hon. Lord Charlie Falconer, Rt. Hon. Liam Fox MP, Field Marshall Lord Charles Guthrie, Rt. Hon. Lord William Hague, Rt. Hon. Lord Michael Heseltine, Rt. Hon. Geoff Hoon, Rt. Hon. Lord Michael Howard, Rt. Hon. Lord Geoffrey Howe, Rt. Hon. Lord David Howell, Rt. Hon. Lord Douglas Hurd, Rt. Hon. Sir Gerald Kaufman MP, Rt. Hon. Lord Tom King, Rt. Hon. Lord Mark Malloch-Brown, Sir David Manning, Sir Christopher Meyer, Rt. Hon. David Miliband, Lord Gus O'Donnell, Rt. Hon. Lord David Owen, Jonathan Powell, General Lord David Richards, Rt. Hon. Sir Malcolm Rifkind, Sir Nigel Sheinwald, Rt. Hon. Jack Straw, Air Marshall Lord Jock Stirrup, Field Marshall Lord Michael Walker and Sir Stephen Wall.

In addition I am very grateful to the large number of parliamentarians, civil servants, party officials and former ministers who chose to speak with me off the record and whose contributions to this book are equally important in its realisation.

I want to pay particular tribute to Lord David Owen who was supportive of this project from the start and encouraged me to further my research beyond its original scope. I would like to thank Sir David Manning and Sir Stephen Wall, who very kindly acted as intermediaries in helping me secure additional interviews. I would also like to acknowledge Lord Peter Carrington for his support and important words of wisdom to a first time author.

Much of this work was researched and written while I have been working in Parliament, first as an intern and later as a parliamentary researcher. This research would not have been possible without the encouragement and backing of those I worked for and I would like to thank Julie Cooper MP, Michael Dugher MP, Mark Hendrick MP and Jack Straw for their indispensable support.

I have found that getting up the courage to begin to write and research can often be one of the most daunting parts, and in this endeavour I was fortunate enough to have the encouragement of Daniel Sleat and Jonathan Fertig. Both advocated early on that I should reach out to the list of prestigious people that I have interviewed and make this book a reality, and for that I am extremely grateful. Dan in particular helped me secure a number of interviews which I would not otherwise have been able to secure, and for that I am in his debt.

Throughout this process I have been fortunate enough to have the advice and counsel of my father, Andrew Goodman who so generously helped edit early drafts of the book. I would also like to thank Khaled Berroum, Megan Purvis and Thomas Henderson Schwarz who each read and reviewed various sections of the book: their feedback was insightful and I appreciate all of the time they generously gave. I would also like to express special appreciation to Tom for kindly finding time to draw the Timeline and James Goodman who helped compile and edit my transcripts.

Writing and researching a book is a long and demanding process: I would also like to thank all of my friends and family for their patience over the last few years in dealing with me talking about British foreign policy non-stop; there have been frustrations along the way but to me this book has been worth it. I appreciate greatly their friendship, support and advice and would like to pay particular thanks to Dami Benbow, Hannah Catchlove, Simon Crossland, Matt Di'Salvo, Sam Gerish, Danny Higgins, Ben Hunte, Nick Jones, Danielle Kileff, Joe Newman, Matt Payne, Josh Stephens and Jon Stowell. I would also like to thank my friends in Washington DC for all their support over the years: Ingrid Gavin-Parks, John Marshall, Lenette Myers, Nishith Pandya, Timothy Robinson, Congressman Bobby Rush and Stanley Watkins. Having the pleasure to work with all of them fed the inspiration and drive to write this book.

I would like to finally thank Manchester University Press for supporting this project and helping make it become a reality.

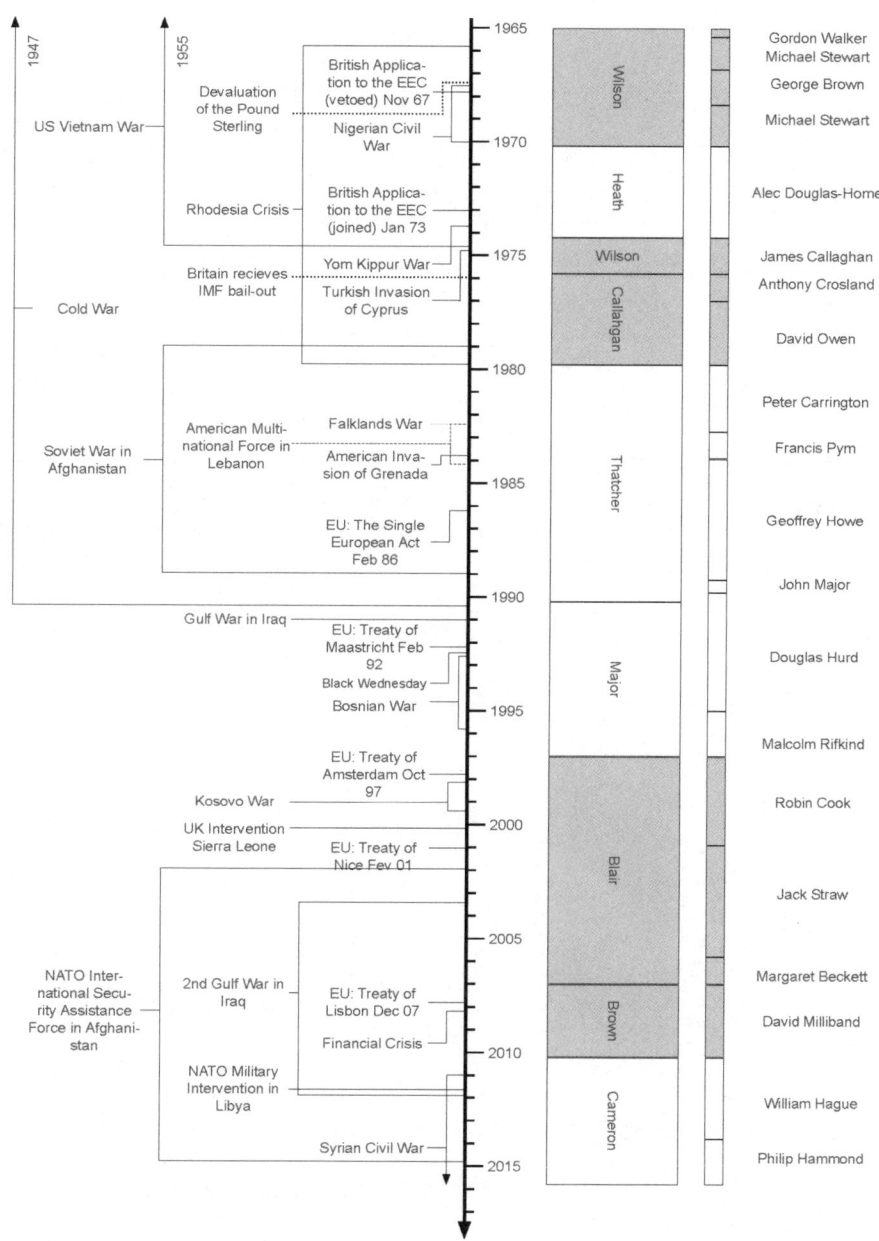

Timeline

Introduction

For the generation that grew up in the aftermath of 9/11 and the subsequent 'War on Terror', foreign policy debate and discussion have become far more common, but no better understood. Plenty of time has been spent watching television and reading papers about British troops deployed in far-off lands with nowhere near enough time spent understanding why and how they came to be *there*.

Since 2003 we in the UK have been consumed by deliberation and argument about one man's decision to commit our country to a war and the consequences of that choice. The 2003 Iraq War is to our generation what Vietnam was for our parents' generation's American counterparts. This comparison is apparent not only in its impact, but also in the way both wars are now viewed. The vast majority of people now believe that the decision to join the American led military intervention in Iraq was taken under a false premise. It has created instability in the region and disillusionment and distrust at home in how our foreign policy is decided upon and conducted.

The Vietnam War was the first time that Americans recognised the true extent of the President's dominance in foreign policy-making terms. In the same way Iraq for us reflected the first time since the Suez Crisis that we began to discuss the Prime Minister's own dominance. At the height of the war in Vietnam, Arthur M. Schlesinger wrote a book entitled *The Imperial Presidency* where he tracked the growth of presidential power in foreign policy. He concluded that, after Vietnam, American foreign policy would be severely weakened and presidents would be adverse to military ventures abroad, particularly those involving ground troops. This prediction, bar a few peacekeeping missions with minimal troops, held true right up until 2001. Schlesinger also added that without reform, this growth of the role would continue despite a period of malaise.

Schlesinger's words ring true in Britain today, where our foreign policy and prime minister is heavily constrained by a public aversion to military ventures abroad, a consequence of Iraq. This book's first premise comes from the original argument that Schlesinger made back in 1973 and the parallel with where we are now.

Despite the parallels, America and Britain are still very different. While the modern President's power flows from a written constitution, the role of the Prime Minister has grown organically through convention and precedent, and, as this book will prove, giving the individual premier freedom to act relatively unconstrained from official oversight in a way the President cannot.

Since 2011 we have had three votes on military intervention in Parliament – in Libya, Syria and Iraq, again. At the time of writing, there is the looming prospect of another vote on the question of expanding military airstrikes against Islamic State to include Syria. The role of the Prime Minister in foreign policy making has never been more topical.

The other impetus for this book came from my own experience of working in Parliament at the time of some of these foreign policy debates. Researching into the topic, I was surprised to find that no one had specifically addressed the growing role of the Prime Minister in foreign policy nor tracked its progress over the last half a century, offering an account of the individual premiers and their personal impact on our country's foreign policy.

To gain a greater understanding of this trend and present a clear and balanced view of the different prime ministers and their individual approach to foreign affairs, I decided to reach out to those who have served and worked with them and had direct involvement in the foreign affairs of the last fifty years. This distinguished group of former foreign secretaries, ambassadors, Cabinet ministers, civil servants, military chiefs, parliamentarians and party officials offered me a unique insight into the often complex nature of foreign policy decision making. This book is a culmination of thirty-seven formal primary interviews, numerous informal off-the-record interviews with individuals who have helped shape British foreign policy and countless documents from the national archives and exhaustive memoirs.

I hope to offer a unique and unprecedented insight into the competing pressures and interests a prime minister has to address in relation to foreign affairs. These interviews offer not only anecdotal evidence that brings the respective premierships to life, but demonstrate the ability of the office holder at times to shape international events through sheer idiosyncrasies.

The Imperial Premiership is underpinned by a simple idea that the Prime Minister as an individual matters and that the best way to write about the growing role of the Prime Minister in foreign policy is by assessing the premierships of the last fifty years and highlighting the personal impact each prime minister has had on key foreign policy decisions.

The book is arranged in a chronological order starting from Harold Wilson's first premiership to that of current Prime Minister David Cameron. Each chapter offers an account and analysis of the biggest foreign policy issues of their premiership, assessing the individual personal approach, looking at their relationship with the Foreign Office, other world leaders and the Cabinet as a whole.

The prologue opens with an account and analysis of the House of Commons vote on Syria on 29 August 2013, exploring the reasons why David Cameron lost the vote and the consequences that vote has had on the role of the Prime Minister in foreign policy making, as well as why this particular vote is still important today.

The book concludes with a number of observations and recommendations for the future I have drawn from my research, interviews and writing the book. They underpin the reforms I believe we need to make for balanced and effective oversight of the conduct of British foreign policy, which takes into account the indisputable importance of the personal traits and personal relationships of those who sit in No. 10 and those around them.

I hope that the content of this book offers the reader the opportunity to pause and reflect, over the premierships of the last fifty years, on where we as a country have been, and where we as a country are going.

Prologue

29 August 2013 is a date that should remain long in the memory of all serious students of foreign policy. That night, David Cameron became the first Prime Minister in 150 years to lose a vote in the House of Commons on an issue of military deployment. Not since Parliament's denouncement of Lord North's continued campaign in the American Revolutionary War has a prime minister suffered such a defeat.[1]

The Syrian civil war

The topic of debate was the authorisation for military airstrikes in Syria against the dictatorial regime of President Basher-Al Assad in response to his use of chemical weapons indiscriminately against both rebel forces and civilians. For two years, Britain, like the rest of the world, had watched as Syria descended into one of the bloodiest civil wars of recent times, prompted by similar pro-democracy protests in Egypt, Tunisia and Libya. Demonstrators called for the overthrow of the Syrian Government in the Arab Spring of 2011.

The UN Security Council was in deadlock and there appeared little western appetite to intervene. Peace talks between the conflicting sides had stalled and in a parliamentary debate, led by the Foreign Secretary William Hague, a proposal to arm the rebels had been met with strong opposition.

In the summer of 2012 in response to the Syrian regime's threats to use chemical weapons on rebel forces, President Obama issued a red line warning of US intervention should such weapons be used. This warning was ignored as the civil war continued to be waged through conventional means.

On 21 August the Assad regime used chemical weapons on three separate sites in the rebel-held areas of Ghouta and Damascus, killing at least 350 people. Images of dead children being held by their weeping mothers and the bodies of whole families caught in the wave of chemicals were beamed around the world on television and across social media.

In response the UN Security Council met in an emergency session and agreed to send a formal request for permission to be granted by the Syrian regime for UN weapon inspectors to inspect the sites of the chemical weapon attacks. The Arab League also held an emergency meeting on 27 August in Cairo, in which it condemned the attack by chemical weapons, accusing Assad of being behind it. The League called for 'the international community to take the necessary measures' against the Syrian Government, stopping short of endorsing military intervention in Syria.[2]

The 'red line' now having been crossed, President Obama found himself under pressure both internationally and domestically from hawkish members of Congress to act, despite public opinion in America being divided about intervention. From 21–27 August, Obama entered into a series of talks with key US allies discussing the possibility of building an international coalition for airstrikes.

Cameron to action

David Cameron's position on Syria was clear. For some time he had been the leading voice on the international stage calling for intervention, and a resolution of the Syrian civil war. He had raised previous concerns about the use of chemical weapons by the Assad regime; such concerns fell on deaf ears. The Prime Minister had already pledged to offer Parliament a vote on the matter. The question therefore was not if he would recall Parliament, but when.

On Wednesday 27 August he returned early from his holiday in Cornwall to chair a meeting of the National Security Council (NSC). Later that day he formally asked the Speaker of the House to recall Parliament, a week before it was due to return from its summer recess.

For many the decision to recall Parliament appeared to point to a US timetable and was not one of Cameron's own making. Cameron faced three obstacles when it came to securing parliamentary approval: his backbenchers were largely sceptical; his coalition partners the Liberal Democrats, were traditionally opposed to interventions; and the Labour Opposition leader, Ed Miliband, was under pressure from his own party to break with the tradition of consensus in foreign policy matters regarding British intervention. The Prime Minister had to cement cross-party support while at the same time attempting to build an international consensus with other countries for intervention through the EU, NATO and the UN to the tune of what was now effectively an American timetable.

Earlier the same day, the three party leaders, Prime Minister David Cameron, Deputy Prime Minister Nick Clegg, and Leader of the Opposition Ed Miliband met to discuss possible intervention in Syria, a fact later leaked to the media. All were in initial agreement on intervention, with Miliband stressing that the Government needed to demonstrate that it had exhausted all possible diplomatic efforts before doing so. Cameron had already drafted a resolution for the UN. However at 5.15 p.m. Cameron received a phone call from Miliband, who informed him that he could now not support the Government until the publication of the UN weapons inspectors' report. He also warned that if the Government pushed forward with its tabled motion his party would have to oppose it.[3]

Miliband's volte-face was the first time in modern day British politics the established convention that the Opposition Front Bench supports the Government on military intervention would be broken.

The House of Commons debate: the Government's case

Government motion on military intervention in Syria

Despite Labour's public refusal to support the Government, Cameron pressed ahead for the vote on 29 August, tabling the Government motion:

This House:
  Deplores the use of chemical weapons in Syria on 21 August 2013 by the Assad regime, which caused hundreds of deaths and thousands of injuries of Syrian civilians;
  Recalls the importance of upholding the worldwide prohibition on the use of chemical weapons under international law;
  Agrees that a strong humanitarian response is required from the international community and that this may, if necessary, require military action that is *legal, proportionate and focused* on saving lives by preventing and deterring further use of Syria's chemical weapons;
  Notes the failure of the United Nations Security Council over the last two years to take united action in response to the Syrian crisis;
  Notes that the use of chemical weapons is a war crime under customary law and a crime against humanity – and that the principle of humanitarian intervention provides a sound legal basis for taking action;
  Notes the wide international support for such a response, including the *statement from the Arab League on 27 August* which calls on the international

community, represented in the United Nations Security Council, to 'overcome internal disagreements and take action against those who committed this crime, for which the Syrian regime is responsible';

Believes, in spite of the difficulties at the United Nations, that *a United Nations process must be followed as far as possible to ensure the maximum legitimacy* for any such action;

Therefore welcomes the work of the United Nations investigating team currently in Damascus. *Whilst noting that the team's mandate is to confirm whether chemical weapons were used and not to apportion blame,* agrees that the United Nations Secretary General should ensure a briefing to the United Nations Security Council immediately upon the completion of the team's initial mission;

Believes that the United Nations Security Council must have the opportunity immediately to consider that briefing and that every effort should be made to secure a Security Council Resolution backing military action before any such action is taken. Before any direct British involvement in such action a further vote of the House of Commons will take place.

Notes that this motion relates solely to efforts to alleviate humanitarian suffering by deterring use of chemical weapons and does not sanction any action in Syria with wider objectives.

This House further notes that such action relates solely to efforts to deter the use of chemical weapons and does not sanction any wider action in Syria.[4] [author's emphasis]

Change in the Government motion and concession

On the morning of the vote in an appeal to both rebel Tory backbenchers and the Opposition, Cameron amended the Government motion at the last minute to include a qualification that British military intervention would only take place if sanctioned by the authority of a UN Security Council Vote. The new amended motion also conceded that MPs would now only be voting on the principle of military intervention and that a further vote would take place after the UN inspectors' finding.

This left many MPs confused. No. 10 that morning had been briefing that there would be one vote on the motion and now they were being told that there would be two. Many felt that this concession undermined the importance of the vote, and they would later remark in the debate that there was little point in having a debate and voting if they would be brought back the following week to do the same again, when more information would be available. The question on every MP's lips before the debate had even started was 'Why couldn't the Government wait for further developments and all the facts?'

The legal case

On the day of the vote the Attorney General, as instructed by the Prime Minister released a two-page summary of his legal advice given in Cabinet. This also happened prior to the parliamentary vote on military intervention in Libya. The UK's case for intervention rested on the Syrian Government committing war crimes, in this instance in breach of the customary international law prohibition on chemical weapons.[5] As with its Libyan Intervention, the UK would seek a resolution of the United Nations Security Council under Chapter VII of the UN Charter, being the right to protect civilians in Syria on the grounds of humanitarian intervention. The Attorney General's advice stressed that any intervention would be qualified as being 'necessary and proportionate', striking specific targets with the arm of 'deterring and disrupting any further attacks'.[6]

Intelligence

The Government also published to the media a letter from the Chairman of the Joint Intelligence Committee (JIC) describing preliminary assessments of who the Committee believed to be behind the chemical weapons attack. The letter stated that:

> There is no credible intelligence or other evidence to substantiate the claims or the possession of CW by the opposition.... We also have a limited but growing body of intelligence which supports the judgement that the regime was responsible for the attacks and that they were conducted to help clear the Opposition from strategic parts of Damascus.[7]

Against this background, the JIC concluded that it was highly likely that the regime was responsible for the chemical weapons attacks on 21 August.

In opening the debate in the Commons, David Cameron was quick to point not only to the JIC's intelligence report, but additionally to the countless pieces of evidence streamed over social media, informing the House:

> the evidence that the Syrian regime has used these weapons, in the early hours of 21 August, is right in front of our eyes. We have multiple eye-witness accounts

of chemical-filled rockets being used against opposition-controlled areas. We have thousands of social media reports and at least 95 different videos – horrific videos – documenting the evidence.[8]

He stated that the use of chemical weapons was not in contention: 'even the Iranian President said that it took place'.

The difference between Syria and Iraq

No single MP could dispel the lingering shadow of the recent war in Iraq from the chamber that evening. Nearly every MP addressed Iraq in some shape or form, with personal anecdotes or views. An observer could have been forgiven for thinking that they were witnessing a debate about the failures of Government policy in Iraq rather than the impending airstrikes on Syria.

The Prime Minister was keen to address the issue directly and early on in his speech. He strived to make clear the differences between the current matter and the 2003 invasion, when he said:

> I am deeply mindful of the lessons of previous conflicts and, in particular, of the deep concerns in the country that were caused by what went wrong with the Iraq conflict in 2003. However, this situation is not like Iraq. What we are seeing in Syria is fundamentally different. We are not invading a country. We are not searching for chemical or biological weapons. The case for ultimately supporting action – I say 'ultimately' because there would have to be another vote in this House – is not based on a specific piece or pieces of intelligence. The fact that the Syrian Government have, and have used, chemical weapons is beyond doubt. The fact that the most recent attack took place is not seriously doubted...
>
> The differences with 2003 and the situation with Iraq go wider. Then, Europe was divided over what should be done. Now, Europe is united in the view that we should not let this chemical weapons use stand. Then, NATO was divided; today, NATO has made a very clear statement that those who are responsible should be held accountable. Back in 2003, the Arab League was opposed to action; now, it is calling for it....
>
> The President of the United States, Barack Obama, is a man who opposed the action in Iraq. No one could in any way describe him as a President who wants to involve America in more wars in the Middle East, but he profoundly believes that an important red line has been crossed in an appalling way, and that is why he supports action in this case...
>
> I remember 2003. I was sitting two rows from the back on the Opposition Benches. It was just after my son had been born and he was not well, but I was determined to be here. I wanted to listen to the man who was standing right

here and believe everything that he told me. We are not here to debate those issues today, but one thing is indisputable: the well of public opinion was well and truly poisoned by the Iraq episode and we need to understand the public scepticism.[9]

Ed Miliband, as Labour leader, also wanted to make clear that this vote would not be like the one made ten years previously:

I am very clear about the fact that we have got to learn the lessons of Iraq. Of course we have got to learn those lessons, and one of the most important lessons was indeed about respect for the United Nations, and that is part of our amendment today.[10]

Labour (amendment) motion on intervention in Syria

Ed Miliband went on to propose the following:

This House expresses its revulsion at the killing of hundreds of civilians in Ghutah, Syria on 21 August 2013; believes that this was a moral outrage; recalls the importance of upholding the worldwide prohibition on the use of chemical weapons; makes clear that the use of chemical weapons is a grave breach of international law; *agrees with the UN Secretary General that the UN weapons inspectors must be able to report to the UN Security Council* and that the Security Council must live up to its responsibilities to protect civilians; supports steps to provide humanitarian protection to the people of Syria but *will only support military action involving UK forces if and when the following conditions have been met*:

1. The UN weapons inspectors, upon the conclusion of their mission in the Eastern Ghutah, being given the necessary opportunity to make a report to the Security Council on the evidence and their findings, and confirmation by them that chemical weapons have been used in Syria;
2. The production of compelling evidence that the Syrian regime was responsible for the use of these weapons;
3. The UN Security Council having considered and voted on this matter in the light of the reports of the weapons inspectors and the evidence submitted;
4. *There being a clear legal basis in international law for taking collective military action to protect the Syrian people on humanitarian grounds*;
5. *That such action must have regard to the potential consequences in the region, and must therefore be legal, proportionate, time-limited and have precise and*

achievable objectives designed to deter the future use of prohibited chemical weapons in Syria;
6. That the Prime Minister reports further to the House on the achievement of these conditions so that the House can vote on UK participation in such action.[11] [author's emphasis]

The Labour opposition to the Government motion rested on three factors, the first being one of timing, the second that of due international process, and the third, the consequences of such an intervention.

Timetable

Parliament was due to return from recess the very next week on 2 September. Many MPs therefore interpreted Cameron's decision to recall Parliament as a sign that airstrikes on Syria were imminent. The Prime Minister's concession of a second vote tied to the findings of the UN weapons inspectors, which would take two weeks, confounded such a timeframe. Sceptical MPs reading tabloids briefed by No. 10's Press Office concluded that the Government would press for a second vote by the end of the weekend.

Dame Joan Ruddock MP typified feeling in the House when she said, 'My reading of his motion tells me that everything in it could have been debated on Monday. I believe that this House has been recalled in order to give cover for possible military action this weekend.'[12]

International process and legality

The legality for intervention as stated by the Government rested on a vote in the United Nations Security Council on the right to protect civilians. However neither Labour's nor the Government's motion mentioned the approval of a UN Security Council Resolution being mandatory for intervention. Instead just that the Security Council merely had to take a vote on the matter.

Cameron, in his statement, had also conceded that it would be 'unthinkable to proceed if there was overwhelming opposition in the Security Council'. Yet China and Russia had by this point already vetoed four separate UN Resolutions on Syria, and had expressed the view that they would do so again on any resolution involving military intervention.[13]

Deadlock, therefore, already existed in the Council, a fact which may well have influenced MPs. Would a majority of members vote for the Resolution despite knowing the likelihood of it being vetoed? One Labour MP remarked that in light of the rushed timetable the UN Resolution merely reflected Cameron 'going through the motions'. This concern Miliband appeared to share, stating:

> I have heard it suggested that we should have 'a United Nations moment'. They are certainly not my words; they are words which do no justice to the seriousness with which we must take the United Nations. The UN is not some inconvenient sideshow, and we do not want to engineer a 'moment'. Instead, we want to adhere to the principles of international law.[14]

The consequences of intervention

The crux of Miliband's speech in opposition to the Government motion focused on the idea that 'evidence should precede decision' and not vice versa. What should be weighed up is the argument 'for why the benefits of intervention and action outweigh the benefits of not acting'. This was entirely characteristic of Ed Miliband as a thinker and academic not disposed to making rash decisions but instead to carefully weighing the pros and cons, and after painstaking thought, coming to the decision he felt was correct.

A view held strongly by many on the Labour backbenches that evening was that any military intervention would undermine the possibility of the Geneva II peace talks, the consequences being summed up rather aptly by John McDonnell MP:

> Military intervention is more likely to undermine the potential for peace talks. Hawks within the Assad regime will be even more intransigent and defiant. The opposition – the so-called rebels – will have no incentive, because they will believe that the US and, yes, the UK and others will be on their side and that they can achieve a military victory. Military intervention would also alienate Iran and the Russians – the very people we look to now to bring Assad to the negotiating table.[15]

Other concerns of MPs raised in opposition to the Government motion included the possibility that intervention would push Russia and Iran into publicly supporting the Assad regime and further arming him. Another fear was that intervention would lead to a proxy war between Russia and America being fought in Syria.[16] Opposition to the motion coalesced around the suggestion that any intervention risked making the situation worse, increasing the loss of lives, and escalating the conflict.

The vote

At the division a large proportion of MPs from all parties did not decide which voting lobby to enter until the last minute. Many sat patiently through the debate waiting to be swayed by the various arguments. The vast majority of Opposition Labour MPs believed that victory for the Government was inevitable. However, for them it was important to get their opposition to airstrikes on record.

Many MPs were therefore shocked when the tellers announced that the Government's motion was defeated by 285 votes to 272, an opposition majority of thirteen. Thirty Conservative MPs and nine Liberal Democrat MPs rebelled against the Government. A long silence in the chamber turned to loud jeering with backbencher Labour MPs shouting for the Prime Minister to resign. Other MPs sat listening cautiously for the Opposition Amendment's result, which was defeated by 332 votes to 220 with a Government majority of 112.

The evening effectively ended in a political stalemate, with the Government and Opposition each rejecting the other's motion. However Cameron losing by such a small margin demonstrated more than a simple setback. It was a disastrous defeat, with many advocates against intervention pointing out that it had been Cameron's to lose. Regardless of Labour opposition, he should have been able to muster the votes to pass the Government's motion. Something had gone terribly wrong.

Cameron could have forced another vote, which is after all the Prime Minister's prerogative. What he chose to do next is at the heart of why this vote matters. Cameron chose to back down and accept defeat stating 'that it is clear that Parliament does not want intervention, I will act accordingly'. Ruling out a second vote laid the issue of UK involvement in intervention in Syria to rest. However it did far more than that: it marked the resigning by a Prime Minister of his greatest foreign policy power, that of military deployment, to Parliament.

Battered, bruised and humiliated, Cameron as Lord Paddy Ashdown referred to him was a 'broken-backed Prime Minister'.[17] The outcome symbolised for many the great diminution in the role of the Prime Minister in foreign policy since 2003. How did this happen? And, more importantly, why?

Timing and whipping

The decision to recall Parliament from recess a week early clearly had an impact on the outcome of the vote. Was it decisive though? Certainly the rushed timetable for pushing through a vote for UK intervention was reflected in the Government's whipping operation itself. The Government simply did not have enough time to prepare its case and get the votes it needed with MPs and whips fractured, both as to policy and geographical location. Government whips were passing notes and sending texts to MPs urging loyalty to the Government throughout the debate and right up until the division was called.

Sir Menzies Campbell, former Leader of the Liberal Democrats and a member of the Foreign Affairs Select Committee, provides an account of the vote which underlines the importance of its timing:

> Why did it happen? Bouncing people, people just straight off the beach at Torremolinos or somewhere more aesthetically pleasing, not really having assimilated what the hell was going on. Not knowing what was happening, and the whips not getting back on time. I mean Douglas Hurd used to have a view that difficult things happened in August. It's quite interesting because some of the worst of Bosnia was in August, and it was August, 1990 when Margaret Thatcher went after the invasion of Kuwait by Saddam. There may be some structural or calendar influence reason for some of these things. People came back without having following this stuff in detail, without the whips being properly organised, a sense of being bounced, and quite a strong manner of complacency. Put all these together and you have problems.[18]

Another sign of the sheer disorganisation and shoddiness of the Government whipping operation was that eight Government ministers missed the vote, as well as two whips and two ministerial aides. Justine Greening, Secretary of State for International Development was discussing aid policy with Mark Simmonds, the Foreign Office Minister for Africa, in the House when the vote took place. Both claim to have missed the vote due to not hearing the division bell, later sheepishly apologising. For anybody who has worked in the House the loud division bell is hard to miss. One would think on such an important international vote as this the relevant Secretary of State and ministers would be seated on the front bench. Kenneth Clarke, Minister without Portfolio and a Tory grandee with a strong interest in foreign affairs similarly missed the vote, offering personal reasons.

Despite a three line whip, a further thirty-one Conservative and fourteen Liberal Democrat MPs were absent. No pairing arrangement had been permitted. If these MPs had voted the outcome would most likely have been different.[19]

Lord Tom King, former Defence Secretary under John Major supports Campbell's analysis: 'The whole thing was an absolute classic summer recess cock-up, these things always go wrong in August and September when people are away, and the whips don't know what people are thinking, they rush back, and we were all over the place.'[20]

Former Defence Secretary, Dr Liam Fox takes a different view. He believes Cameron was damned if he did and damned if he didn't recall Parliament: 'At the time there was a lot of speculation about the Americans' imminent wish to act, and if we had not had a debate in the House of Commons and the US had acted all hell would have broken loose. With people saying why we were not consulted? I don't think it was something that the Prime Minister could have won either way.'[21]

Similarly if intervention was voted on before the summer recess in July, Alistair Burt, then Parliamentary Under Secretary of State at the Foreign and Commonwealth Office, argues that it may not have made much difference:

> I think if a similar vote had been held at the end of July before Parliament left, I think it would have probably had the same answer. Certainly a vote on overt support for military action would have had the same response, whether we had got a first vote just giving the Prime Minister the opportunity to consider that as an option, well maybe that would have been carried at the end of the summer. But there were plenty of colleagues who voted for the Government who would have not voted for a motion a week later, saying now we want to authorise a strike.[22]

A red line

The notion of a red line on chemical weapons left MPs and many international allies confused. It was an awkward halfway house that seemed to reflect a desire to be seen to be doing something while avoiding any deep commitment, a point

Lord Malloch-Brown, former Deputy UN Secretary General and Foreign Office Minister, supports:

> If you want an example of policy made out of the White House or No. 10 red lines around chemical weapons was a good example of it. Nobody in the region understood this red line. It was a tragic incident but a lot of innocent civilians have been lost by other equally brutal weapons. You're either going to draw a line around civilian casualties or you are going to draw a line about the Syrian regime's broader brutal occupation strategy. To pick off chemical weapons was seen as frivolous political strategy by leaders who hoped they could avoid a deeper commitment.[23]

The coalition

Another factor contributing to the defeat was the unique nature of David Cameron's Government. In 2010 he did not gain a parliamentary majority and entered into coalition with the Liberal Democrats. This decision had left many Conservative MPs dissatisfied, questioning whether Cameron's Government was truly Conservative. This has offered opportunities for opposition over a whole swathe of issues, Syria included. Phillip Cowley referred to the 2010–15 Parliament as the most rebellious there has ever been.[24] This is ultimately down to a number within the 2010 Conservative intake who feel that they were elected on the Conservative manifesto and not the Coalition Agreement, and also have little personal loyalty to Cameron. Syria represented for many of them another opportunity to embarrass the Prime Minister and reject the course he wanted Britain to pursue. Their objections fell into two categories: the first, the legacy of Iraq and general belief that it should not fall to Britain to intervene, something Daniel Kawczynski, MP for Shrewsbury, argued in his contribution to the debate: 'Why cannot our allies in the Middle East, such as Saudi Arabia, the Emirates, Qatar and Kuwait, take military action? Why does it fall on us yet again?'[25]

The second objection was scepticism about the urgent moral imperative to intervene in Syria, particularly when other conflicts demanded more urgent action. Many Tory MPs alluded to the difference between the clear moral imperative in Libya and the situation in Syria. David Davis, MP for Haltemprice and Howden, offers such a view: 'When the Prime Minister wanted to take military action in Libya, most of us supported him because there was a clear moral imperative: if we had not acted, tens of thousands of lives would quickly have been lost. That clear moral imperative does not stand in the action we are countenancing.'[26]

However the impact of hardened regular Tory rebels on this particular vote as mentioned earlier could be overstated. John Redwood MP pointed out in a blog at the time that the Syria motion brought out surprising rebels in Fiona Bruce MP, Tracey Crouch MP, Anne Marie Morris MP and Phillip Lee MP, all of whom are often considered 'loyal representatives' of the centre of the Conservative Party.[27]

The role of the Deputy Prime Minister

The decision to have Nick Clegg wind up the debate instead of the Foreign Secretary, William Hague, may also have had an impact on the size of the Conservative revolt. Hague has since referred to the vote as the worst moment of his time as Foreign Secretary.[28] Describing whether Hague would have been more effective in closing, Alistair Burt says:

> I know that he was extremely affected by the vote and everything else. Whether it would have been different if he himself had taken the debate, that is if he had wound up instead of the Deputy Prime Minister I don't know. Maybe he would have taken that as more of a personal rebuff, certainly I think there was a handful of votes that he might have been able to sway, that was not possible for the Deputy Prime Minister to sway, no aspersions to Nick Clegg at all but it wasn't his field, it wasn't his area, and he did the job of bringing Liberal Democrats into the vote.[29]

This is a view that is also supported by former Home Secretary, Charles Clarke: 'The Tories could have won it, even by the trivial decision they took that morning to replace William Hague with Nick Clegg in doing the wind-up speech. Nick did a completely hopeless wind-up speech, and apart from being hopeless didn't address the Tory backbenches who were the people who either failed to vote or voted against and turned it over.'[30]

William Hague is however adamant that it is the prerogative of the Deputy Prime Minister to wind up a debate, for the Prime Minister, on a major national issue, if he would like to do so. He concedes that in the Coalition Government he ranked number three while Nick Clegg ranked number two. It was therefore his choice.[31]

The Opposition

Cameron should have been able to scrape through a majority by relying on enough of his own backbenchers and his coalition partners, the Liberal Democrats, to pass the Government's motion. However failure of the vote can also be blamed on the decision of Ed Miliband to oppose it, an unprecedented breach of the historical parliamentary convention that the Opposition front bench does not oppose Government motions on military intervention.

Why this happened is a matter of considerable debate which is likely to continue. Some argue it reflected nothing but cynical political opportunism. Others consider Miliband took a moral stand which had a real impact on the direction of foreign policy.

As we know the three leaders met and held discussions on Tuesday 27 August and agreed that the use of chemical weapons could not be ignored and that military action if limited, could be justified to stop further use of chemical weapons. It was also felt such action would not trigger wider involvement in the civil war and was legal.[32]

What then, changed for Ed Miliband between that meeting and the following night, when he asked for a second vote on military action to follow? That is a question that many MPs found themselves asking on the day of the vote. Many felt that Labour's Opposition amendment offered nothing that wasn't already in the Government's motion. As Sir Malcolm Rifkind, MP for Kensington, put it:

> The Leader of the Opposition has said that he might be able to support military action of the kind that the Government are contemplating. He has put in his amendment a list of the requirements, virtually all of which, as far as I can tell, appear in the Government's own motion. Why can he not, therefore, support the Government's motion, in order that this House could speak with a united voice to the world on this matter?[33]

Sir Menzies Campbell certainly takes a similar view when discussing the Lib Dem account of Miliband's conversations with Nick Clegg and David Cameron:

> In the end I voted with the Government because the motion was essentially that we should go to the UN and see if we could get a resolution, and if we get the report from the inspectors and support from the Security Council then we'll have a chance to vote again. All one was doing was imposing the UN upon the procedure that is why for the life of me I could not understand Ed Miliband, about whom there is a lot of bad feeling between Cameron and Clegg about Miliband, because their version of events show that they talked to him, and

> every time he raised some point, they said fine, including at the very end the whole question of a second vote. So what was Labour's amendment about? It was about opposing for the sake of opposition, and you can't help thinking that was really looking behind the front bench then in front of the Commons and public.[34]

Hague, who was privy to much of the discussion in the meeting, believes that the Opposition were almost determined not to vote for whatever the Government put forward, because 'what we put forward in the end was pretty much what they were asking for'.[35]

The answer may lie in the internal politics of the Parliamentary Labour Party. One backbench Labour MP told me, 'the Labour party was as divided if not more divided than the Tories over Syria'. Labour's motion therefore offered its own members a way to unite both sides of the argument with a compromise amendment. This however did not do enough to stop the polarising views of those in favour of the Government's position and those opposed. One disgruntled senior political adviser to a Shadow Cabinet Minister remarked to me that 'Miliband's position was a complete betrayal of Labour's ethical foreign policy and Blair's policy of liberal intervention.'

Insiders report that the real split was between Shadow Foreign Secretary, Douglas Alexander and Shadow Defence Secretary, Jim Murphy over supporting the Government's motion. Jim Murphy, who favoured intervention, after the vote argued on his blog that the result actually indicated a parliamentary majority for intervention, writing:

> The unusual thing about Thursday's vote is that most MPs voted for an in principle policy of not ruling out military action in the future. The Labour policy attracted 220 votes and the Government motion won the support of 272, meaning that of the 550-odd MPs who voted 492 supported a version of conditions-based potential use of UK military force if very tight criteria had been met. Just a minority of MPs in all parties opposed any military action in all circumstances for reasons of conscience or concern. Yet that is where our country ended up.[36]

Douglas Alexander however did not share such a view, believing the only way to a resolution of the Syrian civil war would be a negotiated political settlement.[37] Alexander's position won the day, as may be surmised from Miliband's late night U-turn and the demotion of Jim Murphy to Shadow Secretary of State for International Development two weeks later.[38]

Was it simply then about political opposition? Lord Malloch-Brown, a former Foreign Office Minister in Government with Alexander supports this case: 'I think it was political as anything else. It was looking for some way to square the circle, a way of sounding tough and appalled at what was happening while at the same time making sure you weren't being positioned as the Chamberlains of the situation. This was just a politically neat way of doing nothing and dressing it up as meaningful action.'[39]

Alistair Burt agrees, arguing that opposition to the Government's motion may have simply been a clever option particularly when intervention lacked a popular will:

> Well the perception on our side, as I'm sure you know, is that he made an agreement with the Prime Minister because he understood what the circumstances were, and when he went back he was talked out of it, which is within his prerogative as Leader of the Opposition to do. I think his colleagues argued that there is no popular opinion for this, there is no popular will, and maybe there is a cleverer option for an opposition. Clearly it's obvious that certain members of the Shadow Cabinet were unhappy about the decision and where it left foreign policy.[40]

One backbench Labour MP believes this option reflected Douglas Alexander's Brownite approach of strategy over vision, whereby on any given issue he would establish where he didn't want to be and where the public was on the issue, and then move towards the public, rather than deciding a stance on an issue and trying to convince the public of its merits. This argument was echoed by another former Labour Minister who served in the Brown administration, stating that Douglas Alexander 'manages to cloak the thing with a spurious philosophical consistency but completely spurious'.

Labour's position was certainly bolstered by a lack of public support for intervention. After twelve years of military conflict with the UK campaign in Afghanistan winding down and many still feeling burned by Iraq there was no public appetite for intervention in Syria. A *Daily Telegraph* poll reported on the morning of the vote that only 11 per cent of the British public supported becoming involved in a war in Syria,[41] while a YouGov poll found that the public opposed a missile strike two to one; with Labour voters there was a 54–26 split opposing strikes.[42]

The fallout from Iraq for many Labour MPs who had voted for it, or even been in Government at the time, made it impossible to ignore the sense of déjà vu. There was considerable mirroring of the 2003 event: a rushed United States-led timetable; suspect or incomplete intelligence; a lack of clear strategic objectives; and an endgame without any consideration of what that might be. For Miliband it offered a chance to present himself as what he would hope to be: 'a post-Iraq Prime Minister'.[43] This in itself may have been too much of an opportunity to ignore.

What became apparent to anyone who watched the debate was that it was perhaps the most honest and open discussion MPs have had in the chamber about the misconceived notion of the invasion of Iraq ten years before, as much about deconstructing the failures of the invasion of Iraq as discussing intervention in Syria.

The use of intelligence

For many MPs the politicisation of intelligence in the 2003 Iraq debate made it harder for the bare assertions of the Prime Minister and Joint Intelligence Committee, as the former Foreign Secretary, Jack Straw painfully conceded in the debate:[44] 'I simply make the point, which is widely shared across the House, that one of the consequences of the intelligence failure on Iraq has been to raise the bar that we have to get over when the question of military action arises.'

It is a point shared by his former Cabinet colleague, and then Defence Secretary, Geoff Hoon that in the shadow of Iraq, the public will always be sceptical about intelligence and its use: 'I think though part of the same issue in a modern, pluralistic, democratic, information-hungry society, the days in which you can say to the population this is sensitive intelligence we can't tell you how it's been obtained. I'm not sure you can do that any longer, any more can a court decision be simply accepted.'[45]

The strategic objectives

Another factor in Cameron's defeat was the clear failure to outline a defined strategic goal. What did he mean by military intervention? Was he talking about airstrikes, and if so at what targets? Would he commit ground troops? Who else would be involved in this military campaign? Did this mean establishing a no-fly zone as earlier proposed? All these lingering questions existed and David Cameron in the debate did little to demystify the idea of intervention. If MPs, peers and even former Chiefs of the Defence Staff didn't have an idea of what was intended how could the public?

Admiral Lord Mike Boyce, former Chief of the Defence Staff to Tony Blair, raises some of the most important questions about the lack of strategy being shown by Cameron at the time:

> There are a whole heap of questions to which the Government didn't seem to have any answers. Starting with that, if you want to fire a shot across someone's bow, which was what the expression was at the time – if you're firing a shot across someone's bow be aware of what you want your second shot to do. If you were to ask the Prime Minister/Government what the second shot would do, they had no idea…
>
> As far as I can see – and no one I have spoken to since – had the faintest idea of what the consequences of what we were going to launch into were…
>
> Well there is capability there, but people need to be aware of what they are about to go into – the second shot argument for Assad. If Assad, after the first rap across the knuckles, had said 'Go away, I'm not going to listen to you, you don't frighten', what was the next step? Nuke him? What was the next action to be taken? Put boots on the ground? Start a no-fly zone? What was the assessment of the attrition we would take if we tried to set up a no-fly zone? He's got air defences that make Libya look like a prehistoric kindergarten, or even Iraq in the '80s and '90s. Syria has got a very sophisticated capability, so how would you actually impose a no-fly zone without taking quite a lot of attrition, which I suspect people wouldn't want to do? Boots on the ground is a joke. Who is the opposition to the regime in Syria? Who is the opposition today?[46]

Field Marshall, Lord Michael Walker, another former Chief of the Defence Staff makes a similar point about the general ambiguity of military plans:

> I don't think the military knew what he had in his mind when they produced various suggestions which they said was not a good idea. I mean air power on its own without any understanding wasn't going to do it. Again what Cameron, my personal view, is what Cameron was up to was coming up with a plan that would support the United States and anybody else who was up for this as an international coalition presenting a united front to Syria and the Assad regime.[47]

In the chamber, the Prime Minister refused to offer specifics regarding targets or outline his strategy further than this rebuff: 'I do not want to set out at the Dispatch Box a list of targets, but it is perfectly simple and straightforward to think of actions that we could take relating to the command and control of the use of chemical weapons, and the people and buildings involved, that would indeed deter and degrade.'[48]

The only excuse for Cameron's evasion can be that if the Government had won the vote, further details would have been provided in the second vote after further consultation with the USA. However, for many members the vagary over strategy only opened the Government motion up to further criticism. It may have been an unfair charge but for appearance's sake it looked like Cameron was in effect asking for a 'blank cheque' as Angus Robertson an SNP MP put it.[49] It reminded many of the sort of blank cheque that MPs had given to Tony Blair a decade before.

Aftermath of the vote – what happened next?

British foreign policy is irrelevant?

Cameron's defeat in the Commons was quickly interpreted by all media outlets as a blow to President Obama and the 'special relationship'. A number of journalists reported the results showed his personal weakness and was 'a measure of Britain's increasing isolation from its allies – both inside the European Union and now with Washington.'[50] Cameron's private assurances of Commons approval and the shock defeat damaged his credibility in the eyes of the Americans. One of the leading advocates for intervention in Syria was now effectively sidelined by Parliament. Lord Ashdown said at the time that in fifty years of trying to serve his country he had never been so ashamed or depressed at the outcome of a vote.'[51]

On 30 August, the day after the vote, the USA stated that the Commons rejection of intervention did not change US plans for possible intervention and America would continue to seek an international coalition for intervention. Similarly President François Hollande reiterated French support for intervention with the USA, unfazed by the vote in the House of Commons.[52] The fear for many in the Foreign Office and Government was that the US and France would go it alone sidelining Britain to irrelevancy in western policy towards Syria.

This view was reinforced by a comment made by President Vladimir Putin's official spokesman Dmitry Peskov on 5 September at the G20 Summit. Peskov stated in response to the vote, 'Britain is a small island nobody pays any attention to.'[53] David Cameron responded by offering a reminder of Britain's great accomplishments which didn't go far enough to fully disarm the stinging truth and the lingering insecurity raised by the comment.

President Obama conceded to Congress a vote on Syrian military intervention, though constitutionally a President is under no obligation to do so. The White House hoped to appease many of the sceptics in Congress, who inspired by the House of Commons rejection of intervention, would attempt to do the same. The vote was to be just as tight, with many on both sides of Congress undecided.[54]

US Secretary of State John Kerry flew to London to meet with William Hague on a tour of European capitals to whip up support for western intervention. Congress was set to vote at the end of the week. During a press conference Kerry was asked if there was any way for intervention now to be avoided. He stated as an aside that if Assad gave up all of his chemical weapons by the end of the week he might avoid attack, pointing out that it was unlikely that he would do this.[55]

A deal

Then something rather strange happened. A few hours after Kerry's press conference the Russian Foreign Minister, Sergei Lavrov endorsed Kerry's call for Syria to hand over all chemical weapons.[56] The next day the Syrian Government admitted to having chemical weapons and stated it would agree to hand them over and become a signatory to the international convention banning their use.

This was presented by both supporters for and against intervention as a huge diplomatic coup and breakthrough in the conflict. For the more cynical minded this was political spin. Obama halted the vote in Congress on military intervention while Kerry flew to Russia to work out a framework agreement, with Lavrov mediating between the international community and the Syrian Government.

A document was signed on 14 September, which required the Syrian Government to become a signatory to the Geneva international convention banning the use of chemical weapons, to provide a full list of such weapons it currently possessed, and to permit the Organization for the Prohibition of Chemical Weapons (OPCW) access to sites to decommission and destroy weapons. Syrian moderate rebel forces and the regime agreed a ceasefire in certain areas so OPCW inspectors could have access to identified sites and a date was set for the destruction of all weapons and material by the first half of 2014.[57] This deadline was extended numerous times to account for the logistics of removing the chemical weapons in an active war zone and, at times, a lack of cooperation from Assad's regime. For the work of its inspectors, the OPCW would receive the Nobel Peace Prize.

William Hague believes the deal reflected the leverage Russia does have over the Assad Regime: 'Russia was very anxious to avoid military action in Syria, and so as far as one can see, insisted to the Assad Regime that they enter into this program of disarmament overseen by the OPCW.'[58]

For parliamentary opponents of intervention in Syria, the diplomatic solution and UN led destruction of Syria's chemical weapons programme was only possible because of parliamentary opposition to the Government. Diane Abbott, Labour MP for Hackney North and Stoke Newington, said it was one of the few times in her career where individual MPs had impacted on a foreign policy decision. Ed Miliband felt able to tell voters that he stopped a rush to war in Syria.[59] The narrative also suited No. 10 and the Foreign Office. Cameron could tell people that his Foreign Secretary was at the heart of the agreement that saw Assad relinquish his chemical weapons. It was a win–win scenario in terms of both sides being able to claim credit and save face. It is also a falsehood.

Assad's continued use of chemical weapons

This agreement had little to do with ending the Syrian civil war, which at the time of writing rages on through conventional means. Obama's red line on chemical weapons has failed. In May 2014 reports emerged from French intelligence and from the British newspaper, *The Independent* claiming that on 11 and 18 April, chlorine gas canisters packed in barrel bombs were dropped and detonated in the Syrian town of Kafr Zita, near the city of Hama, and again on 21 April in the village of Talmenes.[60] Opposition rebels reported that the gas was used during fierce fighting with regime troops when they appeared to be losing control of the strategic town of Khan Sheikhoun. While chlorine is not listed as a banned chemical weapons agent due to its wide range of industrial uses, as a weapon of war it is prohibited under the 1925 Chemical Weapons Convention.

The OPCW investigated and confirmed in its report in June 2014 that the attacks took place. The UK Foreign Office in a statement issued attributed blame to Assad: 'The systematic and repeated use of chlorine in northern Syria and the consistent reports from witnesses of the presence of helicopters at the times of the attacks leave little doubt as to the Assad regime's culpability.'[61]

Since the attacks in April there has been no parliamentary debate on the issue, nor has any Member raised a point of order or publicly on the record in

Parliament stated that the Syrian Government is in breach of the deal signed in September 2013. A year later the OPCW on 4 September 2014 confirmed in their report that it had successfully destroyed 96 per cent of Assad's chemical weapons programme but could not give a date for completion of the total destruction of Assad's weapons.[62]

The picture on the ground tells a different story. *The Financial Times* and *Washington Post* reported in October 2014 that there had been more chlorine gas attacks, this time in the rebel-controlled Jobar district of Damascus by regime forces.[63] As one Syrian opposition activist put it, 'This whole story of the regime destroying its chemical weapons arsenal is nothing but a lifeline thrown by Russia to the Assad regime'.[64]

To add insult to injury, on 9 July 2014 the Foreign Office released a statement describing the historic role of UK companies in supplying Syria with chemicals which were later weaponised by the regime of Assad Snr in the years 1983–86. The exports included several hundred tonnes of the chemical dimethyl phosphite (DMP) in 1983 and a further export of several hundred tonnes in 1985; several hundred tonnes of trimethyl phosphite (TMP) in 1986; and a smaller quantity of hydrogen fluoride (HF) in 1986 through a third country. The Foreign Office stressed that these chemicals all have legitimate uses but conceded 'they can also be used in the production of sarin. DMP and TMP can also be used for the production of the nerve agent VX'.[65]

In truth the Assad regime has merely switched from using sarin to weaponising chlorine. The West distracted by the ever-growing threat of the Islamic State of Iraq and the Levant has created the perfect opportunity for Assad to gain ground against moderate rebels through any means. The narrative that Assad's chemical weapons have been destroyed and Parliament stopped an overbearing executive rushing to commit the country to war is too seductive to dispel. To this day few MPs, if any, believe or know that chemical weapons are still being used in Syria. Their minds have drifted off to other issues: the economy, immigration, another international conflict, the rise of ISIS. Ultimately the lie suits the Prime Minister and his critics, they get to claim a great victory and he gets to save face.

The loss and its consequences

The parliamentary defeat was a personal rebuff of David Cameron and a wider rejection of prime ministerial dominance in foreign policy.

Many MPs attributed the defeat to Cameron's hands-off 'chairman of the board' approach to all areas of the governance, which critics see as a theme of his premiership. It was this approach that saw the timing of the vote being misjudged, the whipping operation bungled, and Hague, the man who had dealt with British policy on Syria from the start, being benched instead of closing the debate.

The loss of control of a key area of foreign policy is an unprecedented failure but Cameron survived it, limping on. It is not considered a foreign policy moment on a par with that of the parliamentary rebuff of Eden in 1956 as a result of the Suez Crisis, or the Norway debate in 1940, since both of these led to the fall of the respective prime ministers of the day, and Cameron did not regard his defeat as a resigning issue. However, Syria has left its mark on Cameron and his premiership. It demonstrated why he will not be considered a great international statesman. Hague agrees that it was a damaging vote to British foreign policy although not a fatal one.[66]

The vote is considered by some as a victory for legislative restraint on the executive. For parliamentary critics of the growing influence of the executive in the foreign policy it offered a rebalancing, as Douglas Carswell, then a Tory MP, wrote in his blog:

> For decades, our country has been run by a tiny, self-regarding mandarinate in Whitehall. The sort of people who advise the National Security Council – which only the other day told us we had to strike in Syria…
>
> Not for much longer. Parliament is now claiming powers that, thanks to a historic quirk, have given Downing Street the powers of a monarch. If the Commons insists it has the final say over going to war, it won't be much longer before Parliament wants confirmation hearings for senior mandarins and budget hearings.[67]

Crispin Blunt, another Conservative MP who voted against the Government, stated that he hoped the vote would 'relieve ourselves of some of this imperial pretension that a country of our size can seek to be involved in every conceivable conflict that's going on around the world'.[68]

The defeat alone did not weaken the Prime Minister's role; rather it was Cameron's concession after the vote. Tony Blair gave Parliament its first vote on going to war. Gordon Brown carried on supporting the convention pledging to enshrine it into law. David Cameron took it further, conceding the most power. In deciding to call off a second vote and declare that Parliament had spoken Cameron directly relinquished prime ministerial control of foreign policy and in doing so admitted the imperilled state of the office in terms of foreign policy.

That night one could look back over the fifty years of the modern-day premiership, from the first term of Harold Wilson through to David Cameron's stance at the dispatch box and visualise the steady advancement of the Prime Minister's role in foreign policy come shuddering to a halt.

Wilson, Heath, Callaghan, Thatcher, Major, Blair, Brown, Cameron. In analysing and understanding their personal contribution to British foreign policy we can better understand the growth and subsequent slump in modern prime ministerial dominance. Each Prime Minister has strived to control foreign policy against the backdrop of Britain's declining influence on the world stage, often facing opposition from their Cabinets, political party, Parliament and the general public.

Notes

1 R. Hutton and T. Penny, 'Historic Vote Sees Cameron Defeated by Lawmakers on Syria', Bloomberg, 29 August 2013, accessed 9 November 2014: www.bloomberg.com/news/2013-08-29/historic-vote-sees-cameron-defeated-by-lawmakers-on-syria.html.
2 A. Samir and Y. Saleh, 'Arab League Leaders to Blame Assad for Chemical Weapons Attack', Reuters, 28 August 2013, accessed 9 November 2014: www.reuters.com/article/2013/08/28/us-syria-crisis-league-idUSBRE97R12X20130828.
3 D. Hodges, 'The Truth About the Syria Vote: Miliband Changed His Mind', *The Telegraph*, 29 August 2013, accessed 9 November 2014: http://blogs.telegraph.co.uk/news/danhodges/100233087/the-truth-about-the-syria-vote-miliband-changed-his-mind; N. Robinson, 'The Politics of Bombing Syria', BBC News, 28 August 2013, accessed 9 November 2014: www.bbc.co.uk/news/uk-politics-23869303; N. Robinson, 'Why the PM Buckled on the Syria Vote', BBC News, 29 August 2013, accessed 9 November 2014: www.bbc.co.uk/news/uk-politics-23880268.
4 D. Cameron, *Hansard* (HC Deb, 29 August 2013, col. 1425).
5 Rule 74 of the International Committee of the Red Cross, incorporating the Hague Declaration concerning Asphyxiating Gases, the Geneva Gas Protocol, the Chemical Weapons Convention and the Statute of the International Criminal Court.
6 Prime Minister's Office, 'Guidance: Chemical Weapon Use by Syrian Regime, UK Government Legal Position', Cabinet Office, 29 August 2013, accessed 9 November 2014: www.gov.uk/government/publications/chemical-weapon-use-by-syrian

-regime-uk-government-legal-position/chemical-weapon-use-by-syrian-regime-uk-government-legal-position-html-version.
7. Cabinet Office, 'Correspondence: Syria, Reported Chemical Weapons Use, Joint Intelligence Committee Letter', 29 August 2013, accessed 9 November 2014: www.gov.uk/government/publications/syria-reported-chemical-weapons-use-joint-intelligence-committee-letter.
8. D. Cameron, *Hansard* (HC Deb, 29 August 2013, col. 1437).
9. D. Cameron, *Hansard* (HC Deb, 29 August 2013, col. 1428).
10. E. Miliband, *Hansard* (HC Deb, 29 August 2013, col. 1443).
11. E. Miliband, *Hansard* (HC Deb, 29 August 2013, col. 1440).
12. J. Ruddock, *Hansard* (HC Deb, 29 August 2013, col. 1428).
13. L. Charbonneau and M. Nichols, 'UN Security Council Powers Meet Again on Syria: No Outcome', Reuters, 29 August 2013, accessed 9 November 2014: www.reuters.com/article/2013/08/29/us-syria-crisis-un-idUSBRE97S17R20130829; 'Syria Crisis: Russia and China Step Up Warning Over Syria', BBC News, 27 August 2013, accessed 9 November 2014: www.bbc.co.uk/news/world-us-canada-23845800.
14. E. Miliband, *Hansard* (HC Deb, 29 August 2013, col. 1142).
15. J. McDonnell, *Hansard* (HC Deb, 29 August 2013, col. 1462).
16. E. Llwyd, *Hansard* (HC Deb, 29 August 2013, col. 1464); A. Owen, *Hansard* (HC Deb, 29 August 2013, col. 1484).
17. 'A Turning Point for PM and UK', *Evening Standard*, 30 August 2013, accessed 9 November 2014: www.standard.co.uk/comment/comment/evening-standard-comment-a-turning-point-for-the-pm-and-the-uk-8791287.html.
18. M. Campbell, interview with S. Goodman, 9 September 2013, House of Commons.
19. J. Groves, 'Six Ministers Who Missed the Vote: Chief Whip Under Fire for Shambles in Commons is Exposed', *Daily Mail*, 30 August 2013 accessed 9 November 2014: www.dailymail.co.uk/news/article-2406731/Ministers-missed-vote-Chief-Whip-shambles-Commons-exposed.html.
20. T. King, interview with S. Goodman, 10 October 2013, House of Lords.
21. L. Fox, interview with S. Goodman, 10 October 2013, House of Commons.
22. A. Burt, interview with S. Goodman, 3 February 2014, House of Commons.
23. M. Malloch-Brown, interview with S. Goodman, 25 October 2014, private offices.
24. P. Cowley and M. Stuart, 'This Parliament Remains On Course to be the most Rebellious Parliament Since 1945', Conservative Home, 14 May 2013, accessed 9 November 2014: www.conservativehome.com/platform/2013/05/philip-cowley-and-mark-stuart-for-1000am-tuesday.html.
25. D. Kawczynski, *Hansard* (HC Deb, 29 August 2013, col. 1430).
26. D. Davis, *Hansard* (HC Deb, 29 August 2013, col. 1469).

27 J. Redwood, 'Some Thoughts on 5 Big Rebellions in Parliament', John Redwood's Diary, 11 September 2013, accessed 9 November 2014: http://johnredwoodsdiary.com/2013/09/11/some-thoughts-on-5-big-rebellions-in-this-parliament/.
28 K. Cooper, 'William Hague on Humour – and His Worst Moment as Foreign Secretary', BBC News, 18 July 2014, accessed 9 November 2014: www.bbc.co.uk/news/uk-politics-28377955.
29 A. Burt, interview with S. Goodman, 3 February 2014, House of Commons.
30 C. Clarke, interview with S. Goodman, 3 November 2013, private offices.
31 W. Hague, interview with S. Goodman, 2 March 2015, House of Commons.
32 A. Seldon and P. Snowden, *Cameron at 10: Inside the Coalition 2010–2015* (London: William Collins, 2015), pp. 334–6.
33 M. Rifkind, *Hansard* (HC Deb, 29 August 2013, col. 1442).
34 M. Campbell, interview with S. Goodman, 9 September 2013, House of Commons.
35 W. Hague, interview with S. Goodman, 2 March 2015, House of Commons.
36 J. Murphy, 'Thoughts on Syria', Jim Murphy's Blog, 1 September 2013, accessed 9 November 2014: www.jimmurphymp.com/jims-blog/blog.aspx?b=29.
37 D. Alexander, 'Douglas Alexander: Syria- What's Next?', *The Telegraph*, 30 August 2013, accessed 9 November 2014: www.telegraph.co.uk/news/worldnews/middleeast/syria/10277675/Douglas-Alexander-Syria-what-next.html?mobile=basic.
38 P. Wintour, 'Labour Reshuffle: A Victory for Talent or a Purge of the Blairites?', *The Guardian*, 7 October 2013, accessed 9 November 2014: www.theguardian.com/politics/2013/oct/07/labour-reshuffle-victory-talent-blairites.
39 M. Malloch-Brown, interview with S. Goodman, 25 October 2014, private offices.
40 A. Burt, interview with S. Goodman, 3 February 2014, House of Commons.
41 G. Galloway, *Hansard* (HC Deb, 29 August 2013, col. 1471).
42 'Syria and the Shadow of Iraq', YouGov, 28 August 2013, accessed 9 November 2014: https://yougov.co.uk/news/2013/08/28/syria-and-shadow-iraq/.
43 N. Robinson, 'Miliband on Israel, PM plan and Thatcher comparison', BBC News, 12 April 2014, accessed 9 November 2014: www.bbc.co.uk/news/uk-politics-26998207.
44 J. Straw, *Hansard* (HC Deb, 29 August 2013, col. 1451).
45 G. Hoon, interview with S. Goodman, 3 February 2014, private offices.
46 M. Boyce, interview with S. Goodman, 30 March 2014, House of Lords.
47 M. Walker, interview with S. Goodman, 3 February 2014, House of Lords.
48 D. Cameron, *Hansard* (HC Deb, 29 August 2013, col. 1436).
49 A. Robertson, *Hansard* (HC Deb, 29 August 2013, col. 1457).

50 S. Castle and S. Erlanger, 'Britain's Rejection of Syrian Response Reflects Fear of Rushing to Act', *New York Times*, 29 August 2013, accessed 9 November 2014: www.nytimes.com/2013/08/30/world/middleeast/syria.html?_r=0.

51 A. Whithnall, 'Former Lib Dem Leader Paddy Ashdown "Ashamed" by Commons Vote Against War', *Independent*, 30 August 2013, accessed 9 November 2014: www.independent.co.uk/news/uk/politics/former-lib-dem-leader-paddy-ashdown-ashamed-by-commons-vote-against-war-8791383.html.

52 'Syria Crisis: Cameron Loses Commons Vote on Syria Action', BBC News, 30 August 2013, accessed 9 November 2014: www.bbc.co.uk/news/uk-politics-23892783.

53 J. Kirkup, 'Russia Mocks Britain, the Little Island', *The Telegraph*, 5 September 2013, accessed 9 November 2014: www.telegraph.co.uk/news/worldnews/europe/russia/10290243/Russia-mocks-Britain-the-little-island.html.

54 'Obama: US Cannot Ignore Syria Chemical Weapons', BBC News, 7 September 2013, accessed 9 November 2014: www.bbc.co.uk/news/world-us-canada-23999066.

55 P. Wintour, 'John Kerry Gives Syria a Week to Hand Over Chemical Weapons or Face Attack', *The Guardian*, 9 September 2013, accessed 9 November 2014: www.theguardian.com/world/2013/sep/09/us-syria-chemical-weapons-attack-john-kerry.

56 M. Fisher, 'Russia Urges Syria to Give Up Chemical Weapons: Game Changer or Shrewd Bluff?', *The Washington Post*, 9 September 2013, accessed 9 November 2014: www.washingtonpost.com/blogs/worldviews/wp/2013/09/09/russia-urges-syria-to-give-up-chemical-weapons-game-changer-or-a-shrewd-bluff/.

57 T. Cohen and L. Smith-Spark, 'US, Russia Agree To Framework on Syria Chemical Weapons', CNN, 15 September 2013, accessed 9 November 2014: http://edition.cnn.com/2013/09/14/politics/us-syria/.

58 W. Hague, interview with S. Goodman, 2 March 2015, House of Commons.

59 R. Mason, 'Ed Miliband Restores Party Confidence in His Leadership on Syria Motion', *The Guardian*, 30 August 2013, accessed 9 November 2014: www.theguardian.com/politics/2013/aug/30/syria-ed-miliband-labour-party-confidence-leadership.

60 K. Lynch, 'Syria Chemical Weapons: Assad Still Using Chlorine Gas in Attacks, Claims Francois Hollande', *The Independent*, 20 April 2014, accessed 9 November 2014: www.independent.co.uk/news/world/middle-east/syria-chemical-weapons-assad-still-using-chlorine-gas-in-attacks-claims-franois-hollande-9272495.html; M. Esplin, 'Syria Chemical Weapons: The Analysis That Proves Assad Launched Chlorine Gas Attacks', *The Telegraph*, 29 April 2014 accessed 9 November 2014: www.telegraph.co.uk/news/worldnews/middleeast/syria/10795813/Syria-chemical-weapons-the-analysis-that-proves-Assad-launched-chlorine-gas-attacks.html.

61 P. Hammond, 'Press Release: Foreign Secretary Condemns Assad's use of Chlorine in Syria', Foreign and Commonwealth Office, 10 September 2014, accessed 9 November 2014: www.gov.uk/government/news/foreign-secretary-condemns-assads-use-of-chlorine-in-syria.
62 'Ninety-six Percent of Syria's Declared Chemical Weapons Destroyed- UN-OPCW mission chief', The Organization for the Prohibition of Chemical Weapons and the United Nations, 4 September 2014, accessed 9 November 2014: http://opcw.unmissions.org/AboutOPCWUNJointMission/tabid/54/ctl/Details/mid/651/ItemID/341/Default.aspx.
63 B. Daragahi, 'Assad Still Using Chemical Weapons, say Syrian Rebels', *The Financial Times*, 21 October 2014, accessed 9 November: www.ft.com/cms/s/0/9e18f7e8-5460-11e4-84c6-00144feab7de.html; 'Obama Gives Syria's Assad Another Pass on Chemical Weapons', *The Washington Post*, 23 October 2014, accessed 9 November 2014: www.washingtonpost.com/opinions/obama-gives-syrias-assad-another-pass-on-chemical-weapons/2014/10/23/1fe92762-5a05-11e4-bd61-346aee66ba29_story.html.
64 B. Daragahi, 'Assad Still Using Chemical Weapons, say Syrian Rebels', *The Financial Times*, 21 October 2014, accessed 9 November 2014: www.ft.com/cms/s/0/9e18f7e8-5460-11e4-84c6-00144feab7de.html; 'Obama Gives Syria's Assad Another Pass on Chemical Weapons', *The Washington Post*, 23 October 2014, accessed 9 November 2014: www.washingtonpost.com/opinions/obama-gives-syrias-assad-another-pass-on-chemical-weapons/2014/10/23/1fe92762-5a05-11e4-bd61-346aee66ba29_story.html.
65 W. Hague, 'Written Statement on Historical Role of UK Companies in Supplying Dual Use Chemicals to Syria', Foreign and Commonwealth Office, 9 July 2014, accessed 9 November 2014: www.gov.uk/government/speeches/statement-on-the-historical-role-of-uk-companies-in-supplying-dual-use-chemicals-to-syria.
66 W. Hague, interview with S. Goodman, 2 March 2015, House of Commons.
67 D. Carswell, 'Be Happy! The Defeat of the Government will Send a Powerful Message to Whitehall', *The Telegraph*, 29 August 2013, accessed 9 November 2014: http://blogs.telegraph.co.uk/news/douglascarswellmp/100233338/be-happy-the-defeat-of-the-government-will-send-a-powerful-message-to-whitehall/.
68 'Crispin Blunt: UK "Didn't Need To Put Hand on Dagger"', BBC News, 30 August 2013, accessed 9 November 2014: www.bbc.co.uk/news/uk-23895544.

1

Harold Wilson, 1964–70

Harold Wilson ascended to the premiership on 16 October 1964 gaining a parliamentary majority of four in a close fought election. After thirteen years of Conservative Government, marred in the later years by the Profumo scandal and claims of cronyism, the electorate were ready for a change of party. Wilson, at forty-eight years of age, formed the first Labour Government since Clement Attlee.

The left wing of the Labour Party had high expectations of a more left-leaning foreign policy from a Wilson Government. Elected leader on a centre-left platform in January 1963 after the sudden death of Hugh Gaitskell, Wilson already had a long association with the left wing of the Party. Together with Aneurin Bevan, his mentor, and John Freeman, Wilson had resigned as President of the Board of Trade from Attlee's Cabinet in protest against the introduction of fees to the National Health Service to help offset the financial demands of the Korean War.

Labour's 1964 manifesto also offered a return to a more socialist foreign policy, promising 'an end to colonialism', vigorous efforts to relax Cold War tensions, the introduction of new initiatives on disarmament, and leadership at 'the United Nations [as] the chosen instrument by which the world can move away from the anarchy of power politics towards the creation of a genuine world community and the rule of law'.[1] Many at the time questioned whether these ideological manifesto commitments would be sustainable against the pragmatism that foreign policy often requires.

Wilson was thrust into foreign policy literally within minutes of his arrival at No. 10 when he was handed two telegrams: one telling him that the Chinese had tested their first nuclear weapon, the other that Khrushchev had been overthrown in Russia.[2]

Like all premiers, Wilson inherited the foreign policy decisions of his predecessors. Macmillan in his 'Wind of Change' speech had committed Britain to a timetable of decolonisation across Africa, and since 1945 five prime ministers had sustained Britain's Cold War military spending and defence obligations. In both of these areas there was an expectation that he would continue to do the same.

Vietnam

As Prime Minister, Wilson also inherited strained relations with the American President Lyndon Johnson (LBJ), over the growing spectre of Western intervention in Vietnam. His Conservative predecessors, Macmillan and Douglas-Home, had both been close to President John F. Kennedy but neither developed such a relationship with his successor LBJ.

The USA had been involved in Vietnam since the end of the French War in Indochina, when the country was partitioned at the 1954 Geneva Conference. Since then the country had been caught in a fractious civil war between the Communists in the north and the Western-backed military regime of the south. Vietnam was increasingly viewed as a proxy war, with many in the United States citing the fear that if the country fell to the Communists it would create a domino effect in the region. The USA had enacted a policy of committing military advisers to train and assist the south since November 1955.

Prior to his assassination in November 1963, President Kennedy had pledged to remove military advisers by the end of 1964. LBJ initially supported this policy but upon assuming the presidency he soon found himself under pressure from the Joint Chiefs of Staff to commit US troops or watch South Vietnam fall to the Communists.

Britain's role

Under Harold Macmillan, Britain also committed military advisers to help train the South Vietnamese in the form of the British Military Advisory Mission. Running from 1962–64, the Mission advised and trained South Vietnamese soldiers in British counter-insurgency tactics in Malaya.[3]

The strain in relations between No. 10 and the White House first came about over the topic of the US embargo on Cuba. Alec Douglas-Home, on a trip to Washington in the summer of 1964, used a press conference to criticise US policy on Cuba. President Johnson was incensed, later stating that Home had not raised such concerns in their discussions.[4] Instead he felt that the Prime Minister's criticism was an electioneering strategy to win votes and portray himself as independent from the USA. In response Johnson told British newspaper editors that he would never trust a British Prime Minister again.[5]

Wilson criticised Western involvement in Vietnam early on, stating in 1954 that 'not a man, not a gun, must be sent from this country to defend French colonisation in Indo-China...we must not join or in any way encourage an anti-Communist crusade in Asia under the leadership of the Americans or anyone else'.[6] As Leader of the Opposition he pressed the then Prime Minster Alec Douglas-Home in early 1964 to advise LBJ against extending the war in Vietnam. This criticism was noted by the Johnson Administration and created an early distrust of Wilson's premiership in Washington.

Escalation

The war in Vietnam escalated when on 30 July and 4 August 1964, two American navy cruisers on an intelligence-gathering mission in the Gulf of Tonkin were allegedly attacked by North Vietnamese torpedo boats. In response to the attack President Johnson addressed the American people declaring that North Vietnam had attacked the United States. The US Congress, in support of the President passed the Gulf of Tonkin Resolution declaring that 'the Congress approves and supports the determination of the President, as Commander in Chief, to take all necessary measures to repel any armed attack against the forces of the United States and to prevent further aggression'.[7] This resolution effectively gave the President unilateral power to escalate the conflict without requiring a formal declaration of war.

Despite Congressional authorisation, LBJ chose not to escalate US involvement in Vietnam straight away. This restraint was largely due to the upcoming presidential election in November 1964.

A changing position

Early in his premiership Wilson was advised by the Foreign Office to consider changing his position on Vietnam to support the US in 'limited' and 'controlled' action.[8] Fundamentally a pragmatist, he took this advice seriously.

In December 1964, Wilson visited Washington for the first time with his Foreign Secretary Patrick Gordon Walker. Both men were pressed by US officials for a British commitment to the war effort in Vietnam. Walking in the

Rose Garden of the White House, Johnson asked the Prime Minister to send troops to Vietnam, even if it was just a symbolic force like the Black Watch pipers.[9]

The Prime Minister parried his request by pointing out that the UK already had 54,000 troops in Malaya fighting the Indonesian invasion. This UK commitment was already comparable to US forces in Vietnam. Both militarily and politically, Wilson stressed that the UK could not resource war in both Malaya and Vietnam. However he did concede that the UK could increase its commitment in other ways such as increasing the training of the South Vietnamese in jungle warfare as well as providing medical and financial aid to South Vietnam.[10]

US Secretary of Defence, Robert McNamara highlighted Britain's obligations under the South East Asia Treaty Organisation (SEATO) to share the burden of the military effort, particularly when other Commonwealth countries such as Australia and New Zealand were set to deploy troops to Vietnam. To this Wilson argued that a British military commitment would violate Britain's neutral stance as a co-chair of the 1952 Geneva Convention.[11]

Wilson's position was a perilous one. The Labour Party and a large part of his Cabinet were deeply against any involvement in the Vietnam War. If he continued to ignore US demands for a military contribution he risked damaging relations with a key ally, but if he heeded US demands he risked alienating his Cabinet, his party, and possibly destroying his premiership.

The domestic unpopularity of the war explains why much of the UK commitment to the war in Vietnam and at times Wilson's opposition to escalation remained relatively secret. UK material support also included intelligence gathering, the deployment of the SAS to train US Special Forces, and the secret sales of arms to the USA for use in Vietnam including napalm.[12] In the House of Commons when asked about this Wilson dissembled but effectively denied these arms deals took place.[13]

Following escalation of the US bombing campaign to include northern Vietnam on 7 February 1965, Wilson called Johnson to express his concern. This phone conversation reflected the growing gulf between the two men over the war in Vietnam. During the call, the Prime Minister offered to fly to Washington to have direct talks with Johnson on how to avoid further escalation of the conflict. Johnson angrily rebuffed him stating that there was no point 'jumping across the Atlantic' every time a situation arose. Irritated, the President declared 'I won't tell you how to run Malaya, and you don't tell me how to run Vietnam…If you want to help us some in Vietnam send us some men.'[14]

The view in the Johnson Administration was that the phone call was 'outrageous' and had done great damage to Wilson's standing.[15]

Parliamentary and Labour opposition to the war

On 4 March 1965, sixty backbench Labour MPs tabled an emergency motion in Parliament in response to the escalation of the bombing in the north of Vietnam. The motion stated that because UK policy towards Vietnam was based on the 1952 Geneva Declaration and because US policy 'springs from non-acceptance of that declaration', the 'objectives of the two countries cannot be the same'. It urged the Government to 'take an early initiative in order to bring about a ceasefire and a political settlement'.[16]

Parliamentary opposition to the war was exacerbated by the US Department of Defence admitting on 22 March to the use of napalm and CS gas in Vietnam. This announcement caused deep anger in the Labour Party, particularly since at the time of the announcement the Foreign Secretary, Michael Stewart, was in Washington. Six senior Labour backbenchers including Philip-Noel Baker, the Chair of the Labour Foreign Affairs Group, sent a telegram to Stewart demanding he express 'the horror and indignation' felt in Britain at the revelation.[17] They also insisted that Wilson dissociate himself from US policy in Vietnam and warned failure to do so risked detrimental damage to the Party and his Government.

The Prime Minister refused to condemn US action. Instead he stated that Britain would take up the initiative for peace. This did little to settle the growing tensions. At the 1965 Labour Party Conference two motions condemning US action in Vietnam were tabled and after much debate both were defeated.[18] In September William Warbey MP resigned as a Government Whip in protest against Wilson's continued political support of the US war in Vietnam.

The General Election in March 1966 saw Labour and Wilson returned to Government with a much larger parliamentary majority of 98 seats. The Prime Minister hoped this larger parliamentary majority would cool the current in-fighting in the party over Vietnam. However further US escalation through the commitment of more troops and an increase in bombing only heightened it. In response to continued criticism and leaks to the press, Wilson asked the Foreign Secretary to stop attending the Labour Party Foreign Affairs Group.[19]

Wilson did finally dissociate himself and condemn the US bombing of Hanoi and Haiphong in the House of Commons on 29 July with a carefully worded statement. Despite opposition from the Foreign Office on the wording,[20] Wilson called the bombing a step too far but also stressed 'that the United States are right to continue to assist the South Vietnamese'.[21] While the left of the Labour Party welcomed the statement it continued to oppose Government policy on Vietnam at the annual party conferences much to Wilson's irritation. This would be the only time as Prime Minister he ever openly condemned US involvement in Vietnam.

The Cabinet and Wilson's peace plans

The Cabinet, like the Party, was deeply divided over Vietnam and sceptical of Wilson's relationship with President Johnson. While the Prime Minister spoke to Cabinet of his developing friendship with Johnson, some ministers worried that he was allowing himself to be seduced by the Texan's direct ruggedness. Others believed that privately the President regarded Wilson with contempt or at any rate indifference.[22]

The Prime Minister was able to placate the divisions and scepticism early on through his insistence that Britain and he, as an international statesman, would find a peaceful solution to end the war.

North Vietnam refused to talk to the Americans face to face but Wilson deduced that they would talk to the Soviets, who he believed had considerable sway over them. He felt as the Prime Minister of Great Britain he could affect a solution between the Americans and Soviets by displaying his diplomatic skill in creating a peace plan for Vietnam.

Over the next few years of his premiership Wilson dedicated a large proportion of time towards initiatives for peace. The first failed spectacularly. In April 1965 the Prime Minister sent former Foreign Secretary Patrick Gordon Walker on a fact-finding mission to North Vietnam and China to solicit the views of the Chinese communists. He was unfortunately denied entry into both countries.[23]

Wilson's second initiative, and perhaps his most ambitious, occurred in June 1965 at the meeting of Commonwealth prime ministers. Out of the blue he proposed that the Commonwealth send a delegation of three or four prime ministers headed by himself on a tour of Moscow, Washington, Beijing, Hanoi and Saigon to explore the possibility of a peace conference.[24] The Prime Minister had not consulted Cabinet and had only briefly informed Washington of his plan.[25] Wilson reasoned that since the UN could not take the initiative on Vietnam, the Commonwealth should.

The Cabinet Secretary at the time, Richard Crossman, argues in his diaries that the initiative was little more than a 'stunt to mollify the left of the Labour

Party'.[26] The plan did receive positive praise in the left-wing press as well as the Conservative Opposition, although Wilson's sincere wish for peace cannot be dismissed. Unfortunately this initiative, like others before it, failed to get off the ground. The Chinese, Russians and North Vietnamese all refused to meet with the proposed Commonwealth delegation, calling the tour a 'swindle', much to the relief of the White House and Johnson.[27]

Undeterred, in July the Prime Minister secretly prepared another trip. This time the plan was to send left-wing Labour MP Harold Davies, who had previously been to Hanoi and met with the North Vietnamese leader, Ho Chi Minh. Wilson hoped that Davies would be able to gain entry and a meeting with Ho Chi Minh undertaking secret negotiations on behalf of the British Government. The trip was subsequently leaked to the British press. Davies gained entry to the country but was refused a meeting with Ho Chi Minh. Crossman again asserts that the Davies trip was merely another 'gimmick' designed to offer the illusion that the Prime Minister was pursuing peace.[28]

The closest attempt at negotiating a peace deal came during a visit to Britain by Soviet Prime Minister Aleksei Kosygin in February 1967. This trip coincided with the Tet Ceasefire marking the Vietnamese New Year. During talks Wilson and Kosygin came up with a 'Phase A/Phase B Formula' in which the US would cease bombing North Vietnam and in return the North Vietnamese would offer a secret assurance that they would not take advantage of the cessation and move troops into the South. The Prime Minister also raised the possibility of reconvening the Geneva Conference to resolve outstanding issues.[29]

Having been forwarded to Hanoi and Washington, the Johnson Administration responded quickly to point out that the document would have to be changed as the President had just written to Hanoi stating that if they 'assured stoppage of infiltration into South Vietnam, then the United States would cease bombing and stop increasing U.S. troop strength'. This effectively reversed the Phase A/Phase B Formula. It was too late for Wilson to explain the changes to Kosygin who had already left No. 10 for the next stop on his visit.[30]

In his memoirs President Johnson reflected that Wilson's initiatives for peace were 'understandable but not unique' and those who proposed peace 'were all convinced that their moves were the only one that promised success, that their route was the one to take'.[31] The Prime Minister was guilty of this viewpoint.

Wilson had both political and personal reasons for wanting peace. The perception of the Prime Minister personally pursuing peace shielded him from the harsher criticism within the Labour Party and Cabinet. In being seen as proactive he essentially kept a divided Labour Party united. On a personal level, few world leaders can ignore the prestige of peacemaking and with its success, the accolades of the history books. Wilson wanted a legacy and saw himself as an international statesman.

The Prime Minister also understood the growing personal influence of world leaders in foreign policy through multilateral summits like the Commonwealth conference, and through bilateral talks like those with the Russian premier Kosygin. These initiatives offered him the opportunity to further his own personal foreign policy away from the Foreign Office. It also kept Britain relevant and demonstrated British influence. Wilson's biographer, Philip Zeigler writes that Wilson focused a disproportionate amount of time on a problem in which British interest was peripheral.[32]

The economic picture

Another influence on the Prime Minister's position was the looming question of the devaluation of the pound. On taking office, Wilson found British industry to be uncompetitive and failing to reconnect with foreign markets. Much of the problem was the value of sterling being too high. This had led Britain to have a huge trade deficit. Wilson did all he could to prevent devaluation, fearing the long-lasting ramifications. Britain's economic position was precarious, dependent on external help to shore up reserves. The USA did much to support sterling offering two bailout packages in 1964 and 1965 and verbal support for the pound.[33]

Britain was indebted to the USA and Johnson knew it. As Britain's economic woes continued into 1966 talks of a third US bailout began to surface. One adviser to the President suggested that it could be a potential bargaining chip for British military commitment in Vietnam as well as convincing Britain to maintain its military bases East of Suez.[34] Wilson always denied to his Cabinet that any American bailout was linked to a military commitment in Vietnam.[35] However it cannot be denied that in such a weakened economic position the Prime Minister would have found it impossible to openly and vocally criticise Britain's benefactor's war in Vietnam.

Europe

The need for wider markets and greater financial resources paired with strained relations with Washington led Wilson in the summer of 1966 to announce plans to negotiate Britain's entry into the European Economic Community.

The Prime Minister had never been a vocal supporter of the European project nor for that matter a critic. He had generally sat on the fence. In the end he was convinced by then Foreign Secretary George Brown of the economic benefits of membership.[36]

The Prime Minister created a Cabinet Committee chaired by Brown to deal specifically with Common Market membership, to keep under comprehensive review the political, economic and military relations of European countries. Wilson hoped to succeed where Macmillan had failed. Again emphasis was put on his personal diplomatic skills as he and Brown toured European capitals to gather support for Britain's bid. Before going he had to promise to Cabinet colleagues that a full record of all talks would be recorded and circulated to the Cabinet.[37]

Before addressing the Assembly of the Council of Europe, Wilson had in depth talks with French President Charles De Gaulle, the man who had thwarted Macmillan's attempt to join in 1963. Wilson hoped to charm him and prevent a French veto.[38] Unfortunately the Prime Minister's charm wasn't enough, and De Gaulle vetoed Britain's application citing Wilson's Atlanticism and unstable sterling as his reasons.

Decolonisation and Rhodesia

Rhodesia was the second major foreign policy issue which dominated Wilson's first term in office. Macmillan's 'Wind of Change' speech in 1960 had set out a swift timetable for decolonisation across Africa. This meant that by the time Wilson became Prime Minister in 1964 many of Britain's former African colonies had already become independent countries. This included the dissolution of the Federation of Rhodesia and Nyasaland on 31 December 1963, where it was agreed that Northern Rhodesia and Nyasaland would be given independence under majority rule. Nyasaland became the Republic of Malawi on 6 July 1964 followed by Northern Rhodesia becoming the Independent Republic of Zambia on 24 October 1964. Despite pressure from Britain, the white minority government of Southern Rhodesia run by Ian Smith had refused to implement majority rule.[39] This led Britain to refuse to give the colony full independence in retaliation.

The white minority government felt betrayed, having received a number of assurances made by the Conservative Chancellor and Deputy Prime Minister Rab Butler that the Southern Rhodesians too would gain independence if they allowed the dissolution of the Federation of Rhodesia and Nyasaland.[40] When these assurances turned out to be false they were infuriated.

Some in Douglas-Home's Government had had a great deal of sympathy for Smith's position. In negotiations, Butler referred to Smith's Government record as 'exemplary' and tried to persuade Smith to make concessions by warning that failure to do so would risk the possibility of a Labour Government, who would not be so sympathetic.[41]

This political stalemate led to a quick deterioration of relations which only worsened throughout Wilson's first term. He was only a few weeks into taking office, when the white minority in Rhodesia voted in favour of Ian Smith's policy of unilateral independence in a referendum in Rhodesia held on 6 November. Smith used the referendum result to strengthen his argument, stating that the result met Britain's earlier concession that independence must reflect the will of the people.

The Prime Minister's natural reaction was to engage with Smith in talks over independence, much to the chagrin of some members of the Cabinet. He hoped to find a consensus with the Conservative opposition in Parliament.[42] His natural propensity was to negotiate an agreement with Smith through bilateral talks.

Wilson's negotiations rested on five principles:

1 Unimpeded progress towards majority rule as outlined in the 1961 Constitution.
2 Assurances against any future legislation that would be detrimental to the black majority.
3 Improvement of the status of the majority of local Africans.
4 Movement towards ending racial discrimination.
5 Agreement on a settlement that would benefit all of the population.

Where Wilson differed from his predecessors, was in his opposition to the 1961 Rhodesian Constitution.[43] Like the majority of the Labour Party who voted strongly against it, he considered it illegitimate.

Despite regular correspondence between Smith and the Prime Minister little progress was made. In January 1965 Smith flew to Britain for the funeral of Winston Churchill. He and the Prime Minister met in No. 10 to discuss growing tensions. Finding no resolution, they agreed that the UK Commonwealth Secretary Arthur Bottomley and Lord Chancellor Lord Gardiner would visit Rhodesia to assess opinion on the ground.[44] Reporting to the House of Commons after their trip, Bottomley told MPs that he was not without hope of finding a way towards a solution for Rhodesia that all communities could support.[45]

The outcome of the 7 May elections only strengthened Smith's hand with the white governing party, the Rhodesian Front (RF), winning all fifty seats. The RF argued that the outcome of the election gave them a mandate to lead the country to independence, and announced its intention to set up a Rhodesian embassy in Portugal separate from Britain's.[46] In response to these developments Rhodesia was banned from the 1965 Conference for Commonwealth Prime Ministers one month later.

Wilson hoped that through summitry diplomacy he could build a consensus with other Commonwealth countries to put pressure on the Smith Government. However, the Commonwealth was divided over how to deal with the crisis and much of the conference was instead focused on Vietnam and Wilson's peace initiative.[47]

The Prime Minister described the gap between Britain and Smith's Government as 'between different worlds and different centuries'.[48] In early October, as rumours floated of the Rhodesian Government's plan to unilaterally declare independence, Smith flew to Britain for talks with Wilson. Both hoped to settle the issue once and for all. The talks made little progress, but two weeks later the Prime Minister flew to the Rhodesian capital of Salisbury to continue.

During these talks Smith discussed unilateral independence as increasingly a last resort much to the consternation of Wilson. The Smith Government was willing to concede expanding the electorate along the lines of 'one taxpayer one vote' which would enfranchise half a million black voters but still leave a large portion of them disenfranchised.[49] This was rejected as insufficient, the Prime Minister coming to the conclusion that the black majority's rights would be better protected by the British Government directly and by withdrawing the power the colonial Government of Rhodesia had enjoyed since 1923.

Such a prospect alarmed the white minority Government who came to the view that any outcome of talks would not see the maintenance of the status quo. Wilson proposed a Royal Commission to gauge public opinion regarding independence under the principles of the 1961 constitution reporting back to both countries' Cabinets. Both parties agreed and Wilson left Rhodesia on 30 October.[50]

Despite agreeing to the Royal Commission, both sides came away from the talks more distrustful of the other. The Smith Government, sensing the fact that the status quo would not be maintained, saw its choice limited to accepting a Royal Commission or unilateral independence; the latter becoming an increasingly realistic prospect. For the Prime Minister the talks affirmed what many in his Cabinet had said for some time, namely that Smith's Government would never hand control over to the majority.

While both leaders agreed to the principle of a Royal Commission its terms of reference had not been agreed upon. When the British Government's terms for the Royal Commission were presented to Smith, he found that it would operate on the basis that the 1961 constitution was unacceptable without amendments, something the minority Government refused to concede.[51]

In a statement to the House of Commons on 1 November the Prime Minister said he had done 'everything in a man's power' to avert unilateral independence but the Smith Government continued to shift the grounds of negotiation.[52] Therefore, he confirmed his intention to introduce direct British control over the parliamentary structure of Rhodesia to ensure progress towards majority rule.

Hopes of restarting the Royal Commission were all but lost, when in retaliation, the Rhodesian Government announced a State of Emergency which was read as a precursor to declaring unilateral independence (UDI). Four days later in a last minute appeal Smith sent a letter to the Queen stating that whatever happened he would always be personally loyal. On 11 November 1965, Ian Smith's white minority Government declared unilateral independence from Britain.[53] Rhodesia became the first colony to unilaterally break from Britain since the United States Declaration of Independence 189 years before.

The British Government's response to unilateral independence

The Cabinet was divided into two camps over the Rhodesian crisis. One camp was 'obsessed' with trying to avoid UDI at all costs including offering further concessions to Smith, while the other side believed the Prime Minister should ready military preparations for intervention if independence was declared.[54] Many were concerned that Southern Rhodesia might launch a pre-emptive strike against neighbouring Zambia. A number of options were discussed in Cabinet including sending a UN peacekeeping force to Rhodesia and the setting up of a majority African government in exile.[55]

In the end the Prime Minister ruled out military intervention on the grounds that it would be logistically difficult, the UK was not economically in a position to support forces so far afield, and politically Britain would risk being seen as a neo-colonialist.[56] Michael Stewart, Foreign Secretary at the time reflects that domestic opinion was so fragile that intervention might have seen Labour lose its small majority at the 1966 General Election or at least not help them win the kind of majority they did.[57]

Instead the Prime Minister decided Britain would pursue sanctions against Southern Rhodesia in the United Nations Security Council. On 12 November the UN Security Council passed UN Resolution 216 condemning the unilateral declaration of independence as illegal and made by a 'racist minority'; it also urged member states not to recognise or offer the colonial Government any assistance.[58] This was swiftly followed by the passing of UN Resolution 217 on 20 November which described the situation in Rhodesia as 'grave' and called on Britain to 'put an end to it' as 'it constitutes a threat to international peace and security'. It also asked nations not to recognise the 'illegal authority' of the Smith Government and to refrain from diplomatic relations or trade with them.[59]

In Parliament the Government passed a cross party motion condemning the declaration and calling for all Rhodesians to ignore the post-UDI (Universal Declaration of Independence) Government. After much deliberation, on 3 December the British Government suspended the Governors and Directors Reserve Bank of Rhodesia and froze the Rhodesian Government's financial reserves in Britain. This was followed by total economic sanctions which included an oil embargo.

The Prime Minister predicted in January 1966 that it would be a matter of weeks and not months before Smith's Government would give in under the strain of sanctions.[60] Stewart however, believed this assertion was overly optimistic as the sanctions had limited success.[61] This was due to Portugal and South Africa continuing to openly trade with and supply Southern Rhodesia, and a number of other countries doing so in secret.

Wilson's options were back to choosing between a possible military intervention and seeing if there was room for negotiation. The Prime Minister favoured negotiations and between April and September pursued discussion through back channels to establish if any common ground could be found between the two governments.[62] A number of cabinet ministers and members of the party opposed talks, fearing further British concessions to Smith. Suspicious, they believed Wilson had made a secret commitment to push for talks regardless of what the Cabinet said, to the Governor of Rhodesia and the Leader of the Opposition, Edward Heath.

The 'Rhodesia X' Cabinet Committee was established to come up with a solution to the impasse and offer amendments that would lead to independence under majority rule and allay the fears of Smith and the white minority.[63]

Talks on HMS *Tiger* and HMS *Fearless*

On 2 December Wilson met for face-to-face talks with Ian Smith on the warship HMS *Tiger* off the coast of Gibraltar. Present from the Government, were Herbert Bowden, Minister of State for Commonwealth Affairs; Elwyn Jones, Attorney General; and the Cabinet Secretary, Sir Burke Trend. Over two days Wilson and Smith had in-depth discussions covering plans to gradually reform the parliamentary structure towards a higher proportion of non-European seats and the widening of the electoral register.[64] The Prime Minister was also willing to enshrine an amendment stating that regardless of race, there would be no oppression of majority by minority or of minority by majority. Agreement seemed possible but at the last minute Smith refused to sign stating that he did not have the authority to make a deal on behalf of his Cabinet.

This was a huge embarrassment for Wilson, who had only agreed to talks with Smith on the basis that he could speak for the whole of his Government and had done so in the face of some opposition from his own Cabinet. The stalemate continued through 1967 as the Government of Rhodesia rejected the HMS *Tiger* proposal.

On 29 May 1968 the UN Security Council passed Resolution 253 which reiterated the previous resolutions 216 and 217 as well as offering other mandatory sanctions. Wilson was still pushing for the continuation of one-on-one talks with Smith believing that progress had been made on HMS *Tiger*.

The two leaders met again, this time on HMS *Fearless*, to discuss the previous proposal and see if there was any room for manoeuvre. By now the sanctions had become ineffectual. It had been three years since the unilateral declaration of independence and all the horrors people had predicted at the time had not come about. Smith, therefore, felt he had a far stronger position in these negotiations than the Prime Minister and refused to make concessions. This led to deadlock once again.[65]

The failure of the talks was a personal tragedy for Wilson. He truly believed, given enough time, he could convince Smith of the rightness of majority rule. Ultimately he was a believer in bilateral talks, the power of personal relationships and personal diplomacy. And in this instance, as with Vietnam, it was not enough.

The politics of arms exports

Arms ban on South Africa

Before coming to power Wilson pledged that a Labour Government would implement an arms embargo on South Africa,[66] something that previous Conservative administrations had resisted.

South Africa had been a republic since 31 May 1961 after the white minority voted narrowly in favour of independence. Like Ian Smith in Southern Rhodesia, the white minority government in South Africa refused to enact majority rule and ignored pressure to do so from Britain and other Commonwealth countries, instead choosing to leave the British Commonwealth of Nations. A number of countries enacted sanctions against South Africa. Britain was not one of them. The Macmillan Government refused to do so, citing trade with the country as too important to jeopardise.

Less than a month into office, the Prime Minister in keeping with his manifesto commitment announced to the House of Common that the British Government would impose an arms embargo on South Africa, fulfilling outstanding commitments but taking no more.[67] This announcement was well received by the Parliamentary Labour Party (PLP) and generally accepted in Cabinet.

However by December 1967, with the nation's economy in a dire state, George Brown, then Foreign Secretary and Denis Healey, Defence Secretary, wanted the Prime Minister to reconsider selling arms to South Africa.[68] A slip-up by Jim Callaghan, when speaking at the 'under-40s' Labour club, led to the question of arms being reopened: a response he gave to a member about the possibility of future sales to South Africa ended up being leaked to the press.[69]

The issue divided the Cabinet and the Party with Barbara Castle, Minister for Transport, threatening to resign.[70] Wilson was taken by surprise since it appeared that Brown and Healey had convinced a majority of the Cabinet.[71] However the Prime Minister refused to be beaten.

Gerald Kaufman, at the time his press officer and a member of his 'Kitchen Cabinet', recalls:

> When the Labour party came to office in 1964, it came in on a policy of among many other things refusing to sell arms to South Africa which was then an apartheid state. As time proceeded some Cabinet ministers wanted to abandon this ban, and they included the Foreign Secretary, and they included the Defence Secretary Denis Healey, and they began manoeuvring to gain a majority in the

Cabinet. So Harold asked me to contact a Labour backbencher Alex Lyon the Member of Parliament for York. He asked me to contact him and to ask Alex Lyon to put down an Early Day Motion opposing a resumption of arms sales to South Africa, and to get as many signatures for it as possible. Alex Lyon got well over a hundred signatures immediately, and that was the end of sales of arms to South Africa.[72]

Wilson's greatest asset as Prime Minister was his political instinct and in this instance he saw that he would have a better chance of winning the support of the Parliamentary Labour Party than the Cabinet. He therefore delayed the vote in Cabinet, suggesting that it could not take place until George Brown returned from Brussels.[73] This gave him time to build up opposition in the PLP. His prediction was that if the PLP showed a strong objection to lifting the arms ban this would be communicated to the Cabinet, and sway the argument against. He was correct.

Arms to Nigeria

In the case of Nigeria, the Prime Minister found himself with the opposite problem, hoping to send arms to support the Nigerian Government in its civil war in the face of Cabinet and parliamentary opposition.

The civil war started on 30 May 1967 when the eastern region broke from the rest of the country declaring itself the Republic of Biafra. Wilson was keen to sell heavy weaponry to the Nigerian Government to help them win the war, citing the 17,000 British citizens still in Nigeria as well as a desire to support the republic it had helped create. The Prime Minister argued that in the absence of British assistance, the Soviet Union would send arms to the Government of Nigeria in Britain's stead and consequently gain influence over the region.[74] The decision was carried through Cabinet with the help of the Foreign Secretary, Michael Stewart (his first of two appointments to the post) who was ready to resign over the issue.[75]

The Parliamentary Labour Party (PLP) was split on the matter. Wilson recalls in his memoirs that he came under bitter attack from 'young and idealistic members' who supported Biafra and were against British intervention.[76] Like with the war in Vietnam, there were mass demonstrations across the country against the civil war.

A year later and the debate around an arms embargo began to emerge again both in the House of Commons and the Cabinet. Lord Gardiner, the Lord

Chancellor, on 5 December 1968 argued that Britain should strike a deal with France, by which Britain would stop arming the Nigerian Government if France stopped sending arms to Biafra. The general consensus in Cabinet was to try to establish an international arms ban with the cooperation of the Russians and French, however no agreement was reached.[77]

The Six Day War

Despite heated debates in Cabinet over Vietnam, Rhodesia and the question of arms bans against Nigeria and South Africa, the greatest split came over the Six Day War between Israel, Egypt, Syria, Jordan and Lebanon. Tensions between Israel and her neighbours had been strained since independence in the 1948 Arab–Israeli War. They were exacerbated by the 1956 Suez Crisis when Britain along with France and Israel invaded Egypt with the hopes of removing Egypt's President Nasser. The Suez Crisis saw the fall from grace of Anthony Eden who was forced to resign when it became clear that he had lied to the House of Commons about colluding with the French and Israelis.

Since the crisis a United Nations peace keeping force was stationed across the Sinai border between Israel and Egypt. Despite their presence there were a number of incursions and raids into Israel by Arab Fedayeen. These tensions were brought to a head when on 19 May 1967 UN Secretary-General U Thant bowed to pressure by President Nasser and withdrew UN forces from Egypt. Four days later Nasser announced the closing of the Straits of Tiran, at the entrance to the Gulf of Aqaba to Israeli shipping. This effectively blockaded Israel's main port of Eilat, her outlet to the Red Sea.

This declaration sparked an international crisis with Israel interpreting it as a possible precursor to invasion. Nasser's announcement also stated that no foreign ship from any country carrying goods towards Israel would be allowed through. Wilson called an emergency Cabinet on 23 May to discuss a possible response. The Prime Minister along with the Foreign Secretary, George Brown advocated that the maritime powers needed to enforce the right of passage for civilian ships through the Gulf, with force if necessary.[78] The USA was determined to stand by Israel and Wilson advocated that Britain should too.

Jim Callaghan, then Home Secretary, challenged the Prime Minister's view cautioning that there was no way of knowing what sending the navy would lead to.[79] Some in Cabinet, listening to the proposal, felt it was reminiscent of the

Suez Crisis and feared Wilson was about to make the mistake of his predecessor Eden. Others were uncomfortable with the Prime Minister's pro-American position as he argued that the USA would certainly intervene, and if Britain did not back them they would write it off. Denis Healey as Defence Secretary also opposed intervention because he thought it would be difficult logistically to move the naval forces into position in time and even then Nasser could simply close the Suez Canal.[80]

In the end the Prime Minister's stance was defeated and overruled by the Cabinet. He conceded that no decision or statement would be made until he had consulted with the Americans and reported back to Cabinet, and that under no circumstances would he get tied up in an Anglo-American ploy. Patrick Gordon Walker argues that this was an example of the Cabinet's ability to check the role of the Prime Minister in foreign policy.[81] Richard Crossman in his *Diaries* also supports this view, writing that this was a case where prime ministerial government certainly did not work.[82] Wilson later reflected on it as one of the gravest discussions his Cabinet ever had.[83]

After defeat in Cabinet, the Prime Minister's position changed to favouring diplomacy over military action. Wilson now supported French President Charles De Gaulle's call for a four-power summit with Britain, France, the USA and the Soviet Union to resolve the Middle East crisis. The proposal was rejected by the Soviet Union.[84] Any prospect of Britain sending arms to Israel was also quashed in Cabinet. This however had little impact on the balance of the conflict as the USA continued to send arms.

On 5 June 1967, Israel attacked Egyptian and Syrian airfields in a coordinated pre-emptive strike. Egyptian forces responded by invading from the Sinai and Gaza strip. Both Jordan and Syria who had defence pacts with Egypt joined the invasion under the assumption that Egypt was winning the war. This was not the case. After only six days of war Israel had made huge territorial gains capturing the West Bank, Gaza Strip, Golan Heights and the Sinai Peninsula up to the Suez Canal. A ceasefire was signed on 11 June.

In response to Western support of Israel in the Six Day War, the Arab-dominated Organisation of Petroleum Exporting Countries (OPEC) announced an oil embargo against western countries including the USA, Britain, Japan, Canada and the Netherlands. The oil embargo put further strain on Britain's economy with many in Government fearing a recession.[85] Enacted on 6 June, the embargo was only officially ended later that year on 1 September 1967 with the Khartoum Resolution that allowed moderate oil producing nations to restart oil exports to the West in return for aid to Egypt and Jordan.

Wilson and his foreign secretaries

At the beginning of his premiership, Wilson caused controversy with his appointment of Patrick Gordon Walker to the Foreign Office after the latter had lost his parliamentary seat. Walker had been Shadow Foreign Secretary for a year before the election of 1964, and prior to that he was a junior foreign affairs minister under Attlee. It was assumed that Walker would head to the Foreign Office in a Wilson Government. However, on election night he lost his seat to a local anti-immigration election campaign.

Against advice, the Prime Minister chose to appoint Gordon Walker to the position of Foreign Secretary rather than finding another candidate. Walker would become the first Foreign Secretary who was neither an MP nor a peer and therefore not personally answerable to Parliament. To settle this problem the Prime Minister exerted his influence to get Walker selected for the safe Labour seat of Leyton where there was a by-election in January 1965, by offering the current MP there a peerage. This however left Wilson open to criticism that there was no parliamentary oversight of the Government's foreign policy and that this decision was ultimately undemocratic.

In a shock result Walker lost the Leyton by-election by 205 votes and was forced to resign as Foreign Secretary. Stewart in his memoirs reflected that Walker's defeat was largely down to resentment by the voters of Leyton who felt he was being parachuted in and they were being used.[86] This result caused the Prime Minister huge embarrassment and damaged his reputation having given Walker the full support of No. 10. Many felt that Wilson had wasted political capital and time on fighting for the appointment of Gordon which could have been better focused elsewhere.

Walker was replaced by Michael Stewart who had previously been Secretary of State for Education and Science. Stewart would serve two stints in the Foreign Office stepping down in August 1966 so that George Brown could take the position, before replacing Brown in March 1968 after Brown's resignation. Wilson and Stewart were a strong partnership in balancing demands from the Labour Party to condemn the Vietnam War with those from President Johnson to commit troops. Stewart and the Foreign Office believed that Britain should offer more vocal support for American policy in Vietnam.[87] As Foreign Secretary he went so far as to argue in Cabinet that Britain should support the expansion of bombing in the North, much to the chagrin of the Prime Minister.

In August 1966, George Brown was elevated to Foreign Secretary having been Secretary of State for Economic Affairs after threatening to resign from the Cabinet over Wilson's refusal to devalue the pound. Brown had coveted the position for some time and the Prime Minister calculated that this appointment would stop Brown from rocking the boat. Charismatic, Brown had a huge following in the party but a damaging propensity for alcohol. Some in Cabinet believed that he did not have 'precisely the right temperament for the Foreign Office'.[88] Brown was passionate about UK entry into the European Economic Community and was the main driving force behind the Wilson Government's application to join.[89]

Brown's behaviour became erratic and unpredictable as his drinking problem became more pronounced. Unhappy with the Government's position on devaluation, Brown felt shut out and slipped into depression. In March 1968, as sterling came under further pressure, Wilson called a Cabinet meeting to discuss declaring an emergency bank holiday to give the economy breathing space. Brown was unreachable and missed the meeting. Incensed, he gathered ministers who had also not been invited, to challenge Wilson. A row broke out between the Prime Minister and his Foreign Secretary. Brown stormed out of that meeting and wrote the Prime Minister a letter stating that it would be better if the two parted company. The Prime Minister accepted this letter as a resignation.[90]

The Inner and 'Kitchen Cabinet'

In his memoirs, Brown claimed that he resigned because of what he perceived to be a worrying trend of Wilson introducing a 'presidential system into the running of the Government that is wholly alien to the British constitutional system'. Brown believed 'decisions were being taken over the heads and without the knowledge of Ministers and far too often outsiders in his entourage seemed to be almost the only effective Cabinet'.[91] Wilson in his memoirs reflects his bemusement that only a few days earlier Brown had been pressing him to take more decisions as Prime Minister by himself and not refer so many issues to the collective decision of Cabinet.[92]

The resignation damaged Brown's credibility and many at the time saw this as an excuse for irrational and drunken behaviour. In his memoirs, Michael Stewart said that he believed the facts did not support Brown's claim of a presidential system.[93]

These allegations are not without merit. What has become known as Wilson's 'Kitchen Cabinet' consisted of a group of inner advisers whom the

Prime Minister would meet with informally.[94] Gerald Kaufman, one of them, remembers:

> He didn't have such a thing as Kitchen Cabinet. He had a very small number of us at No. 10, on the whole only two, his secretary Marcia Williams [afterwards ennobled as Lady Falkender] and me. Then he had a different group, which constituted itself and which met at homes of various people one night in the week. There were four or five of those, and they included Tony Benn and Tommy Balogh, as well as a few others and he would occasionally let them meet at No. 10 in the kitchen in the private Prime Minister's residence. Now you wouldn't call that a Kitchen Cabinet, though I'm sure they liked to think of themselves as one.[95]

These groups were considered to be more of a sounding board for the Prime Minister than having any decision-making power. That is not to say that other ministers did not feel shut out by the Prime Minister. Both Patrick Gordon Walker and Barbara Castle discuss in their diaries Wilson's use of an 'inner' Cabinet composed of Jim Callaghan, George Brown and Wilson which consulted specifically on the devaluation of the pound.[96] In July 1966 a number of Cabinet ministers complained that too many issues were being settled by a few senior ministers. In response Wilson set up the Steering Committee on Economic Policy to incorporate more members into the decision-making process.[97]

Denis Healey argues in his memoirs that 'no Prime Minister interfered so much in the work of his colleagues as Wilson did,'[98] in his first term. Richard Crossman, former Housing and Local Government Minister asserts that this was particularly true of foreign policy. In his *Diaries* Crossman writes that 'one of the abiding facts about Harold's foreign policy is that he always sees himself as being able to help. He wants to run a foreign policy that enables him to shine as a negotiator, to intervene...he sees himself influencing events personally.'[99]

Wilson was a Prime Minister who was happy to display his dominance in foreign policy making. He was driven by the belief that he was not only capable of being a great international statesman but that personal relationships underpinned the vast majority of foreign policy. To that end he believed that no issue was insoluble through personal diplomacy, backed by consensus at bilateral summits, as was seen with his attempt at the Commonwealth Conference to establish a joint effort to solve the Rhodesian Crisis and Vietnam War. In his mind the road between Washington and Moscow crossed through his office. Having good relations with both, he truly believed that Britain could be the ultimate peacemaker. This proactive approach towards foreign policy was often taken in partnership with his foreign secretaries but not always. At times Wilson's clumsy approach to diplomacy left his foreign secretary on the outside looking in.

That being said we cannot discount his collegiate approach and management of Cabinet. A small parliamentary majority in 1964 and a divided Labour Party meant that Parliament and the Cabinet had an abundance of opportunities to debate foreign policy. There are clear instances where the Prime Minister's proposed course of action was defeated, as with the Six Day War, or where he conceded more to Cabinet colleagues and to MPs to maintain discipline in the Party, as with Vietnam. Wilson frequently sought the permission of Cabinet for his many diplomatic initiatives over Rhodesia and the negotiation of membership of the European Community.

In all his actions he appears to have understood the growing dominance of the Prime Minister in foreign policy, conceding far more to Ian Smith in negotiations than the Cabinet wanted, and still publicly and privately supporting the USA in Vietnam despite strong objection in the halls of Westminster and on the streets of Britain. Wilson's premiership can be seen as a turning point of what was possible.

George Brown, in his memoirs, foresaw a future of prime ministerial dominance in foreign policy which would be defined by a bypassing of Cabinet, replaced with unofficial advisers. Discussing the problem he wrote:

> It places too much power in the hands of one man. It also places power where it shouldn't be, in the hands of friends or unofficial advisers to the President or Prime Minister, who are not accountable to Congress or Parliament while reducing the real Cabinet to the level the others should occupy. I suppose it could be argued and no doubt some people would argue – that concentrating things in this way at No. 10 in these modern rather hectic times when events move so fast, may well be better than our tradition system just so long as the man at No 10. runs things well. It may be said that, whatever the constitutional niceties, no great damage has been done. But what if he doesn't run things well? After all the hectic pace the greater the chance that one man, with a handful of irresponsible advisers around him will go wrong. Look at what we have been allowed to know of Mr Eden's actions and relations with his then Ministers and in the consequence, the way Britain got into the Suez disaster.[100]

Whether he knew it at the time, he had written an accurate prediction of things to come.

Notes

1. Labour Party, '1964 Labour Manifesto', 16 October 1964, accessed 1 August 2015: www.politicsresources.net/area/uk/man/lab64.htm.
2. J. Barber, *Who Makes British Foreign Policy?* (Milton Keynes: Open University Press, 1976), p. 14.
3. Peter Davies, 'Sterling & Strings', *London Review of Books*, 30:22 (20 November 2008): 17–18, accessed 1 August 2015: www.lrb.co.uk/v30/n22/peter-davies/sterling-and-strings.
4. H. Wilson, *The Labour Government 1964–70: A Personal Record* (London: Weidenfeld, Nicolson/Michael Joseph, 1971), p. 46.
5. *Ibid.*, pp. 46–7.
6. P. Foot, *The Politics of Harold Wilson* (Harmondsworth: Penguin, 1968), p. 203.
7. United States Congress, 'The Gulf of Tonkin Resolution'(H.J. RES 1145), 4 August 1964, accessed 1 August 2015: www.ourdocuments.gov/doc.php?doc=98.
8. Wilson, *The Labour Government*, pp. 83–5.
9. *Ibid.*, p. 48.
10. British National Archives, PREM 13/104, The Prime Minister's Office, 'The Prime Minister's Visit to the United States and Canada', 6–10 December 1964, p. 31. See also 'Memorandum of Conversation', 8 December 1964, in *Foreign Relations of the United States, 1964–1968*, vol. I, p. 985.
11. M. Tiley, 'Britain, Vietnam and the Special Relationship', *History Today*, 63:12 (12 December 2013), accessed 1 August 2015: www.historytoday.com/marc-tiley/britain-vietnam-and-special-relationship.
12. S. Dorril, *MI6: Fifty Years of Special Operations* (London: Harper Collins, 2000), pp. 718–19; K. Connor, *Ghost Force: The Secret History of the SAS* (London: Cassell, 1998), pp. 109–10; B. Pimlott, *Harold Wilson* (London: Harper Collins, 1992), p. 385.
13. H. Wilson, *Hansard* (HC Deb, 17 May 1966, vol. 728, col. 1119).
14. Wilson, *The Labour Government*, p. 80; Pimlott, *Harold Wilson*, p. 387.
15. Lyndon Baines Johnson Presidential Library, Texas, USA, M. Bundy, 'McGeorge Bundy memo to President Johnson', 22 March 1965, in vol. 4, Memoranda to the President, NSF.
16. Bennett, F., *Hansard* (H.C. Deb., 4 March 1965, vol. 707, C1530).
17. Wilson, *The Labour Government*, p. 85; The Prime Minister's Office, 'Telegram from Philip Noel-Baker to Michael Stewart', 22 March 1965, British National Archives, in PREM 13/693.
18. R. Vickers, 'Harold Wilson, the British Labour Party, and the War in Vietnam', *Journal of Cold War Studies*, 10:2 (Spring 2008): 43–72.
19. H. Wilson, 'Speech by Harold Wilson to the Meeting of the PLP on 15 June 1966', in File PLP Minutes 1964–Box of PLP Papers, Labour Party Archives.

20 Wilson, *The Labour Government*, p. 297.
21 H. Wilson, *Hansard* (HC Deb, 29 June 1966, vol. 730, cols 1796–7).
22 Pimlott, *Harold Wilson*, p. 387.
23 P. Gordon Walker, *Patrick Gordon Walker: Political Diaries 1932–1971*, ed. Robert Pearce (London: Historians Press, 1991), p. 302.
24 Wilson, *The Labour Government*, p. 108; Pimlott, *Harold Wilson*, pp. 389–90.
25 B. Castle, *The Castle Diaries: 1964–70* (London: Weidenfeld & Nicolson, 1984), pp. 40–2.
26 R. Crossman, *The Diaries of a Cabinet Minister, vol. 1, Minister of House 1964–66* (London: Hamish Hamilton and Jonathan Cape, 1975), pp. 252–5.
27 C. Cooper, *The Lost Crusade: America in Vietnam* (New York: Dodd, Mead & Company, 1970), p. 329.
28 Crossman, *The Diaries of a Cabinet Minister, vol. 1*, p. 269; Pimlott, *Harold Wilson*, p. 390.
29 Wilson, *The Labour Government*, pp. 347–66; Pimlott, *Harold Wilson*, pp. 461–2.
30 Wilson, *The Labour Government*, pp. 356–7.
31 L. Johnson, *The Vantage Point: Perspectives of the Presidency 1963–1969* (New York: Holt, Rinehart & Winston, 1971), p. 255.
32 P. Ziegler, *Wilson: the Authorised Biography* (London: Weidenfeld & Nicolson, 1993), p. 219.
33 Johnson, 'The Vantage Point', p. 318; Davies, 'Sterling & Strings'.
34 Tiley, 'Britain, Vietnam and the Special Relationship'; Pimlott, *Harold Wilson*, pp. 385–6.
35 Wilson, *The Labour Government*, p. 264; Pimlott, *Harold Wilson*, p. 387.
36 Wilson, *The Labour Government*, p. 293.
37 P. Gordon Walker, *The Cabinet* (London: Jonathan Cape, 1972), p. 103.
38 Wilson, *The Labour Government*, pp. 338–40.
39 I. Smith, *Bitter Harvest: The Great Betrayal* (London: Black Zed, 2001), p. 51
40 *Ibid.*, p. 50.
41 Smith, *Bitter Harvest*, pp. 53 and 50.
42 Castle, *The Castle Diaries*, p. xv.
43 Wilson, *The Labour Government*, p. 311.
44 Smith, *Bitter Harvest*, pp. 86–8.
45 A. Bottomley, *Hansard* (HC Deb, 8 March 1965, vol. 708, cols 35–40).
46 Smith, *Bitter Harvest*, p. 90.
47 Wilson, *The Labour Government*, pp. 114–16.
48 J.R.T. Wood, *A Matter of Weeks Rather Than Months: The Impasse Between Harold Wilson and Ian Smith: Sanctions, Aborted Settlements and War 1965–1969* (British Columbia, Canada: Trafford Publishing, 2008), p. 5.

49 J.R.T. Wood, *So Far and No Further! Rhodesia's Bid For Independence During the Retreat From Empire 1959-1965* (British Columbia, Canada: Trafford Publishing, 2005), pp. 411-14.
50 Wilson, *The Labour Government*, pp. 166-7; Smith, *Bitter Harvest*, pp. 97-101.
51 Castle, *The Castle Diaries*, p. 62; Smith, *Bitter Harvest*, p. 101.
52 H. Wilson, *Hansard* (HC Deb, 1 November 1965, vol. 718, cols 629-48).
53 Smith, *Bitter Harvest*, p. 103.
54 Castle, *The Castle Diaries*, p. 59.
55 Wilson, *The Labour Government*, p. 182.
56 *Ibid.*, p. 182; Pimlott, *Harold Wilson*, p. 374.
57 M. Stewart, *Life and Labour* (London: Sedgwick & Jackson, 1980), p. 169.
58 The United Nations Security Council, Resolution 216, 12th November 1965, accessed 1 August 2015: www.un.org/en/ga/search/view_doc.asp?symbol=S/RES/216(1965).
59 United Nations Security Council, UN Resolution 217, 20 November 1965, accessed 1 August 2015: www.un.org/en/ga/search/view_doc.asp?symbol=S/RES/216(1965).
60 Wood, *A Matter of Weeks Rather Than Months*, p. 47.
61 Stewart, *Life and Labour*, p. 172; Pimlott, *Harold Wilson*, p. 380.
62 Castle, *The Castle Diaries*, p. 120.
63 *Ibid.*, p. 182.
64 Wilson, *The Labour Government*, pp. 310-21; Smith, *Bitter Harvest*, pp. 128-33.
65 Wilson, *The Labour Government*, pp. 570-7; Smith, *Bitter Harvest*, pp. 143-6.
66 Labour Party, '1964 Labour Manifesto'.
67 Wilson, *The Labour Government*, p. 311.
68 G. Brown, *In My Way: The Political Memoirs of Lord George-Brown* (London: Gollancz, 1971), pp. 172-4.
69 Wilson, *The Labour Government*, p. 470.
70 Castle, *The Castle Diaries*, p. 336.
71 Wilson, *The Labour Government*, pp. 470-3; Pimlott, *Harold Wilson*, p. 493.
72 G. Kaufman, interview with S. Goodman, 11 October 2013, Houses of Parliament.
73 Wilson, *The Labour Government*, pp. 470-3.
74 Wilson, *The Labour Government*, p. 556; Pimlott, *Harold Wilson*, pp. 491-2.
75 Stewart, *Life and Labour*, p. 241.
76 Wilson, *The Labour Government*, p. 557.
77 Castle, *The Castle Diaries*, pp. 566-7.
78 Brown, *In My Way*, pp. 136-7.
79 Castle, *Castle Diaries*, p. 258.
80 *Ibid.*, p. 258.

81 Gordon Walker, *The Cabinet*, p. 103.
82 Crossman, *The Diaries of a Cabinet Minister*, vol. 1, p. 352.
83 Wilson, *The Labour Government*, p. 396.
84 *Ibid.*, p. 397.
85 *Ibid.*, p. 415.
86 Stewart, *Life and Labour*, p. 138; Pimlott, *Harold Wilson*, p. 357.
87 Stewart, *Life and Labour*, pp. 152–5.
88 Wilson, *The Labour Government*, p. 272.
89 *Ibid.*
90 *Ibid.*, pp. 507–10; Brown, *In My Way*, pp. 175–81.
91 Brown, *In My Way*, p. 169.
92 Wilson, *The Labour Government*, p. 512.
93 Stewart, *Life and Labour*, p. 205.
94 Pimlott, *Harold Wilson*, pp. 340–1.
95 G. Kaufman, interview with S. Goodman, 11 October 2013, House of Commons.
96 Gordon Walker, *The Cabinet*, p. 45; Castle, *The Castle Diaries*, p. 142.
97 Gordon Walker, *The Cabinet*, pp. 102–3.
98 D. Healey, *Time of My Life* (London: Politicos, 2003), p. 331.
99 Crossman, R., *The Diaries of a Cabinet Minister, vol. 2, 1966–1968* (London: Holt, Rinehart & Winston, 1977), p. 414.
100 Brown, *In My Way*, p. 183.

2

Ted Heath, 1970–74

Edward Heath was an established figure in both the Conservative Party and in government long before he became Prime Minister on 19 July 1970. Under the premierships of Eden, Macmillan and Douglas-Home, he had spent thirteen of the twenty years prior to 1970 in Government rising through the ranks. During this period he had a first-hand apprenticeship in foreign policy.

Serving as Chief Whip to Anthony Eden, he witnessed close up the folly and mistakes of the Suez Crisis. He only managed to stay out of the controversy due to the parliamentary convention that Government Whips cannot speak in the House of Commons.

Heath played a pinnacle role in the selection of Eden's successor, Harold Macmillan in January 1957. He reported on the opinions of the majority of Conservative backbench MPs, which largely favoured Macmillan. This helped him secure the party leadership's backing. Macmillan never forgot Heath's support and the two became close under his premiership, sharing a common interest in reassessing the United Kingdom's relationship with Europe.

In 1960 Macmillan appointed Heath to Lord Privy Seal with special responsibility for negotiating Britain's entry into the European Economic Community. Over the next few years he led in depth discussions with a number of European and Commonwealth Heads of State; these negotiations and experiences would shape his later premiership. In his memoirs, Heath writes that in February 1963 it was calculated that during eighteen months of negotiations he had made twenty-seven visits to Brussels, eleven to Paris, and twenty-seven to other countries, covering a total of 50,000 miles in all.[1]

Despite his efforts and that of Macmillan's, on 29 January 1963 French President Charles De Gaulle publicly vetoed Britain's membership application in a state address. The veto damaged Britain's standing in the world and Heath's within the Conservative Party, ensuring that when an ill Macmillan stepped down from the premiership in October 1963, he was not a contender to succeed him. Instead the Foreign Secretary Alec Douglas-Home succeeded him despite being a hereditary peer. This was highly controversial at the time with many considering it cronyism. Under Douglas-Home, Heath received little of the patronage that he had enjoyed under both Macmillan and Eden. Outside of the Prime Minister's inner circle he was appointed President of the Board of Trade.

After the Conservative defeat in the October election in 1964, Douglas-Home conceded to pressure and changed the party leadership rules to allow selection by a ballot of MPs for the first time. There was no pressure for Douglas-Home to step down right away and he continued as leader until 22 July 1965. As Shadow Chancellor, Heath threw his hat in the ring to succeed Douglas-Home, going head to head with the popular Shadow Foreign Secretary and former Chancellor, Reginald Maudling, who many considered the favourite. The result saw him become the youngest Tory leader, beating Maudling by 150 to 130 votes with Enoch Powell gaining 15.

Heath was relatively popular in the Conservative Party and his leadership survived the defeat of the General Election of 1966. In April 1968 Heath sacked Powell from the Shadow Cabinet after his famous 'Rivers of Blood' speech in which he criticised mass immigration.[2] There was a huge backlash against the speech. In his memoirs, Heath recalls that outrage in the Party was so strong that if he did not sack Powell the Party would not have had a Shadow Cabinet.[3] Powell had been a thorn in the party leadership's side for some time. A potential rival to Heath for power and influence, his removal cleared another hurdle to No. 10.

Wilson and the Labour Party expected the electorate to return them with another majority on 18 June 1970. Instead they found the Conservatives were the largest party with 330 MPs to their 288, a comfortable majority of 31. The decision to devalue the pound greatly damaged Labour's economic credibility. The high rate of unemployment and high inflation became the key themes of the election, with the public supporting Heath's pledge of a free market approach.

The rebalancing act: European economic community membership

Heath had long decided that the main foreign policy goal of his premiership would be to successfully negotiate UK entry into the European Common

Market. The failure of the Macmillan Government haunted him. He believed that he would succeed where they had failed.

The British public was still open to the possibility of membership. Before the General Election in February 1970, Heath had undertaken some private polling which found that while accession no longer had strong support, 67 per cent of people still believed that the next government should attempt to negotiate membership.[4]

The polarising effect of the US War in Vietnam only reaffirmed to him that Britain's future led towards Europe and away from the USA. Heath differs from all modern day prime ministers in that he was genuinely a pro-European, enthusiastic about the idea of a federal Europe with Britain at the centre. This was reflected in Heath's first trip abroad. The Prime Minister chose to visit Paris and Berlin instead of Washington. This was symbolic. Deliberately chosen to demonstrate the seriousness Heath placed on Britain gaining European membership, it also was a message to US President, Richard Nixon, that his administration would not be as pro-American as his predecessors.

The US war in Vietnam had now dragged on officially for five years and unofficially for far longer. Richard Nixon had been elected to the presidency in November 1968 on a pledge to bring peace to Vietnam and unify the country. By 1970 it was clear that he had no intention of ending the war and rather began expanding US bombing to include areas of Cambodia. This expansion further alienated the USA from her allies, including Britain.

Nixon as a man was a divisive figure, and the lack of chemistry between him and Heath may also have played a factor in reaffirming to the Prime Minister that Britain's destiny lay in Europe and not clinging on to the 'special relationship'. Kissinger asserted that in Heath, the USA faced the curiosity of a more benign British version of De Gaulle.[5]

Heath, like Wilson, understood the importance of personal diplomacy and had a similar belief in his ability to convince other leaders in Europe of his sincerity for British membership of the Economic Community. Since De Gaulle's veto in 1963 he had spent years nurturing pre-existing relationships with European politicians, civil servants and diplomats, as well as building new ones. He believed these relationships would be the key to a successful negotiation.

Another factor that favoured the Prime Minister's efforts was the election of a new French President, Georges Pompidou. Charles De Gaulle, the popular Second World War hero and President stepped down in April 1969 after a decade in power. De Gaulle had been a barrier to British entry. The French feared that Britain would use membership to destroy what the original six founding members had painstakingly achieved.[6]

France's current position as chair of the Economic Community's Ministerial Council meant that its support would be even more crucial than last time. The path to membership once again ran through the Élysée Palace. An early concern for the Prime Minister was the timetable for negotiations. The six members of the EEC were still in disagreement over their negotiating positions and the size of the UK's possible contribution late into the summer of 1970.[7] Heath feared that the longer negotiations took, the higher the risk would be of scepticism of membership at home. He was advised by Permanent Secretary to the Cabinet, Sir William Neld, that negotiations would have to be completed by early 1972 at the latest.[8] In private, the Prime Minister told advisers that a third failed membership bid would firmly put the British public off any future membership.[9]

The main discussions in Cabinet surrounding membership focused on how best to outline the case for joining as well as the possible economic requirements. In a memo to the Prime Minister, Willie Whitelaw, Lord President of the Council outlined ten reasons Britain should join the EEC: 'for real independence and sovereignty, for a rising standard of living, for a fuller life, to improve our foreign earnings, for economic growth, to develop our industry and technology, for our way of life, for peace and security, for world prosperity, and for our children's future'.[10] These arguments would largely be used by the Government in Parliament to defend the application.

The financial requirements of membership were discussed frequently between the Prime Minister and his chancellors Ian Macleod and Anthony Barber. EEC requirements would include Britain paying off its deficit and outstanding debts, as well as running a surplus of £500 million. Barber was concerned that this might not be possible. The question then, Barber summed up in a letter to the Prime Minister, was if the British economy 'was in such a state that we couldn't afford to enter, can we with such a weak economy afford to stay out and endure increasing American, European, Japanese, and other competition?'[11]

Another focus in Cabinet was the size of Britain's contribution to the overall EEC budget. The general position was that Britain's opening bid should be 13–15 per cent of the total budget but be willing to concede to a higher percentage of 17 per cent. The Prime Minister was particularly concerned about how this figure would be presented to the public.[12] He argued that they should worry first about the principle of EEC membership instead of dwelling on whether they could afford it, taking the view that a debate about the cost would only force the negotiations to stall.

Negotiations for membership had the added dimension and complication of the Commonwealth. Britain's leadership of the Commonwealth, a rival trading bloc, had long been cited by the French as a reason why she could never be a fully committed member of the EEC. Commonwealth countries were also distrustful of the EEC, fearing that British membership would result in a decline in trade between their countries. The Prime Minister had the tough job of convincing both parties of Britain's commitment without upsetting the other; something which was only possible with the high level of shuttle diplomacy Heath displayed throughout 1970 and 1971.

Heath held bilateral talks with the Canadian Premier and the Prime Minister of New Zealand both of whom held the greatest concerns about UK membership. In a meeting on 16 December 1970 the Canadian Premier, Pierre Trudeau warned Heath that the EEC agricultural policies could harm British and Canadian interests. He also raised Canadian concerns of a possible future trade war between the USA and the EEC.[13]

New Zealand's concerns were focused on trade. In 1970, the country's exports to the UK as a proportion of total exports stood at 34.45 per cent.[14] Prime Minister Keith Holyoake argued that successful membership would see a decline in British imports of New Zealand sheep meat and butter, as European tariffs would make it cheaper to import from other member states. This would have a huge impact on the country's economy. To allay fears, Heath conceded to Holyoake that Britain would continue to buy New Zealand meat and butter for a transitional period after joining.

Britain's renewed application was welcomed by Italy, Germany and the Benelux countries. The Prime Minister used his pre-existing relationship with German Chancellor Willy Brandt to great effect. The two men shared regular correspondence about the best strategy for dealing with the French President. Frequently Heath stressed to Brandt the importance that the terms of membership appear fair to Parliament and the British public.[15]

The Prime Minister was suspicious about Foreign Office involvement in the talks. While he had deep respect and admiration for the Foreign Secretary, Alec Douglas-Home, he did not trust the institution. He believed it still held an ingrained view of the French as rivals and not partners. Heath feared that there were still some in the Foreign Office who wanted to use membership to isolate the French, by working with the five other members against them.[16] Douglas Hurd, his press secretary at the time, recalls that the Prime Minister was particularly irritated and critical of anti-French mutterings originating from the Foreign Office.[17]

Heath and Pompidou agreed to two days of talks scheduled for May 1971. The idea of holding bilateral talks with the French President was hotly debated within No. 10. The Prime Minister's advisers feared that if the talks ended in failure they would kill any further talks with other EEC leaders.[18] To avoid this and play down their importance in the media, Heath sandwiched his visit to Paris between similar visits to Washington, Berlin and Rome.

The Prime Minister reflects in his memoirs that 'once again, we had to convince a French President that Britain was sufficiently "European" and would not exploit membership to disrupt or dilute the Community'.[19]

The talks were intensive, with ten out of the twenty-four hours of talks involving only the Prime Minister, French President and their respective interpreters. Both men had known each other since 1962 when Heath, negotiating on behalf of Macmillan's Government, met Pompidou, then French Prime Minister. The Prime Minister hoped this pre-existing relationship would create a trust between them that might make the talks a success.

Both agreed that discussion should largely focus on creating the right atmosphere regarding Anglo-French relations, with each man speaking at length about a general understanding of the importance of negotiations for both countries.

The Prime Minister was keen to address French concerns about American influence over Britain, telling the French President that 'there could be no special partnership between Britain and the United States, even if Britain wanted it, because one was barely a quarter the size of the other'.[20]

This did not stop either side bringing up specific issues. Both felt obliged to talk about defence issues and the possibility of future collaboration, including possible nuclear cooperation, with American permission. Heath voiced concerns about the EEC fishery policy as well as the possible negative effect of trade tariffs on New Zealand's exports to Britain.[21] Pompidou raised French fears that British membership would lead to sterling becoming the reserve currency of the EEC. Aligned against the dollar this would damage competition.[22]

The President also raised wider concerns about the state of the British economy and whether the country could financially afford to be a member. As a precondition of French support the UK would have to give up its right to invoke articles 108 and 109, which would allow member states to apply for financial assistance regarding balance of payment difficulties. Another demand was that Heath end Britain's Exchange Control Discrimination policy in favour of the Commonwealth.[23]

The Prime Minister agreed to both, as well as allaying French concerns over any move to make sterling a reserve currency of the EEC. In reading his report of the talks to Cabinet it is easy to take the view that Heath was largely willing to concede anything to Pompidou in exchange for his blessing.[24] The only problem he foresaw was how best to sell it to Parliament.

Emerging from the talks, Pompidou and Heath announced to a stunned press corps French support for UK membership. The Prime Minister described it as his proudest moment; standing in the very room where De Gaulle had vetoed Britain's applications in 1963 and 1967.[25] Both men would meet on four further occasions to continue the talks and iron out specifics, twice in Paris and twice at Chequers.

The outstanding issue of Britain's contribution to the Community's budget was settled in June. It was agreed that Britain would pay 8.64 per cent of the budget of the enlarged community in the first year. This would rise to 18.92 per cent in the fifth year, a figure comparable to the country's proportion of the gross national product of the enlarged community. Heath called this 'a favourable compromise'.[26]

June 1971 also saw an agreement reached over Britain's access to Commonwealth goods. This would include in the fifth year after entry, 80 per cent of New Zealand butter quotas and 20 per cent of existing trade in cheese. The Prime Minister was told there would possibly be scope for a review of the terms over butter during the third year of UK membership.[27]

Kissinger argues that Britain's acceptance into the EEC had much to do with power politics and the long-standing rivalry between France and Germany. Pompidou's argument was that everybody wanted Britain in the Common Market to restrain Germany, while Brandt favoured British entry to answer critics who charged him with being one-sided, leaning towards the East.[28] Kissinger believed this long-standing rivalry and distrust between France and Germany was the reason they supported British entry.

The case for entry

The Prime Minister now focused his efforts back home on gaining parliamentary support for entry. Each minister in Heath's Government found more of their time increasingly consumed by the European Communities Bill and the campaign to convince their Conservative colleagues and the general public of its merits.[29] In a paper circulated to Cabinet on 2 August 1971 the Prime Minister advocated that the Government should proceed on the assumption of Parliamentary support.[30]

The paper outlined that joining the EEC would require a change in attitude, arguing that 'in all problems of policy whether political, strategic, or economic in character we have to learn how to "think European". We have to think and decide in terms of the inter-action of our policies with Community policies and developments.'[31] Heath was in effect asking for a revolution in the way British Government and ministers thought, away from a colonial or pro-American outlook and more in line with his own thinking. He called it the great challenge of transforming the British administrative system into something truly European.[32]

Between July and October 1971, ministers made nearly 300 speeches explaining the implications of the settlement for their particular departments and the country at large.[33]

The Government allocated a four day 'take-note' debate in July before the House of Commons rose for its summer recess. On the MPs return on 28 October 1971 Parliament began scrutinising the European Communities Bill. This debate would be the longest parliamentary debate since the Second World War, with a total of ten days dedicated to arguing the principle of membership.

There was much internal discussion over whether the Prime Minister should impose a three-line whip or not. While the vast majority of Conservative MPs supported membership there were some who opposed it strongly on grounds that Parliament would lose sovereignty. Heath feared that this minority of Conservative MPs could band together with Labour and gain a majority in opposition to the bill.

The Government Chief Whip Francis Pym recommended a free vote estimating that there were twenty-six 'hard-line antis', six doubtful MPs who would vote with them, and thirteen uncertain MPs, with a good chance of remaining loyal. This left a total of 281 Conservative MPs in favour of entry.[34] Pym argued that a three-line whip may alienate wavering MPs making it more likely that they vote against the Government.

The Prime Minister, acting on Pym's advice, relinquished his early decision to whip the vote, instead allowing Conservative MPs a free vote. This would mean that a minority of his own MPs would vote against the bill, but Heath calculated that their votes would be offset against the portion of Labour and Liberal MPs who were in favour of membership.

Estimates on the number of Labour rebels varied enormously, making it impossible for Government whips to assess with any accuracy Labour's position. If the Labour Party imposed a three-line whip there was a risk that only twenty opposition backbenchers might join the Government, not enough to give a substantial majority. Heath's decision was therefore a huge gamble.

Labour opposition

Harold Wilson, as Leader of the Opposition had decided to put a three-line whip on the vote to oppose the bill despite deep divisions in his own party. He pledged that a future Labour Government would offer a referendum on membership as a way of keeping the party united in its opposition. Wilson and his then Shadow Foreign Secretary Jim Callaghan were particularly critical of Heath's handling of the negotiations.

Callaghan in his speech in the debate argued that the Government had misled the British people on the matter of agricultural policy, arguing that Heath had given into Pompidou, who, 'in the interests of French agriculture... has successfully denied us access to food that is cheaply and efficiently produced by New Zealand, Australia, the United States, and other countries'.[35] Wilson went even further, stating that 'The condemnation of this Government is not that they failed to secure terms which would have ensured that the Labour Government's stated requirements were met. The condemnation of them is that they did not even try. The pass was sold in the Elysée. Some would say that that is arguable. I believe the pass was sold first in the British Cabinet by the right hon. Gentlemen opposite.'[36]

Wilson was keen to establish the differences between his own negotiations and that of his successor's, arguing that 'although the Labour Government saw great political advantage in entry on the right terms, a Britain strong through her own efforts, with an unchallengeable trade and payments position such as we handed over to right hon. Members opposite – £600 million surplus, very different from £800 million deficit – was not prepared to see that strength destroyed by crippling terms of entry'.[37]

He went on,

> There is a further factor. The suggestion has been made in the House in debate, and outside, that the terms that the Government have negotiated represent or are in some way related to a negotiating position, paper or statement agreed to by the Labour Government before we left office. This is, indeed, asserted in the present Government's White Paper. This I categorically repudiate. No

negotiating position, no statement, was ever submitted to the Labour Cabinet in the June, 1970, negotiations, or to any Cabinet Committee of which I was chairman or, indeed, to any representative body at top Ministerial level of which I had any knowledge, and no paper was submitted to me for approval which could be regarded as in any way a statement of our negotiating position.[38]

The former Prime Minister's greatest criticism was that Heath had failed to gain a mandate to take Britain into the EEC, concluding that the Prime Minister 'has no mandate, for he sought none and obtained none, to take Britain into the Common Market except with the full-hearted consent of the British people. That is not at his command, and no vote of this House can of itself redeem his personal pledge to the British people.'[39] These carefully chosen words reflect Labour's position in favour of a referendum on entry.

In summing up the debate, the Prime Minister was keen to stress the importance of the EEC for Britain's relevance in the world. Heath argued that regardless of the vote, the next European Community summit would still make decisions that impacted on Western Europe. Rejecting membership 'would not be a sensible way to go about protecting our interests or our influence in Europe and the world'.[40]

Responding to the criticism that EEC membership may damage US–UK relations, Heath outlined the argument that he would continue to make throughout his premiership that 'Our relationship with the United States is close, friendly and natural, but it is not unique. It is not fundamentally different from that of many other countries of Western Europe, except, again, for our natural ties of language and common law, tradition and history'.[41]

In finishing he touched on a personal note discussing his own vision of 'a Britain in a united Europe; a Britain which would be united economically to Europe and which would be able to influence decisions affecting our own future, and which would enjoy a better standard of life and a fuller life'.[42]

Eventually the bill passed with a majority of 112. Conservative MPs overwhelmingly supported the Government with only 39 MPs voting against the bill. These rebels were substantially outnumbered by Roy Jenkins and the 68 Labour MPs who joined the Government in the voting lobbies. The Prime Minister was particularly pleased with the vote in the House of Lords where the bill passed resoundingly, by 451 votes to 58, a majority of almost 400.[43]

In January 1972 the Prime Minister signed the Treaty of Accession committing Britain to the pre-existing Community treaties. However the Treaty would still have to be ratified by Parliament. This presented a problem. The bill would easily be several hundred clauses long including all pre-existing EEC laws and this offered the Opposition plenty of opportunities to object to the bill. Even if they could not oppose the passing of the clauses they could bring the process to a standstill and use objections to filibuster and effectively use up the whole timetable on the bill.

A compromise was reached between the two parties. A short twelve-clause bill would be presented to the House for second reading on 15–17 February. The bill passed by 8 votes, 309 to 301, with 15 Conservatives rebelling. This didn't stop Labour and Conservative rebels mounting rearguard opposition to the bill. Over five months there were no less than 85 votes. In each of these votes there were rebellions against the Government, with the Government majority falling in sum to as low as four or five.[44]

EEC membership and the USA

President Nixon admired Heath from the outset. He had been openly supportive of the Conservatives throughout the General Election of 1970. A believer in the 'special relationship' between Britain and the United States, Nixon looked forward to working closely with a Conservative Prime Minister with whom he shared a similar ideology.[45]

He was therefore disappointed to find that Heath had no plans for the normal meeting between a British Prime Minister and American President immediately after the General Election. Instead the Prime Minister headed to Paris and Berlin. The two exchanged very few personal phone calls.

Kissinger recalls that Nixon offered Heath the preferred status in consultation for which his predecessors had struggled. He chose not to avail himself of the opportunity and by making his rejection explicit, he both smoothed Britain's entry into Europe and constrained his relationship with Washington.[46] Heath was the leader that Nixon respected the most, yet the Americans felt that he was probably the Prime Minister least committed emotionally to America.[47]

There is evidence to suggest that Britain's membership of the EEC and Heath's pro-European outlook did create tensions between Europe and the USA. In a letter to the Prime Minister dated 16 July 1973 President Nixon wrote of becoming increasingly 'disturbed that Europe has developed an attitude of almost adversary bargaining towards America'.[48]

In his response Heath stressed that in his mind there was no incompatibility between the bilateral relationship between the UK and the USA and the multilateral relations between Europe and the USA. He wrote that the 'two are complementary and both should serve to reinforce the trans-Atlantic link on which, you and I believe the peace and security of the world are based.'[49]

The Yom Kippur War (arms embargo)

The Prime Minister quickly demonstrated Britain's newfound commitment to the EEC, when in October 1973 Syria and Egypt led a surprise attack on Israeli forces in occupied Sinai and the Golan Heights, starting the Yom Kippur War.

The British Government immediately implemented an arms embargo on the region. This had huge implications for Israeli forces, preventing them from getting spare parts for their British-made Centurion tanks. It received criticism from Margaret Thatcher, then Education Secretary and Lord Hailsham, the Lord Chancellor, who told Douglas-Home that the British attitude was 'ignoble and immoral'. If you sell weapons, he maintained, you implicitly undertake to provide spare parts and ammunitions.[50]

Heath, following the example of other European countries, also refused to allow US aircraft carrying arms to Israel to refuel at British bases, and denied the US access to Cyprus for intelligence gathering.[51] Like many European leaders he feared another Arab oil embargo, which would be catastrophic to the British economy. The other concern held by the nine leaders of the EEC was that the Arab–Israeli war was in effect a proxy war between the Soviet Union and the USA, with each rearming their respective sides. They took the view that Europe had no business getting involved or to allow the use of their ports or airbases to prolong the war.[52]

Needless to say the USA and Israel took a dim view of Heath's decision, which greatly damaged Britain's relationship with Israel. It reinforced concerns in the White House that Heath was adamant on a downgrading of the 'special relationship'.[53]

The American reaction was to accuse European counterparts of failing in their NATO responsibilities. Henry Kissinger angrily complained that Europeans had acted as if the alliance did not exist.[54] The Yom Kippur War demonstrated to Nixon that there was a clear divergence between European and American interests. Their approach reflected the contrasting levels of oil dependency. European countries relied heavily on Arab oil while the USA's dependence was marginal. The economic risk of a boycott for European countries was too severe and that is why EEC ministers viewed themselves as in a different position to the USA.

The Prime Minister saw the conflict as a defining moment to prove to other European leaders that Britain was serious about its EEC membership. He masterfully used the war to reposition British foreign policy away from unilateral action and towards the European view of a collective response.[55]

This new EEC approach was embraced by a meeting of the nine foreign secretaries from the respective countries of the EEC and the release of a joint statement on 6 November 1973. This called for both sides to desist from military action, return military prisoners, for Israel to return to its pre-1967 borders and for the conflict to be mediated by the UN.[56]

In response to the crisis in the Middle East, French President Pompidou suggested that the EEC needed further institutionalisation of political consultation between member states and the Community in dealing with crises.[57] At the heart of these reforms would be the establishment of regular summits between the heads of government to deal with emergencies, as well as regular meetings for finance ministers to deal with overall economic policy. These reforms would fundamentally change the nature of summitry diplomacy, reducing the prestige attached to such events and making them the norm for European leaders.

The Arab nations responded, as many EEC countries had feared, with a complete oil embargo on the USA and the Netherlands. They also decided that consuming nations would have to pay more for what they received, regardless of whether they were 'friendly' or 'hostile'. A barrel of crude oil which had cost around $2.40 would now cost more than $5.00.[58] A month later OPEC threatened to go further and cut supplies by an additional 25 per cent.

Rising oil prices had a catastrophic effect on the British economy. As 1973 turned into 1974, the Government faced a shortage of oil supplies, a run-down of coal stocks, and the possibility that key electricity workers would strike in sympathy with coal miners and paralyse the power stations.[59] The introduction of a three-day week to eke out supplies as far as they could be stretched was the final straw. The oil crisis had now pushed the Prime Minister into a corner where he finally had to face the trade union movement head on.

The tale of two Prime Ministers

Perhaps one of the most striking features of Heath's foreign policy was his relationship with his foreign secretary, former prime minister and Conservative leader Alec Douglas-Home. The two had never been close but on taking over the leadership in 1965 Heath kept Douglas-Home in the Shadow Cabinet, seeing a role for him in the Foreign Office as an experienced hand. The Prime Minister, thinking towards British membership of the EEC, felt that having Douglas-Home as Foreign Secretary with his own existing relationships and diplomatic skill would yield a greater chance of success. His appointment clearly had a political aspect, since he was still popular in the party, with prestige and influence; he was a strong ally.

However with Douglas-Home as Foreign Secretary, Heath would not be able to dominate the Foreign Office in the way that many of his successors would come to. Rather, as Prime Minister, he would offer deference to Douglas-Home taking his advice and experience seriously. Douglas-Home took the lead on the issue of a negotiated settlement with Smith over Rhodesia and in establishing diplomatic relations with the Peoples' Republic of China (PRC). The Prime Minister was comfortable in delegating these foreign policy decisions as he knew that Douglas-Home was not a rival for his job.[60]

The two worked closely together, with Douglas-Home actively making sure that the two met outside of Cabinet to discuss policy and get on the same page. Douglas-Home's experience meant that he understood and respected the Prime Minister's right to interfere in foreign policy as and where he saw fit.[61] All in all it was a positive relationship recounts Lord Robert Armstrong, Cabinet Secretary at the time:

> He had great regard for his foreign secretary, and his foreign secretary had been Prime Minister and it was a perfectly good and open, friendly relationship. No, he had a respect for Alec Douglas-Home, and valued him as a foreign secretary, but particularly on Europe he conducted the policy himself. I don't think that Douglas-Home resented that, or felt that he was being elbowed out. It was clearly a supremely important area of policy, and it was clearly something with which Heath was very closely associated.[62]

Relations with China

Heath, like President Nixon at the time, came to the conclusion that the West should engage diplomatically with the Peoples' Republic of China. He visited China twice in 1974 and 1975, meeting Chairman Mao. The Prime Minister considered the establishment of relations with China a diplomatic coup that demonstrated his status as an international statesman. However it also later met with criticism from home. Many Conservative backbenchers were horrified at the idea of Heath meeting and shaking Chairman Mao's hand, a man many believed as bad as Stalin. This was why the initial discussions were largely kept secret. The Prime Minister managed to parry such criticism with his Conservative credentials; something that a socialist like Wilson did not have.

A key factor in his success may have been down to the coincidence of American overtures to the Chinese. Unbeknown to Heath, the Nixon Administration had been in secret talks with the PRC since American table tennis athletes visited China in April 1971.[63] In July Nixon announced to the world that he had been invited by the PRC to visit Beijing and that he had accepted. Nixon had built his reputation as a rabid anti-communist subscribing to McCarthyism. These credentials, the President argued, were the reason only he could get away with doing this. The Americans calculated that by establishing friendly relations with China they could draw them away from the Soviet Union. It was a policy of triangulation.[64]

Douglas-Home has argued that the other factor that opened up the possibility of diplomatic relations with China was Britain's new role in the EEC. He wrote that China took the view that a united Europe could be a counterweight to the USA and offer a moderating influence on US foreign policy.[65]

Britain was not informed of the Nixon Administration's talks with the Chinese. Instead by his own devices the Prime Minister asked Alec Douglas-Home to approach the Chinese in early 1971 to indicate a willingness to negotiate on establishing diplomatic relations. He undertook the necessary talks, which appeared to be going satisfactorily until the Chinese suddenly halted them without any explanation. The Prime Minister found out some months later of Henry Kissinger's trips to China and America's similar overtures.[66] He had been beaten to the punch.

Discussing the talks in Bermuda over Christmas 1971, the Prime Minister welcomed Nixon's lead on the issue and his plans to visit Beijing in 1972.[67] The crux of Britain's negotiations with the PRC was the acknowledgement that Taiwan was part of the mainland and therefore the PRC should rightfully have China's United Nations seat.[68] While Britain and the USA differed over a timetable for enacting this, both sides agreed it, as part of establishing diplomatic relations and sending their respective ambassadors. The process was completed in late 1972 when Alec Douglas-Home made a trip to Beijing on behalf of the British Government; this trip was the forerunner for a later trip by the Prime Minister.

A rethinking on South Africa and Rhodesia

The Conservative Party had always largely been sympathetic to the former colonial white minority regimes of South Africa and Southern Rhodesia. Both Macmillan and Douglas-Home had strived to find an acceptable accommodation with Ian Smith on the basis of the 1961 Rhodesian Constitution, which a Conservative Government had drafted, despite the criticisms of many in the Labour Party who viewed it as unequal and largely in favour of the white minority.

In opposition the Conservative Party was deeply divided over sanctions against Rhodesia. On the vote to enact oil sanctions on 21 December 1965, Heath wrote that the differences of attitudes could not be contained. The Shadow Cabinet and the majority of backbenchers abstained from the vote in line with the Conservative position that sanctions were punitive measures, but fifty MPs voted against the Government and thirty-one MPs supported these new sanctions.[69]

Heath believed, like many in his party, that the solution to the crisis was still direct talks with Smith and sanctions were largely counter-productive. Overtures were made by the Conservatives when in opposition to the Smith Government, and it is reasonable to believe that the Rhodesian Government may have felt that they could achieve a better deal with a Conservative Prime Minister.

Upon taking office, there was pressure on the Prime Minister from within the party to consider the lifting or weakening of the sanctions enacted by Wilson. The party had openly been critical of sanctions in opposition but there was no way the Prime Minister could unilaterally pull out of sanctions which were imposed by a UN resolution without what Lord Carrington called a 'disproportionate row'.[70]

Home was keen to negotiate with Smith and use his pre-existing relationship. The Prime Minister was happy for him to do so. Their initial discussions got off to a bad start. Smith was suspicious of the Foreign Office who he believed was out of step with Douglas-Home.[71] Smith stated that he would only negotiate on the basis of independence for Rhodesia being recognised. Home replied that no country in the world regarded Rhodesia as independent and the achievement of international recognition of its independence would be dependent on an Act of Parliament.[72]

Home flew to Rhodesia, and talks were held between him and Smith from 15–24 November 1971 at which time both men signed an agreement setting out the proposals for a settlement. They included: progress beyond the current parity of representation in both Houses of the Assembly, unimpeded progress to majority rule, an increase of African voters, the abolition of the current income tax regulation used to deter African voters, a pledge that new African seats would be added as the proportion of African voters rose, an introduction of a declaration of rights, and the set up of a three-man commission including one African to look at the Land Tenure Act. Britain in response would lift sanctions if the Rhodesian Government in return lifted the state of emergency. The United Kingdom would also provide £50 million in aid over ten years for economic and educational development.[73]

Both men agreed that these proposals should be submitted to the Rhodesian people for a vote in a referendum. It seemed that the Rhodesian question might be finally settled. However before leaving to return to London, Douglas-Home discovered that Smith had been in discussions with the minority Government of South Africa. He had also been sitting on a number of bills that if passed into law would put Rhodesia firmly in the South African camp as an apartheid state. In response the British Government immediately rescinded the agreement.[74] Smith argued that the change of position was political, Heath scrapping the deal as the price for Liberal and some Labour support for EEC membership. Writing in his memoirs he says 'the problem was I made a deal with Alec Home, the Foreign Secretary and not Heath the Prime Minister'.[75]

The other change in position the Heath Government settled on was over arms sales to the apartheid regime in South Africa. His predecessor was strongly in favour of an arms ban and this was the subject of much debate in Cabinet, despite being enacted early on in his Government.

In opposition Heath had criticised this move. South Africa was a huge market for arms exports and like Rhodesia many in his party were sympathetic to the minority regime. It was therefore no surprise that the Prime Minister changed Britain's position, repealing the arms ban and stating that the British Government was willing to supply arms to South Africa that could be used for external defence, but not those that could be used internally against the civilian population.[76]

This change in position caused a large amount of friction within the Commonwealth. He faced open criticism at the Prime Minister's Commonwealth Conference in Singapore in January 1971. African countries were particularly critical of Britain, arguing that South Africa would only change by imposing full economic sanctions and, if necessary, force.[77] Heath repudiated these claims, believing Britain to be unjustly criticised. Lord Carrington recalls that this was an instance where Heath proved that he was a tough Prime Minister and a harsh opponent.[78]

East of Suez

The Prime Minister took the view that Britain's membership of the EEC and its continued imperial presence were not mutually exclusive. While he was determined to see Britain at the heart of Europe he still supported the view that Britain should maintain its military presence across the world.

In opposition he was heavily critical of the Wilson Government's announcement in January 1968 of the withdrawal of British forces in 1971 from military bases in Malaysia, Singapore and the Maldives, ending the role of British forces East of Suez. Heath on coming to power chose to reverse this decision and maintain a small force East of Suez in keeping with the Five Power Defence Arrangements.

A dominant Prime Minister

Heath was Prime Minister at a time when the Conservative Party was in transition between generations. Many who had served under Douglas-Home and Macmillan had also served Eden and Churchill and were now retired. This meant that he had a young Cabinet who were on the whole loyal to him. His election victory, together with the sudden death of his main rival and Chancellor, Iain Macleod, in the summer of 1970, meant that Heath's political position was impregnable.

This strength meant that Cabinet Government suited Heath who could easily get his own way. Lord David Howell, a junior minister at the time, recalls that these meetings were largely procedural: 'Ted Heath was very correct and liked to hear everybody's views in advance and operated in a very collegiate way. There was a feeling that too many of his meetings were with the civil servants and not with the ministers but he was a very correct procedural chap'.[79]

Anthony Barber, his Chancellor, believes this accounts for there being no resignations from Heath's Government. Whenever a controversial issue arose he always allowed a full discussion, the result of which was that ministers could not complain that they had not had the opportunity to put forward their case.[80]

Lord Carrington recalls that as Prime Minister, Heath could be abrasive and sometimes contrived to seem at the same time both touchy and autocratic, though he concedes that the majority of prime ministers tend to be autocratic.[81]

Like his predecessor, Heath was interested in getting alternative advice and counsel outside of Cabinet. Lord Armstrong remembers vividly many of the late night discussions in Heath's study:

> He liked to get streams of advice on any particular subject coming in from different quarters and he would listen and read it. I can remember meetings with Mr Heath where the members of the staff of No. 10 would go up to the study and sit around with the Prime Minister and throw a subject around. The Prime Minister would be sitting there, very often he wouldn't say much while the discussion was going on, after it had gone on for a certain length of time he had absorbed the views, and reached a view of his own. When that happened he'd say thank you very much and then go on to the next subject but of course that all takes time and effort.[82]

Where Heath differed was in the nature of the advice. The Prime Minister largely took a dim view of Wilson's informal 'Kitchen-Cabinets' believing that advice should be given in a formal setting and recorded. This belief led to the creation of the Central Policy Review Staff (CPRS). Lord Geoffrey Howe, Minister for Trade and Consumer Affairs under Heath, describes it as being 'a special study group which could be directed to look at a whole range of things, semi detached from the ordinary Cabinet structure'.[83] It was the first time a modern Prime Minister set up an official independent unit to offer formal advice on specific policy outside the pre-existing Cabinet structure. This would fundamentally change the power of the office of the Prime Minister and that of the Cabinet.

The Prime Minister encouraged the CPRS to 'think the unthinkable' and 'at least to express the uncomfortable'. It had three main functions, the first being to keep under review the country's economic performance; the second, was to undertake studies on long-term issues which transcended departmental boundaries; and the third function was to provide collective briefs for the Cabinet and sometimes personal briefs for the Prime Minister.[84]

Douglas Hurd describes the setting up of the CPRS as the creation of the 'anointed rebel within the system'.[85] The Prime Minister was unwavering in his support of the CPRS even when it criticised his own performance. This was perhaps one of Heath's most striking innovations and certainly paved the way for future policy units and the idea that more power could be centralised in No. 10.

It was originally suggested to Heath that the CPRS should report to and serve the Prime Minister. He dismissed this idea in favour of the Cabinet, reflecting again his belief in collective government. Hurd argues that had the CPRS survived it could have helped prevent the recent dangerous erosion of responsible Cabinet Government.[86]

Did Heath dominate foreign policy?

One could argue that Heath was one of the last modern Prime Ministers who believed in the power of Cabinet Government. All foreign policy decisions were open to discussion and debate in Cabinet. The Prime Minister had no rivals and a relatively young and inexperienced Cabinet which made them largely malleable to his positions.

Alec Douglas-Home, as a former Prime Minister was one of the most powerful modern day foreign secretaries, and with that in mind Heath would never dominate the Foreign Office in the way his successors did. However, the two of them rarely disagreed and both were happy to defer to the other. Douglas-Home, having been in No. 10, understood the difficulties of the job and was clearly happy to give Heath the space he needed when it came to the larger issues of foreign policy. Likewise the Prime Minister allowed Douglas-Home to continue talks with Ian Smith; a project he knew the Foreign Secretary was passionate about.

British membership of the EEC is no doubt the biggest foreign policy decision since the Second World War, and the biggest change in the British constitution for hundreds of years. Although both Macmillan and Wilson had tried to get Britain to join unsuccessfully, it was Heath who successfully changed the course of British history. In this area he was dominant. Despite the talks being led by Geoffrey Rippon and overseen by Douglas-Home, it was Heath who negotiated for hours on end with the French President Pompidou. In these talks the terms of British membership were struck. While there were many discussions in Cabinet over Britain's stance, they did not authorise Heath to negotiate the terms; he did so on his own.

Many ministers in his Government have conceded that while the members of the Cabinet were all committed to EEC membership, it was Heath and his determination that made it possible. His pro-European nature coloured his Government's foreign policy. We see this reflected in the cooling of relations with the USA. He personally attempted to rebalance Britain's foreign policy towards Europe and a united European foreign policy and away from the Anglo-American relationship. Perhaps one of the only truly pro-European

Prime Ministers his preference and ambitions for Europe were reflected by his Government's foreign policy and in that regard one cannot deny that they dominated it.

Heath made the case that it was possible for Britain to engage with Europe and move away from relying on the USA. In that light his legacy and his foreign policy live on. To this day many pro-Europeans make the case that a Prime Minister can once again tip the balance in favour of Europe.

Notes

1. E. Heath, *The Course of My Life* (London: Hodder & Stoughton, 1998), p. 236.
2. E. Powell, 'Rivers of Blood Speech', Birmingham Conservative Association Meeting, 20 April 1968, accessed 1 August 2015: http://www.telegraph.co.uk/comment/3643823/Enoch-Powells-Rivers-of-Blood-speech.html.
3. Heath, *The Course of My Life*, p. 293.
4. *Ibid.*, p. 363.
5. P. Riddell, *Hug Them Close: Blair, Clinton, Bush and the Special Relationship* (London: Politicos, 2004), p. 44.
6. Heath, *The Course of My Life*, p. 364.
7. British National Archives, London, PREM 15/62, The Prime Minister's Office, 'EEC Negotiations 1970: Secret Memo 1970', 19 June 1970–30 December 1970.
8. *Ibid.*
9. Heath, *The Course of My Life*, p. 364.
10. British National Archives, London, PREM 15/62, Memo by Willie Whitelaw, 'EEC Negotiations 1970: Memo – Willie Whitelaw, Lord President of the Council – 10 Reasons for joining EEC', 19 June 1970–30 December 1970.
11. British National Archives, London, PREM 15/62, Memo from William Neld, 'EEC Negotiations 1970: Memo to Prime Minister William Neld', 8 December 1970.
12. British National Archives, London, PREM 15/62, The Prime Minister's Office, 'EEC Negotiations 1970: Memo negotiating objectives', December 1970.
13. British National Archives, London, PREM 15/62, The Prime Minister's Office, 'EEC Negotiations 1970: Minutes of meeting with Canadian Premier', 16 December 1970.
14. Heath, *The Course of My Life*, p. 373.
15. British National Archives, London, PREM 15/62, Telegram from Heath, 'EEC Negotiations 1970: Telegram Heath to Brandt', 12 December 1970.
16. Heath, *The Course of My Life*, p. 364.
17. D. Hurd, *Memoirs* (London: Abacus, 2003), p. 219.

18 British National Archives, London, PREM 15/370, Memo from Nicholas Barrington, 'UK EEC Application: Strategic memo about the meeting with Pompidou', 21 April 1971.
19 Heath, *The Course of My Life*, p. 364.
20 *Ibid.*, p. 370.
21 British National Archives, London, PREM 15/372, The Prime Minister's Office, 'EEC Policy Memo 1971: Telegram to Downing St Copy of PM's talks with Pompidou, A M Palliser', 10 May 1971–24 May 1971.
22 British National Archives, London, PREM 15/62, The Prime Minister's Office, 'EEC Negotiations 1970: Minute of meeting with Pompidou & Soames to Foreign Office', 23 November 1970; Heath, *The Course of My Life*, p. 374.
23 British National Archives, London, PREM 15/370, Memo from Anthony Barber, 'UK EEC Application: Chancellor of Duchy memo to No.10', 27 March 1971–21 April 1971.
24 *Ibid.*
25 Heath, *The Course of My Life*, pp. 371–2.
26 *Ibid.*, p. 372.
27 *Ibid.*, p. 374.
28 H. Kissinger, *White House Years* (London: Weidenfeld & Nicolson/Michael Joseph, 1979), p. 422.
29 P. Hennessey, *The Prime Minister: The Office and its Holders since 1945* (London: Penguin Books, 2000), p. 346.
30 British National Archive, London, CAB 129/158, The Cabinet Office, 'The European Economic Communities Memorandum Cabinet Meeting', 2nd August 1971.
31 *Ibid.*
32 *Ibid.*
33 Heath, *The Course of My Life*, pp. 377–8.
34 *Ibid.*, p. 379; W. Whitelaw, *The Whitelaw Memoirs* (London: Aurum Press, 1991), p. 92.
35 J. Callaghan, *Hansard* (HC Deb, 28 October 1971, vol. 823, cols 2076–217).
36 *Ibid.*
37 H. Wilson, *Hansard* (HC Deb, 28 October 1971, vol. 823, cols 2076–217).
38 *Ibid.*
39 *Ibid.*
40 E. Heath, *Hansard* (HC Deb, 28 October 1971, vol. 823, cols 2076–217).
41 *Ibid.*
42 *Ibid.*
43 Heath, *The Course of My Life*, p. 380.
44 Whitelaw, *The Whitelaw Memoirs*, p. 95.
45 Riddell, *Hug Them Close*, pp. 42–3.

46 Kissinger, *White House Years*, p. 934.
47 *Ibid.*, p. 935.
48 British National Archives, London, PREM 15/1981, The Prime Minister's Office, 'UK/US relations telegrams 1973: Nixon to Heath July 16th letter', 2 July 1973–10 November 1973.
49 British National Archives, London, PREM 15/1981, The Prime Minister's Office, 'UK US relations telegrams 1973: Message Heath to Nixon September 1973', 2 July 1973–10 November 1973.
50 P. Ziegler, *Heath: The Authorised Biography* (London: Harper Press, 1993), p. 386.
51 Heath, *The Course of My Life*, p. 501.
52 *Ibid.*, p. 501; D. Mockli, *European Foreign Policy During the Cold War: Heath, Brandt, Pompidou and the Dream of Political Unity* (London: I.B. Tauris, 2008), pp. 189–90.
53 Ziegler, *Heath: The Authorised Biography*, p. 384.
54 *Foreign Affairs Magazine*, 'The Year of Europe?' The Council on Foreign Relations, January 1974, accessed 1 August 2015: www.foreignaffairs.com/articles/24476/z/the-year-of-europe).
55 Heath, *The Course of My Life*, p. 501.
56 CVCE, 'Declaration of the Nine Foreign Ministers, 6th November 1973, in Brussels, on the Situation in the Middle East', Press & Information Office of the Federal Government of Germany, 1977, Bonn, Germany, accessed 1 August 2015: www.cvce.eu/content/publication/1999/1/1/a08b36bc-6d29-475c-aadb-0f71c59dbc3e/publishable_en.pdf).
57 *Ibid.*
58 Heath, *The Course of My Life*, p. 501.
59 A. Douglas-Home, *The Way The Wind Blows* (London: Collins, 1976), p. 273.
60 Zeigler, *Heath: The Authorised Biography*, p. 388.
61 Douglas-Home, *The Way The Wind Blows*, pp. 69–71.
62 R. Armstrong, interview with S. Goodman, 18 December 2013, House of Lords.
63 British National Archives, London, PREM 15/1988, The Prime Minister's Office, 'US Relations with China 1972', 16 July 1971–21 February 1973.
64 Kissinger, *White House Years*, pp. 1049 and 1053.
65 Douglas-Home, *The Way the Wind Blows*, p. 264.
66 Heath, *The Course of My Life*, p. 494.
67 British National Archives, London, PREM 15/1981, Telegram from Edward Heath, 'UK/US relations telegrams 1973: Heath to Nixon', 25 April 1973.
68 Douglas-Home, *The Way the Wind Blows*, p. 263.
69 *Ibid.*, pp. 277–8.
70 P. Carrington, *Reflect on Things Past: Memoirs of Lord Carrington* (London: Collins, 1988), p. 247.
71 Smith, *Bitter Harvest*, pp. 154–5.

72 Heath, *The Course of My Life*, p. 479.
73 Douglas-Home, *The Way the Wind Blows*, pp. 255–6.
74 Heath, *The Course of My Life*, p. 479.
75 Smith, *Bitter Harvest*, p. 156.
76 Heath, *The Course of My Life*, p. 478.
77 *Ibid.*, p. 478.
78 Carrington, *Reflect on Things Past*, p. 253.
79 D. Howell, interview with S. Goodman, 15 May 2012, Foreign Office.
80 A. Barber, *Taking the Tide: A Memoir* (Norwich: Michael Russell, 1996), p. 76.
81 Carrington, *Reflect on Things Past*, p. 252.
82 R. Armstrong, interview with S. Goodman, 18 December 2013, House of Lords.
83 G. Howe, interview with S. Goodman, 25 June 2012, House of Lords.
84 Heath, *The Course of My Life*, p. 315.
85 Hurd, *Memoirs*, p. 228.
86 *Ibid.*

3

Harold Wilson, 1974–76

Harold Wilson was returned to the premiership in February 1974 when, in response to the growing industrial action by the trade unions, the Heath Government called an election on the question of 'who governs Britain?' Many opinion polls predicted a Conservative majority but instead Labour won the largest amount of seats, 301 to the Conservatives 297. Both shy of a parliamentary majority, neither could form a Government. Heath entered negotiations with Jeremy Thorpe, the leader of the Liberals, over the possibility of a coalition. When these talks failed, Heath resigned, paving the way for Wilson's second term. Labour governed as a minority Government for seven months until calling a snap election on 7 October, which saw Labour returned with a parliamentary majority of three.

A different approach

Wilson's second premiership could not have been more different from his first. In four years he and the country had greatly changed. Britain was becoming largely ungovernable as industrial action brought much of the country to a standstill. The economy had gone from dire to worse and much domestic action was needed. Labour had pledged to reform public services and committed to increased spending in healthcare, education and welfare. This would take up much of the Prime Minister's attention.

His approach had also changed. Wilson, now an elder statesman, had spent much of his time in opposition reflecting over his Government's record and the path a future Labour administration should take. He took the view that in his second term he should take a less dominant role in government, summing it up by analogy, his economic policy adviser Lord Bernard Donoughue recalls: 'Wilson said to me, he knew I'd played football so he used a football image about when he came in '64 he was a centre forward trying to score all the goals, "Now I play at the back as a sweeper up and leave everything else to the ministers."[1]

The reason for this change, he confided, was that 'his ministers were more experienced'.[2] In 1964 'most didn't have any experience and so needed him to take a lead because of his own Cabinet experience'.[3] Another reason may have been his age and health. At fifty-eight, Wilson was acutely aware that he could not dedicate the same energies to the office. He took the view that it would be better for him to direct his focus to the things having top priority. Denis Healey, Chancellor of the Exchequer in Wilson's second Government, attributes the Prime Minister's change of approach to the prospect of early retirement. He had told Healey during a trip to Helsinki in 1972 that he did not plan to serve more than three years next time he was Prime Minister.[4]

Underpinning this relaxation of power was an informal agreement between the Prime Minister and his then Foreign Secretary, Jim Callaghan. The agreement saw Callaghan gain control over large swathes of foreign policy, making him one of the most powerful foreign secretaries of the modern age. Some would argue this elevated him to the position of a co-premier.

Callaghan was considered by Wilson to be more supportive by the time Labour regained power in 1974. Callaghan, in his memoirs, attributes this factor largely due to his own acceptance that he was himself now too old to be Prime Minister.[5] The two men who had been considered rivals, now both of a similar age and heading towards the end of their careers, established a trust and reliance that would define the latter half of British foreign policy of the 1970s. There was no ambiguity over who held the foreign policy reins. Donoughue remembers, 'My feeling was right from 1974 foreign policy was for Callaghan.'[6]

Renegotiation (European Economic Community membership)

The Prime Minister's main priority, aside from focusing on stabilising the economy, was the renegotiation of British membership of the European Economic Community. Labour, throughout its time in opposition, had criticised the way in which Heath had handled negotiations. Wilson reminded him that the 1970 Conservative Manifesto asked for a 'mandate to negotiate no more… no less' and therefore the people were entitled to a say.[7]

This criticism was particularly fierce in the debate over the Communities Bill when both men clashed over the terms of entry. The Labour Party's February 1974 manifesto argued that Heath had made a 'profound political mistake' by entering the Common Market 'without the consent of the British people'. Instead Labour pledged to renegotiate the terms and offer 'the British people the right to decide the issue through a General Election or a Consultative Referendum'. Wilson therefore saw Labour's victory as a mandate to renegotiate and offer the people a referendum.

However the Party was deeply divided over the prospect of entry and the notion of a referendum. The left wing of the Party was set on opposing entry. Wilson threatened to resign as Leader in October 1973, if the National Executive of the Party voted for a policy of withdrawal. The right of the Party was led by Roy Jenkins, Deputy Leader, who favoured entry and defied a three-line whip to vote in favour of entry. The policy of having a referendum was therefore a compromise between the left and the right which would allow both sides to fight it out. It was the only thing that maintained the Labour Party in opposition. However this compromise was not universally accepted, with Roy Jenkins choosing to resign from the Shadow Cabinet in protest.[8]

In 1974 Britain was facing a crisis as global prices increased due to the growing demand for food as well as inflation caused by the Arab oil embargo. Membership of the EEC had seen the price of British food imports double due to existing tariffs. For the original six nations these tariffs had never been an issue as they were largely self-sufficient.

The Prime Minister was determined to secure a renegotiation of the Common Agricultural Policy, specifically so the country could cut import prices. A key Government proposal was that the Community should cap rising farm prices so that food prices wouldn't fluctuate. Wilson also wanted to extend the opt-out Heath had secured for British access to New Zealand sheep meat and butter which would run out in 1977.[9]

Wilson and Callaghan worked effectively as a team throughout the renegotiations at the Paris summit in December 1974 and at the Dublin summit in March 1975. The Prime Minister was even said to have taken a step back, entrusting his able foreign secretary to deal with the detail of Britain's proposal, as Lord Donoughue remembers: 'When we were doing in '75 the European Community renegotiations, although Wilson took part and had a key role in selling it, he basically left much of it to Jim, who knew most of the detail'.[10]

The Prime Minister writes in his memoirs that the Foreign Secretary was put in the Chair of an operating committee, for the tactical handling of negotiations and the supervision of briefing material, reporting back to the Prime Minister's committee if necessary. This structure gave Callaghan a large personal role in renegotiations but did so outside of the Foreign Office.[11] At the time Wilson was concerned that if the official work on renegotiation was concentrated in the Foreign Office, the policy would run into difficulties with other ministers. It was largely suspected that the Foreign Office was so committed to membership of the EEC that they would tend to use their position to overrule the interests of other departments.[12]

A change in the British Government's position over EEC membership also came at a time of change in both French and German politics. A month after Wilson took office again, French President Pompidou died, and a few weeks later in May 1974 Willy Brandt, the German Chancellor, resigned. France elected Valery Giscard d'Estaing to replace Pompidou and Helmut Schmidt succeeded Brandt as Chancellor. Callaghan recalls that these changes while being beneficial to Europe in the long run, naturally led to a certain hiatus for any appetite in either European capital to discuss British renegotiation.[13]

The first aim was to make it clear to the existing members of the EEC and their respective governments that Wilson was hoping for a renegotiation and not a withdrawal. The Prime Minister favoured an outcome which meant continued membership. As in 1963, 1967 and 1970, the Prime Minister planned a tour of European capitals to convince European leaders of Britain's sincerity for renegotiations. 1974 differed from the previous demonstrations of shuttle diplomacy in that the Prime Minster took a back seat, leaving much of the trips and bilateral talks to Callaghan. During this period Wilson only paid five visits to capitals, three of them to Paris, of which one was for the memorial service of President Pompidou. The other two were to Bonn and Brussels.[14]

Callaghan found on his first European trip as Foreign Secretary to Bonn there seemed to be a shared sympathy for Britain's difficulties but little enthusiasm for renegotiation. This was mainly due to the fact that the German Government, already the largest contributor to the Community budget, understood that any reduction in Britain's contribution would lead to Germany paying more.[15] In reporting to the Prime Minister, both men deduced that despite their uncertainty over the new French President's position, the greatest obstacle to renegotiation would be the objections of Germany.

Despite these early misgivings, the German Chancellor turned out to be far more amenable to renegotiation than previously thought. Schmidt even agreed to speak at the Labour Party conference on 27–30 November in favour of Britain's continued membership of the EEC. Afterwards at Downing Street, Schmidt informed Wilson of French President Giscard d'Estaing's scepticism over British plans; the French President did not believe Britain was earnest about renegotiation.[16]

It was France and not Germany who would present the greatest obstacle to renegotiation. French President d'Estaing wanted the European Economic Community to focus on further integration rather than renegotiation.[17] He was particularly concerned about the timetable of any renegotiation fearing that it would interfere with his desire for a French 'initiative' when the country took over the EEC Presidency. The French President was set on pushing for what he called a 'European Confederation', which would see the creation of European minsters with delegated powers over specific briefs. In a meeting with Wilson and Callaghan on 18 July in Paris he advocated that renegotiations should be out of the way by November or December, so the Community could focus on further integration. Both Wilson and Callaghan explained to the President that the timetable was simply unrealistic.[18] The British Prime Minster also argued that the European Commission should not interfere in the affairs of national governments, particularly in foreign affairs. He was, however, prepared to contemplate the establishment of some kind of political secretariat if it could lead to common positions in respect of foreign political problems.[19]

Roy Jenkins believes Wilson's conversations with Schmidt renewed his interest in foreign policy involvement, engaging him in a way he had not been since his relationship with President Johnson. Unlike previously, the Prime Minister could play an equal hand with Schmidt and d'Estaing rather than being the junior partner with LBJ.[20]

In response to the information from Schmidt, Callaghan pushed for an informal dinner between Britain and France's opposing numbers before the Paris Summit to discuss their differences. At the dinner, the French Foreign Minister was keen to stress France's opposition to changes to the EEC budget that would include a self-adjusting mechanism.[21]

Expectations going into the Paris Summit on 9–10 December were therefore quite low. British renegotiation was last on the agenda and the meeting nearly broke down before it even got to the topic, over the Commission's proposed regional fund which was designed to help struggling economies. The proposal would see specific allocations of money for Italy and Ireland, with Italy receiving 40 per cent and Ireland 6 per cent. The problem was the regional fund would have to be provided mainly by Germany. In the end a compromise was reached which saw Britain surprisingly get a 28 per cent portion of the allocation.[22]

Callaghan recalls that throughout the Paris Summit Wilson was experiencing a number of minor indispositions and was not wholly well.[23] Although the Prime Minister persevered, the Foreign Secretary took the lead on his behalf. On renegotiation all countries favoured that whatever Britain's issues they could be resolved through compromise, even budgetary issues. Germany's Schmidt was keen to point out that the term renegotiation was misleading, as it did not mean Treaty revision. This, he argued, needed to be made clear to national Parliaments.[24] All of the nine EEC countries agreed that any specific deal would be negotiated and agreed upon at the European Council meeting in Dublin in March 1975.

An 'agreement to differ'

The Prime Minister reported favourably to Parliament that the renegotiations were at hand and would lead to a correcting mechanism for the budgetary contribution. Both those in favour of the EEC, the pro-Marketeers and those against membership, the anti-Marketeers saw the negotiations as most likely to end with the Government recommending the British people support continued membership.[25]

This presented a huge problem for those against, who felt unable to accept the Government's position under the convention of collective Cabinet responsibility, and were therefore presented with the dilemma of resigning from the Cabinet. Wilson conceded that members of the Cabinet would have to be free to express their own views.[26] The Prime Minister therefore proposed a position that there should be an 'agreement to differ' in Cabinet, which would be announced to the House, allowing ministers to break with the normal rules of collective responsibility.[27] This would include junior ministers, a considerable number of whom were considered to be anti-Marketeers.

At the time some argued that the unprecedented loosening of Cabinet responsibility was dangerous and would lead to disorder but Bernard Donoughue believes it was essential:

> It was a perfectly sensible thing for Harold to do, to allow members of his Cabinet to break the then tight rules of collective responsibility; they are very loose now, but then were very tight, and allow people to speak on different sides, and not to have a Government position for the referendum. So it was an excellent device. It got us through two elections. It kept the Government together because people didn't argue about Europe. There was no need to, as we had a means of solving it.[28]

The Prime Minister and Foreign Secretary had to balance domestic scepticism as well as European concerns over the consequences of a referendum. German Chancellor Schmidt worried that a British exit could see Ireland and Denmark choose also to leave.[29] President d'Estaing questioned whether a referendum would be constitutional or whether it was legally possible so soon after concluding a Treaty to join and also whether the verdict would be binding on the government.[30] Callaghan conceded in a meeting with him that it was uncharted territory, but he felt sure that MPs ignored the popular will at their own risk.[31] He said if Britain remained in the Community in spite of a negative vote she could only be a reluctant partner which would inhibit the Community's development.[32] Despite these worries both Wilson and Callaghan were optimistic about renegotiations and the campaign to come.

At the European Council meeting in Dublin, on 10–11 March 1975, agreement was finally reached on acceptable terms for continued British membership of the EEC. Germany, having its own budgetary problems, supported the idea of criteria for the assessment of a budget refund if in any year budget contributions were larger than would be fair in relation to the country's GNP.[33] The German Chancellor proposed a maximum refund of 250 million units, the equivalent of £125 million in one year. This was considered to be an appropriate budget mechanism. The Foreign Secretary calculated this would mean that Britain's net contribution for 1974 would be around £70 million.[34]

In the case of the Commonwealth, the Prime Minister had fought long and hard to explain the importance of the Commonwealth to sceptical Community countries who did not understand the nature of Britain's relationship with its former colonies. That being said, in the end they conceded that Britain could continue to import New Zealand's dairy products after 1977.[35]

Recommendation and referendum

Wilson announced at a press conference that the negotiations had resulted in a great improvement for British membership. He was satisfied that no more could be achieved at that time, but it would be for Parliament and the people to decide whether the terms were good enough. This success, he argued, was down to a team effort between himself and Callaghan, describing them as in complete partnership 'we pass the ball from one to the other and break through the opposition'.[36]

The recommendation of the Prime Minister and Foreign Secretary was accepted by a substantial proportion of the Cabinet, with sixteen voting in favour. The Prime Minister then requested the names of the Cabinet ministers who felt unable to support the decision and would wish to disassociate themselves in the referendum campaign to come. Seven chose this course: Michael Foot, Barbara Castle, Eric Varley, Willie Ross, Tony Benn, Peter Shore and John Silkin.[37]

Wilson was keen to dismiss criticism from the left of the party who argued that he had packed the Cabinet with a pro-Market majority. In his memoirs, Wilson argued that when he took office he calculated that the make-up of his Cabinet was a twelve anti-Market majority, with nine in favour, and himself and Callaghan as undecided depending on terms of renegotiations. By March 1975, five Cabinet ministers had clearly changed their minds.[38]

There was much confusion over the Prime Minister's policy of agreeing to differ when it came to the debate on the EEC renegotiations in Parliament. Wilson was away at the time in Belfast. In his absence the Cabinet was chaired by Ted Short, Leader of the House. In the Prime Minister's absence, the Cabinet decided the policy meant that senior and junior ministers would be free to vote against the Government's recommendations. Wilson, in his memoirs writes of his shock of learning of this misinterpretation, since he believed the policy should have seen ministers abstain, something that seemed both 'right and to me obvious'.[39]

This confusion caused the Government great embarrassment and only served to heighten tensions as seven Cabinet ministers and thirty-one ministerial and other ranks, exactly half of the junior ministers, voted against the Government motion.[40] The Cabinet did however agree to place a ban on ministers speaking in the debate who had not otherwise been requested to. The only person to ignore this ban was Eric Heffer, the Minister of State for Industry, who later tendered his resignation as requested by the Prime Minister.

The debate on the acceptance of the Government's position on the outcome of the renegotiations lasted three days from 7–9 April 1975. The result saw 396 MPs vote for the Government's motion and 170 against. The Government was sustained by the Conservative Opposition. The Parliamentary Labour Party was split down the middle, with 137 voting in favour and 145 against, with another 33 failing to vote.[41]

The Prime Minister now diverted his attention to the outline of the referendum campaign. It had been agreed for some time that the date of the referendum would be the first Thursday in June 1975, but there had been little agreement on 'the question'. In consultation with ministers, it was agreed that the referendum campaign would follow the same model as a General Election, with Government grants of £125,000 of funding available to both sides. Government would also pay the costs of distributing leaflets presenting both sides of the argument to voters.

Both the Liberals and the vast majority of the Conservative Party, including its leader Margaret Thatcher and former Prime Minister Ted Heath, campaigned in favour. Under the terms of the Prime Minister's policy of 'agreement to differ' Labour MPs and Cabinet ministers were allowed to campaign on either side of the argument. However Wilson laid down a further two rules, the first being no personal attacks – stick to the issues and not personalities. Secondly, ministers were told that the 'agreement to differ' ended on 6 June, the day following the poll. From then on full collective responsibility would apply to the EEC as on all other issues.[42] The rules were largely followed except for a *Question Time* debate between Tony Benn and Roy Jenkins, which descended quickly into personal attacks likened by Wilson to 'a public brawl'.[43] The debate became iconic and representative of the wider national debate but both men were rebuked by the Prime Minister.

Cabinet ministers in large part behaved themselves. Wilson's biggest problem throughout the campaign came in the form of the Labour National Executive Committee, who decided to support the No lobby. The NEC were talking of an outright campaign against the Government. In his concern, Wilson threatened once again to resign his leadership if a compromise could not be reached. In the end a special one-day conference was called whereby the whole of the Party was given an opportunity to vote on the official position. In the end 3,724,000 voted against the Market and 1,986,999 for continued membership. This was practically 2 to 1 against.[44]

At the Commonwealth Prime Ministers Conference a week before the vote, the Conference released a statement endorsing British membership as being in the best interests of the Commonwealth. This was due mainly to the Lomé Convention, which saw the EEC offer aid to developing Commonwealth countries.[45] This endorsement was used effectively to counter criticism that membership was harmful to the interests of the Commonwealth or betrayed developing countries.

On Thursday 5 June the country voted by 67.2 per cent against 32.8 per cent to stay as a member of the EEC and accept the terms of renegotiation. 64.5 per cent of the electorate turned out to vote. It was a resounding defeat for the No campaign. Each individual country in the Union recorded their vote as a clear majority for membership.

The anti-Marketeers argue with the benefit of hindsight that they always had a tough battle. As Wilson himself agrees in his memoirs, the national and provincial press were in favour of a Yes vote almost without exception.[46] In terms of campaign spending the final tally showed that the pro-Marketeers had spent £1,365,583 to the anti-Marketeers £133,629, outspending them 10 to 1.[47]

The Cabinet ministers sceptical of membership accepted the result, and the Prime Minister declared on the steps of Downing Street that fourteen years of national argument was over.

The politics of arms

On taking office, Wilson was again keen to place a ban on arms exports to South Africa, after his predecessor had lifted the ban for weapons that were for external defence only. This was not an easy task as a number of items were at different stages of building and shipping, already bought and paid for by the Government of South Africa.

The Prime Minister called a meeting with the ministers concerned to take immediate decisions about a blanket ban. The first of these was to cancel a helicopter still on order. The ministers then went down a list deciding on each item to determine whether they had military or civilian use. The Secretaries of State for Defence and Trade were delegated to meet and draw up a list of permitted and banned items for the future. If there was any disagreement they would refer this to the Prime Minister's Committee for settlement.[48] The Labour Government also moved forward with plans to rescind the Simonstown Agreement, which set out naval cooperation between South Africa and Britain.[49]

Despite this, the Royal Navy did take part in exercises off the coast of South Africa. This created a row between Jim Callaghan and the Defence Secretary, Roy Mason with both men claiming they had no prior knowledge. As a result, the London *Evening Standard* ran the headline, 'Who runs the navy?' Both the Foreign Office and the Labour Party blamed the Ministry of Defence, and the National Executive Committee of the Labour Party censured the Government. In the end, it was discovered that the Foreign Office had organised the joint naval exercises with the Charge d'affaires in South Africa. Somehow, Mason writes in his memoirs, the arrangements hadn't been transferred to the Foreign Secretary until it was too late.[50] Needless to say the incident brought great embarrassment to the Government and its policy of an arms ban.

In the case of Chile, both Wilson and Callaghan had made it clear in opposition of their wish to see a change in foreign policy regarding the military junta then in charge of the country. On regaining office, Callaghan reported to the Commons on 27 March 1974 of the new Government's desire to see democracy in Chile restored and human rights upheld. To this end, he said, the UK will support any future representations to the UN regarding human rights abuses in Chile.

The Prime Minister immediately suspended aid as well as a projected naval training exercise arranged by his predecessor. As with South Africa, a review of pre-existing defence contracts was undertaken for the implementation of a weapons ban. The problem for Britain was some of the ships Chile had ordered had already been handed over, and were engaged in trials; under international law the UK had no recourse for retrieving them.[51]

The Conservative opposition, being close with Chile and sympathetic to the military junta, criticised Wilson's decision. So did a number of Labour MPs, who asked Wilson why similar action was not being taken over the Soviet Union. The Prime Minister responded that the UK had not traded with the Soviets since just after the Second World War.[52]

Cyprus

Wilson's second term was not without foreign policy crises. On 15 July 1974, a fanatical Greek politician called Nikos Sampson, a member of the EOKA Greek Cypriot nationalist group, started a revolt in Cyprus attacking the presidential palace. In response, the Greek National Guard intervened, supporting Sampson in a coup which forced the Cypriot President, Archbishop Makarios III, to flee the country to the UK.[53] The Prime Minister welcomed him and offered the hospitality due to any visiting Head of State.

The Foreign Secretary reported to the House. Discussing the crisis, he said that the UK had no responsibility under the independence treaty granted by Britain to Cyprus for internal security, though there was a contingent of British troops as part of a UN force on the island, as well as the two military bases at Akrotiri in the south and Dhekelia in the East.[54]

Both the British and Turkish Governments refused to recognise Sampson's regime. Callaghan dispatched a note to the Greek Government, then led by a military junta, to do the same and remove the Greek National Guard from the island.

In response to the coup and in fear for the safety of the Turkish minority, the Turkish Prime Minister, Bülent Ecevit, headed to London on 17 July for urgent talks regarding the instability in Cyprus. In discussions with the Prime Minister and Foreign Secretary, Ecevit argued that because of the coup Turkey no longer recognised Greece as a Guarantor of Cyprus. This therefore meant that the mechanism for consultations under the 1960 Treaty was invalid. Instead he demanded there must be a Turkish presence on the island to save Turkish civilians.[55]

Ecevit asked for British support for Turkish plans to invade the island to protect the Turkish minority there. For this purpose he requested the use of the British military base at Akrotiri, something which Wilson immediately refused. The Prime Minister argued that the legal status of the bases differed from the rest of the island and to allow their use by a third country's troops would certainly give rise at some stage to a direct challenge to their status as British sovereign territory.[56]

The Prime Minister felt that Britain had a special obligation to Cyprus as both a member of the Commonwealth and former colony, and more importantly under the obligations of the 1960 Treaty of Guarantee. The Treaty allowed Britain to keep her bases as the price of guaranteeing the island's independence and security. Therefore he held a strong belief that the only solution to this crisis would be for all of the signatories of the Treaty to uphold their obligations. The Prime Minister invited both Turkey and Greece for talks in London. Both governments refused. Wilson was faced with the fact that two of the three guarantors of Cyprus's security and independence had failed to fulfil their obligations under the Treaty.[57]

Over the next few days the Prime Minister and Foreign Secretary both worked to increase converging pressure on Athens, through the European Community, through NATO, and above all by reaching out to the USA to pressure the Greek military Government.[58] The hope was that getting Greece to remove its National Guard would remove any pretext for a Turkish invasion. However the Nixon Administration was then in turmoil over the Watergate scandal, which was reaching its finale. Owing to this, Nixon's Secretary of State, Henry Kissinger, was unreachable during the crucial hours of the crisis and when he was, could not gain any clear guidance from the President.[59]

The Greek Government did not respond to the pressure; instead it also threatened intervention in Cyprus to get the situation under control. However before anything could be done, on 19 July Turkish military forces began their invasion and bombing of Cyprus. Responding, the Prime Minister directed military air support at British bases in Cyprus to be strengthened and naval vessels in the Mediterranean, the Atlantic, and at UK bases to proceed towards Cyprus. On arrival the navy was largely engaged in humanitarian relief rescuing Greek Cypriots in the north of the island threatened by the advancing Turkish military forces, whom Wilson argued sought to occupy areas of Cyprus which could not by any stretch of the imagination be regarded as Turkish Cypriot territory.[60]

In response to the Turkish invasion, the Greek Government demanded the withdrawal of Turkish troops from Cyprus or Greece would declare war and a state of Enosis that would permanently unite Cyprus with Greece.[61]

Britain attempted to push through a UN resolution to increase the pre-existing UN forces already on Cyprus. This was prevented by a veto from the Soviet Union. Instead, on 20 July, the UN Security Council passed UN Resolution 353, which demanded an immediate cessation of military intervention and called on both Turkey and Greece to respect the island's sovereignty.

The ceasefire came into effect on 22 July. The following day the humiliated military junta in Greece resigned and Sampson was removed from power in Cyprus, being replaced by Greek Cypriot leader, Glafcos Clerides. The Greek, Turkish and Cypriot governments all agreed to talks in Geneva, chaired by Britain. The hope was that all sides could find a resolution.

However on the evening of 24 July, the Turkish Government informed Wilson of their plans to bomb Nicosia airport where UN forces were stationed, including British and Canadian troops. Wilson, encouraged by Callaghan, spoke with Ecevit and demanded an explanation. The Turkish Prime Minister told Wilson that he planned to go ahead with the action but conceded that the Turkish air force knew the location of the British troops and could avoid bombing this sector.[62]

The Prime Minister informed his Turkish counterpart once again in strong language that he would not accept this and had a responsibility as a UN member to protect UN forces. He would not enter into collusion whereby British troops were safeguarded and the lives of Canadians endangered. He told the Turkish Prime Minister that if he continued down this path then he would not hesitate to order fighters to shoot down Turkish aircraft.[63]

In the end the Turkish Government backed down and cancelled their plans. Wilson in his memoirs reflects that aside from Suez, this was probably the nearest Britain had come to war with another nation since 1945.[64]

At the first round of talks on 25–30 July, both Greece and Turkey agreed on a buffer zone with the existing UN force in charge of maintaining it. Clerides argued that Cyprus needed a level of autonomy to protect both Turkish and Greek citizens. The talks reached a deadlock over the question of Cyprus's autonomy, with neither side happy.

Turkey threatened to derail the whole Geneva process and advance her troops to capture the rest of the island, despite UN, US and British pressure. Greece argued that if Turkey did so they would invoke Article 5 of the North Atlantic Treaty.

Britain, with the rest of the international community pushed for a second round of Geneva talks taking place from 12 August. These talks did not yield any further agreement and by 14 August both the Greeks and the Turkish had broken the ceasefire. On 16 August the UN Security Council passed UN Resolution 360 declaring respect for the sovereignty and integrity of the Republic of Cyprus and condemning Turkey's unilateral action. Despite all Callaghan's diplomatic skills he was unable to find a resolution. He and the Prime Minister both lamented what they considered a failure on their part.

The creation of a policy unit

Like his predecessor, Wilson was interested in gaining as much independent advice as possible, particularly in regard to dealing with Britain's economic woes. Heath's Central Policy Review Staff was a good start, but Wilson wanted to take it a step further with the creation of a policy unit in No. 10 directly under his control.

Political advisers had been attached to various departments for some time and the idea of a Prime Minister having a political adviser was not something new. What was different about this particular development was for the first time there was to be a specific delegated unit that had the authority of the Prime Minister which had the power to coordinate policy and direct other departments.

Wilson appointed Dr Bernard Donoughue to lead a team of seven other advisers; their role was focused on both departmental administration and political coordination as well as picking up the CPRS role of policy research. Donoughue says that this was 'an early sign of strengthening No. 10 in a policy role'.[65] This was largely down to the fact that Wilson was distrustful of the Treasury and wanted independent advice. He wanted the policy unit to specifically come up with alternative policies for the economy and effectively shadow the Treasury. Wilson drew from his experiences in the 1960s and the decision to devalue sterling, which he felt reflected that the Treasury and Chancellor were poor at economic policy. 'It was ultimately about giving the Prime Minister the ability to quiz the Treasury but not necessarily to replace them'.[66]

This represented a huge step in the evolution of the power of No. 10. While this focused heavily on domestic policy, it set the path for a designated foreign policy unit later.

Conspiracy, illness and resignation

Wilson had decided long before his re-election that he would only serve in the position for two years, being just enough time to use his stewardship to get the Labour Party through renegotiation and a referendum.[67] It cannot be said for certain when he learnt of his diagnosis but by 1976 Wilson was beginning to show the early symptoms of Alzheimer's disease.

He had always been a believer in conspiracies. His suspicion of plots and fears of being spied on grew throughout his second term. Many attributed this growing paranoia to ill health and eccentricity. His accusations rested upon three forms: the first, that he was being bugged by foreign intelligence services; second, that MI5 was doing the same; and finally that former members of the armed forces were preparing a *coup d'état*.

When George H. Bush visited No. 10 as the head of the Central Intelligence Agency, he left thinking Wilson was crazy, after being told by him that the Cabinet room was bugged.[68] In fact much of the literature for a long period was sceptical of these claims, even going as far as to mock Wilson. There was an inquiry in 1977 and the Callaghan Government concluded in a statement to the House 'The Prime Minister is satisfied that at no time has the security service or any other British intelligence or security agency, either of its own accord or at someone else's request, undertaken electronic surveillance in No. 10 Downing Street'.[69]

In 2010, historian Christopher Andrew published a book entitled *Defence of the Realm: the Authorised History of MI5*.[70] In a first draft he intended to reveal evidence that MI5 had bugged the Cabinet Office from 1963 until the listening devices were taken out in 1977.[71] The *Mail on Sunday* reported on 18 April 2010 that this section of the book had been excised for national security reasons.[72] Around the same time as the publishing of the book, MI5 admitted that they did have a file on Wilson and his association with known Communists. While this does not support Wilson's claim of bugging, it certainly presents his claims in a more fair and balanced way.

Perhaps the more damaging claim was of plans by members of the military establishment to remove him in a *coup d'état* and install Lord Mountbatten. The alleged plans were devised between disgruntled members of the military and intelligence services, who suspected that Wilson was a secret Communist. Only weeks after leaving Downing Street he spoke to journalists about his concerns over plans to remove both his governments in the 1960s and 1970s.[73] A number of books and documentaries have been written about these claims with many people lending their voices to argue their credibility, including Baroness Falkender, his political secretary at the time.

As with the charges levied against MI5, if these claims were ever found to be true they would have a shattering effect on the way we view the conduct of our foreign policy and the military and intelligence relations with Government. While the true extent of them will probably never be known, it is clear they cannot be dismissed as fantasy when talking about Wilson and his premiership. If he was viewed to be such a threat that he needed to be bugged and possibly removed by the military, then was he not by that definition a powerful and dominant Prime Minister?

Notes

1 B. Donoughue, interview with S. Goodman, 26 November 2013, House of Lords.
2 *Ibid.*
3 *Ibid.*
4 Healey, *Time of My Life*, p. 388.
5 J. Callaghan, *Time and Chance* (London: Politicos, 2006), p. 300; Pimlott, *Harold Wilson*, p. 653.
6 B. Donoughue, interview with S. Goodman, 26 November 2013, House of Lords.
7 H. Wilson, *The Final Term: the Labour Government 1974–76* (London: Wiedenfeld & Nicolson/Michael Joseph, 1979, London), p. 51.
8 Wilson, *The Final Term*, p. 51; R. Jenkins, *Life at the Centre* (London: Politicos, 2006), p. 344; Healey, *Time of My Life*, p. 360.
9 British National Archives, London, CAB 129/182/18, The Prime Minister's Office, 'Memorandum: EEC White Paper – Harold Wilson', 21 March 1975.
10 B. Donoughue, interview with S. Goodman, 26 November 2013, House of Lords.
11 Callaghan, *Time and Chance*, pp. 302–3.
12 Wilson, *The Final Term*, p. 54.
13 Callaghan, *Time and Chance*, p. 305.
14 Wilson, *The Final Term*, p. 56.
15 Callaghan, *Time and Chance*, p. 302.
16 Wilson, *The Final Term*, pp. 88–9.
17 British National Archives, London, PREM 16/74 ,The Prime Minister's Office, 'Record of Meeting between British Prime Minister and French President Giscard d'Estaing', 19 July 1974.
18 British National Archives, London, PREM 16/74, The Prime Minister's Office 'Extract of Note on the Lunch Given by President of France for the Prime Minister', 18 July 1974.

19 *Ibid.*
20 Jenkins, *Life at the Centre*, p. 400.
21 Wilson, *The Final Term*, pp. 88–9.
22 *Ibid.*, p. 93.
23 Callaghan, *Time and Chance*, p. 315.
24 Wilson, *The Final Term*, p. 95.
25 Jenkins, *Life at the Centre*, p. 399.
26 Callaghan, *Time and Chance*, p. 319.
27 Wilson, *The Final Term*, p. 98; Jenkins, *Life at the Centre*, p. 400.
28 B. Donoughue, interview with S. Goodman, 26 November 2013, House of Lords.
29 British National Archives, London, PREM 16/76, German Foreign Ministry, 'Extracts from the German Chancellor's remarks on British Membership of EEC, Bonn, Germany', 16 November 1974.
30 British National Archives, London, PREM 16/76 , The Prime Minister's Office, 'Summary Note of Foreign Secretary meeting with French President at Elysee Palace', 19 November 1974.
31 *Ibid.*
32 British National Archives, London, PREM 16/76, Foreign & Commonwealth Office, 'Summary Note of Foreign Secretary meeting with French President at Elysee Palace', 19 November 1974.
33 Wilson, *The Final Term*, p. 102.
34 Callaghan, *Time and Chance*, p. 323.
35 *Ibid.*, p. 313.
36 *Ibid.*, p. 324.
37 Wilson, *The Final Term*, p. 103.
38 *Ibid.*, p. 103.
39 *Ibid.*, p. 104.
40 *Ibid.*, p. 104.
41 Wilson, *The Final Term*, pp. 104–5.
42 Jenkins, *Life at the Centre*, p. 407; T. Benn, *Against the Tide: Diaries: 1973–1977* (London: Hutchinson, 1989), p. 349.
43 Wilson, *The Final Term*, p. 105; Jenkins, *Life at the Centre*, p. 411; Benn, *Against the Tide*, p. 384.
44 Wilson, *The Final Term*, pp. 106–7.
45 *Ibid.*, p. 107.
46 *Ibid.*, p. 105.
47 *Ibid.*, p. 105.
48 *Ibid.*, p. 59.
49 R. Mason, *Paying the Price* (London: Robert Hale, 1999), p. 132.
50 *Ibid.*
51 *Ibid.*; Benn, *Against the Tide*, pp. 128 and 135.

52 Wilson, *The Final Term*, p. 59.
53 Callaghan, *Time and Chance*, p. 338; Mason, *Paying the Price*, p. 128.
54 Wilson, *The Final Term*, p. 62.
55 Callaghan, *Time and Chance*, p. 339.
56 *Ibid.*, p. 340.
57 *Ibid.*, pp. 340–1.
58 *Ibid.*, p. 341.
59 *Ibid.*, p. 344; Benn, *Against the Tide*, p. 266.
60 Wilson, *The Final Term*, p. 63.
61 Callaghan, *Time and Chance*, p. 343.
62 Wilson, *The Final Term*, p. 63; British National Archives, London, PREM 16/19, The Prime Minister's Office, 'Record of Telephone Conversation between the Prime Minister and the Prime Minister of Turkey', 25 July 1974.
63 British National Archives, London, PREM 16/19, The Prime Minister's Office, 'Record of Telephone Conversation between the Prime Minister and the Prime Minister of Turkey', 25 July 1974.
64 Wilson, *The Final Term*, p. 64.
65 B. Donoughue, interview with S. Goodman, 26 November 2013, House of Lords.
66 *Ibid.*
67 P. Hennessey, *The Prime Minister: The Office and its Holders since 1945* (London: Allen Lane, Penguin Press, 2000), pp. 362–3.
68 *Ibid.*, p. 357.
69 Security Service Mi5, 'The Wilson Plot', accessed 1 August 2015: www.mi5.gov.uk/home/about-us/who-we-are/mi5-history/the-cold-war/the-wilson-plot.html; K. Morgan, *Callaghan: A Life* (Oxford, Oxford University Press, 1997), p. 610.
70 C. Andrew, *Defence of the Realm: The Authorised History of MI5* (London, Penguin Books, 2010).
71 R. Norton-Taylor, 'No 10 Downing Street Bugged by MI5, Claims Historian', *The Guardian*, 18 April 2010, accessed 1 August 2015: www.theguardian.com/uk/2010/apr/18/mi5-bugged-10-downing-street.
72 T. Harper and J. Lewis, 'Revealed: How MI5 Bugged 10 Downing Street, the Cabinet and at least five Prime Ministers for 15 YEARS', *The Mail on Sunday*, 18 April 2010, accessed 1 August 2015: http://www.dailymail.co.uk/news/article-1266837/Revealed-How-MI5-bugged-10-Downing-Street-Cabinet-Prime-Ministers-15-YEARS.html#ixzz3PYvFTp9N.
73 B. Wheeler, 'Wilson "plot": The Secret Tapes', BBC News, 9 March 2006, accessed 1 August 2015: http://news.bbc.co.uk/1/hi/uk_politics/4789060.stm.

4

James Callaghan, 1976–79

While he had consulted in private with some of his close colleagues, many of the Cabinet were still shocked at Wilson's announcement of his plans to resign.[1] At a Cabinet meeting on 16 March 1976 he told stunned colleagues before leaving the Cabinet room abruptly. His plans for resignation had been set for after the completion of renegotiations and a referendum however they were delayed by economic instability.

Callaghan had for some time been taking a lead on foreign policy and in Wilson's mind it seems clear he always favoured Callaghan to succeed him. Both of them worked closely throughout the EEC renegotiations and referendum. In fact there were few meetings that Wilson had with Heads of State, diplomats, foreign ministers, or other Cabinet colleagues at which Callaghan was not present. Roy Jenkins recalls that he once raised this topic with Callaghan to which the latter responded 'Oh, Harold will see nobody without me at present.'[2] Wilson, when announcing his resignation, tactfully stated that the fact he was leaving at the age of sixty should have no bearing on the choice of his successor, a clear pivot to his Foreign Secretary.[3]

Despite the Prime Minister's informal endorsement and Callaghan's considered status as heir apparent, six candidates put themselves forward to succeed Wilson: Callaghan, Roy Jenkins, Michael Foot, Tony Benn, Denis Healey and Anthony Crosland. In the end the choice was whittled down to Foot and Callaghan, who represented the opposite wings of the Party. Callaghan beat Foot by 176 to 137 votes to secure the leadership of his party and premiership of the country.

Callaghan had perhaps the easiest transition of any modern day Prime Minister into the realms of foreign policy. Already established and with long-standing personal relationships, Wilson had given him much of a free hand over the past two years, where many argued that he had effectively ran foreign policy with Wilson's backing.

The Cabinet

The new Prime Minister's first point of business was reshuffling the Cabinet. He decided to keep Denis Healey as Chancellor, feeling that he had the experience and a good understanding of the role. The question of his successor at the Foreign Office was more carefully weighed up. Callaghan ruminates in his memoirs that Roy Jenkins would have been a natural successor but the wounds of his resignation had not healed. His role as the lead spokesman for the 'yes' campaign in the referendum meant that all his actions as a Foreign Secretary would be viewed through his pro-European paradigm.[4] In the end Callaghan appointed Anthony Crosland to the role and instead nominated Jenkins to be President of the EU Commission.

Callaghan reflected that the period of March 1976 marked the end of the triumvirate that had dominated British politics. Wilson was now retired, George Brown was in the Lords, and with Jenkins heading to Brussels, a Cabinet of great minds and great characters had now fragmented.[5]

Economic crisis

While Callaghan's experience made him the most suited for a dominant prime ministerial role in foreign policy, any thought of possible foreign policy aims were quickly subjugated by an economic crisis.

The British economy was facing three major problems: hyper inflation due to high wage settlements, a high level of public expenditure and Government borrowing, and the weak position of sterling. Early on Callaghan had stated it was not his intention to over-involve himself in economic policy; however he soon found this position untenable.

The first issue at hand was the renegotiation of a pay restraint deal with the trade unions. High wage settlements of up to 30 per cent had led to rapid inflation. In 1974, Michael Foot as Secretary of State for Employment reached an agreement with the unions that would see excessive wage claims abandoned in return for a voluntary income policy, giving union members a maximum increase of £6 per week for a period of twelve months.[6]

When Callaghan came to office this period was almost over and therefore a new deal was needed as soon as possible to consolidate the lowering of inflation. Wage restraint policy had achieved and to an extent kept down domestic manufacturing costs. Healey and Foot had already begun to engage with the TUC in wage discussions.

The second issue was the high level of public expenditure, which would require the Government to borrow £12 billion to finance its programme for the year 1976/77. This had a knock-on impact on the third issue, the position of sterling, which had been in decline since February 1976. Set unrealistically high at two dollars to the pound, in February the Bank of England contrived to edge it down. Foreign exchange dealers soon cottoned on and began selling sterling. The Bank of England was forced to spend substantial reserves to hold the exchange rate.[7]

All three of these issues were interlinked and were together creating economic uncertainty verging on crisis. The Chancellor informed the Prime Minister that inflation would again start rising over the next few months and forecast that the Government would have to restrain public spending for 1977/78.[8] He also added that they may have to approach the International Monetary Fund during that summer for a loan.

Initial talks with the unions dragged. Healey hoped to agree a package of a modest 3 per cent increase per annum. In the end both sides settled for a 5 per cent wage increase at £2.50 per week. The Treasury estimated that the final effect of the agreement would be an increase in the Retail Price Index of 7.5 per cent which Callaghan considered 'a miracle by comparison with the Summer of 1975 when it was as high as 26.5 per cent'.[9]

The value of sterling once again created uncertainty and pressure. At $1.80, sterling holders recommended further devaluation by 5 or 10 per cent, arguing that this was inevitable. Callaghan found himself witnessing a sense of déjà vu, reminiscent of 1967.

Other countries began to worry about their own currencies – the fall in sterling was blamed on unreasonable exaggeration of foreign markets. In June 1976 in an attempt to arrest the fall of sterling and avoid damage to their own currencies, the Group of Ten industrial countries offered Britain a short-term loan of $5 billion. The Prime Minister consulted with the Cabinet and accepted.[10]

The tactic worked and the markets reacted favourably to the news of the loan. However speculators grasping the short-term nature of the loan and that Britain would be required to repay it in December soon began reasserting pressure on sterling.

Sterling was held at $1.77 for several months in early 1977; however it became evident that once Britain paid back the $5 billion loan it would not be able to sustain sterling at such a level. This news came as forecasts from the Treasury showed a balance of payments deficit of about $3 billion for 1977 as well as a public sector borrowing requirement of some £10.5 billion for 1977/78, a substantial increase of £1.5 billion from the initial figure of £9 billion.[11]

The Prime Minister and Chancellor agreed that the only solution would be to apply to the IMF in late autumn for standby credit sufficient to finance the expected deficit of £3 billion in trading and other accounts with overseas countries for 1977 while also reviewing the Government's future expenditure, looking to reduce it by about £1.5 billion.[12]

The Government had the added pressure of a falling pound, which by 25 September was at $1.63. The Bank of England forecasted that it could fall futher to $1.50, and from there no one could tell where it would stop. The Cabinet authorised an application for standby credit from the IMF amounting to £2.3 billion to pay off the expected £3 billion of trade deficit payments.[13]

At this time Callaghan reached out to President Ford. Despite ideological differences both men had a friendly relationship. Callaghan explained that the UK needed two things: an early declaration from the IMF that a standby loan would be forthcoming, and second, sterling needed long-term protection against the volatility arising from the low ratio of sterling reserves compared to foreign held reserves. The President assured Callaghan that he would do all he could despite the US Treasury Department being sceptical of the idea of a safety net.[14]

The Americans were concerned that Britain might enact import restrictions to balance the trade deficit. Ford was keen to express reservations over such a course of action. Callaghan conceded that this would be the alternative action if sterling could not be secured but felt that import restrictions would call into question Britain's role in the transatlantic relationship, something which he was anxious to preserve.[15]

A few weeks later on 2 November 1976, Ford lost to Jimmy Carter in the presidential election and with it his influence. The US Treasury Department, despite Ford's backing, refused to enter into safety net talks until the IMF talks were completed.[16] The problem was that the IMF was suspicious of the idea of a safety net which it feared would mean that Britain would not reduce public sector borrowing.

This stalemate brought Britain to a dangerous impasse. Callaghan reached out to German Chancellor Schmidt who in turn spoke to the USA on Britain's behalf, proposing a possible plan to recall some of Germany's dollar reserves paired with similar assistance from the USA and one or two other countries. This could possibly offset the instability of the sterling overseas balances. Now with a lame duck President the plan seemed unlikely to happen, but the Chancellor still reached out to Callaghan offering that if ever an acute danger of necessity should arise Britain could call on Germany and within twenty-four hours the German Government would make whatever improvised arrangements were necessary.[17] This unprecedented offer reflected the depth of trust and warmth between the two leaders.

The Prime Minister faced even greater opposition from the Cabinet, many of whom while sanctioning the Government's position in reaching out to the IMF, opposed cuts to public expenditure. Tony Crosland in particular argued that there was no economic case for cutting back on forward plans, the Government's existing strategy was working and the IMF could not risk denying Britain a loan or would risk pushing Britain into a siege economy accompanied by protectionism.[18] Other members of the Cabinet felt that Callaghan was pursuing his own externally directed policy by using his links with Ford and Schmidt in order to bypass the IMF.[19]

Tony Benn argued that Britain should voluntarily embrace some form of protection through import quotas which could bring controlled industrial investment and compulsory planning agreements with companies. The Cabinet as a whole argued that they would agree to no less than £9.5 billion for 1977/78. In the end an agreement was reached that borrowing in the public sector would be limited to £8.7 billion in 1977/78 and £8.6 billion 1978/79. This would be met by selling £500 million of British petroleum shares of North Sea oil and by cutting public expenditure by £1 billion.[20]

Callaghan was able to quell dissent in Cabinet by allowing alternative views to be put forward and debated, but also by reminding them that while negotiations preceded it was in all their interests to remain united in public, lest they find themselves arguing for preferred alternatives from the Opposition benches.

1977 brought further problems for Callaghan. Firstly the unexpected death of his Foreign Secretary, Tony Crosland, on 19 February, left him with the tough decision of finding a successor. Callaghan in the end made the bold decision to promote the junior foreign office minister, David Owen. The second headache and perhaps the largest, was the decline of Labour's thin majority whittled away in by-elections. Callaghan was effectively running a minority Government for a large period of time.

However the prospect of a Vote of No Confidence in the Government forced Callaghan into talks with the Liberals and Irish Ulster Unionist MPs. These talks finished on 23 March when both sides announced that the Liberals would offer a supply vote to the Government in Parliament to prevent them facing a Vote of No Confidence. In return, Callaghan would offer referendums on devolution for Wales and Scotland as well as accepting a proportional representation electoral system for members of the European Parliament. The Cabinet was divided over the pact but agreed when the Prime Minister argued that the bleak picture was a pact or face a Vote of No Confidence, which would lead to a General Election they would probably lose.

Sterling had stabilised by June 1977, to $1.72 from the low of $1.56 in the autumn of 1976. Britain's account was virtually in balance, with a surplus forecast for 1978. The Prime Minister predicted that if the Government could keep pay settlements to about 10 per cent, inflation levels would be reduced from over 17 per cent to 8 per cent by the end of 1978.[21]

This wasn't to be. The USA was now enduring its own problems with the dollar, which was unstable due to the country's levels of debt and rising inflation. This had a direct countervailing effect on other currencies, causing sterling to appreciate in January 1978 to 1.93, a level which the Prime Minister considered too high for the competitive position of British exports. President Carter was unwilling to take the lead, instead devoting his energies to repairing relations between Israel and Egypt.[22]

At the EEC summit in Bonn on 16–17 July, the climate of global economic uncertainty led Giscard d'Estaing and Helmut Schmidt to begin discussions about the creation of a European Monetary system, which would bring closer economic union within the EEC. Callaghan told both leaders that while he supported the scheme, it would be unlikely that Britain could enter. Far too many in the Labour Party were suspicious of further integration with Europe, and just after the European question had been settled it could reignite divisions once again. The Treasury supported this position and argued that the current standing of sterling was too high for entry to be advantageous.[23]

While Britain could not join a monetary union, the Prime Minister did commit the country to the European Currency Unit which saw sterling included in the new composite unit for the purpose of determining its value. He also agreed to deposit a proportion of Britain's gold and dollar reserves as security and to accept European Currency Units in their place. Ironically, the Leader of the Opposition, Margaret Thatcher, would later criticise Labour's lacklustre position in regard to a monetary union.

Bonn was the last summit Callaghan attended as Prime Minister. In his memoirs his reflections on the change of summitry diplomacy are poignant, and demonstrate their changing nature and the ability to get things done as he writes:

> Bonn was the last Summit I attended, and with the passage of time their character has changed. The participants of the 1970s have now left the scene, and their successors seem to regard Summits as media events or opportunities to enhance their election prospects, with thousands of photographers and journalists jostling for the best angle. The leaders make speeches to each other which are intended for public consumption back home. All of this is a far cry from our original intention.[24]

A statesman

The sadness of Callaghan's premiership is that so much of his energies were distracted by averting both national and global financial crisis. This meant that there was little room to deal with foreign policy in a traditional sense.

Having been Shadow Colonial Secretary in the 1950s and Foreign Secretary in the second Wilson Government, Callaghan had long-standing and friendly relations with many African leaders. He had hoped that in using these relationships he could settle once and for all the question of Rhodesia. In the end he delegated this task to his Foreign Secretary, David Owen.[25]

Callaghan's role in the Camp David Summit is often understated but it was pivotal. Having long-standing relationships with the Israeli Prime Minister, Menachem Begin and Egyptian President, Anwar Sadat, he worked as an effective and impartial go between with the two leaders.[26] President Carter turned to Callaghan for guidance on the accord and believed his help was indispensable in injecting momentum and trust into discussions thereby helping the diplomatic breakthrough.[27]

As Prime Minister his prestige was undeniable and throughout his term many argue that he represented a bridge between Europe and the USA, in a way that later successor Tony Blair could only dream of. Callaghan kept together a distant White House set on its own foreign policy objectives and a Europe led by German Chancellor Schmidt who was set on focusing on its own internal development. The Prime Minister utilised his strong relationship with both men.

Schmidt and Callaghan had known each other for a long time and had an immediate rapport. The Prime Minister describes himself and the Chancellor as both believers in the Atlantic Alliance, despite Germany being impatient with American shortcomings.

Both as Prime Minister and Foreign Secretary he was keen to strengthen the Atlantic Alliance which he believed Heath had significantly weakened through his deep and lasting commitment to Europe. Callaghan had close relations with Ford despite their ideological differences, and later with Carter. They both were Baptists and ex-sailors. Callaghan sensed that Carter was not immediately at home with foreign affairs. On some areas Carter naturally turned for a second opinion to the wise and knowledgeable British Prime Minister. Callaghan freely confessed later on, he 'cultivated' Carter and turned to him for support in areas of mutual concern.[28]

Cabinet style

Callaghan was a believer in a collective style of governance allowing ministers to debate and discuss issues freely. He was happy to delegate work and allow ministers to get on with it. Like Heath, this may have been largely down to the fact that except Denis Healey, he was largely unrivalled in Cabinet. David Owen recalls that Callaghan always expected consensus from the bigger figures in Cabinet: 'Jim Callaghan did take a view that there were four big beasts in Cabinet, and they were the Chancellor, the Foreign Secretary, the Home Secretary and the Prime Minister, and he used to say to me I don't think it's right for any of us four disagreeing in Cabinet without trying to get those areas of dissent dealt with beforehand.'[29]

In that regard he was more than happy to delegate to his able foreign secretary. In one instance Owen remembers that Callaghan received a distressing phone call from Kenneth Kuanda, President of Zambia, who was struggling to deal with raiders from Ian Smith's forces in Rhodesia. Kuanda needed more weapons and was calling to inform the Prime Minister that he might have to buy Soviet ones.[30] Callaghan calmed him down and agreed to meet with him at an airport in Kano in Northern Nigeria. The Prime Minister then called Owen to apologise for speaking to Kenneth without him and invited him to the meeting. Owen asks 'can you imagine a Prime Minister we've had since then behaving like that to the Foreign Secretary?'[31]

This reflected Callaghan's style and confidence in his colleagues, something which Donoughue also supports:

> Under Jim as Prime Minister he remained very driven by foreign affairs and to some extent was his own foreign secretary, but he had great confidence in David Owen and quite rightly so. Owen was very good, but I would say during those five years of a Labour Government, Callaghan was decisive on foreign affairs and still at that time it was the view of the Prime Minister that on the whole you left things to your foreign secretary. Callaghan was a great believer in letting ministers get on with the job.[32]

Notes

1. Callaghan, *Time and Chance*, p. 391.
2. Jenkins, *Life at the Centre*, p. 404.
3. Callaghan, *Time and Chance*, p. 392.
4. *Ibid.*, p. 399.
5. Morgan, *Callaghan*, p. 16.
6. Callaghan, *Time and Chance*, p. 413; Healey, *Time of My Life*, p. 395.
7. Callaghan, *Time and Chance*, p. 414.
8. *Ibid.*, p. 414.
9. *Ibid.*, p. 416.
10. Healey, *Time of My Life*, p. 427; Callaghan, *Time and Chance*, p. 419.
11. Callaghan, *Time and Chance*, p. 422.
12. Healey, *Time of My Life*, p. 428; Callaghan, *Time and Chance*, p. 423.
13. Callaghan, *Time and Chance*, pp. 427–8; Morgan, *Callaghan*, p. 538.
14. Callaghan, *Time and Chance*, p. 429.
15. *Ibid.*, p. 430.
16. Morgan, *Callaghan*, p. 542.
17. Healey, *Time of My Life*, p. 430; Callaghan, *Time and Chance*, p. 432; Morgan, *Callaghan*, p. 538.
18. Callaghan, *Time and Chance*, pp. 434–5; Healey, *Time of My Life*, p. 432.
19. Morgan, *Callaghan*, pp. 22–3.
20. Callaghan, *Time and Chance*, p. 435–40; Benn, *Against the Tide*, p. 672.
21. Callaghan, *Time and Chance*, p. 462.
22. *Ibid.*, p. 486.
23. *Ibid.*, p. 493.
24. *Ibid.*, p. 497.
25. Morgan, *Callaghan*, p. 595.

26 Callaghan, *Time and Chance*, p. 486.
27 Morgan, *Callaghan*, p. 608.
28 *Ibid.*, pp. 590–1.
29 D. Owen, interview with S. Goodman, 11 May 2012, private offices.
30 Morgan, *Callaghan*, p. 597.
31 D. Owen, interview with S. Goodman, 11 May 2012, private offices.
32 B. Donoughue, interview with S. Goodman, 26 November 2013, House of Lords.

5

Margaret Thatcher, 1979–90

As the years have passed since her premiership the myth of Margaret Thatcher as the Iron Lady has grown, yet it shrouds the true nature of her time in office, particularly the early years. Margaret Thatcher became leader of the Conservative Party in a unique set of circumstances.

After the two electoral defeats of 1974, Conservative MPs were largely fed up with Ted Heath. He had taken them into government in 1970, but many now felt that he had become a liability. The decision to make the 1974 election based around the issue of 'who governs Britain?' had been a disaster, and many believed this to be the sole reason the Conservatives lost the election.

In truth, Heath had never been personable. He was awkward and could sometimes come across as condescending or patronising. These traits did not warm people to him. In October 1974, he was pressured into setting up a commission to propose changes to the rules for the election of the party leader and to resubmit himself for election.

There was no real challenger to Heath. Keith Joseph, the former minister, Shadow Home Secretary, and long-standing critic of Heath ruled himself out of contention. Instead, along with Airey Neave MP, he approached Margaret Thatcher to stand.

Becoming an MP in 1959, she had served in Heath's Cabinet as Secretary of State for Education but was largely considered in the party to be a political lightweight. This was no doubt in part due to her being one of the few women in the Cabinet at the time. Like Joseph, she was largely in disagreement with the party leadership over economic policy, believing that they should be taking a more anti-Keynesian approach towards the welfare state.[1]

She was considered to have little chance of winning. In fact much of her support came from disaffected Conservatives who wanted Heath to listen more to his backbenchers. They believed by voting for Thatcher they would send a strong message to Heath and force him to change his attitude. It was therefore a huge shock, when on 4 February 1975, she defeated Heath in the first ballot by 130 votes to 113. Although not a large enough margin for the 15 per cent needed to win outright on the first ballot, it was so damaging to Heath that he immediately withdrew his candidacy.[2]

The second ballot saw Thatcher beat Willie Whitelaw – Heath's preferred candidate, Geoffrey Howe, Jim Prior and John Peyton to become leader of the Conservative Party. She offered Heath any position he wished in the Shadow Cabinet. He initially seemed receptive, agreeing to wait six months before announcing his decision, but in the end refused.

Many of those who had supported her did not believe she would win and her shocking victory created unease in the party. This was not simply because she was a woman but also because of her radical views on reshaping the economy.

On the question of Europe, the Conservative Party in opposition was united. Thatcher campaigned alongside her predecessor, successfully, for Britain to stay in Europe in the referendum of 1975. As 1978 rolled into 1979 and the trade unions brought the country to a standstill in the Winter of Discontent, it seemed that a Conservative victory was inevitable.

A General Election was called after Callaghan's Government lost a Vote of No Confidence and on 4 May the Conservatives won 339 seats to Labour's 269, a parliamentary majority of 44.

Like many Prime Ministers before her, Thatcher came to the premiership with little knowledge or interest in foreign affairs. As Lord Peter Carrington, her first Foreign Secretary recalls:

> After all, there was no reason why Mrs Thatcher when she first became Prime Minister [should] know a great deal about foreign affairs. When she became leader of the Conservative party unexpectedly, with a good deal of opposition because she was a woman, unknown and all the rest of it, she very sensibly realised her priorities were to control and dominate the party and worry about domestic affairs to win the next election. At that time she wasn't interested in foreign affairs. She was certainly less expert on foreign affairs than domestic affairs.[3]

She had never held a previous position in Government or in opposition with international responsibilities and had travelled little in her pre-political life. Associates felt that she was neither interested in specific knowledge about the outside world nor the niceties of foreign diplomacy.[4]

As Prime Minister she found herself with a largely hostile Cabinet many of whom had served under Ted Heath. As Sir Stephen Wall, the Private Secretary in the Foreign Office at the time remembers: 'She had to be more careful in the beginning. There were a lot of Tory old boys she had to have in her Cabinet who disliked her, disliked the fact she had beaten Heath, disliked her inexperience and thought they could get rid of her.'[5]

Lord Michael Heseltine, who served as Secretary of State for the Environment and later for Defence agrees, suggesting that the seniority of Cabinet members meant that she was far less dominant:

> Mrs Thatcher...came to dominate the Cabinet in later years. She didn't dominate the Cabinet in early years. After all, you have to only think of the background, the early Cabinet was a rerun of Ted Heath's Cabinet; she was not the choice of most of them as leader and was not held in that particularly high regard by those who had served under Heath. There were some very senior people there, like Peter Carrington and Quentin Hailsham and Willie Whitelaw together with others who were more her contemporaries like Jim Prior who were certainly not going to be overruled by her.[6]

In Peter Carrington, she had a skilled and experienced Foreign Secretary. He had been Defence Secretary under Heath, and had also served in the administrations of Churchill, Eden and Macmillan. Carrington was considered the archetypal party grandee and a skilled diplomat. The Prime Minister in those early years had a great deal of respect for the Foreign Office, largely in part due to her respect for Carrington.[7] She took his advice seriously and often deferred to his judgement, as Douglas Hurd, a junior Foreign Office Minister at the time, recalls: 'I knew that Peter Carrington's influence over her, which was very substantial, was based on private chats and not having officials around'.[8]

She formed an effective partnership with Carrington. This was in part due to the fact that as a peer he was not a competitor or a personal rival.[9] Their varying styles complemented each other. This was particularly evident in the renegotiations over the European Economic Community Budget.

EEC budget

Britain's contribution to the EEC has always been a cause of much debate. Despite Callaghan and Wilson's renegotiation in 1975, Margaret Thatcher was keen that her first foreign policy aim should be to secure a larger rebate for Britain. Like her predecessors she believed the problem was twofold: first, Britain's role as the largest importer of food in the EEC meant a large contribution to the budget in the form of tariffs; secondly the fact that up to 70 per cent of the EEC budget was spent on the Common Agricultural Policy, despite the British economy being far less dependent on agriculture than other member countries.[10]

At her first EEC Summit as Prime Minister, in Dublin on 29–30 November 1979, Margaret Thatcher argued that the 1975 Budget Correction Mechanism had failed to cut British payments and more needed to be done. The EEC Commission proposed reviewing the Community's expenditure on programmes and proposed specific spending on UK projects to boost receipts. Britain was offered a refund of £350 million implying a net contribution of £650 million.[11] The Prime Minister rejected the offer as simply not large enough.

A decision was postponed until the next summit in Luxemburg on 27 April 1980. There was general concern in those months between the two summits amongst other EEC countries that if they did not reach a solution Britain might withdraw her contribution to the Community's budget. The Prime Minister deduced the main stumbling block to renegotiation was France and Germany's desire to see higher agriculture prices. A factor on her side was predictions from the Treasury that the EEC would run out of funds by 1982 and any further increase in the budget would need unanimous approval.[12]

No consensus could be reached; instead it was agreed the issue would be best dealt with at the next meeting of the Community Foreign Ministers. Carrington received a mandate from the Prime Minister and flew to Brussels on 29 May to undertake negotiations. The deal arrived at, saw Britain's net budget contribution rise in 1980 but Britain would pay less under the new package in 1981. A three-year solution was offered, which would see a major review of the budget problem. If by mid-1981 this had not happened, the Commission would make proposals along the lines of the formula for 1980/81. Britain would concede to a 5 per cent rise in farm prices but overall the deal would see it gain a refund of two-thirds of its net contribution.[13]

The Prime Minister was wary of accepting such a deal. John Nott, former Secretary of State for Trade and afterwards Defence recollects that the issue of the EEC budget set Margaret Thatcher at her most determined and the Foreign Office at its most feeble, appeasing self.[14] Yet Carrington pulled off the impossible feat of convincing a new Prime Minister set on standing up to Europe that the deal was actually a pretty good one.

He did this by outmanoeuvring her and appealing to a Prime Minister's vanity, by briefing the press that the agreement was a great personal foreign policy success for Margaret Thatcher.[15] It was a move only an experienced hand could pull off. As Foreign Secretary he did not seek the limelight nor chase headlines, and in this instance understood that his role was to work behind the scenes and offer the Prime Minister the praise.

Rhodesia and the Lancaster House Summit

This is not to say that their relationship always ran smoothly. The second pressing foreign policy issue when entering government was to finally solve the question of Rhodesia. The situation since the white minority Government of Ian Smith had declared Unilateral Independence had drastically deteriorated. The Rhodesian Government had undertaken cross-border raids into Zambia, which sparked armed resistance from black nationalists using guerrilla tactics from both Zambia and Mozambique.

In April 1979, Rhodesia held its first election under a new constitution, which allowed many in the black majority to vote for the first time. The result saw the formation of a black majority Government headed by Bishop Abel Muzorewa. However the Patriotic Front parties of the guerrillas Robert Mugabe and Joshua Nkomo refused to take part.

Many African nations felt that Muzorewa's Government was nothing more than a facade for white minority rule, and in July 1979 the Organisation of African Unity endorsed the Patriotic Front as the sole legitimate authentic representative of the people of Rhodesia. Many of these states as members of the Commonwealth believed that it was Britain's responsibility to bring the issue to a close.[16]

Carrington took the view that it was essential to secure the widest possible recognition of a Rhodesian regime, since the country held the key to the whole of the South African region.[17] The Prime Minister under his advice recommended at her first Commonwealth Conference that a Constitutional Conference be set up to bring the conflicting sides together. Despite scepticism, African Commonwealth countries signed a joint communiqué in favour of a conference.

The Conservative Party had been historically divided on the issue of Rhodesia and support for the white minority Government of Smith; the idea of a constitutional conference was no different. Many backbenchers and some in the

Cabinet believed that the Patriotic Front were terrorists and should not be invited to the conference. Instead the British Government should be doing more to support and offer legitimacy to Muzorewa's Government. Margaret Thatcher as Prime Minister was swayed by some of these arguments.[18] Carrington concedes that their opposing views did create difficulties on the outcomes of a conference.[19] A great many people in the Conservative Party were on her side.

Despite a divided Party the conference went ahead all the same. The interested parties met at Lancaster House in London on 10 September 1979. Peter Carrington chaired the summit which had forty-seven plenary sessions. In the end all sides agreed upon a new constitution, fresh elections and a ceasefire between the guerrillas and the Government which would come into effect on 17 December. The Prime Minister pushed for the reinstatement of British rule until the elections were over and a British Governor was appointed once again.[20]

At the time, the agreement was heralded a great success, which finally brought a resolution to an episode which had haunted British foreign policy for some time. In the elections that followed Robert Mugabe and his party won an overwhelming majority victory and on 18 April 1980 Rhodesia became Zimbabwe. At the time of writing Mugabe has effectively ruled Zimbabwe as a dictator in all but name for thirty-five years; with that in mind the author asked Lord Carrington if the Lancaster House Agreement really was the best deal at the time:

> Well it depends what you think would have happened if we didn't have a Lancaster House Agreement. I mean the fighting would have gone on, the Conservative Government would have had to recognize Muzorewa, which would have been a disaster, the Commonwealth would have been totally against recognition of Muzorewa, the Americans and President Carter would have been against it. The only ally we would have had would have been South Africa; the killing would have carried on, Mugabe would have won in the end after more killing and bloodshed and I think the consequences would have been worse.[21]

The Falklands

Many people cite the Falklands as the defining moment in Margaret Thatcher's premiership, when she transcended the boundaries of simply being a British Prime Minister and became instead an international statesman.

By 1982 the Falkland Islands had been a British territory for 149 years. Argentina for some time had claimed ownership of the islands, which they considered the Malvinas. Their claim on the islands and demands for a settlement had become more vocal from 1974 onwards when a military junta took over the Argentinian Government.

In 1971, the Heath Government signed a Communications Agreement with the Argentine Government, establishing air and sea links in the hope of warming relations and with an eye to negotiating a settlement. This agreement quickly fell apart when the Argentine Government argued that they would not support the deal unless sovereignty over the islands was also agreed.

In 1979, when Thatcher took office she inherited Foreign Office policy which under Wilson/ Callaghan argued for some kind of accommodation with Argentina in the form of a 'lease back' arrangement. Under this plan, sovereignty for the islands would pass to Argentina but the way of life of the islanders would be preserved by the continuation of a British administration. The Prime Minister was not keen on this proposal but was willing to consider it.[22]

Another option the Government considered was the recommendation put forward by Lord Shackleton in 1976, which would see an enlargement of the airport on the Falklands by lengthening the runway. It was considered that this would send a message to the Argentine Government that Britain would not have serious talks about sovereignty and would increase the capacity for the islands to be defended.[23]

Argentina had maintained a military presence on Southern Thule, in the South Sandwich Islands, since 1976. The driver for military action came in the form of a military coup in Argentina in December 1981, when a three-man military junta replaced the previous military Government. One of those men, General Leopoldo Galtieri was appointed President. Galtieri relied heavily on the Argentine navy for support whose Commander-in-Chief, Admiral Anaya held a particularly hard line on Argentina's claim to sovereignty over the Falklands.

Indebted to the Argentine navy and with a weakening and unstable domestic situation, in hindsight Galtieri's decision to invade the islands seems to some historians inevitable. This was particularly evident when the Argentine Government abruptly changed their negotiating position over the islands at talks in New York at the end of February 1982.

The precursor to invasion came on 20 December 1981, when Argentine scrap metal dealers made an unauthorised landing on the island of South Georgia. They subsequently left and the Argentinian Government denied any knowledge of the event. On 20 March 1982, in mirroring the prior incident, Argentine scrap metal dealers made another unauthorised landing this time raising the

Argentine flag and firing shots. Once again the Argentine Government denied any knowledge. The Prime Minister and Foreign Secretary attempted to negotiate with Argentina to resolve what at the time was considered an awkward diplomatic incident.[24]

As tensions grew over the following days, the Prime Minister agreed to send a nuclear submarine to reinforce HMS *Endurance*, which was already in the area, and made preparations to send a second. The hope of dissipating tensions seemed slim. On Wednesday 31 March the Prime Minister received intelligence that the Argentine fleet looked set to invade the Falklands on Friday 2 April, which by the time she received the information was already under way.

Could the islands be retaken? This was the question she posed to her inner circle. On one hand the Defence Secretary John Nott gave the Ministry of Defence's view that they could not. On the other hand Chief of the Naval Staff and First Sea Lord, Admiral Sir Henry Leach argued that they could. He proposed assembling a naval task force comprising of some 100 ships and 25,000 men that could be ready to leave in 48 hours to retake the islands.[25] Thatcher chose to agree with her Chief of the Naval Staff and gave him the authority to begin assembling the fleet but reserved for Cabinet the final decision as to whether it should sail.

The Prime Minister faced criticism from both the public and Parliament over her Government's inability to prevent the invasion of the islands. An instant opinion poll found that 60 per cent of the public blamed her personally for allowing the invasion to occur.[26] The debate in the House of Commons was marked by anger from many MPs including her own backbenchers who blamed the Government for inaction and a lack of foresight.[27]

This anger and criticism was not confined to the Commons or limited to the Prime Minister. Both John Nott and Peter Carrington found themselves the subject of scathing attacks from Conservative backbenchers and the British press.[28] Carrington, being a peer, received the brunt of the attacks. In the end he chose to resign, arguing that his resignation would allow the party to unite and the country to focus on the task at hand.[29] This act of self-sacrifice would later be dubbed the last honourable resignation in history.[30]

Carrington proved to be right. Both Parliament and the Cabinet unanimously backed the idea of a naval task force which left Britain on 15 April,[31] although the Prime Minister concedes in her memoirs that at the time she was aware that some considered it a purely diplomatic armada that would bring Argentina back to the negotiating table.[32]

To replace Carrington, Margaret Thatcher appointed Francis Pym as Foreign Secretary. Well qualified as a former Defence Secretary and well liked, the Prime Minister believed he had the 'requisite experience'[33] for the position. However she considered Pym an old-style Tory and a by-product of the Heath Government and not 'one of us'.[34] This was the beginning of a dysfunctional and painful relationship, as neither of them liked or trusted the other. After his own resignation she was faced with a real dilemma, recalls Lord Carrington:

> I mean poor Francis Pym, for example, when I resigned. She was faced with a dilemma with who to appoint. I mean she disliked Francis Pym and they didn't get on and never had. Therefore it was a very difficult position for him. Hell of a nice guy, and she sort of made it more difficult for him by being a bit rough on him, but you know people. It depends so much on the Prime Minister of the day and whether the foreign secretary can bark back [laughs].

A diplomatic response

The task force would take a number of weeks to reach the island. Therefore the Prime Minister's first priority was to apply diplomatic pressure on Argentina to buy time for the fleet. She did this both bilaterally and unilaterally. Utilising her long-standing relationship with American President Ronald Reagan, she convinced him to apply pressure on Argentina to negotiate a withdrawal. He was just one of many world leaders she convinced to support Britain's cause.

While she did this, Anthony Parsons, the British Ambassador to the United Nations, attempted to negotiate a difficult tightrope between securing a UN Resolution condemning the invasion and attempting to limit UN involvement in negotiating sovereignty of the islands. The fear was that UN interference might lead to unsatisfactory terms for peace. While Britain could veto this, the Prime Minister concedes it would have diminished international support for her position.[35] His efforts were not in vain when on 13 April the UN Security Council passed UN Resolution 502, which condemned the invasion and demanded an immediate withdrawal.

The Prime Minister asked the USA, the European Community, Japan, Canada, Australia and New Zealand for support by banning arms sales, Argentine imports, ending export credit cover for new commitments and to give no incentive or encouragement for banks to lend to Argentina. The USA refused to do so out of fear of toppling Galtieri. Despite this, her diplomatic efforts were largely successful. The European Community, less Italy and Ireland, imposed a ban on Argentine imports from April onwards. The Commonwealth also enacted economic sanctions, less India.[36]

The War Cabinet

Following the advice of her predecessor Harold Macmillan, the Prime Minister set up a War Cabinet composed of herself; Francis Pym as Foreign Secretary; John Nott the Defence Secretary; Willie Whitelaw her Deputy Prime Minister; Cecil Parkinson, a Cabinet Minister and close adviser; Admiral Sir Terence Lewin, Chief of the Defence Staff; and Sir Michael Havers the Attorney General.[37] She purposely left out the Chancellor of the Exchequer taking the view that discussions over the funding of the war would be a distraction from the purpose of military strategy.

The War Cabinet would meet every day and sometimes twice a day. It would become characterised by the differences of opinion between the Prime Minister and her Foreign Secretary Francis Pym over a negotiated settlement. These disagreements were not kept to the confines of No. 10 as Sir Malcolm Rifkind, at the time a junior minister in the Foreign Office recalls:

> It has been public knowledge for many years that he wanted to explore the possibilities of a negotiated compromise with the Argentinians. Margaret Thatcher took the view that the Argentinians would never agree to a compromise that did not enable them to continue occupying the islands; any compromise would be face saving, no more than that, but she wasn't going to tolerate that. Now I think most of us actually would agree with Thatcher not with Francis Pym, but what surprised me was the extent – in front of junior ministers – he exposed the deep divisions between the Prime Minister and the Foreign Secretary, instead of that being kept in the confines of No. 10. So it was quite obvious to us that there was deep disagreement, and that was a genuine policy issue where at the end of the day Francis Pym was in a minority.[38]

John Nott writes that sometimes Francis, in his determination for a negotiated settlement, perhaps allowed his emotions to get the best of him but it was ultimately his job As Foreign Secretary to seek and propose a diplomatic exit.[39]

The problem arose from the USA's desire to see a quick settlement to the conflict that would avoid the collapse of the Argentine Government. The Reagan Administration had gone to great lengths to foster relations with Galtieri as a counterbalance to the influence of Communist Cuba. They therefore wished to remain neutral and see a diplomatic settlement.[40]

General Alexander Haig, the US Secretary of State, headed US diplomatic efforts, proposing that both sides accept a neutral interim administration after an Argentine withdrawal while the islands' future was decided with a decision to be made by 31 December 1982. The War Cabinet debated these proposals with Pym advocating they accept. The Prime Minister however felt that Haig's plan would put Britain at a huge disadvantage, as Argentina could resend her forces when she liked, while the task force would have to return to Britain. There was also no underpinning of the islanders' wishes.[41]

Thatcher believed Argentina was using Haig's proposal as a diversionary tactic and that the main issue was still a military one, believing that the military junta had a better hand if they could negotiate before the task force made it to the Falklands.[42]

The Prime Minister was fortunate in that the military junta liked Haig's proposal even less then she did. Their argument stemmed from the Communications Agreement in 1971, that Argentinian citizens deserved to have the same rights to reside on the islands and own property as part of a 'de-colonialisation' process. Argentina's list of demands included the appointment of an Argentinian Governor, the Argentinian flag to continue to be flown, and that the USA should offer assurances that when negotiations ended they would recognise Argentine sovereignty over the islands.[43]

These unrealistic demands certainly bought the taskforce time but did not stop growing tensions between the USA and Britain over the use of the Ascension Islands, particularly when Haig wanted to release a statement stating that the USA would restrict Britain's access to them.[44] The Prime Minister needed to be seen to be cooperating with Haig and the US proposals or risk alienating her greatest ally, while also hoping the military junta in Buenos Aires would break off negotiations and allow the USA to openly support Britain.

This strategy created a further gulf between the Prime Minister and her Foreign Secretary. Pym felt that instead of feigning a desire to negotiate Britain should genuinely do so. The Prime Minister debated with him in private and rebuked him in public when she felt in a Commons statement he insinuated that Britain would not use force as long as the negotiations were continuing.[45]

The breaking point between the two came when Pym went to Washington on 22 April to negotiate a deal. The Prime Minister, in consultation with the War Cabinet, gave him an amended proposal of terms which would be acceptable. It was on this basis he was instructed to negotiate. On his return on 24 April the Prime Minister was both shocked and perplexed at the negotiated proposals. Under the new terms the taskforce would have to withdraw to defined zones within a designated period of days, sanctions against Argentina would be lifted on the signing of the deal, and Argentina would be allowed to place settlers on the island as well as have representatives in local government. She argued that these proposals were unacceptable and would surrender British leverage both military and economic over the Argentinian Government and rob the Falklanders of their freedom and Britain of its honour.[46]

Despite the Prime Minister's opposition, Pym put the terms to the War Cabinet, who agreed that it would be best not to comment and instead wait for an Argentinian response. This strategy was a gamble since if they responded favourably, Britain would have to accept the terms. However if the military junta, as predicted, rejected them, then the USA could finally come firmly down on the side of Britain. Luckily the gamble paid off, and Argentina rejected the proposals. However Margaret Thatcher would not forget what she considered a betrayal from both Pym and the Foreign Office. The incident resonated in her mind and helped build the firm view that the Foreign Office could not be trusted and was 'wet'.

Things could have been different. Nigel Lawson, Secretary of State for Energy at the time and later Chancellor of the Exchequer, believes that if the military junta had accepted the proposals it would have been possible that the recall of the taskforce may have commanded a majority in Cabinet. However they did not do so, and because of this, there was no dissention within Cabinet throughout the war, even if one or two members may have nursed private doubts.[47]

The taskforce reached the islands on 20 April and began the military campaign. The island of South Georgia was swiftly retaken. The turning point of the naval campaign came when the submarine HMS *Endurance* sank the *General Belgrano*, an Argentinian cruiser which was in the British maritime exclusion zone. In retaliation Argentinian bombers sank the destroyer HMS *Sheffield*. Despite this, the sinking of the *Belgrano* demoralised the whole of the Argentine navy and saw the vast majority of their ships return to port. The Argentinian air force continued to attack the taskforce but the lack of naval engagement allowed British special forces to land on the main island, and on 13 June British forces retook Port Stanley. A ceasefire was agreed by both sides the very next day.

Britain's victory subsequently led to what many people argued was a resurgence of British foreign policy and influence in the world. The Falklands effect is what many believe led to the landslide victory for the Conservatives in the June 1983 General Election seeing them gain 58 seats and a parliamentary majority of 144.[48]

Now at the height of her political power, the Prime Minster chose after the election to replace Pym with her loyal Chancellor Geoffrey Howe.[49] The hope was to realign the Foreign Office with the thinking of No. 10. But this was not to be the case. Thatcher concedes in her memoirs that she had her doubts about Howe's suitability.[50] He was not her first choice, as she favoured Cecil Parkinson, who at the time was embroiled in a domestic scandal and was therefore not able to take the job.

Hong Kong

Despite private doubts, Thatcher and Howe worked effectively on the issue of Hong Kong. Initial discussions over the handing back of Hong Kong came about rather by chance. Britain had administered the islands as an overseas territory since the Treaty of Nanking, signed in 1842. The Second Convention of Peking in 1898 leased the New Territories of the Chinese mainland to Britain for ninety-nine years.

On a visit to China by the Prime Minister in January 1983, the topic of Britain's lease on the islands was raised in informal discussion. At the time there was still fifteen years remaining on the lease. This was the first time any discussion about their future had been raised, and the Prime Minister offered a willingness to open formal negotiations over the islands' future. The Prime Minister hoped to exchange sovereignty over Hong Kong in return for continued British administration.[51]

This was a non-starter for the Chinese, who declared that they would not negotiate over sovereignty and intended to recover control over the whole of Hong Kong, both the island and New Territories, by no later than 1997. Despite this clear deadlock both sides agreed to sign a communiqué officially setting a date to start talks.[52]

Many in Britain feared that if Hong Kong's future was not negotiated, the fear of a Communist takeover would lead to a loss of financial confidence in the Hong Kong Market well before the lease ran out. On 28 January, the Prime Minister proposed to ministers and the Governor that in the absence of talks they should develop the democratic structure in Hong Kong as if it were to achieve independence or self-government, as Britain had similarly done with Singapore.[53] This move quickly came to the attention of the Chinese Government, who feared that Britain would democratise Hong Kong before any such handover. The Prime Minister knew this too. Whether this was truly a plan of last resort or a political ploy to get the Chinese to negotiate is still debated to date.

The first round of talks in September 1983 produced little results, with neither side willing to give an inch. This was despite the Foreign Office arguing that Thatcher should concede early in the talks that British administration would not continue. In October the second round of talks were far more productive, with the Prime Minister reaching out to Chinese Premier, Zhao Ziyang, about possible positive involvement of China in Hong Kong's future. Ziyang put forward a counter-offer that Hong Kong could become a special administrative zone run by the local people with its existing social and economic system unchanged. The Prime Minister agreed in principle, however argued that it would depend largely on the detail of what a 'special administrative zone' would entail.[54]

The Foreign Secretary was sent to Beijing to negotiate on Britain's behalf the details of such an arrangement. Howe argues that the concessions in the final agreement were largely based on the high respect the Chinese leadership had for Margaret Thatcher and her adversarial style: 'On the Hong Kong negotiations, the fact the Chinese respected the Prime Minister, who had already spoken about it…in that particular case she expressed in a BBC interview a robust defence of Hong Kong which meant they knew when I was pressing for further compromises I was being pushed from back home'.[55]

The Sino-Anglo Agreement negotiated in April and signed in December 1984 saw a Joint Liaison Group operate in Hong Kong from 1988 onwards. From 1997 Hong Kong would become a special administrative zone with its freedoms and way of life kept intact for fifty years. The agreement would be an international binding treaty which would be stipulated in the Basic Law to be passed by the Chinese People's Congress and effectively be a constitution for Hong Kong.[56]

Many considered Margaret Thatcher's international prestige after the Falklands War led to this successful negotiation and created a solution that could otherwise have ended with a foreign military invading a British territory. However some criticised the move, arguing that in theory Britain could have kept the island of Hong Kong and handed back the New Territories after their lease was up.[57] John Major, a backbencher at the time and later Chancellor and Foreign Secretary under Thatcher, defends the decision believing that Britain's negotiating position was hopelessly weak. The only point of issue was whether the handover would take over with an agreement or not.[58]

Reform of No. 10

Changing her foreign secretary was not the only reform the Prime Minister had in mind when it came to the formation of foreign policy. If the first lesson she took from the Falklands War was that the Foreign Office could not be trusted, the second lesson was that No. 10 needed more influence over the conduct of foreign affairs.[59] At the heart of this was a desire to gain information from a number of different sources rather than relying solely on the Foreign Office.

This was not the first time that a Prime Minister had taken such a view. Both Ted Heath and Harold Wilson at the height of the country's economic difficulties felt they could no longer trust the Treasury. They therefore sought independent advice which came in the form of the Central Policy Review Staff and later a policy unit in No. 10. However neither of them dared to interfere with the Foreign Office and the advice they were receiving.

Margaret Thatcher chose to reward Anthony Parsons for his role in negotiating a UN resolution in the Falklands by appointing him as a special foreign policy adviser. Parsons on his retirement would later be replaced by Percy Craddock the former Ambassador to China.

While Thatcher took the advice of her appointed foreign policy advisers seriously there was no one she listened to more than Charles Powell. Like Parsons and Craddock he originated in the Foreign Office, and served there until 1983 when he was appointed to be Margaret Thatcher's private secretary. Powell over the next few years would amass huge influence and power in Government, so much so that he would in some instances usurp the Foreign Office. As Lord David Owen recalls, it came to the point where he would choose if the Foreign Secretary would see the Prime Minister or not:

> Thatcher used the official machinery…she didn't bypass Cabinet until really quite near the end. She used the dominance of Charles Powell…he would decide whether the Foreign Secretary saw her, and he knew she didn't want to see him (Geoffrey Howe). It wasn't totally Charles's fault…I mean he loved being in power, but he was basically doing the job, the traditional job of the diplomatic secretary.[60]

Powell's role of private secretary was not something unique. Lord Robert Armstrong, Cabinet Secretary at the time is keen to point out that many prime ministers had private secretaries often with a background in the Foreign Office.[61] What was unique in the Powell–Thatcher relationship was just how in sync their minds were. Powell came to No. 10 at a time when the Foreign Office and

Foreign Secretary were out of favour and found himself helping the Prime Minister enact her own foreign policy. This suited Powell, as Stephen Wall concedes, 'Charles liked to have power in his hands'.[62]

A special relationship (Thatcher and Reagan)

Despite her many achievements, Thatcher will always be credited most with reviving the 'special relationship' with the USA. Her relationship with American President Ronald Reagan went well beyond shared foreign policy interests.[63] They often considered themselves political soulmates sharing a similar domestic outlook on taxation and economics.

On coming to office in 1979, while she struck up a cordial relationship with President Carter they were ideological poles apart. In foreign policy they both found themselves at odds in the aftermath of the Iranian hostage crisis in November 1979. The disagreement surrounded freezing Iran's financial assets in Britain. The President wanted Thatcher to do so as part of a way to put financial pressure on Iran. She flatly refused, arguing that it would be devastating for international confidence in the City of London as a world financial centre.[64] She did however agree to soft sanctions on the USSR in retaliation to their invasion of Afghanistan but she was also deeply critical of the USA for allowing it to happen.[65]

The Prime Minister welcomed the election of California Governor and former actor Ronald Reagan to the presidency in November 1980. While many in NATO were sceptical of his credentials the Prime Minister was his greatest cheerleader.[66] Both of them shared a similar view of the Soviet Union and believed that the best way to beat Communism was to outspend their military.

Part of this strategy was the signing of an agreement, on 12 December 1979, which would allow American missiles to be deployed across Europe in NATO countries.[67] The plan was initially for Belgium and Holland to take a share of the missiles but in June 1981 the Prime Minister announced to the chagrin of those in favour of nuclear disarmament that Britain would take her share too.

Strategic Defence Initiative (SDI)

The crown jewel of the West's arms race with the East came in the form of Ronald Reagan's Strategic Defence Initiative often dubbed 'Star Wars'. The plan was to research a satellite that would be able to shoot down and disable ballistic missiles, with the aim of stopping the Soviet's nuclear arsenal if they were deployed. Margaret Thatcher believed this was 'the single most important decision of his presidency'.[68]

Reagan's announcement was offered a mixed reaction and the Prime Minister decided to keep tight personal control over decisions relating to SDI and any British reaction to it.[69] The 1972 Anti-Ballistic Missile Treaty as amended by a 1974 Protocol, allowed the USA and the Soviet Union to deploy one static ABM system with up to 100 launchers in defence of an intercontinental ballistic missile or a national capital. Whether this allowed for what Reagan envisioned was where the crux of the debate came in. His administration took a broader interpretation of the treaty which placed no effective restraint on SDI's development or deployment.

Both the Foreign Office and the Ministry of Defence argued for the narrowest possible interpretation that SDI would be in breach of the agreement.[70] The Prime Minister sided with the Americans and supported SDI, although, she told Reagan in private that both the 1972 ABM Treaty and 1967 Outer Space Treaty would most likely have to be renegotiated. Where she disagreed with him, was the use of the technology, arguing that the USA should do all it could to keep the technology out of the Soviets' hands and not surrender a hard won technological lead.[71]

Sir Percy Craddock reflects in his memoirs that Thatcher's decision to support SDI was far more pragmatic then ideological. Reagan's emotional attachment to SDI made it a top American foreign policy priority. The Prime Minister deduced that there was little to be gained personally or for the transatlantic relationship in opposing it.[72]

Whether SDI ever would have worked we do not yet know. The policy, however, was effective in that it stretched the Soviet Union economically as it struggled to keep up with the US program. Both Thatcher and Reagan felt that it would push the Soviets to the practical limit of how far they could keep their people from austerity.[73]

The Cold War reflected both their personal and their two countries' relationships at their best. However it was not always plain sailing. Like all relationships there was strain put on them; this was particularly evident in the Falklands War when the USA chose to stay relatively neutral. Relations were strained once again on 19 October 1983, when a pro-Soviet coup took place on the Caribbean island of Grenada and a suicide bomber attacked the US marine headquarters in Beirut, Lebanon.

Lebanon

American troops had been deployed as part of an American Multi-National Force in Lebanon since August 1982, as part of a UN plan to stop the civil war that was engulfing the state. The mandate was to assist the Lebanese Government and the Lebanese Armed Forces to restore their authority over the Beirut area.

The Lebanese Government had approached Britain to make a contribution. The Prime Minister argued at the time that Britain was overstretched, but in the end agreed that 100 British servicemen stationed in Cyprus could join the force.[74] On 23 October a suicide truck bomb attacked the US marine headquarters in Beirut, killing 241 American servicemen and another bomb on the same day killed a further fifty-eight French servicemen. The bombing was a wake-up call for both Reagan and Thatcher. The Prime Minister saw it as a sign for British servicemen to leave Lebanon. For some time now she had questioned the purpose of the mission and now, with such a high cost, an ineffectual American response in Lebanon to the bombings reinforced in her mind; the question was no longer whether there should be a withdrawal but how to effect one.[75]

Grenada

In response to the pro-Soviet coup which saw the Prime Minister and five of his ministers killed, both Jamaica and Barbados immediately called for military intervention from Britain and the USA. The Prime Minister's initial reaction was that it would be unwise to intervene, fearing that it would risk the 200 British civilians on the island.[76] The main organisation of Caribbean States, CARICOM, also stated that they would not support military intervention. However the organisation of Eastern Caribbean states, the OECS, voted unanimously to put together a force.

The USA viewed Grenada through the prism of Cuba, and Reagan felt an obligation to stop the spread of Communism and prevent a wider Cuban/Soviet influence in the region. The USA diverted the USS *Independence* to the area with 1,900 marines on standby. On Monday 24 October Reagan wrote to Thatcher to confirm that the USA was thinking about accepting the call from the OECS. The Prime Minister warned him that it would be seen as the USA interfering in a smaller country, something which Britain wished to avoid.[77]

American marines launched their invasion of Grenada in the early hours of the morning on Tuesday 25 October. The Prime Minister was not notified in advance. This led the British Government to being criticised harshly by the press, Parliament and the public. Thatcher claimed that it made them look impotent and at worst deceitful – the Monday before Howe had told the Commons that he had no knowledge of any American plans to intervene.[78] Howe recalls that both he and the Prime Minister were shocked at the US action: 'If you take the reaction to the US invasion of Grenada for example, we were both astonished by that since they had not indicated they were going to do it. Our reaction was a common one, but the Prime Minister had a greater instinct for the American, than perhaps I would have because the foreign secretary is living in a multilateral world while the Prime Minister is focusing on one issue then another.'[79]

The Prime Minister publicly rebuked the US invasion, and found her criticism of their actions and desire not to intervene badly damaged relations with Caribbean members of the Commonwealth. The President called the Prime Minister to apologise claiming that by the time he received her response to his letter operations were already under way.[80] However the Prime Minister and many around her believed that the USA's invasion of Grenada was a demonstration of US power in the face of the bombings in Lebanon. In her memoirs, she writes 'just as events in Lebanon had affected American action in Grenada, so what I had seen in the crisis over Grenada affected my attitude to Lebanon.' In February 1984 British forces withdrew from Lebanon.[81]

A direct consequence of the US invasion of Grenada was that Parliament put pressure on the Government to renegotiate the arrangement for the deployment of cruise missiles in Britain. The Labour opposition argued that if the Americans did not consult the British Government about Grenada then why would they do so in regard to the use of cruise missiles.[82]

Despite Grenada and Lebanon, the Prime Minister remained a staunch ally of the USA, sometimes even to the point of positioning herself against members of her own party and the Cabinet. This was the case over the US bombing of Libya.

Libya

Libya's leader, Muammar Gaddafi, had a reputation for financing terrorism including the Irish Republican Army (IRA). Britain had tried in the past under

Wilson to dis-incentivise these activities by effectively paying him not to and by conducting anti-terrorism operations, although these had mixed results.

On 5 April 1984, a bomb was detonated in a discotheque in West Berlin frequented by US servicemen, killing two people and one US soldier and injuring 200 others including sixty American civilians. US intelligence confirmed that the Libyan Government was involved. In response Reagan announced the USA's intention to bomb Libya in retaliation. The President requested the Prime Minister's support for the use of American F1-11 military aircraft and the support of aircraft based in Britain for the airstrikes.

Thatcher met with her Foreign Secretary and her Secretary of State for Defence, George Younger, to discuss the request. The Prime Minister agreed to support in principle Reagan's request but expressed anxiety over the targets.

This anxiety over an American retaliation was not confined to No. 10. Other European leaders offered their concern and scepticism. German Chancellor Kohl warned the President that he could not expect the wholehearted support of European leaders.[83]

Reagan responded that the USA was legally justified in striking Gaddafi's primary headquarters and immediate security forces rather than the Libyan people. The Prime Minister sent a further message offering Britain's 'unqualified support for action directed against specific Libyan targets demonstrably involved in the conduct and support of terrorist activities'.[84]

The issue was taken to Cabinet where Margaret Thatcher argued that the USA was justified to act in self-defence under Article 51 of the UN Treaty. She also stressed to colleagues that Britain had to stand by the USA as they stood by Britain over the Falklands. John Dickie, in his book *Inside the Foreign Office* recalls that the Prime Minister found herself opposed not only by Howe but by the whole Cabinet, who were concerned about the public reaction to an American airstrike as well as the possibility of retaliations by Libya. Despite this the action went ahead and Margaret Thatcher won the vote in Cabinet.[85]

Other European countries, while politically supportive of the USA, refused access to their airspace. This included both France and Spain. The airstrikes were conducted on the evening of 14 April. As the Prime Minister had been warned, the reaction was largely critical.[86] The British public were largely critical of the loss of civilian life and feared reprisals. One poll found that up to 70 per cent opposed her position making it one of the most unpopular foreign policy decisions in her tenure as Prime Minister.[87]

An emergency debate was called in the House of Commons, in which both Labour and the Liberal parties criticised the Prime Minister for allowing the

US access to the bases. They argued that she should have followed the example of other European countries and refused.[88] The Government faced further attacks when Libya in retaliation killed two British hostages in Lebanon.

However the Prime Minister was adamant that Britain's support of the USA was not only morally required but strategically important. She argued that because of this, Britain's voice in arms control negotiations was accorded special weight and that the American administration offered strong support for the extradition treaty that would bring back IRA suspects from the USA against Congressional opposition.[89]

Sanctions and South Africa

Libya was not the only instance when Thatcher found herself against the grain of public opinion. When it came to foreign policymaking, she had a tendency to support regimes of all colours, whether in favour or not. This included befriending General Pinochet, the dictator of Chile, whose regime was renowned for human rights abuses and murdering opposition figures, as well as supporting the Khmer Rouge by allowing them to keep Cambodia's seat in the UN, despite reports of mass killings.

She drew particular criticism when it came to the apartheid government of South Africa. The Conservative Party had always been sympathetic to the South African Government and had consistently repealed old sanctions put in place by the Labour Governments of Wilson and Callaghan while resisting pressure for new ones.

Despite growing international and domestic criticism of the regime in South Africa, Margaret Thatcher was unwilling to impose sanctions. She believed that it was the established Foreign Office view that Britain's national interests required going along with the 'radical black African states in the Commonwealth'.[90] She did not share this view, arguing that even if it was morally acceptable to pursue a policy which would have led to the collapse of South Africa it did not make strategic sense.

Reflecting on her position Geoffrey Howe concludes: 'I think sanctions in South Africa are a good example [of the way] in which Margaret had undoubtedly a less emotional commitment to hostility toward apartheid, but she would never have defended it.'[91]

In 1985 Reagan, under pressure from Congress, introduced a limited package of sanctions on South Africa. The Prime Minister found herself under similar pressure from Commonwealth countries who wanted Britain to sign a communiqué criticising the Government of South Africa. At the Commonwealth Heads of Government meeting in the Bahamas a compromise was reached that a group of 'eminent people' should visit to report on the situation.[92]

The Prime Minister sought to persuade Howe to attend, as Britain's 'eminent person'. However he was reluctant to do so, believing that it had a poor chance of success. He protested that as Foreign Secretary he could not do both jobs. The Prime Minister responded that she could cope with his job as well while he was away. Writing in her memoirs, she confirms that at this point she was now firmly in charge of Britain's foreign policy towards South Africa, making the main decisions directly from No. 10:[93] an unprecedented conformation that foreign policy was now firmly in her grasp and the Foreign Secretary irrelevant.

The trip turned out to be a disaster. The South African armed forces launched raids against the African National Congress (ANC) in Botswana, Zambia and Zimbabwe at the same time as the visit. Geoffrey Howe was pushed by the Prime Minister to visit bilaterally, as Britain would be taking the Presidency of the European Economic Community. Again reluctant to go, Howe was to press for reform and the release of Nelson Mandela. His trip was ultimately a failure since Howe found himself brushed off by President Botha of South Africa and insulted by President Kuanda of Zambia. The Foreign Secretary felt that the Prime Minister had set him up for an impossible mission.[94] This incident added to the growing personal isolation between them and the growing gulf between No. 10 and the Foreign Office.

The European monetary union: the Lawson–Howe pact

By 1985 it was clear that there was a rift developing between the Foreign Office and No. 10. The regular briefings that the Prime Minister received from the Foreign Secretary became far less frequent and when they did happen, they lasted only a perfunctory half hour.[95]

Percy Craddock, foreign policy adviser at the time, writes that by the second half of the 1980s no foreign affairs decision of any significance was made without reference to No. 10. The instinctive sympathy and understanding between the Prime Minister and Foreign Secretary was lacking.[96]

Nowhere was this more evident then on the growing question of Britain's future relationship with the European Economic Community. The June 1984 European Council summit at Fontainebleau saw leaders meet to negotiate the new budget. This left a particular strain on No. 10's relations with the Foreign Office.

The Prime Minister was keen to secure a rebate of well over 70 per cent of Britain's contribution to the budget. Negotiations were handled by the Community's foreign ministers. The French pushed for a rebate system that would give back a simple percentage of a country's net contribution. This system would mean that there was no link between net contributions and relative prosperity unlike the 'threshold' system Britain had argued for. The formula would acknowledge only the payments made under VAT and ignore sums contributed through tariffs and levies. In the end this means of calculation was accepted.[97]

Britain was offered a rebate of between 50–60 per cent with a temporary two year sweetener which would bring the refund up to 1,000 million ecus a year for two years. The Prime Minister was shocked at the offer, writing that she could not understand how Geoffrey Howe had allowed the Foreign Ministers to reach such a conclusion.[98] She announced that while she was willing to accept the new system of calculation she would not concede any figure below 70 per cent.

The main session broke up and in the bilateral meetings the Prime Minister found President Mitterrand of France would not move above 60 per cent but Chancellor Kohl of Germany would go as far as 65 per cent. She came to the conclusion that she could negotiate a deal on the basis of two-thirds refund but was determined to get the full 66 per cent, arguing that it would be absurd to deny her 1 per cent.[99] In the end her negotiations succeeded. Yet she perceived her success to be in spite of the Foreign Office, viewing the episode as another instance of Foreign Office 'appeasement'.

Now that the budget was out of the way, the member states of the Community wanted to press ahead with enlargement and with the measures to create a Single Market. The Prime Minister supported in principle the idea of the Single Market, believing it would revive the real ambition of the Treaty of Rome which was its literal free trade and deregulatory aim. However she was concerned about the growing push for a European Monetary System.[100]

The introduction of such a system would require changes to the original treaty itself which, under the current rules, would need unanimity. France and Germany being concerned about delay, pushed instead for an inter-Governmental Conference which would allow the changes to be passed by a simple majority instead. Despite British, Greek and Danish opposition the decision to push for an inter-Governmental Conference was passed.

In her memoirs, the Prime Minister believes that Geoffrey Howe would have agreed to it. She argued that his willingness to compromise reflected partly his temperament, partly the Foreign Office's déformation professionnelle but it may also have reflected the fact that Britain's membership of the Community gave the Foreign Office a voice in every aspect of policy that came under the Community.[101]

Ultimately, Margaret Thatcher believed that the Foreign Office was in favour of a federal Europe as a way of centralising power in Whitehall. She thought it was a power grab by the Foreign Office and for that reason Geoffrey Howe as Foreign Secretary had a slightly more accommodating view of European federalism than her.

Despite this, the Prime Minister was confident that a European Economic and Monetary Union would not happen with both British and German opposition. However this changed at the Luxemburg Council meeting on 2 December 1985 when Germany withdrew its opposition and allowed the amendment of the Treaty to add the phrase; for the first time allowing the EEC to push ahead with the Single European Act, later signed on 17 February 1986.[102]

The European Exchange Rate Mechanism (ERM) was created as a step towards European Monetary Union (EMU) by pegging Community members' currencies to reduce the exchange rate variability. Margaret Thatcher's scepticism of both the ERM and the EMU remained unchanged throughout the latter half of the 1980s. She believed her Chancellor, Nigel Lawson shared this view. The Prime Minister was therefore surprised to find, in May 1989, both her Foreign Secretary and Chancellor pushing for her to reconsider Britain's position on joining the ERM.[103] This was largely in response to the publication of the Delors Report on EMU which pushed for greater political and economic integration.

Howe publicly mentioned a commitment to ERM in his speech at the Scottish Conservative Party Conference and privately pushed for a meeting with Lawson, himself and the Prime Minister to discuss the issue. She refused to meet both, instead meeting with Lawson separately.[104]

Twelve days before the EEC Madrid summit, Howe and Lawson sent a minute to the Prime Minister, arguing for a compromise on the Delors EMU proposals. They made the case that Britain should agree to stage 1 but make no commitment to the later stages, accepting a 'non-legally binding reference' to sterling joining the ERM by the end of 1992, provided that certain conditions were met. The Prime Minister saw both of them on 20 June and again both argued that she set a date for Britain joining.[105]

In the end she relented and at the Madrid conference did spell out the conditions for Britain joining but the price of this concession cost Geoffrey Howe his job.[106] The Prime Minister concluded that she could not have Howe at the Foreign Office while Lawson was at the Treasury, and so moved him to Leader of the House, compensated with the title of Deputy Prime Minister. Howe was replaced in the Foreign Office by John Major, who would succeed where Howe had failed.

John Major was considered a rising star and a potential successor to the Prime Minister. Major's stay in the Foreign Office was brief but in his short time he utilised his personal relationship with the Prime Minister to try and mend the now heavily damaged bridge between the Foreign Office and No. 10. He saw both sides of the fence.[107]

The Foreign Office initially distrusted Major, considering him to be the Prime Minister's man. Sir Stephen Wall recalls that early on Major told Foreign Office officials that he wasn't surprised that they were cut off from No. 10:

> I remember him saying early on, 'I'm not surprised you haven't been getting anything out of the PM. From her perspective...you're sending her advice saying this is our recommendation and she feels like you're not giving her the full facts. What you need to be doing is say, look this is what it looks like; here is the bad, it's not very good, but we think what we're recommending is better than the alternative. If you do that you have a better chance of her saying OK.' We started to do that, to get better results.[108]

Three months later, Nigel Lawson resigned as Chancellor. This forced the Prime Minister to appoint Major to replace him. Initially Thatcher wanted to put Cecil Parkinson in the Foreign Office, as she had wanted all along but Major convinced her to appoint Douglas Hurd.[109]

Major in his memoirs writes that on taking over the Treasury he noticed the extent to which the policy dispute over ERM was damaging the Prime Minister. He believed that it was not so much the policy but the dogmatic way she advocated it. She was flatly hostile to a single currency without any idea of how committed the other Community members were to it.[110]

During this period Major and Hurd worked together to convince the Prime Minister to accept the arguments for UK entry into the ERM. They believed that she needed to be coaxed and not browbeaten into accepting a different point of view.[111] Major and Hurd both recognised the pro-ERM tide, with the majority of political opinion favouring entry, as well as business and economic commentators. They relayed their fears to the Prime Minister that if Britain used its veto the other countries would proceed with a Treaty of Eleven, leaving the UK behind.

Both men deduced that the Prime Minister could not afford to lose either another Foreign Secretary or Chancellor, and with that in mind she would have to listen to their case.[112] However they wanted to avoid a Howe-like ultimatum and instead focused on convincing her of the merits of their argument while recognising that they would need to help her save face.[113]

At the end of March 1990, Major began the task of talking Thatcher round to the merits of British entry. Laying out his case, he argued that it would be wrong to publish a future date for joining as it would leave Britain at the mercy of the markets. It would also be wise if the country enter within wide bands for rate fluctuation and not be confined to a narrow straitjacket. He also made it clear that sterling was in a vulnerable position and that the foreign exchange markets were getting used to high interest rates to sustain it.[114]

The severity of the last point had a particular impact on the Prime Minister who some months later conceded that Britain would join the ERM when the right conditions were met. Lord David Owen argues that Major is an example of someone who understood the Prime Minister, he got on because he stood up to her, she was amused to find a younger person able to speak his mind and unafraid of her.[115]

The ending of the Cold War and German reunification

Margaret Thatcher played an indispensable role in the resetting of relations with the USSR and in essence vetted Gorbachev on behalf of President Reagan.[116] She famously declared that he was someone the West could do business with.

Throughout 1983 the Prime Minister began to have seminars at Chequers with experts on the Soviet Union to help formulate policy. Out of these seminars she began researching possible future leaders. One of these was Mikhail Gorbachev, to whom the Prime Minister instructed her then Foreign Secretary Geoffrey Howe to reach out.[117] This led to him being invited to London and the opening of relations between the West and East; when Gorbachev ascended to the Presidency of the Soviet Union in 1985 this would eventually bring about the end of the Cold War.

The Chequers seminars also represent an example of Thatcher and Howe working together at their best. Sir Malcolm Rifkind, a junior Foreign Office Minister at the time recalls:

> Her relationship with Geoffrey Howe was much better. For example the single most important thing I was involved with during that period under Geoffrey

Howe, was the very major resetting of our relationship with the USSR and the invitation to Gorbachev. It was in the UK which led to the Thatcher/Gorbachev relationship. Thatcher had initially, since the Soviet invasion of Afghanistan, been disinterested in any bilateral relationship with the Soviet Union. I had discussions with Geoffrey Howe and together we put representations to the Prime Minister that it was time to look again at our relationship with the Soviet Union, and she decided to have a seminar at Chequers which is now well reported and recorded. The results of that seminar was that the Foreign Office had the authority to pursue an invitation to Gorbachev, who at that time was a relatively unknown junior member of the Politburo but we had identified as a potential future Soviet leader and then it happened all very quickly. So that was a good example of a constructive relationship between Thatcher and her foreign secretary, quite different from the final relationship when he resigned. By that time it had deteriorated very badly.[118]

Two events marked the beginning of the end of Cold War tensions between the Soviet Union and the West. First, the signing by the USSR and USA in December 1987, of the Intermediate-Range Nuclear Force Treaty after two years of talks, and secondly, the announcement by Gorbachev of the withdrawal of Soviet forces from Afghanistan in February 1988. Domestically the Soviet Premier's *Perestroika* reforms were taking hold and the general belief was that the Soviet Union would eventually dismantle. This process was speeded up by the collapse of the Berlin Wall, on 9 November 1989.

Lord Tom King, Defence Secretary at the time recalls that the Government did not have a policy on our attitude to a united Germany. The Prime Minister was personally hostile to a reunified Germany. As part of the generation that fought the Second World War, she instinctively felt that a united Germany would take Europe back to the old trouble. She believed Germany was a country far too big and far too powerful.[119]

Thatcher deduced that the Soviets would also be opposed to a reunified Germany and she therefore sought out Gorbachev's support to establish democracy and a separate Government in eastern Germany. However she found herself outmanoeuvred by Chancellor Kohl who negotiated bilaterally with the Soviet Premier and gained an agreement for reunification.[120]

Her resistance put her at odds with other EEC leaders, the Americans and domestically with the Foreign Office. Hurd describes the question of reunification as his biggest dispute with the Prime Minister.[121] Sir Stephen Wall, still in the Foreign Office, argues that her rigid opposition went so far as to risk her relationship with the German Chancellor, ceding it instead to Hurd:

She thought she could make an alliance with Mitterrand and then with Gorbachev to stop it happening and it became increasingly clear that was a non starter. Douglas Hurd eventually was instrumental in persuading her that this was a reality that we had to be part of it rather than on the side lines. Equally as her relationship with Kohl, the German Chancellor, broke down, Douglas was effectively the man who would go and see Kohl and he would go to Germany. Kohl made the point at EEC council meetings that he didn't know Douglas at all. There's a bit in the Foreign Office documents published about German reunification, where Charles Powell says to Thatcher 'We can't have Douglas take over your relationship with Kohl' and she agreed in practice. She let it happen otherwise there would be no contact at that level between the British Government and the German one.[122]

Hurd describes the Prime Minister's unrelenting position as a moment where we were heading for the cliff edge but then the situation changed and her attitude changed with it. Two things happened, he recalls:

The actual situation objectively moved. Two things happened. There was an American plan for discussion. What had been a rather chaotic summit with lots of people talking about it was formalised into a 2 plus 4 discussion. So that we British knew that there would be a meeting on a date and what we would discuss, as soon as that became properly organised so that she didn't any longer feel that we were being outmanoeuvred she began to move. The other point was Chancellor Kohl proved to be much more resolute on a range of things that she thought were crucial, the NATO issues and as soon as she realised that she began to think well it's not the end of the world if this plan leads to a united Germany.[123]

Thatcher's decline and foreign policy legacy

What the Prime Minister's stubborn opposition to German reunification reflected was what many considered her growing difficulty. It was not so much what she said but how she said it. It was not so much about the positions she took but her dogmatic approach that ultimately alienated her colleagues. During this time, Lord Armstrong says the strain was evident: 'In the last years of her [Margaret Thatcher's] prime ministership [she] was clearly beginning to flag a bit under the strain. You might not notice it from the outside but from the inside she was a little less zealous about reading the papers at night and that kind of thing. The pace was beginning to tell.[124]

In the end it was the question of Britain's role in Europe and her broken relationship with her former Foreign Secretary, Geoffrey Howe that saw her resign from the premiership. Her Commons performance on 30 October 1990, in the reading of a statement from the Rome European Summit was the final straw. The debate was defined by the infamous moment of her shouting 'No, no, no!' to any discussion of the European Commission increasing its powers.

In response, Geoffrey Howe resigned from the Government. This prompted Michael Heseltine to launch the leadership challenge which would see Margaret Thatcher forced to resign. Howe argues that their disagreement was ultimately based on a different analysis of the European question.[125] Although Lord Carrington contends that while Europe caused her a lot of trouble it did not finish her off.[126] In the end her downfall was, many believe, a culmination of grievances and the general belief that she had become hubristic and out of touch.

Thatcher's premiership has now become defined by her dominance over Cabinet and wider Government itself. Many point to her time in No. 10 as the defining moment where power, particularly in foreign policy terms, was centralised. Margaret Beckett, later Foreign Secretary and Acting Leader of the Labour Party, believes this to be the case, stating: 'To my mind it is Margaret Thatcher who tore up most of the conventions, who made the Prime Minister more one among equals rather than an all powerful figure. She drove a coach and horses through all the constitutional conventions and the press smiled because they all loved her.'[127]

However that is not how the men who worked in her Government necessarily saw it. Lord Armstrong believes Margaret Thatcher preferred the endorsement of her colleagues either in the Cabinet or a Cabinet committee but she made sure in advance that she would get it. 'She certainly led in Cabinet but there were times where she led with her chin, where she defied them to knock her.'[128] Sir Malcolm Rifkind outlines her approach as 'we have to decide X or Y. This is my view. What does everyone else think, basically challenging each person to disagree with her'.[129] 'She never bore any malice to those who disagreed with her', says Lord Carrington, 'and in that regard people were quite wrong. What she wasn't prepared to do was to listen to people who didn't know what they were talking about'.[130]

One can easily make the case that Margaret Thatcher was perhaps the most dominant modern day Prime Minister through the force of her personality alone. The historical decline of the Foreign Office in prominence was sped up in this period by her personal distrust and dislike of it as an institution. She questioned the advice she was given and often came to the conclusion that the occupants one by one went 'native'.[131]

In constitutional terms she respected convention. She did not seek to bypass the Cabinet even if at times the view could be that she bullied it. The collegiate style of governance certainly seemed to be lacking, replaced by an adversarial style at No. 10, pitted against other Whitehall departments. Part of her legacy was that more power rested in No. 10 when she left office then before she came in. In this essence she was the pinnacle 'imperial' Prime Minister, using her personality and standing in the Conservative Party and the country to dominate foreign policy.

However we have to take into consideration two unique factors. First, that she was the longest serving Prime Minister of the twentieth century, spending eleven years in office. There is clearly a natural trend that a more experienced Prime Minister will dominate foreign policy as time goes on, mainly because they are safe and secure in their foreign policy experience and see it as an escape from domestic policy. Some will argue therefore it is inevitable that she would be dominant as the longest serving minister in Government. Secondly she is our only female Prime Minister, a woman in the top job surrounded by men, many of whom had Victorian values when it came to women's role in society, let alone the idea of a woman leading. Her feminine charm was exercised in many instances as a factor in her domination, whether that was challenging many of the Conservative Heath grandees in Cabinet, many of whom thought it inappropriate to debate with a woman, or using it to charm other world leaders; we cannot discount her gender as a factor.

Returning to her personality, Margaret Thatcher was a force of nature. Her dominance in foreign policy is directly linked to her personality, her adversarial, strong and often dogmatic style. Ultimately this style led to the centralising of power in No. 10 as an alternate to the Foreign Office which she distrusted more and more. It also inevitably led to her downfall.

Notes

1 M. Thatcher, *The Autobiography* (London: Harper Collins, 1995), p. 159.
2 *Ibid.*, p. 172.
3 P. Carrington, interview with S. Goodman, 19 April 2012, House of Lords.
4 S. Dyson, 'Cognitive Style and Foreign Policy: Margaret Thatcher's Black-and-White', *International Political Science Review*, 30:1 (2009), 33–4.

5 S. Wall, interview with S. Goodman, 7 June 2012, private offices.
6 M. Heseltine, interview with S. Goodman, 30 May 2012, Department for Business, Innovation and Skill.
7 C. Moore, *Thatcher: The Authorised Biography Volume 1: Not For Turning* (London: Allen Lane, 2013), p. 429.
8 D. Hurd, interview with S. Goodman, 18 June 2012, private residence.
9 K. Theakston (ed.), *British Foreign Secretaries Since 1974* (London: Routledge, 2004), p. 31.
10 Thatcher, *The Autobiography*, p. 282.
11 *Ibid.*, p. 291.
12 *Ibid.*, p. 292.
13 *Ibid.*, pp. 292–3; Moore, *Margaret Thatcher*, p. 493.
14 Nott, J., *Here Today Gone Tomorrow: Recollections of an Errant Politician* (London: Politicos, 2002), p. 186.
15 Theakston, *British Foreign Secretaries Since 1974*, p. 31.
16 Thatcher, *The Autobiography*, p. 286.
17 P. Carrington, interview with S. Goodman, 19 April 2012, House of Lords.
18 Moore, *Margaret Thatcher*, p. 451.
19 P. Carrington, interview with S. Goodman, 19 April 2012, House of Lords.
20 Thatcher, *The Autobiography*, p. 288.
21 P. Carrington, interview with S. Goodman, 19 April 2012, House of Lords.
22 Thatcher, *The Autobiography*, p. 340.
23 *Ibid.*, p. 341.
24 *Ibid.*, p. 343.
25 *Ibid.*, p. 344; Moore, *Margaret Thatcher*, p. 667.
26 J. Campbell, *Margaret Thatcher Volume Two: The Iron Lady* (London: Jonathan Cape, 2003), p. 133.
27 Thatcher, *The Autobiography*, p. 347.
28 *Ibid.*, p. 348; Nott, *Here Today Gone Tomorrow*, p. 246.
29 P. Carrington, interview with S. Goodman, 19 April 2012, House of Lords.
30 P. Osborne, 'Lord Carrington: "I wish David Cameron would stop holding his wife's hand"', *The Telegraph*, 19 May 2013, accessed 1 August 2015: www.telegraph.co.uk/news/politics/10065066/Lord-Carrington-I-wish-David-Cameron-would-stop-holding-his-wifes-hand.html.
31 Campbell, *The Iron Lady*, p. 134.
32 Thatcher, *The Autobiography*, p. 347.
33 *Ibid.*, p. 348.
34 Campbell, *The Iron Lady*, p. 135.
35 Thatcher, *The Autobiography*, p. 346.
36 *Ibid.*, pp. 351–2.
37 *Ibid.*, p. 350; Campbell, *The Iron Lady*, p. 156.

38 M. Rifkind, interview with S. Goodman, 18 April 2012, House of Commons.
39 Nott, *Here Today Gone Tomorrow*, p. 245.
40 R. Reagan, *An American Life* (London: Hutchinson, 1990), p. 360.
41 Thatcher, *The Autobiography*, pp. 355–6; Moore, *Margaret Thatcher*, p. 691.
42 Dyson, 'Cognitive Style and Foreign Policy'.
43 Thatcher, *The Autobiography*, p. 357.
44 *Ibid.*, p. 359.
45 *Ibid.*, p. 361.
46 *Ibid.*, pp. 362–3; Moore, *Margaret Thatcher*, pp. 700–1.
47 N. Lawson, *Memoirs of a Tory Radical* (London: Biteback Publishing, 2010), p. 93.
48 F. Pym, *The Politics of Consent* (London: Hamish Hamilton Publishers, 1984), p. 27; Thatcher, *The Autobiography*, p. 392.
49 N. Allen and A. King, 'Off with their heads: British Prime Ministers and the Power to Dismiss', *British Journal of Political Science*, 40:2 (2010), 249–78; Thatcher, *The Autobiography*, p. 418.
50 Thatcher, *The Autobiography*, p. 420.
51 *Ibid.*, p. 390.
52 *Ibid.*
53 *Ibid.*, p. 525.
54 *Ibid.*, pp. 526–7.
55 G. Howe, interview with S. Goodman, 25 June 2012, House of Lords.
56 Thatcher, *The Autobiography*, p. 528.
57 Reagan, *An American Life*, pp. 87–8.
58 J. Major, *The Autobiography* (London: Harper Collins, 1999), p. 119.
59 N. Ridley, *My Style of Government* (London: Hutchinson, 1991), p. 43; P. Craddock, *In Pursuit of British Interests* (London: John Murray, 1997), p. 8.
60 D. Owen, interview with S. Goodman, 11 May 2012, private offices.
61 R. Armstrong, interview with S. Goodman, 18 December 2013, House of Lords.
62 S. Wall, interview with S. Goodman, 7 June 2012, private offices.
63 British National Archives, London, PREM 19/944, The Prime Minister's Office, 'Telegram from President Reagan to the Prime Minister', 7 August 1981.
64 Thatcher, *The Autobiography*, p. 294.
65 *Ibid.*
66 *Ibid.*, p. 335.
67 *Ibid.*, pp. 381–3.
68 *Ibid.*, p. 512.
69 *Ibid.*
70 *Ibid.*, p. 313.
71 *Ibid.*, p. 314.
72 Craddock, *In Pursuit of British Interests*, p. 64.

73 Thatcher, *The Autobiography*, p. 515.
74 *Ibid.*, p. 426.
75 *Ibid.*, p. 432.
76 *Ibid.*, p. 427.
77 *Ibid.*, p. 428.
78 *Ibid.*, p. 430.
79 G. Howe, interview with S. Goodman, 25 June 2012, House of Lords.
80 'Reagan's Apology to Thatcher over Grenada Revealed', BBC News, 10 November 2014, accessed 1 August 2015: www.bbc.co.uk/news/uk-29986729.
81 Thatcher, *The Autobiography*, p. 431.
82 *Ibid.*, p. 430.
83 *Ibid.*, p. 501.
84 *Ibid.*
85 J. Dickie, *Inside the Foreign Office* (London: Chapmans, 2000), pp. 272–3.
86 Craddock, *In Pursuit of British Interests*, p. 75.
87 Dickie, *Inside the Foreign Office*, p. 273.
88 Thatcher, *The Autobiography*, p. 503.
89 *Ibid.*, p. 503.
90 *Ibid.*, p. 534.
91 G. Howe, interview with S. Goodman, 25 June 2012, House of Lords.
92 Thatcher, *The Autobiography*, p. 536.
93 *Ibid.*, p. 536.
94 *Ibid.*, p. 359.
95 Theakston, *British Foreign Secretaries Since 1974*, p. 29.
96 Craddock, *In Pursuit of British Interests*, pp. 24–5.
97 Thatcher, *The Autobiography*, pp. 547–8.
98 *Ibid.*, p. 548.
99 *Ibid.*, p. 549.
100 *Ibid.*, p. 551.
101 *Ibid.*, p. 553.
102 *Ibid.*, p. 555.
103 *Ibid.*, p. 630.
104 *Ibid.*, p. 637.
105 *Ibid.*, p. 641.
106 N. Allen and H. Ward, '"Moves on a Chess Board": A Spatial Model of British Prime Ministers' Powers over Cabinet Formation', Briti*sh Journal of Politics and International Relations*, 11:2 (2009), 238–58.
107 Major, *The Autobiography*, p. 116.
108 S. Wall, interview with S. Goodman, 7 June 2012, private offices.
109 S. Wall, interview with S. Goodman, 7 June 2012, private offices.
110 Major, *The Autobiography*, p. 142.

111 *Ibid.*, pp. 155–6; D. Hurd, interview with S. Goodman, 18 June 2012, private residence.
112 P. Dunleavy and R.A.W. Rhodes, *Prime Minister, Cabinet and the Core Executive* (Basingstoke: Macmillan Press, 1995), p. 96.
113 Major, *The Autobiography*, p. 155.
114 *Ibid.*, p. 156; Thatcher, *The Autobiography*, p. 651.
115 D. Owen, interview with S. Goodman, 11 May 2012, private offices.
116 British National Archives, London, PREM 19/1656, The Prime Minister's Office, 'Record of the meeting between the Prime Minister and President Reagan at Camp David', 22 December 1984.
117 Thatcher, *The Autobiography*, p. 504.
118 M. Rifkind, interview with S. Goodman, 18 April 2012, House of Commons.
119 T. King, interview with S. Goodman, 31 January 2014, House of Lords.
120 Thatcher, *The Autobiography*, p. 685; D. Hurd, interview with S. Goodman, 18 June 2012, private residence.
121 D. Hurd, interview with S. Goodman, 18 June 2012, private residence.
122 S. Wall, interview with S. Goodman, 7 June 2012, private offices.
123 D. Hurd, interview with S. Goodman, 18 June 2012, private residence.
124 R. Armstrong, interview with S. Goodman, 18 December 2013, House of Lords.
125 G. Howe, interview with S. Goodman, 25 June 2012, House of Lords.
126 P. Carrington, interview with S. Goodman, 19 April 2012, House of Lords.
127 M. Beckett, interview with S. Goodman, 22 May 2012, House of Commons.
128 R. Armstrong, interview with S. Goodman, 18 December 2013, House of Lords.
129 M. Rifkind, interview with S. Goodman, 18 April 2012, House of Commons.
130 P. Carrington, interview with S. Goodman, 19 April 2012, House of Lords.
131 Major, *The Autobiography*, p. 153.

6

John Major, 1990–97

The sudden and unexpected demise of Margaret Thatcher's premiership created the conditions under which for the first time since Churchill, a Prime Minister ascended to the office in the middle of preparations for war. On the day John Major entered No. 10 on 28 November 1990, there were 29,000 British troops stationed in Saudi Arabia. Faced with a foreign policy baptism of fire, Major had to weigh up both domestic political concerns and international concerns coming from Britain's allies.

The Prime Minister's main focus was on uniting a deeply divided Conservative Party that had just removed one of their most popular leaders. As her successor, his position was less stable. He was more reliant on figures in the Cabinet with their own bases of power within the party. With this in mind, he chose to keep Thatcher's Cabinet intact, only firing two junior ministers from their positions.[1] Lord Michael Heseltine, Deputy Prime Minister under Major believes he wanted a break from the past: 'John wanted to avoid any repetition of the tensions of the Thatcher years; he was himself a much more consensual character'.[2]

Preparations for the Gulf War were in their final stages and members of the European Community were in the middle of negotiations for a new treaty to create a common currency. These two pressing foreign policy challenges meant that Douglas Hurd as Foreign Secretary and a rival in the leadership challenge to succeed Margaret Thatcher would be indispensable. Major knew from the outset that he would need him. Hurd had significant influence over Major, as Sir Stephen Wall, Major's Private Secretary at the time recalls: 'Hurd had huge authority, having been in the Foreign Office before. He had been a senior minister before Major, was the Secretary of State for Northern Ireland and Home Secretary. That made their relationship much more equal'.[3]

The Gulf War

Western preparations for war had been set in motion since the Iraqi army, under the orders of their ruler Saddam Hussein, had invaded the neighbouring country of Kuwait on 2 August 1990. At the time, Margaret Thatcher was being awarded the American Medal of Freedom by President George H. Bush at the White House. Both quickly offered a robust response, condemning the invasion and demanding an immediate withdrawal of Iraqi forces. The USA and Britain committed troops to the border of Saudi Arabia to protect its oil fields, at the behest of Saudi King Fahd.[4]

On the day Major became Prime Minister the UN Security Council passed UN Resolution 678. This set 15 January 1991, as the final date for an Iraqi withdrawal and authorised the use of 'all necessary means'[5] to compel Iraqi troops to go – in essence authorising the use of force.

Major inherited the 'War Cabinet' Margaret Thatcher had established. The Overseas Defence (Gulf) Cabinet Committee included Douglas Hurd as Foreign Secretary, Tom King as Defence Secretary, John Wakeham as Energy Secretary, Patrick Mayhew as Attorney General, and Chief of the Defence Staff, Air Marshall Sir David Craig. This group of ministers was supported by Sir Percy Craddock, Foreign Policy Adviser and Charles Powell who the John Major kept on as Private Secretary after Margaret Thatcher resigned, as well as the Cabinet Secretary, Robin Butler, Len Appleyard from the Cabinet Office and his then Press Secretary, Gus O'Donnell. They would meet twenty-six times throughout the Gulf War.[6]

Early discussion in the War Cabinet was dominated by two fears, the first being how good were the Iraqi armed forces, and the second the looming concern that Saddam may use chemical or biological weapons on the battlefield. In response, the group agreed to vaccinate British troops on a voluntary basis against possible attacks.[7]

With the help of Saudi Arabia, the USA and Britain had brought together a coalition of nineteen nations, the majority of which were Arab countries. Major's first priority on the world stage was reassuring the members of the coalition and the British soldiers already deployed of the British Government's continued support. Many of them were concerned about Margaret Thatcher's departure, as Lord Tom King remembers:

> The build up of our forces was slow but steady; the pressure was on; we were putting our people out there, and they were out in the desert; it wasn't terribly

comfortable. In the middle of this we then had a change of Prime Minister. I had already assured our troops of the new Prime Minister and the Government's full backing. I now had to repeat the message for a new Prime Minister, to reassure them that there would not be a change. I said it also to the Americans, 'don't doubt the Prime Minister, he's fully behind you'. I had to answer a lot of questions amongst our Arab friends. They all had tremendous respect for her, and were quite bewildered to hear that she had lost her position.[8]

At home Major was keen to build a consensus for the war as well. Parliament had been recalled in September for a two-day debate in response to the invasion, and the need for military action was approved by an overwhelming majority of 437 to 35. However in the New Year, a number of Labour backbenchers were keen for Parliament to be recalled to debate the situation. Tony Benn and Ted Heath had been to Baghdad to argue for the release of hostages. Both men opposed the principle of war and in turn their trip ignited similar calls from a minority of Labour MPs led by former Secretary of State for Defence, Denis Healey.

Labour's Shadow Foreign Secretary, Gerald Kaufman warned that Labour would not support the early use of force. Despite the warning, which some perceived to be placating backbenchers, there was cross party support for the use of force designated under the UN resolution. At the end of the debate 534 MPs of all parties voted in favour of military action to some 55 Labour MPs who voted against, including two junior opposition spokesmen, who resigned from the front bench.[9]

Similarly the Prime Minister was keen to seek out the opinions of his Cabinet colleagues on the final decision to go to war. Lord Michael Howard, then Secretary of State for Employment, remembers this clearly: 'When it came to the first Iraq War John Major went round the Cabinet table asking each individual Cabinet member their views as to whether we should go to war'.[10]

On 16 January, rushing from the chamber of the Commons, the Prime Minister took a phone call from President Bush to confirm the beginning of military operations. The plan would see massive airstrikes designed to degrade Iraqi defences followed up by a ground onslaught. UK forces would essentially be in support of the American military, accepting US tactical command. So tightly was the timing of the beginning of the campaign kept, that the Prime Minister only informed close ministerial colleagues hours before it began – Chief of the Defence Staff Sir David Craig, General Sir Peter de la Billière, Tom King and Charles Powell had advance notice. Douglas Hurd was only informed an hour before the first bombs fell.[11]

The Prime Minister made the decision to keep in close touch with senior political figures. He offered the customary briefings for former prime ministers to Margaret Thatcher and Ted Heath but also arranged for Neil Kinnock, the Labour Leader of the Opposition, and Paddy Ashdown, Leader of the Liberal Democrats, to be regularly briefed and met with them to seek out their views.[12] This was the highest level of contact and discussion between a Prime Minister and opposition leaders since the Second World War.

Major in his memoirs writes that he was at home with this consensual approach, and was well rewarded for it. Both Kinnock and Ashdown remained supportive of the Government in public and despite a few backbenchers, the Commons was united on the prosecution of the war. In fact many of their exchanges at Prime Minister's Questions were orchestrated. This reflected the bipartisan nature that foreign policy can often be conducted in as well as the collective approach of the Prime Minister. He concedes that the experience of the Gulf War turned him away from many of the cruder forms of party political conflict, which he had never had much attraction to.[13]

The air campaign lasted five and half weeks and support from Parliament, the Cabinet, the Party, and the public largely held. On 23 February, the second phase of the conflict began with a ground invasion to drive Iraqi forces out of Kuwait. Both the Prime Minister and the President were taken aback at how fast the ground battle was won.[14] Five days later on the 28 February a ceasefire was in place and Kuwait was liberated.

The military objectives agreed in relation to the UN Resolution were met. Iraqi forces were evicted from Kuwait and the Iraqi Republican Guard's capability had been degraded to the point where they would not be able to re-invade.[15] Despite this, many argue even to this day, that Coalition forces should have gone on to Baghdad and removed Saddam Hussein, with hindsight sparing much later anguish. Margaret Thatcher, perhaps the most vocal on this topic in Britain, later claimed that she certainly would have gone all the way to Baghdad.[16]

Despite criticism, Major is clear that there was little support from the heads of government in the Coalition or the generals responsible for prosecuting the war to go to Baghdad. The conflict was undertaken under a UN mandate which set out the war aims. On that basis Parliament supported the liberation of Kuwait. Both Labour and the Liberal Democrats had frequently argued for full compliance with the resolutions but nothing further.[17]

The Prime Minister argued at the time, 'that if nations who had gone to war on the basis of international law were themselves to break that law, what change would there have been in future of order rather than chaos? What authority in the future would the great nations have had against law-breakers if they themselves broke the law and exceeded the United Nations mandate? They would never be trusted again'.[18] In hindsight his argument seems almost like a premonition of the things to come.

The ceasefire talks centred on removing Iraqi forces and assets from Kuwait and did not address Saddam's assets within Iraq. Lord Tom King recalls that they were over very quickly with General Norman Schwarzkopf taking it upon himself to negotiate terms. Chemical weapon stockpiles were not discussed in these talks, and the General allowed Iraq to keep its helicopter gunships.[19]

Safe havens

Saddam's defeat was not the end of the crisis, as many had envisaged. Instead it continued in the form of a humanitarian disaster. On 15 February, before the beginning of military action, President Bush had appealed directly to Iraqis to overthrow Saddam and stop the impending bloodshed of the Coalition forces intervention. Two days after the liberation of Kuwait he made a similar appeal that the Iraqi people should put aside Saddam and join the international community.[20] In response to these calls and the general feeling of dissatisfaction amongst the Iraqi army, on 1 March there were uprisings in the south of Iraq. A few days later there were similar uprisings amongst the Kurdish population in the north of the country. At the height of the uprisings the Iraqi Government lost control of fourteen of Iraq's eighteen provinces.

Initially Saddam offered the Kurds and the Shia, who dominated the army, a share in central government in exchange for their loyalty, however no agreement was reached. He turned to the Republican Guard who by now had regrouped, and using gunships, artillery barrages and chemical weapons indiscriminately put down the uprisings. Throughout March and early April 1991, approximately 2 million Iraqis, 1.5 million of them Kurds fled Northern Iraq to the mountains along the northern border to Turkey and Iran, and in the south fled to the marshes. Their situation was dire, since hundreds of thousands were stranded with little supplies. On foot they were not only vulnerable to the elements but to Iraqi armies in pursuit.[21]

The international community watched as the situation worsened. On 21 March the Prime Minister raised his concerns over the plight of the Kurds in Cabinet. Major believed that the world could not stand aside and began coming up with a plan to help the Kurds. After consulting with the Ministry of Defence and the Foreign Office, he proposed a plan consisting of creating safe areas or 'safe havens' where Kurds would be protected from attack and could be fed and housed safely. The policy would require both American and European support due to its size and cost, and the Prime Minister was determined to secure it.[22]

The upcoming European Community Summit in Luxembourg offered the perfect opportunity for the Prime Minister to win over European support. In bilateral discussions throughout the summit, Major was able to convince both German Chancellor, Helmut Kohl and French President, Francois Mitterrand to support the plan.[23]

The USA was far more reluctant to support the safe haven proposals, feeling that its commitment to the war effort had been substantial and was unenthusiastic about a proposal that would require a larger troop commitment, more expense and no guarantee of an end plan.[24] Major reached out to Bush and using his personal relationship with the President convinced him of the merits of the plan and with it secured an American commitment.[25]

The US sent 5,000 troops as the largest contingent; Britain sent 2,000, and France would send 1,000. Food, water, clothing and shelter were provided on a massive scale and a humanitarian catastrophe was averted. Part of the plan was the establishment of a no-fly zone over Northern Iraq in 1992; this would later be extended to most of Iraq under the auspices of UN Resolution 688.[26]

For Major the Gulf War was seen as a great foreign policy success. He had been thrown in to the deep end and proven himself to be a credible statesman. There was much talk within the Prime Minister's close circle of going to the polls in the spring of 1991. This discussion had begun even before the ceasefire had officially been declared. Major rejected such advice, arguing instead that the idea of a 'khaki election' would be cynical and that a victory won off a successful military campaign would be a false one.[27] Whether he would have won or not we do not know; what we do know however is that it takes a rare individual to give up such an advantage.

Maastricht

The second foreign policy decision Major inherited from his predecessor was the pending European Community negotiations on further economic and monetary union, with the final aim of a single currency. The case for a single currency had been set long in advance. The 1989 Delors Report had set out the future direction of Europe towards greater political and economic integration and the Single European Act of 1986 had created a single market for goods and services across Europe.

The six Christian Democrat Leaders in the European Community, German Chancellor Kohl and the prime ministers of Italy, Belgium, Greece, Holland and Luxembourg, had already established a consensus over the future direction of Europe. They were keen to ensure that no outcome of the negotiations for a new treaty on European Union could question the irreversibility of the democratic and federalisation of the future union. The draft treaty included a European Social Chapter underpinning workers' rights and more powers for the European Parliament.[28]

Domestically, the Prime Minister found himself in a particularly difficult position. The Conservative Party had become increasingly unstable over the issue of European integration and that instability had in the end led to his predecessor's ejection from office. He understood that the party was still reeling from the battles of the Thatcher years and there was little appetite for more infighting on the topic. The Prime Minister also knew that the Eurosceptic wing of the party would not accept any treaty that ceded further powers to the Community.

Yet the current in Europe was undoubtedly in favour of integration. Once again Britain risked being the awkward partner, something which Major wished to avoid. His first goal was to re-establish good working relationships with his European counterparts, something which he acknowledged had been in decline for some time. What he wanted to make clear was that he was not Margaret Thatcher, both in style and outlook. Sir Malcolm Rifkind, Secretary of State for Defence and Secretary of State for Transport under Major, describes him as having by temperament and by conviction many eurosceptic views but being a pragmatist, believing ultimately that if you are part of an international organisation then diplomacy requires compromise.[29]

The Prime Minister came to the conclusion that Britain would need allies to break its European isolation since even when right, few countries would agree with Britain due to its poor reputation. Ultimately personal relationships between leaders matter, and, as Prime Minister, Major set out to establish important ones of his own. Writing in his memoirs, he is quick to point out that it is cynical to believe that personal chemistry between leaders counts for nothing when the chips are down.[30]

On the European front he began lobbying potential allies and dispelling many of the old fears concerning a retreating Britain. Domestically, the Premier set up a Cabinet Committee to examine the proposals likely to be put into a treaty. Douglas Hurd was entrusted to chair these meetings except on issues that were highly contentious, which Major chose to preside over himself to ensure that each Cabinet member was consulted and able to have input into deliberations.[31] This format copied the one used by Wilson during the European renegotiations in 1974/75, with Callaghan chairing the Committee and Wilson intervening as and when was necessary.

Like Wilson before him, he took up the task of engaging in difficult European negotiations while managing a divided Cabinet and a divided Party. The Cabinet reflected largely the differing views in the Conservative Party on the subject and the Prime Minister understood that he would need to establish a negotiating position that was acceptable to everyone.

The Prime Minister was fundamentally opposed to a European single currency and also believed that in practical terms it was too early for the introduction of one. The political implications, would, he argued, be untenable to the UK. A single currency, a central bank and unified monetary policy would remove key economic power from Government and Parliament. From a Conservative perspective, it would lead to the harmonisation of taxes which, due to the left-leaning nature of much of Europe, would see taxes rise. Major's second objection derived from his belief that the Community should be enlarged to include the Central and East European nations. An early move to monetary union would be likely to delay their entry as the Community's attention would be focused on EMU.[32]

Major outlined Britain's negotiating strategy as two tier; first, to try and delay the single currency and if that failed, then to insert safeguards. In no circumstances, he argued, should the Government commit sterling to enter, although they should retain the right to negotiate entry later on. He conceded to the more Eurosceptic Cabinet colleagues and backbench MPs that there was little point in blocking the whole treaty, as the Community would simply create their own, leaving Britain out,[33] making the argument, echoed since entry, that Britain would be isolated and have no influence over the Community's plans.

The second issue of the Maastricht Treaty came in the form of the Social Chapter, which would standardise labour laws across Europe. This would include the number of hours employees should work as well as the level of wages. The Prime Minister, like the vast majority in the Conservative Party, was ideologically opposed to this. He argued that the Social Chapter would reverse Conservative domestic reforms, and also it reinforced fears that Brussels wanted to take over large swathes of domestic policy.[34]

Major decided to hold a Commons debate to gain approval of the Government's negotiating stance. This was a risky strategy but reflected his desire to build a broad consensus behind his approach. It also provided the opportunity to flush out opposition from the Conservative backbenches. His personal inclination was to build cross-bench support even with a parliamentary majority of 125 seats.

At the end of the debate the Government received a majority of 101, with six Conservative MPs voting against. During the debate Margaret Thatcher made a rare intervention, advocating a referendum on the issue of a single currency. While publicly popular, many in the Cabinet opposed the idea on constitutional grounds, while others considered it to be an attempt to undermine her successor. This would not be the end of discussion surrounding a referendum.[35]

Before the summit, Major met with German Chancellor Helmut Kohl and Ruud Lubbers, the Dutch Prime Minister and current occupant of the EEC Presidency. In these meetings, the Prime Minister stated that he would not accept current proposals but would agree to a treaty if Britain could obtain her concessions.[36]

Throughout Maastricht Hurd and Major worked in perfect partnership. In Cabinet they set out all the areas of the draft treaty that were still in serious dispute and gained approval on their final negotiating position. This was only possible after the 'private coaxing' of Michael Howard and Peter Lilley. Hurd and the Chancellor Norman Lamont, flew out with the Prime Minister on Sunday 8 December 1991.[37]

On the first day of the summit, Kohl was quick to put forward that the Community should be ready for monetary union by 1996–97, if a critical mass of states could meet the conditions. In response to this the Prime Minister made it clear that Britain would not agree to enter a single currency. Instead he proposed a two-tier Europe – stressing that there should be no suggestion of compelling unwilling countries to enter the new currency.[38] French President Mitterrand agreed with Kohl, and stated that the currency must be irreversible and that the Community must fix a date for entry. He favoured the later date of 1999. On a side note Belgian Prime Minister, Wilfried Martens argued for a common defence policy and more importantly an end to decision-making by unanimous agreement.[39]

The second day saw the Social Chapter take the spotlight, as the single currency was put to one side. The Prime Minister started by setting out the UK position in relation to the Social Chapter arguing against its inclusion in the treaty. The Dutch attempted to amend the draft but French President Mitterrand opposed such measures, stating that if the chapter was watered down he would vote against the whole treaty. This drew clear sides; the UK would veto a treaty with the Social Chapter in it, while the French would veto a treaty without it. Both the Belgian and Italian prime ministers offered their support to Mitterrand.[40]

To compromise, the Chairman offered incentives to water down the treaty or add amendments, but the Prime Minister refused, arguing that as they had not been prepared adequately in advance they would be open to legal challenge in the courts. After much debate, the end result was an agreement with the other eleven Community countries outside of the treaty. This was possible mainly because Major managed to sway German Chancellor Kohl in private bilateral discussions, convincing him that there was no way he would budge. Minsters also conceded to a UK opt-out on EMU largely because of their preoccupation with the Social Chapter.[41]

At home Major's opt-outs were seen as a great success. The Times ran the headline 'Major wins all he asked for at Maastricht'. The Prime Minister recalls that in Cabinet it was all 'sweetness and light', describing it as the modern equivalent of a Roman triumph. Both Hurd and Lamont too, received standing ovations at meetings of Conservative backbenchers.[42]

On 9 April 1992, John Major was returned to the premiership with a parliamentary majority of 21, despite many polls predicting a Labour victory. Within the Conservative Manifesto was a commitment to the passing of the Maastricht Treaty with the relevant opt-outs. The Conservatives polled more votes than any party in British political history, winning half a million more votes than Labour in their 1997 landslide and a third of a million more than Thatcher managed in 1987.[43]

The Prime Minister was riding high and enjoyed a renewed honeymoon period within the Conservative Party, until Black Wednesday (16 September 1992), when the pound fell out of the European Exchange Rate Mechanism. There were a number of factors that played into one of the worst days for the British economy since the 1970s.

In June 1992, the Treasury forecast that the UK trade deficit would widen, government borrowing would grow and unemployment would continue to rise. The sudden announcement by the Danish Government that it would hold a referendum on the Maastricht Treaty led Mitterrand to also concede one to the French people, where opinion polls favoured a French rejection. The stakes were raised days later, when the Danish people voted on 2 June against the treaty. Confidence in the markets was badly damaged by the uncertainty which began to cause fright. Sterling sank steadily from DM 2.91 in May to DM 2.80 in August, close to the floor of the ERM set at 2.778.[44]

The situation was exacerbated by a weak dollar and a strong deutschmark. Over the summer of 1992, the dollar weakened substantially as the US Federal Reserve Bank lowered interest rates in order to increase the rate of growth in the US economy. An unforeseen consequence of this was capital flight from Wall Street, as investors moved their money into deutschmarks, the foundation of the ERM. In doing so, this strengthened the price of the deutschmark and in turn put a strain on all other European currencies that could not keep up as the Bundesbank, the German national bank, adjusted interest rates to favour Germany. The pound was stuck in the middle.[45]

The Prime Minister was faced with a tough decision. To stay in the ERM the Government would have to increase interest rates by 1 per cent. However if Britain decided to do so, the fear was that France would do so too and this would lead to French votes rejecting Maastricht. Major also feared it would stifle the economic recovery and encourage Conservative backbenchers into the small anti-Maastricht camp.[46]

G4 finance ministers of Britain, French, Italy and Germany met to discuss the situation while Major spoke privately to Kohl, pressing that Britain would leave the ERM if Germany did not lower its interest rates.[47] The Chancellor argued that the Bundesbank was independent of Government. Progress was slow. This led Norman Lamont to announce that the British Government would take a foreign currency loan of 10 billion ecus (over £7 billion) to support sterling[48] as a short-term stop gap.

The Italians decided to increase their interest rates to 15 per cent which again raised the prospect that France and Britain would follow, continuing the uncertainty in the market. On Sunday 13 September, Kohl conceded that Germany were finally willing to cut interest rates, however this was only by a miniscule amount, the Lombard rate by 0.25 per cent and the discount rate by 0.5 per cent. In the end it was too little too late and without any sign of intervention by European banks. The decision was made to leave the ERM. In attempting to prop up sterling the Government had spent £3.4 billion.[49]

A few days later French voters narrowly voted yes in their referendum on the Maastricht Treaty. However the damage from Black Wednesday and the Danish rejection of the treaty was already done. Conservative backbenchers opposed to the treaty were enthused and ready to do battle. What would follow was a unique moment in British parliamentary history where for a time there were two separate parties within the Conservative party.

Prior to the Danish referendum, the Maastricht Bill had swiftly been approved in both first and second reading in Parliament. Denmark's rejection of the treaty raised the possibility of the treaty being opened once again for discussion, unless the Danes could be convinced to change their minds. This came just as Britain took over the presidency of the EEC.

After the Danish result Michael Spicer MP laid down an Early Day Motion calling for a new approach to Europe. Sixty-nine Conservative MPs signed it, a third of Tory backbenchers. The Bill was about to enter the Committee stage to enact the legislation, and in response to the EDM, Government whips cautiously advised the Prime Minister to delay this stage; Major agreed with their assessment. The bill was kicked into the long grass until the end of 1992.[50]

However, the Prime Minister had made a deal with Labour leader, Neil Kinnock that in the result of a yes vote in the French referendum, he would allow a one-day paving debate before reintroducing the Bill. In hindsight this deal would only offer eurosceptic backbenchers a platform to voice their opposition, but Major did not want to break his word. Instead he made a deal with his backbenchers, promising to delay the bill's third reading until after the second Danish referendum. This was effective and the Government survived the crucial vote in November 1992.[51]

While the delay gave the Government a reprieve from the difficult internal debate within its party, it also allowed the Eurosceptic rebels time to prepare. Their composition was a mixture of ideologues who opposed in principle the European Union, those who disliked the treaty and some who opposed Major's leadership. The rebels were encouraged by Major's predecessor, Margaret Thatcher, who used her old allies, Gerald Howarth and Lord Norman Tebbit, as intermediaries to openly encourage the defeat of the bill.[52] The struggle to pass the Maastricht Treaty reflected a unique occurrence in British parliamentary politics, of a former Prime Minister openly opposing and inciting rebellion against a successor of the same party.

The rebels were well financed and well organised. They had their own informal whips James Cran and Christopher Gill. Norman Tebbit served as a go between for Margaret Thatcher, inviting potential rebels to meet with her in her office in the Lords. Their plan was to firstly delay the bill in the hope that external events would render it irrelevant; secondly they sought to add an amendment requiring a referendum on the treaty, and finally they wanted to add a further amendment forcing the Government to abandon the whole treaty.[53] At the heart of their campaign was the belief that while the Prime Minister has the power to negotiate treaties on Britain's behalf, Parliament as the legislative body should have the final say, independent of government.[54]

In the opposition Labour Party, the rebels hoped to find willing allies. Although officially supportive of the Maastricht Treaty and sceptical of referendums, many Labour MPs would do anything to defeat and bring down the Major Government.

An internal dispute within a political party was now having a clear impact on British foreign policy. Major believed that if Britain repudiated a treaty it had helped negotiate while holding the chair of the community, it would create long-term damage to Britain's national prestige. He argued that at stake was Britain's reputation as an 'honest nation'.[55]

The Prime Minister found that he was unable to re-establish party discipline over the rebel members, due to the decentralised nature of the party. Area Chairmen reported that when they tried to persuade constituency parties to bring their rebellious member into line, the response was often that 'what is right for Margaret Thatcher is right for our Member'.[56]

At the European Summit in Edinburgh, in December 1992, European Community leaders agreed a series of opt-outs of the Maastricht Treaty for Denmark. These opt-outs, they hoped would convince Danish voters to vote yes in the pending second referendum. They were proved right, when in May 1993 voters, by a healthy margin, agreed to ratify Maastricht. The agreement now freed the British Government to continue its own ratification process and put the legislation to its third reading.

Meanwhile, the rebels had found mixed results in achieving their aims of stopping the treaty. In April they had managed to get their referendum amendment debated in the chamber but Labour's formal opposition to it ensured their defeat.

May saw the largest number of Conservative rebels vote against the Government's third reading of the bill. The stories of backbenchers being invited to Margaret Thatcher's office and lobbied by a lurking Norman Tebbit in the Members' Lobby came back to the Prime Minister. The rebellion was in full steam with forty-one Conservative MPs voting against the Government. It was not enough however to stop the bill passing and being given Royal Assent on 20 July 1993.[57]

In response, the rebels announced their intention to seek a judicial review of the Government's right to ratify the treaty. Douglas Hurd argued that under the Crown prerogative the Social Chapter did not need Parliament's approval; instead it fell into the category of foreign undertakings, which the Prime Minister executed under the Royal prerogative.[58] This dispute over the power of the executive to negotiate on Britain's behalf is at the heart of the Maastricht rebellion.

There would be a further two votes on 22 July, the first on a Labour opposition motion that the bill should not be ratified without the inclusion of the Social Chapter, the second vote on the Government's opt-out. No one could predict the outcome of the vote. Journalists recounted Cabinet sources as split between victory and defeat. Some hinted that the Cabinet was split on continuing with the ratification process irrespective of the result.[59]

The Labour amendment was defeated as the Conservative Party united. However the Government opt-out was a different matter; the rebels saw it as the perfect moment to defeat the Government and twenty-four Conservative MPs shuffled into the opposition division lobby, joining with Labour and the Liberal Democrats to defeat the Government's motion 324 to 316.[60]

In response to the Government defeat, Major decided to table an emergency Motion of Confidence in the Government to the existing motion on the Social Chapter, telling his backbenchers if the Government was defeated by another rebellion he would seek a dissolution of Parliament and trigger an immediate general election. The choice was clear. They could vote for the treaty or fight an election that would bring into office a government more strongly committed to Maastricht and many of them, deprived of the party whip, would lose their seats.[61]

In the end the confidence vote was won by thirty-nine votes. Even though committed to their cause, many of the rebels were more afraid of the electorate. Maastricht was passed. This however did not stop the divisions in the party over Europe through 1994. On 22 June 1995 John Major called a leadership election, telling the Eurosceptic backbenchers that they had a choice: 'put up or shut up'. He would handily defeat the 'stalking horse' opponent John Redwood MP, by 218 to 89 votes.[62]

The Balkans: Bosnia

Instability in the Balkans would bring Major the greatest heartache of his tenure in No. 10, as well as testing his foreign policy skills to their limits. The disintegration of the Federal Republic of Yugoslavia and the descent into war among her former states was prominent throughout Major's premiership.

The inability to find a quick solution was largely the product of a clear split between the USA and Britain over intervention. The USA largely saw it as a 'European' problem,[63] as American Secretary of State, James Baker, famous stated, 'we [America] got no dog in this fight'. Lord Richard Dannatt, a colonel at the time, in charge of running the High Command Training Course and tasked with drafting the campaign plan for the United Nations Protection Force recalls: 'The Americans were determined to keep out of Bosnia, seeing the Cold War having so recently ended. How are we going to make the Europeans stand on their own feet? Let the Europeans handle the Balkans.'[64]

The collapse of Communism across Europe in 1989, as well as the death of the long-serving leader Marshal Tito, had put extreme strain on the Yugoslavian Federation. Serbia had come to dominate the other states. Serbian leader, Slobodan Milosevic was determined that Yugoslavia should be transformed into a 'Greater Serbia', on the basis that there were large Serb populations in Croatia and Bosnia-Herzegovina.

Milosevic's ambitions created great unease amongst the other republics of Yugoslavia. They would not wait around for Serbia to dominate them and chose instead to pre-empt Serbian ambitions. Slovenia and Croatia declared independence in June 1991, splitting from Yugoslavia.

Belgrade responded militarily and fighting broke out, by August becoming full-scale war. Milosevic used the Yugoslav army to fight against Zagreb for control of Serb-dominated areas of Croatia. The international community favoured the stabilisation of Yugoslavia. Lord Peter Carrington, former Conservative Foreign Secretary, was sent to mediate a settlement, while the UN imposed an arms embargo on the region. Despite his best efforts, neither side would enter talks, so the fighting continued.[65]

In December the Prime Minister faced a dilemma. Douglas Hurd informed him that eleven members of the European Community wanted to recognise Croatia's independence. They argued that a delay in recognition would only encourage the Serbs to further wage war. Germany's Foreign Minister, Hans-Dietrich Genscher, made it clear to Major that Germany would recognise Croatia unilaterally if other Community members did not agree unanimously to do so.[66]

The Prime Minister, in the middle of Maastricht negotiations and relatively new, could not afford to oppose other Community members but at the same time Peter Carrington, the UN Envoy was asking for more time. There was also the further question of the protection of minorities in Croatia. After the EEC foreign ministers met to agree on terms of recognition, the Prime Minister agreed. Many have raised the coincidence that Britain's concession to Germany over recognition came at the same time as Germany's concession to Britain over Maastricht opt-outs.[67]

Peter Carrington felt undermined. He argued that by the European Community endorsing Croatian independence they were throwing away their only opportunity to oblige the Yugoslav republics to agree to a settlement prior to independence, and offer real protection to minorities.[68] On the other hand, Percy Craddock believes the opposite, namely that acknowledging secession was unavoidable and followed by an immediate deployment of peace-keeping troops could have avoided further bloodshed,[69] although he notes that Yugoslavia must have been one of the first instances of Britain siding with Europe against the USA in a major international crisis. The commitment to Europe was such, he argues, that Hurd was apparently prepared to sacrifice Lord Carrington's peace plan for the sake of a common front with Germany.[70]

In recognising Croatia and Slovenia as independent states the EEC set a precedent for Bosnia, which was faced with the choice of whether to stay in a Serb-dominated Yugoslavia or follow the example of their neighbours and leave. After a referendum, Bosnia declared its independence on 6 April 1992.

In response, Radovan Karadžić, the leader of the Serbian population in Bosnia declared a Serb state within Bosnia, with Sarajevo as the capital which, he argued, was under 'enemy occupation'. Fighting broke out in Eastern Bosnia, and in May 1992 Serbia launched an assault on Sarajevo which would last three years. The Serb-dominated Yugoslav Army had overrun 70 per cent of Bosnia-Herzegovina.[71]

On 21 February 1992, the UN passed UN Resolution 743, mandating a UN protection force (UNPROFOR) in Serbian areas of Croatia to create safe havens and ensure conditions for peace talks. Brokered by former US Secretary of State, Cyrus Vance, the force consisted of 39,000 military personnel.[72] UNPROFOR's role in Bosnia was, by comparison, unclear. It was not there to manage an existing ceasefire but stuck in the middle of a humanitarian crisis.

By June 1992, three quarters of a million refugees were fleeing advancing Serb forces in Bosnia. In August, reports were immerging of 'ethnic cleansing' of both sides murdering members of the different ethnic and religious groups. Many faced expulsion from their homes and others were put in detention camps.

On 18 August, the Prime Minister cut his holiday short to hold a six-hour emergency meeting of the Cabinet, asking the assembled ministers how Britain could save lives and limit the conflict. After much discussion, it was agreed that Britain would send 1,800 men to protect humanitarian convoys and the Prime Minister convinced France and Canada to also send troops.[73]

Politicians and commentators alike were sceptical of this decision, arguing that Britain had no strategic interest in the Balkans. The Conservative Party was largely split between those connected to the right wing of the party, normally considered to be pro-military who did not support action and others who were urging military intervention. It was not clear cut. Some favoured delivering aid but not at the cost of troops meeting opposition.[74] There was a certain amount of unease about the risk of military disaster.

Major notes in his memoirs that this reflected a shift in the left/right-wing fracture which had dominated British foreign policy. Those on the right were considered more hawkish while those on the left advocated peaceful alternatives. This had been a reliable barometer throughout the Cold War but now seemed to be shifting.[75] A broad ideological coalition against intervention emerged, composing of MPs on the left like Tony Benn, to one-nation pragmatic Conservatives like Ted Heath, and right-wing Conservatives like George Gardiner.

Cabinet reflected the divided opinion of parliamentarians. Hurd along with the Prime Minister was committed to the use of troops. Defence Secretary, Malcolm Rifkind along with other Cabinet colleagues Ken Clarke, Michael Portillo and Robert Cranborne all held reservations. The Prime Minister chose to set up a Cabinet subcommittee with himself, Hurd and Rifkind, in what became an informal triumvirate. The three would monitor the situation on the ground and find a consensual agreement. Sir Stephen Wall, Private Secretary to the Prime Minister at the time recalls that Bosnia was discussed in depth frequently. There were, he says, umpteen papers about what the policy should be.[76]

The triumvirate worked well, Hurd believes, because they had the same three ministers and this meant there were rarely any head-on clashes. Recalling his discussions with the Prime Minister in these meetings: 'There were no major sort of clashes really because he was very ready to listen and to accept my view. There were issues particularly on Bosnia where we had a slightly different view; then you had a third character in the room, in the discussion was Malcolm Rifkind as the Defence Secretary.'[77]

The question of intervention loomed throughout. Hurd recalls that the Bosnian issue was perhaps the most difficult issue of his time in the Foreign

Office, reflecting on the letters that Margaret Thatcher sent to him throughout the crisis:

> I think if Margaret Thatcher had remained Prime Minister she would have done a good deal more than the interventionists and indeed after she resigned she did send letters and talk to me about Bosnia. Always on the line that we must be prepared [to] intervene or take a stronger line. I just didn't think that was sensible or would lead anywhere and John Major agreed with me with certain reservations which he had.[78]

A week after the decision to commit troops, the Prime Minister chaired a conference on Bosnia in London with the UN Secretary General, Boutros Boutros-Ghali, in Britain's capacity as the current chair of the European Union. Around thirty nations attended, together with representatives from the warring parties. Anthony Seldon, in his biography of Major writes that he was the dominant personality at this summit, deploying considerable negotiating skills, taking the individual Yugoslavian leaders into a private room to persuade or cajole them, or offer compromises, and driving the plenary sessions through with his blend of force and charm.[79]

At the end of the summit, the warring parties had virtually agreed to all the demands for a swift end to the fighting, including UN supervision of heavy weapons, recognition of the borders of Bosnia, a no-fly zone over Bosnia, and the return of refugees. *The Times* called the conference 'a triumph for international diplomacy' with much of the praise going to Major and his diplomacy skills. The problem however was with the implementation of the agreement, since the Serbs did not want to stop their aggression and the sanctions and no-fly zone were not enforced.[80]

The Prime Minister was also tasked with appointing a new European Union representative after Lord Peter Carrington stepped down. He chose to approach Lord David Owen, Callaghan's former foreign secretary for the position. He already had a large amount of foreign policy experience and had worked closely with Cyrus Vance, the UN Representative, in the past. Owen was sceptical. Carrington had been undermined in his attempts to negotiate a settlement by Germany and some would argue by the Foreign Office. In taking the role Owen wanted assurances that it would be made clear to the Foreign Office that he was there because the Prime Minister wanted him and not the Foreign Secretary. Owen remembers that he knew that the power structures had shifted: 'I didn't want to be in a position where I was off in Bosnia making some compromise on the end of some branch and the Foreign Office would be sawing off that branch and I was out in the extremity.'[81]

He found that the Foreign Office did do this to him but it never worked because he had an entrée through Stephen Wall and could speak with the Prime Minister any time he liked. Owen was therefore never at what he would consider 'the mercy of the Foreign Office'.[82] Owen and Vance set up a conference organisation in Geneva and began developing a proposal to secure a resolution to the conflict.

British troops arrived in Bosnia in November 1992. In December, the USA put forward a four-point plan to protect the aid convoys; this would include the enforcement of a ban on military flights over Bosnia and a lifting of the UN arms embargo. While the Prime Minister agreed with the objective, he worried that the plan was ambiguous about how to enforce the no-fly ban and was concerned for the vulnerable position British troops were in, defending a 150-mile stretch.[83]

The USA was largely distracted by domestic politics. November had seen a change of President. George H. Bush had been defeated by a young southern Governor, Bill Clinton, in what many considered to be a huge upset. Major had got on well with Bush; the Republicans and Conservatives had always been ideologically similar and both men liked each other personally. His relationship with Clinton would be far frostier and started largely on the wrong foot. The Conservatives had helped Bush in the election and leaked negative information about Clinton's time as a student at Oxford University. Clinton's people were therefore distrustful of Major.[84]

The two met in February 1993 for the first time, and Clinton made it clear that the US position was largely unchanged. There was no appetite domestically for intervention. The prevailing opinion amongst US foreign policymakers was that of 'lift and strike', lifting the arms embargo and starting airstrikes against the Bosnian Serbs.[85] This view concerned the Prime Minister, who argued that such a policy would put British troops in harm's way and compromise neutral missions to deliver humanitarian aid.[86] Lift and strike appealed to the White House as it would allow the USA to avoid a troop commitment while maintaining their concern and offering the appearance of engagement.

Vance and Owen in January 1993 announced their proposed plan to divide Bosnia between the conflicting parties and in effect create barriers between them using troops. The hope was to create breathing space, which could spur on a diplomatic settlement. It would require a high number of troops that only a military as big as the USA could provide. Of course the USA was opposed to any discussion of ground troops, arguing that not only was the issue in Europe's backyard but there was little strategic interest.[87] These concerns were exacerbated by the failed US mission in Somalia.

Instead advocates in the USA turned their attention back to the idea of 'lift and strike'. Russia and France were both opposed to the idea of airstrikes and the lifting of the arms embargo. The Prime Minister chaired a Cabinet committee to discuss options, the consensus opinion being that the lifting of the embargo would not offer the Bosnian Muslims a decisive advantage and air attacks were unworkable. Airstrikes risked retaliations from Serbs aimed at UN troops from NATO countries on the ground.[88]

Both sides met privately on 25 July 1993 to attempt to bridge the gulf between US and British opinions. The USA offered to help implement an agreement between Serbs, Croats and Muslims under a credible threat of airstrikes, and conceded that they would not rule out ground troops but did not offer any idea of a final settlement.[89] The conflict therefore continued on through 1993.

However 1994 brought with it the need to act. On 5 February 1994, Serbs fired a mortar into a market in Sarajevo killing 70 and wounding 200. The international community responded quickly, giving the Serbs ten days to withdraw from Sarajevo and place their heavy weapons under the control of UN forces. NATO airstrikes began on 12 February and would last until the autumn of 1995.[90]

The airstrikes had limited success but failed to bring the conflict to an end. The Bosnian Serbs refused to hand over their heavy weaponry or stop the siege. In May 1995, they took 250 UN personnel hostage, including 33 Royal Welsh Fusiliers. The hostages were used as human shields chained to heavy guns to warn off future airstrikes.[91]

Parliament was recalled in an emergency sitting to discuss the crisis on 31 May and the Prime Minister sent a warning to Bosnian Serbs that there would be severe consequences if the hostages were harmed.[92] This instance, paired with the fall of Srebrenica and the slaughter of many of its Muslim inhabitants in July, left many in the Cabinet shaken and questioning Britain's next step. Lord Richard Dannatt believes that Srebrenica was the result of a weak UN mandate: 'We sort of struggled our way along through the UN mandate from '92–'95 but it was a very weak mandate, and it was the weakness of the mandate that resulted in Srebrenica. You declare a safe haven, a safe area but don't mandate the troops or the equipment to make it safe. The people think it's safe, they go there and they get massacred.[93]

The London Conference was reconvened on 14 July in response. This conference, co-chaired by the Prime Minister, would be vital in breaking the western stalemate on action in the Balkans. After intense talks, the Americans dropped their insistence on generalised bombing and all sides agreed on the deployment of an Anglo-French Rapid Reaction Force of 1,700 to Sarajevo to defend the city against attack. All Bosnian/Serb aggression would be met by punitive military attacks.[94]

Another mortar attack on 29 August on a Sarajevo market saw the intensifying of the air campaign and more importantly saw Serbia lose the political sponsorship of Russia. The sanctions enacted on Belgrade were beginning to take effect and Milosevic's own position of power was in jeopardy. The tide was turning as Serbs were facing the UN Rapid Reaction Force in Sarajevo whilst the Croat army were defeating and ethnically cleansing Serbs in Croatia.

The Dayton Peace Conference began on October 1995 in Ohio, USA, out of which an agreement was formed which would be implemented by 60,000 NATO troops, a large portion of which would be American. All parties signed the agreement which created the Federation of Bosnia and Herzegovina and the Republic of Srpska. It also maintained the autonomy and protection of all minorities within Bosnia.[95]

As time would later show, the Dayton Agreement had its own shortcomings and did nothing to prevent the expansionist ambitions of Milosevic. It allowed Serbia to largely maintain its influence in the area and did not address the issues of Croatia either. As Dannatt concludes, it was a pretty good ceasefire but was actually a rotten framework for peace in the region.[96]

The consensual approach

Did Major's premiership see a rebalancing of power between the Premiership and the other actors in government? Some may believe yes, but in doing so they may miss the distinction between a prime minister who has the power and seeks agreement anyway and a prime minister who has no power and therefore has to seek agreement. Which out of the two is true? The office or the man?

Major's very nature was consensual and this fed into his approach to foreign policy. His personal style of governance was inclusive. As Hurd recalls, John Major really liked listening to people, he liked drawing people out. This was a personal inclination but also a matter of survival. As prime minister, he knew by offering everyone a say he would get them on board and could not later be accused of ignoring his Cabinet.[97]

This approach reflected an undercurrent of pragmatism that was a large part of Major's character. He was not strongly ideological. He had a kind of methodical approach, says Wall, 'as prime minister, he would literally take a sheet of paper and draw a line down the middle and put the pros and cons on either side and think about them'.[98] This was in stark contrast to Margaret Thatcher who in her later years would go with her gut reaction.

The Foreign Office, once seen as the enemy, was now considered a strong ally under Major. Hurd acknowledges that under his premiership there was a great change in the role of the Foreign Secretary. He found himself intimate with the inner thoughts of a prime minister.[99] Sir Malcolm Rifkind agrees that Major, not on every issue, but generally speaking, saw the Foreign Office as an asset rather than a liability.[100] The stabilisation of relations between the Foreign Office and No. 10, underpinned by the Prime Minister's close relationship with his foreign secretary, saw some powers returned to the Foreign Office. Even Lord David Owen, critical of the recent trends, concedes that some powers were returned, 'not a lot but a bit'.

In that sense Major was keen to break from the past. If his predecessor had been the pinnacle of an 'imperial' premier dominating foreign policy with sheer willpower and personality, he was quite the opposite. In the telling of this story his premiership should be viewed as a period of steadiness where the growth of the premier's role in foreign policy stabilised and he did not seek to speed up the pace of change.

His relationship with his predecessor and his party seemed to dominate British foreign policy. As prime minister he had many of his decisions second guessed by the spectre of Margaret Thatcher. On the Gulf War she advocated that she would have gone all the way to Baghdad. On Maastricht she would have opposed it all the way. On Bosnia she would have intervened faster and more decisively. Her interventions were rarely helpful, and in the case of Maastricht fanned the flames of rebellion. There can only be one prime minister and yet throughout his premiership, Major found his decisions second guessed by a predecessor who still believed they should rightfully be in No. 10.

Instead John Major chose to be his own man. He directed a foreign policy built on consensus and collaboration with Cabinet colleagues and world leaders alike. Often understated and modest, his foreign policy had at the heart of it a moral compass. This was reflected by Britain's leadership in both the Safe Havens policy in Iraq and Bosnia, which in both instances had the hallmarks of Major's personal leadership in private and in public. He presided at a time when European and American foreign policy interests were clearly diverging after the end of the Cold War; veering apart, he attempted to maintain the Atlantic Alliance and keep Britain engaged in the European Community. Not an easy task.

Unfortunately much of his premiership's energy and memory is lost to the constant battle between his Eurosceptic backbenchers over Maastricht and the question of Britain's role in Europe as a whole. We forget the accomplishments of a man who genuinely believed in putting consensus above all else, who maintained the survival of not just his party but Britain's role as a world leader.

Notes

1 K. Theakston, 'Political Skills and Context in Prime Ministerial Leadership in Britain', *Politics and Policy*, 30:2 (2008), 283–323.
2 M. Heseltine, interview with S. Goodman, 30 May 2012, Department for Business, Innovation and Skill.
3 S. Wall, interview with S. Goodman, 7 June 2012, private offices.
4 C. Powell, *My American Journey* (New York: Random House, 1995), p. 463; G.H. Bush and B. Scowcroft, *A World Transformed* (New York: Alfred A. Knopf, 1998), p. 319.
5 The United Nations Security Council, United Nations Security Council Resolution 678, passed 29 November 1990, accessed 1 August 2015: www.un.org/Docs/scres/1990/scres90.htm.
6 Major, *The Autobiography*, p. 222.
7 Ibid., p. 223; J. Hill and S. Hogg, *Too Close to Call: Power and Politics John Major in No. 10* (London: Warner Books, 1995), p. 40.
8 T. King, interview with S. Goodman, 31 January 2014, House of Lords; Bush and Scowcroft, *A World Transformed*, p. 430.
9 Major, *The Autobiography*, pp. 232–3; G. Kaufman, interview with S. Goodman, 11 October 2013, House of Commons.
10 M. Howard, interview with S. Goodman, 5 November 2013, House of Lords.
11 Major, *The Autobiography*, p. 233; D. Hurd, interview with S. Goodman, 18 June 2012, private residence.
12 A. Seldon, *Major: A Political Life* (London: Phoenix, 1998), p. 155.
13 Major, *The Autobiography*, p. 237; P. Ashdown, *A Fortunate Life* (London: Life Aurum Press, 2009), p. 254.
14 T. King, interview with S. Goodman, 31 January 2014, House of Lords; Bush and Scowcroft, *A World Transformed*, p. 587.

15 Major, *The Autobiography*, p. 240.
16 Thatcher, *The Autobiography*, pp. 706–7; Craddock, *In Pursuit of British Interests*, p. 179.
17 Major, *The Autobiography*, p. 240.
18 *Ibid.*
19 T. King, interview with S. Goodman, 31 January 2014, House of Lords; Norman Schwarzkopf (with Peter Petre), *The Autobiography: It Doesn't Take A Hero* (London: Bantam Press, 1992), pp. 599–600.
20 Powell, *My American Journey*, pp. 530–1; Bush and Scowcroft, *A World Transformed*, p. 472.
21 Major, *The Autobiography*, p. 243.
22 Major, *The Autobiography*, p. 242; Craddock, *In Pursuit of British Interests*, pp. 181–2.
23 Major, *The Autobiography*, p. 243; Seldon, *Major: A Political Life*, p. 162; Dickie, *Inside the Foreign Office*, pp. 227–8.
24 Bush and Scowcroft, *A World Transformed*, pp. 489–90; Seldon, *Major: A Political Life*, p. 163.
25 Major, *The Autobiography*, p. 243; Seldon, *Major: A Political Life*, p. 163; Dickie, *Inside the Foreign Office*, pp. 227–8.
26 Major, *The Autobiography*, p. 243.
27 *Ibid.*
28 *Ibid.*, p. 264.
29 M. Rifkind, interview with S. Goodman, 18 April 2012, House of Commons.
30 Major, *The Autobiography*, pp. 266–7; Hill and Hogg, *Too Close to Call*, p. 142.
31 Major, *The Autobiography*, p. 271.
32 *Ibid.*, pp. 271–2.
33 *Ibid.*, p. 272; N. Lamont, *In Office* (London: Little Brown and Company, 1998), p. 112.
34 *Ibid.*, p. 273.
35 Major, *The Autobiography*, p. 275; Seldon, *Major: A Political Life*, p. 244.
36 Hill and Hogg, *Too Close to Call*, p. 47; Seldon, *Major: A Political Life*, p. 246.
37 Major, *The Autobiography*, p. 276.
38 *Ibid.*, p. 278.
39 *Ibid.*, p. 279; Hill and Hogg, *Too Close to Call*, p. 149.
40 Major, *The Autobiography*, p. 281.
41 *Ibid.*, p. 287; Hill and Hogg, *Too Close to Call*, p. 155; Seldon, *Major: A Political Life*, p. 248.
42 Major, *The Autobiography*, p. 288; Lamont, *In Office*, p. 134.
43 Major, *The Autobiography*, p. 307.
44 *Ibid.*, p. 313; Seldon, *Major: A Political Life*, p. 310.
45 *Ibid.*, p. 313; Lamont, *In Office*, p. 239.

46 Major, *The Autobiography*, p. 319; Seldon, *Major: A Political Life*, p. 297.
47 Major, *The Autobiography*, p. 320.
48 *Ibid.*, p. 322; Seldon; *Major: A Political Life*, p. 309.
49 Major, *The Autobiography*, pp. 325–7; Lamont, *In Office*, p. 240.
50 Major, *The Autobiography*, p. 349.
51 *Ibid.*, p. 330.
52 *Ibid.*, p. 350.
53 D. Baker, A. Gamble and S. Ludlam, 'The Parliamentary Siege of Maastricht 1993 Conservative Divisions and British Ratification', *Parliamentary Affairs*, 47:1 (1994), 37–60.
54 T. Gorman and H. Kirby, *The Bastards, Dirty Tricks and the Challenge To Europe* (London: Pan Books, 1993), p. 47.
55 Major, *The Autobiography*, p. 363.
56 *Ibid.*, p. 362.
57 *Ibid.*, pp. 376–7.
58 Baker, Gamble and Ludlam, 'The Parliamentary Siege of Maastricht'.
59 *Ibid.*
60 *Ibid.*
61 Major, *The Autobiography*, p. 382.
62 *Ibid.*, p. 645.
63 Seldon, *Major: A Political Life*, p. 306.
64 R. Dannatt, interview with S. Goodman, House of Lords, 21 October 2014.
65 Major, *The Autobiography*, p. 533; Ashdown, *A Fortunate Life*, pp. 264–5.
66 *Ibid.*, p. 533; Seldon, *Major: A Political Life*, pp. 304–5.
67 Major, *The Autobiography*, p. 533.
68 *Ibid.*, p. 533; Seldon, *Major: A Political Life*, p. 304.
69 Craddock, *In Pursuit of British Interests*, p. 187.
70 *Ibid.*, p. 191.
71 Major, *The Autobiography*, p. 534.
72 *Ibid.*, p. 534; Seldon, *Major: A Political Life*, p. 306.
73 *Ibid.*, p. 535.
74 Major, *The Autobiography*, p. 535.
75 *Ibid.*, p. 536.
76 S. Wall, interview with S. Goodman, 7 June 2012, private offices.
77 Hurd, D., interview with S. Goodman, 18th June 2012, private residence.
78 Hurd, D., interview with S. Goodman, 18th June 2012, private residence.
79 Seldon, *Major: A Political Life*, p. 307.
80 *Ibid.*, p. 307.
81 Owen, D., interview with S. Goodman, 11th May 2012, private offices.
82 Owen, D., interview with S. Goodman, 11th May 2012, private offices.
83 Major, *The Autobiography*, p. 538; Seldon, *Major: A Political Life*, p. 353.

84 Clinton, B., *My Life* (London: Hutchinson, 2000), p. 333; Seldon, *Major: A Political Life*, p. 353.
85 Clinton, *My Life*, p. 510.
86 Major, *The Autobiography*, p. 539.
87 *Ibid.*, p. 539; Clinton, *My Life*, p. 513.
88 Major, *The Autobiography*, p. 541; Seldon, *Major: A Political Life*, p. 373; Clinton, *My Life*, p. 510.
89 Major, *The Autobiography*, p. 543.
90 *Ibid.*
91 *Ibid.*, p. 544.
92 *Ibid.*; Seldon, *Major: A Political Life*, p. 559.
93 R. Dannatt, interview with S. Goodman, 21 October 2014, House of Lords.
94 Major, *The Autobiography*, p. 545; Seldon, *Major: A Political Life*, p. 592.
95 Major, *The Autobiography*, p. 546; Seldon, *Major: A Political Life*, p. 593.
96 R. Dannatt, interview with S. Goodman, 21 October 2014, House of Lords.
97 D. Hurd, interview with S. Goodman, 18 June 2012, private residence.
98 S. Wall, interview with S. Goodman, 7 June 2012, private offices.
99 D. Hurd, interview with S. Goodman, 18 June 2012, private residence.
100 M. Rifkind, interview with S. Goodman, 18 April 2012, House of Commons.

7

Tony Blair, 1997–2007

When Tony Blair ascended to the premiership in May 1997, he did not have any grand strategy or vision for foreign policy. He had just been elected to office with a landslide victory. The Labour party gained 418 seats and the largest majority in its history. His first concerns were the implementation of a manifesto packed with promises from reform of the House of Lords, and the adoption of the Human Rights Act, to devolving power to Scotland, Northern Ireland and Wales.

The north London barrister had little prior experience in foreign policy making and as Jonathan Powell, his Chief of Staff, points out, had not actually travelled much before he became Prime Minister.[1]

Sir David Manning, his foreign policy adviser and later Ambassador to the USA, recalls that he showed an early interest in foreign policy particularly in the Middle East:

> Tony Blair had shown a keen interest in foreign policy from the time he came into office and, in my experience, he had a really passionate interest in the Middle East. The first time I met him was when I was ambassador in Tel Aviv and he came to Israel. It was clear then that he was very interested in, and exercised about, the Middle East. I think he was also fascinated intellectually about the problem of conflict, and by the challenge of resolving outstanding conflicts. The Irish example is, of course, always quoted.[2]

This interest was paired with certain moral views over what the UK should and should not be doing; Powell refers to this moral compass as more of a factor than 'deep embedding in diplomacy' when it came to his foreign policy outlook.[3]

Blair's early involvement in foreign policy was guided by his relationship with President Clinton, a relationship that had been nurtured through a shared ideological ground, the 'third way', throughout Blair's time in opposition. Many in Blair's Government at the time speak of a natural affinity between the two men, who held frequent conversations on foreign policy.

Clinton and bombing Iraq

Like his predecessors before him, Blair set about focusing on domestic policy. However foreign policy decisions were soon thrust upon him, in this case rapidly, with the US decision to bomb Iraq. Since the end of the Gulf War in 1991 the Iraqi dictator Saddam Hussein had effectively been in a game of cat and mouse with UN inspectors regarding Iraq's chemical and nuclear weapons programme. As part of a deal with the UN following his defeat, Saddam agreed to adhere to UN Resolution 687 calling for Iraq to declare its nuclear and chemical weapons and allow for inspectors to inspect and destroy them.

During the next few years Saddam would switch between allowing the UN inspectors in and accepting disarmament to refusing to cooperate with inspectors and kicking them out. The UN would pass seven resolutions in a period of seven years demanding that Iraq declare and dismantle its nuclear and chemical weapons programme and allow UN inspectors to inspect Iraqi facilities.

At the beginning of 1998 the picture was of a weary international community tired of an obstructive Saddam and an increasingly concerned US administration weighing up the use of force. It was at this point when serious discussions between Tony Blair and President Clinton took place, over the UK joining the USA in bombing Iraq to get Saddam to comply with the multiple UN resolutions. On 31 October, Clinton signed the Iraq Liberation Act authorising the removal of Saddam and the support of Iraqi opposition forces in the creation of democracy in the country. The act officially adjusted US policy openly to support regime change.

In the face of the threat of force, twice in 1998, the Iraqi Government appeared to bow to international pressure. In February, Saddam agreed to a negotiated settlement with UN General Secretary Kofi Annan, to allow the inspectors back. After this fell apart, in November he agreed to allow the inspectors in again to prevent imminent US airstrikes, which the UK was set to join.

Blair recalls that the suspension of action was much to the relief of his foreign secretary Robin Cook, who had been troubled by the possibility of military intervention. He, however was determined to keep the US alliance intact and functioning at this crucial moment.[4]

Despite these concessions, Saddam once again reverted to obstruction, stopping UN inspectors from inspecting sites in late November. This time the USA had had enough, and Blair was presented with the dilemma of whether the UK should join with Clinton in the airstrikes and the UK stick with the Americans, a question that was to dominate his premiership. In this instance the answer was relatively simple. As Jonathan Powell puts it: 'In our own time we went ahead and bombed Iraq with Clinton. It came as a bit of a surprise to us. We came into power and hadn't thought about it a lot. Clinton kicked the spectres out and said we've got to do it and we went along with it.'[5]

On 16 December US and UK air forces launched Operation Desert Fox, striking targets in Iraq. Blair had his first taste of foreign intervention. The bombing campaign lasted four days, with the British air force accounting for 15 per cent of sorties flown. By 19 December the joint campaign had struck ninety-seven targets and it was declared a success.[6]

The reaction to the joint airstrikes was mixed. Clinton's opponents in Congress accused the President of using Iraq as a way to distract from the impeachment proceedings against him. Russia, China and France responded to the airstrikes by demanding the lifting of the oil embargo on Iraq and the reordering of the UN inspector's team through the firing of its head. At the time the campaign was seen as a successful containment of Saddam and Iraq's nuclear and chemical weapons programme, although Blair recalls his general feeling was that Saddam had got away with it again.[7]

More importantly, the campaign solidified the relationship between Blair and Clinton. Blair admired the President, as one former adviser put it, the relationship 'fed something very natural in him'. Charles Guthrie, the Chief of the Defence Staff at the time, witnessed their relationship first hand, and describing it he said, 'Blair got on very well with Clinton, in fact I thought sometimes too well. If Clinton wanted something we tended to do it. Sometimes I don't think it was always in our interest'.[8]

Robin Cook and an ethical foreign policy

Blair found in Robin Cook, his Foreign Secretary, an intellectual with his own power base within the party and the media. 'He was the self appointed leader of the left and was a very big figure and a powerful foreign secretary' recalls a former Government Special Adviser. Sir Christopher Meyer, US Ambassador at the time describes their relationship as 'slightly awkward and prickly ... It was a relationship that couldn't last'.[9] This was illustrated when within a few hours of his taking over the post Cook announced that the Labour Government would pursue an 'ethical foreign policy'.

In a statement, Cook set out that the Foreign Office's long-term strategy would supply an ethical content to foreign policy and recognise 'that the national interest cannot be defined only by narrow realpolitik'.[10] The announcement blindsided No. 10 and the Prime Minister who had not been consulted at all. The statement touched on many areas, but it was the press that picked up on the ethical dimension. The problem arose of what exactly does constitute an ethical foreign policy. As Charles Clarke, a backbench Labour MP at the time points out: 'He got into difficulty in the idea of an ethical foreign policy. Obviously there is a whole series of questions about what do you mean by it and how it relates to realpolitik and people's actual lives. I think he was simplistic in the way that he looked at it, actually. I also don't think he behaved very much on the ethnical foreign policy, with arms sales'.[11]

Another senior Cabinet colleague argues that Robin Cook's announcement was based on self-interest and left the Government open to attack, stating:

> He was so determined to have publicity for him going to the Foreign Office; he made a statement about how we were going to have a foreign policy with an ethical dimension. When I heard it I thought, you idiot! Everything we do from now on, they'll say 'I thought, you were supposed to be ethical, that is not ethical'. You have hung a milestone around the neck of the Government and a weapon of every critic to bash us over the head. No one knew he was going to do that, so I think that didn't do his standing any good as being a skilful politician.

It was seen by No. 10 as Cook attempting to cut a separate political profile by appealing to the left of the party. The announcement was one of many initiatives that he came up with, which were designed to please his constituency within the party. This reflected the view that Cook was considered 'Old Labour and not New Labour, so he wasn't one of us as it were'. What was No. 10's reaction to Robin Cook's independent initiatives? One adviser to Blair recalls 'to be honest we never really paid much attention to him'.

One former special adviser at the time believes that 'they rated his intellectual ability but didn't like him politically'. Sir Stephen Wall, European adviser to Blair agrees that 'Robin Cook was extremely clever, and to that extent Blair did rely on his advice. For example if Cook was at a meeting of the European Council with Blair his command of the subject matter was brilliant but there wasn't that element of trust'.[12] It seems that Robin Cook had his independence but at the price of being on the outside looking in. However it was still a partnership based on mutual respect, at its strongest through the NATO intervention in Kosovo.

The Balkans: Kosovo

Albanians residing in Kosovo had wanted greater autonomy and independence since Kosovo lost its autonomous status in 1989. However with a huge Serbian population, Belgrade pushed for Albanians to integrate into a Serbian model of society and government, giving Serbian Kosovars prominent positions in society. These tensions were exacerbated by the break-up of the Federal Republic of Yugoslavia and the influx of thousands of Serb refugees from Croatia in the early 1990s.

In February 1996, the Kosovo Liberation Army (KLA) was formed and began conducting attacks on Government offices and police stations. Over the next two years attacks and reprisals would continue between the police and the KLA. In March 1998, the situation escalated when Yugoslavian President, Slobodan Milosevic authorised the Yugoslavian army to use military force to tackle the KLA. The army undertook anti- terrorism operations which included the shelling of whole villages and there were reports of whole families of ethnic Albanians being taken away or shot by soldiers.

It was impossible for the Yugoslavian Government to target specific KLA members, with so many Albanians sympathetic to the KLA's aim, so the Government enacted collective punishment of the whole Albanian community. Serbs suffered too, with the KLA undertaking reprisal attacks which forced many to flee their homes.

The Contact Group countries (UK, US, Russia, France, Germany and Italy) met in London on 9 March 1998, to agree on the need for sanctions and an arms ban on Serbia which included Kosovo. Two weeks later the UN Security Council passed UN Resolution 1160, condemning the violence in Kosovo and enacting an arms embargo on Serbia and the Kosovo region. The hope was that the UN resolution would put pressure on both sides to negotiate an end to the bloodshed. However the Serbs were not keen on the idea of foreign intervention and in a referendum held on 23 April, 95 per cent of Serbs rejected foreign mediation to solve the crisis.

In response to heightened violence and continued fighting throughout the summer, the UN passed another Resolution demanding an immediate ceasefire and the allowance of UN observers.

In October 1998, a temporary agreement was reached between the warring sides which would allow civilians to return to their homes under the assurance of the international community. Despite the agreement the displacements and killings continued. In December it was estimated that around 2,000 people had been killed and hundreds of thousands had been displaced.[13]

Blair's case for intervention

In December 1998, the Prime Minister received a note from Paddy Ashdown, the leader of the Liberal Democrats summarising his recent visit to Kosovo. He wrote that the situation was deteriorating as both sides were re-arming and the Serbian military looked set to invade.[14]

For Blair the UN reports of ethnic cleansing in Kosovo and the scars fresh from the failures of intervention in Bosnia quickly led him to the belief that the West needed to intervene. As Sir David Manning recounts: 'He was absolutely determined that, after the horrors of the 1930s, this could not happen again in Europe. There was a strong impulse in him, a moral vision about what foreign policy should be trying to do, and this translated into absolute determination that this could not be allowed to happen in the Balkans'.[15]

The massacre of forty-five ethnic Albanian civilians in the village of Racak, on 15 January 1999, brought the conflict into the homes of the British public. Appalled, they pressed the British Government to act. At a conference in Rambouillet, France, the international community tried to broker an agreement. Blair recalls in his memoirs that the result of this summit saw resolutions passed, statements issued and daily declarations against the unacceptable nature of the situation in Kosovo, but the killings and ethnic cleansing continued. He felt frustration with an international community whose desire was to pacify but not resolve the situation.[16]

From the outset the Prime Minister was keen to persuade both his European colleagues and the American President to back the case for military action. He wanted a strong declaration of support and to keep the diplomatic negotiations going but in the event of those failing there had to be a commitment to military action. Blair argued that failure to intervene effectively in Bosnia had led to the situation in Kosovo, and if the international community did not resolve the situation it would only lead to further conflict.[17]

Early on in the crisis both Blair and Clinton were in agreement on the use of airstrikes if Milosevic was unwilling to accept a political solution to the violence. Similar to the campaign in Iraq, the aim of the airstrikes would be to contain and degrade.

However, while in agreement on the need for airstrikes, Blair's and Clinton's political fortunes could not be more different. Clinton found himself with a Republican-controlled Congress, in the middle of impeachment proceedings against him for allegedly lying about having a sexual relationship with a White House intern. The Congressional leadership was deeply sceptical of intervention in Kosovo. Many, as with the bombing of Iraq, accused Clinton of creating a distraction from the impeachment proceedings. This was paired with a view held by the US public that Europe should begin to deal with its own security issues rather than relying on the USA.[18]

Blair, still riding high from his historic landslide victory in 1997 and the quick enactment of many of Labour's manifesto promises, found his popularity at an all time high. The Cabinet was solidly behind him on the issue of intervention in Kosovo and so was the vast majority of the Labour Party. For Blair, the legacy and inheritance of a flawed foreign policy approach towards Bosnia reinforced the need to demonstrate the willingness to show force.

In his statement to the House of Commons, on 23 March 1999, the Prime Minister was keen to stress that this was not a case of unilateral action but a joint NATO effort with a broad coalition of countries. He emphasised the limited nature of the strikes, which would not involve an active ground force except in a peace keeping role.[19] This was a concession he had to make to the President and his European allies to gain their support, but he believed that No. 10 could work out how to unravel that commitment later.[20]

The BBC likened his intensity and claims of certainty in the debate to that of Margaret Thatcher, a comparison that would continue to be made throughout his premiership.[21] William Hague, the Leader of the Opposition at the time was quick to offer his party's support for the proposed airstrikes to help implement a diplomatic settlement.[22]

Both Russia and China were quick to condemn the prospect of NATO airstrikes and the legal argument of a general right of humanitarian intervention. The Chinese Foreign Minister stated that intervention would violate the UN Charter and other universally acknowledged norms of international law.[23]

The case for intervention, Blair argues, rested on three main pillars: first, to avert a humanitarian disaster in Kosovo, second to prevent the risk of the instability spreading, and third the real threat that walking away may not only destroy NATO's credibility but the faith of thousands relying on NATO to maintain the peace.[24]

The use of force rested on the passing of UN Resolution 1199 which stipulated 'should the concrete measures demanded in this resolution and resolution 1160 not be taken, to consider further action and additional measures to maintain or restore peace and stability to the region'.

Robin Cook believed at the time that Milosevic would not have committed himself to full compliance of the resolution if it was not backed up by the credible threat of military intervention.[25] The resolution itself did not give explicit authorisation for the use of force, but objections from China and Russia obstructed efforts at the time for a more unambiguous mandate.

NATO commenced its airstrikes on 23 March. At the outset of the bombing campaign US and NATO expectations were that Milosevic would give in after a few days of essentially symbolic bombing, estimating that he would not hold out for more than twelve days. After three weeks of bombardment it became clear that this estimate was wishful thinking, as the violence in Kosovo and the Serbian offensive, pushing ethnic Albanians out of Kosovo, continued.

Blair writes in his memoirs, two weeks into the bombing campaign, after talks with NATO generals and after another report on the situation from Ashdown, it was clear the campaign was not working. He had to get Clinton to commit to ground troops and was willing to lose his premiership on it.[26]

The prospect of a drawn-out bombing campaign put President Clinton particularly in a difficult position. Congress was critical of airstrikes from the beginning and had offered its approval on the basis that it would be a short campaign. Its position was one of supporting the armed forces while opposing the President. Ground troops would heighten the risk of American military casualties, the very reason Congress opposed intervention in the first place.[27] At the same time Clinton's impeachment hearing had left his popularity with the American people at an all time low. Clinton was boxed in. Kosovo divided public and Congressional opinion even before the discussion of ground troops.

As early as 1999, Blair had worked out that US commitment to military action would rest on his relationship with the President. If he could be persuaded, Blair had a chance. If not, he believed the Europeans would never act on their own.[28] As Prime Minister, he understood the power of personal relationships and the importance of his own with Clinton.

This was the backdrop when Blair spoke in Chicago on 22 April. The speech would be one of the pinnacle foreign policy speeches of his career. On one level it was deliberately designed to persuade public opinion in the USA to get behind the deployment of ground troops, even if the President himself would not. On another level, it outlined his unique foreign policy approach, often dubbed 'liberal interventionism'. Many of his Cabinet colleagues believe that his strategic vision is best encapsulated by this speech.

The wider context of the Chicago speech

Blair in his speech suggested that the crisis in Kosovo could not be seen in isolation, and that the rise of global interdependence through globalisation demanded an international approach to security. With that in mind, he stated that acts of genocide could never be purely an internal matter, given the instability to neighbouring countries in the form of refugees.[29] He therefore argued that western intervention should be supported for moral and mutually self-interested reasons.

The most important part of this speech in understanding Tony Blair's foreign policy is the section discussing when and whether to intervene. He stresses five major considerations:

> First, are we sure of our case? War is an imperfect instrument for righting humanitarian distress; but armed force is sometimes the only means of dealing with dictators. Second, have we exhausted all diplomatic options? We should always give peace every chance, as we have in the case of Kosovo. Third, on the basis of a practical assessment of the situation, are there military operations we can sensibly and prudently undertake? Fourth, are we prepared for the long term? In the past we talked too much of exit strategies. But having made a commitment we cannot simply walk away once the fight is over; better to stay with moderate numbers of troops than return for repeat performances with large numbers. And finally, do we have national interests involved? The mass expulsion of ethnic Albanians from Kosovo demanded the notice of the rest of the world. But it does make a difference that this is taking place in such a combustible part of Europe.[30]

These considerations reflect his own thinking in regard to intervention in Kosovo and also his wider philosophy. They offer a rare glimpse into the thought process behind Blair's foreign policy decisions. Although he is keen to stress that international cooperation must have the UN as its central pillar, the speech represents Blair's own legal background and what former Lord Chancellor, Charlie Falconer believes is his barrister-like approach:

> His style in politics is very much down to the fact he was a barrister before he became a politician. Tony is a totally different type of politician. He is constantly thinking about what is the right kind of argument, unlike a barrister in the sense

that he is not representing a client but like a barrister constantly shaping the debate in a way that he will win the argument. He is much more focused on what is the right argument, while the traditional politician is focused on what is politically doable.[31]

In this case Blair was keen to advocate the right argument for intervention over a constrained Clinton looking for what is 'politically doable' in Washington. The speech also highlights another pillar at the foundation of Blair's foreign policy: his belief in being a 'bridge' between Europe and the USA. He considered himself one of the few modern prime ministers who was both pro-European and an Atlanticist, David Manning recalls: 'He always saw himself as a bridge, a role and an image that personally I don't like. He felt it was very important that the international community, the western community in particular, should stick together with the Americans. We should try to manage these crises together.'[32]

The Chicago speech in the context of Kosovo

In relation to the bombing campaign in Kosovo, Blair was keen to stress in his speech that the airstrikes were a success, pushing Milosevic and his armed forces to breaking point. Blair outlined five campaign objectives: 'A verifiable cessation of all combat activities and killings; the withdrawal of Serb military, police and paramilitary forces from Kosovo; the deployment of an international military force, the return of all refugees and unimpeded access for humanitarian aid; and a political framework for Kosovo building on the Rambouillet accords.'[33]

All NATO partners broadly agreed with these objectives. What they did not all agree with was the next paragraph of the speech in which Blair stated that they would not succeed without an 'international force entering Kosovo', something the Clinton Administration was particularly divided over – Blair knew this too, and that is why he ended the speech with a direct appeal to the American public:

> You are the most powerful country in the world, and the richest. You are a great nation. You have so much to give and to teach the world; and I know you would say, in all modesty, a little to learn from it too. It must be difficult and occasionally irritating to find yourselves the recipient of every demand, to be called upon in every crisis, to be expected always and everywhere to do what needs to be done. The cry 'What's it got to do with us' must be regularly heard on the lips of your people and be the staple of many a politician running for office.

Yet just as with the parable of the individuals and the talents, so those nations which have the power, have the responsibility. We need you engaged. We need the dialogue with you. Europe over time will become stronger and stronger; but its time is some way off.[34]

The Chicago speech was given a popular reception and days later a US opinion poll found Blair with higher approval ratings as US President than Clinton; *Time* magazine printed a cover entitled 'President Blair?' Clinton saw this as an attempt by Blair to undermine and pressure him into supporting ground troops by appealing directly to the US public. In his book, Jonathan Powell recounts that Clinton called Blair from Air Force One and heatedly demanded that he cease from publicly pressing for a ground invasion. Both No. 10 and the White House played down their divisions over Kosovo.[35]

Throughout this time Blair pushed Clinton to put together a draft plan for a ground invasion. He argued that the logistics would take some time and would therefore need to be put together in advance. Clinton rebuffed this, arguing that the plans would leak.

Despite this the Prime Minister went ahead with his own plans, in consultation with Chief of the Defence Staff, Charles Guthrie. Blair discussed the possibility of mobilising 50,000 British troops. In a note to Clinton he advocated a force of 150,000 with half coming from Europe and half of that from Britain. He believed that there was no reason that other European nations would not commit, and if the USA did not, they would be shamed into committing. Blair ordered the preparation of 30,000 letters calling up Britain's army reserves.[36]

By late May, the President had moved towards Blair's view on ground troops and directed his National Security Team to discuss a timetable for a ground invasion, declaring all options on the table.[37] Russia's long-term support of Serbia had begun to wane and Russian President Yeltsin began to show signs that they might support a UN resolution. In response the Prime Minister proposed that an Italian proposal of a forty-eight hour ceasefire should be amended to include an ultimatum to Milosevic to take it or leave it, and if he refused, to reconvene the UN with a prospect of a ground invasion.[38]

On 3 June 1999, UN mediators headed to Belgrade where Milosevic accepted the terms for a new Kosovo peace plan, in effect conceding his defeat. The prospect of a real and lasting ground war with NATO forces led Milosevic to agree to NATOs terms. The UN adopted Security Council Resolution 1244 authorising a UN peacekeeping force to enter Kosovo. Over 600,000 refugees returned in the coming weeks, and by 20 June Serbian forces had completely withdrawn from Kosovo. Blair visited weeks later and was greeted with a hero's welcome and to chants of 'Tony!' To this day many argue the road to Baghdad started with the bombing of Belgrade. Sir Malcolm Rifkind, former Foreign Secretary at the time of the crisis in Bosnia supports this argument:

> It's worth remembering when NATO began its operation on Kosovo they said it would take only 3 days. It took 78 days of bombing before Milosevic bent. You had an operation that grew out of all proportion than what had been anticipated and one of its single most important consequences was a new state called Kosovo, which still is not recognised by half of the EU never mind by half the world, and is unresolved. Now I'm not saying there weren't good things as well. I don't believe it was a great example of international intervention. Sierra Leone was, but Sierra Leone was at the invitation of the Government. That wasn't like Iraq or Kosovo. Kosovo and Iraq were closer. The road to Baghdad started in Belgrade.[39]

Those in Blair's Government would instead argue that it was the inheritance of a 'spineless policy in Bosnia that led to a very large number of people dying by doing nothing' that propelled Blair into a much more activist and interventionist foreign policy. His critics however, say that he used Kosovo as an opportunity to 'milk his image as a war leader' although they concede that much of Kosovo policy was led by the Foreign Office.[40]

Sierra Leone

Blair's interventionist approach to foreign policy continued in 2000, when he decided to send British Special Forces to intervene in Sierra Leone and end a bloody civil war. The small West African country had experienced eleven years of conflict between the Revolutionary United Front (RUF) rebels backed by Liberia, and the Sierra Leone Army directed by the President, Ahmad Tejan Kabbah.

In July 1999, both sides signed the Lome Peace Accord enacting a ceasefire and power sharing agreement between the RUF and the army. A UN mission already present in Sierra Leone, UNAMSIL, oversaw the enacting of the agreement. The first thing UNAMSIL did was to set up disarmament camps with the purpose of allowing all sides to hand in their weapons.

In April 2000, RUF members, acting of their own accord, entered one of the disarmament camps and demanded the return of their weapons. When the UN observers refused the camp was besieged. The RUF then took UN observers hostage and began advancing into previously held Government areas, taking the town of Kambia on 3 May. The Government estimated that the RUF could take the capital of Freetown in a week with the vast majority of the army disarmed and confined to barracks.

Blair writes in his memoirs that preceding the decision to intervene, there was the usual round of negotiations, agreements, declarations and general attempts to find common ground between two factions that had none. This dragged on until the RUF renounced the ceasefire and President Kabbah came to see the Prime Minister asking for his help.[41]

On 5 May, the Government began to debate the feasibility of intervening in Sierra Leone. The Foreign Office advocated a full intervention to assist UNAMSIL, arguing that simply evacuating personnel would undermine the UN. However the Ministry of Defence believed that the armed forces would be unable to sustain a larger-scale operation.[42] A meeting in the Cabinet Office Briefing Room (COBRA) was convened and Blair approved the military recommendation for an operational reconnaissance and liaison team to be sent to Sierra Leone, to assess the situation on the ground and evacuate personnel.

The Cabinet was divided on how to proceed, with the Department for International Development, the Foreign Office and the Ministry of Defence struggling to agree on clear objectives post-evacuation. A consequence of British involvement was that it halted the RUF advance to Freetown, but a British withdrawal risked a return to violence. The Prime Minister conceded that British troops would therefore have to stay at least until UNAMSIL troops were reinforced.

This decision faced cross-party parliamentary opposition. Menzies Campbell, the Foreign Affairs Spokesman for the Liberal Democrats, said it was proof the operation was falling prey to 'mission creep'.[43] The Conservative Shadow Foreign Secretary, Francis Maude, argued that Britain should not get involved shoring up a UN mission on the verge of collapse.[44]

Blair however chose to continue further, giving British troops authorisation to send a small contingent to help free the captured UN observers and provide RAF Chinook helicopters to pick them up. By 14 May there were approximately 4,500 British personnel in the area, providing the embattled Government forces with air cover, reconnaissance missions and transport.

On 17 May, the RUF came directly into contact with British forces at Lungi Lol, a small village. The ensuring fire fight resulted in thirty RUF casualties and forced them to withdraw. The same day, the leader of the RUF was captured by

Government forces, creating a power vacuum in the RUF. The British Government, on 23 May 2000, laid out clear long-term objectives for military intervention in Sierra Leone which included to establish sustainable peace and security in Sierra Leone; to support UNAMSIL operations; to prevent another humanitarian disaster in Freetown; to see the release of captive UN personnel; and finally to avoid British casualties and devise an exit strategy that avoided 'mission creep' without undermining UNAMSIL or the Sierra Leonean Government.[45]

British involvement in Sierra Leone was still unpopular in Westminster, and the Ministry of Defence believed that forces could not be assembled while maintaining its other commitments. They therefore began training Sierra Leonean Government forces to take on the RUF.

Tensions were exacerbated on 25 August, when a patrol of the 1st Battalion, the Royal Irish Regiment, were taken captive by the West Side Boys, a local militia. Negotiations saw the release of five of the soldiers but another six remained. This led to Operation Barras, which saw British Special Forces assault the village of Gberi Bana, where the soldiers were being held and extract them, killing twenty-five West Side Boys and losing one British soldier in the process. The operation's success was seen as a shifting point in the campaign, with some arguing a failure would have led to the pressure for withdrawal being unable to avoid.

The intervention was bolstered by the passing of UN Security Council Resolution 1313 on 4 August, which cited multiple breaches of the Lome Peace Accord by the RUF and authorised an increase in the size of UNAMSIL and a strengthening of its mandate. The newly trained and supported Government forces soon began making military gains and by late October entered into talks with the RUF. A ceasefire was declared on 10 November 2000.

The legacy of intervention in Sierra Leone is one of success. British forces stayed in one form or another to train the Sierra Leone armed forces until 2013. The UK, in the form of international aid contributions still gives Sierra Leone more money per capita than any other African country. For Blair it is one of his proudest accomplishments.

Why did Blair feel the need to intervene, particularly in the face of such strong parliamentary opposition? It was the fusion of personal moral vision and the case for intervention, David Manning points out:

> He became heavily involved in Balkan issues, but was focused on Africa too. I don't know Africa well but when I was Foreign Policy Adviser I travelled with

him to Sierra Leone. He had taken quite a risk to send British forces in to deal with rebels there, but it had paid off. When I went to Sierra Leone with him I was struck by how emotionally charged it was for him. He had lived there for a time as a child when his father was teaching there. As well as this personal connection, there was the moral dimension for him of ending the conflict.[46]

Sierra Leone represented the practical action of the sort of ethical foreign policy that Robin Cook had talked about. The country had no strategic or commercial interest to the UK, but it was of symbolic importance for Blair to continue the philosophy outlined in Chicago of liberal interventionism and the duty to protect. For Blair there was the moral imperative of Britain intervening because it could.

The legacy led Blair, with the French, to push for the creation of EU Battle Groups, able rapidly to deploy in Africa to help prevent crises and civil wars. It also led him to consider further interventions in both joining the French mission in the Democratic Republic of Congo and intervening against Robert Mugabe in Zimbabwe. In both these instances he was cautioned against such action by his Chief of the Defence Staff, Charles Guthrie. Guthrie was concerned that intervention in Zimbabwe would be a logistical nightmare, with the white farmers spread out and the country landlocked. He warned the Prime Minister: 'If we do this, the whole world will be against us, and the Africans will not help at all because they will be bound to be sympathetic to Mugabe'.[47]

Blair took this advice seriously and concedes in his memoirs that he would have loved to have removed Mugabe but ultimately he heeded the advice of Guthrie and accepted that it was not practical.[48]

9/11 changed the world

In June 2001, Tony Blair became the first Labour Prime Minister to be re-elected for a full second consecutive term. His victory, another landslide with a small net loss of five seats, reinforced the view that Blair was unrivalled as a dominant force in UK politics. Before the eventful day in September, Blair was focused on making his second term about public sector reforms, as Michael Dugher, a special adviser at the time, points out: 'Tony Blair after 2001 wanted to make his second term about home department delivery. So you know, Transport, Education, and Health all these key public services – he wanted to show that we were making real change in all of those areas and that we were also making reforms in those public services. He wanted it to all be about that domestic agenda.'⁴⁹

Blair had lost an ally and a mentor in Clinton, who, meeting his term limit, was replaced by Republican Governor of Texas, George W. Bush. Bush was elected in one of the closest and most controversial elections in America's history. Many in Blair's Government presumed that Clinton's Vice-President, Al Gore would succeed him. He was considered another believer in their 'third way' project. Therefore the election of Bush, a man with little experience in international relations, who had run on a platform of reducing the USA's role in the world, came as a bit of a surprise. Many believed that their opposite ideologies would see a cooling of relations at worst or at best a cordial relationship that would not be as close as the former relationship with Clinton. These fears were quickly put aside, as David Manning attests:

> The relationship with Bush had already worked well. The first time I saw it was in the summer of 2001. They clearly got on fine. But the relationship really began to deepen after 9/11. Bill Clinton, before stepping down as President, had allegedly said to Tony Blair that he hoped he would get close to Bush and be an ally. Clinton seems to have calculated that his successor in the White House was someone inexperienced in international affairs who would need support. I think Tony Blair would have taken Clinton's request seriously and would have thought that he should respond accordingly.⁵⁰

As Manning points out, the relationship started off fine, but was solidified by the events of 11 September 2001 when four planes were hijacked, two flown into the World Trade Center in New York, another into the Pentagon, and the last one brought down by passengers in a Pennsylvania field en route to attacking the White House or Congress. The total number of victims from the 9/11 attacks, including those in the hijacked planes, the Pentagon and the World Trade Center, came to 2,977 excluding the 19 hijackers.

Many believe the events of 11 September 2001 changed the world but what do they mean by that? Jonathan Powell points out that the events changed American foreign policy: 'They (the United States) responded in a different way and expected different things from their allies. If you're under attack you do expect your allies to come to your aid, that's the attitude the Americans took'.⁵¹

This change in attitude would affect other countries' foreign policy. Jack Straw, Foreign Secretary at the time recounts: 'I mean the world was different. Threats which the US had tolerated before that – Afghanistan self-evidently; Iraq more debatable; but that was their perception and many others – those threats changed in the American calculus. That's what changed and then everyone else. The US foreign policy affected Russian foreign policy, China's foreign policy, it affected everything.'[52]

Al Qaeda and the War on Terror

Evidence found after the attacks linked the hijackers to the terrorist group Al Qaeda whose training camps were situated in Afghanistan, then ruled by the Taliban who originated around the time of the Soviet Afghanistan War in 1979 as an offshoot of the Mujahideen. Trained and armed by the CIA at the time, the Soviet invasion attracted fighters from all over the Middle East.

One of Al Qaeda's leaders and principal financier, Osama Bin Laden, was behind the planning of the 9/11 attack. Al Qaeda was also considered to be behind the US embassy bombings in Kenya and Tanzania in the early 1990s, the 1993 attack on US troops in Somalia, and an earlier failed attempt to blow up the World Trade Center.

For some time in the late 1990s Al Qaeda had formed an alliance with the Taliban in Afghanistan, providing troops, arms and money to fight the Northern Alliance. In return the Taliban allowed Al Qaeda to create terrorist training camps and base their operations there.

Richard Clarke, the US's first counter-terrorism expert from 1980–2004, served under four Presidents and has written vividly about Al Qaeda and its origins. In his book, *Against All Enemies: Inside America's War on Terror*,[53] he talks of many missed opportunities by President Reagan, President H.W. Bush, President Clinton and President George W. Bush, to address the threat. Bill Clinton was the closest, with a plan in 2000 to destroy the Al Qaeda training camps in Afghanistan with cruise missiles. He later said domestic political pressure made it all but impossible for the plan to be enacted.[54] A more important revelation is the lack of consultation that Bush received about Al Qaeda, with Richard Clarke only meeting the Vice President, Dick Cheney twice to discuss the issue before 9/11.[55]

Did Tony Blair receive similar briefings about Al Qaeda before 9/11? Charles Guthrie, Chief of the Defence Staff at the time recalls:

> I honestly don't know the answer about that. We certainly talked to him about it. I talked to him a lot about it. I had a rocky relationship with my Russian number, a typical Russian General. We never got on until the last week, when he said to me that you have no idea about the problem you are going to have

with extreme Muslims. You have the three Chechen warlords living in North London. He said you are all targets, and you have a large number of people in your country who are potential troublemakers. I came back and I talked to Blair about it a bit, and I went to the Foreign Office and their attitude was well they would say that because of Chechnya. I think Blair thought about it but not particularly hard.[56]

In the case of Bush, many have since argued that he was somewhat manipulated in the days that followed 9/11 by his Vice-President Dick Cheney and Defence Secretary Donald Rumsfeld. Sir Christopher Meyer, the UK Ambassador to the USA at the time disputes this depiction, highlighting the personal effect 9/11 had on Bush:

First of all the President was not an idiot and not a dupe. He was an extremely astute man with a great deal of American political experience who was not particularly articulate in public. This man was no fool at all, and the idea that he was a sort of puppet and Cheney and Rumsfeld were pulling the strings is wholly false. But after 9/11 which was a traumatic event, leave aside the American people for a moment, for the administration, and personally for the President. We've never cut Bush enough slack. We never tried to put ourselves into his brain. Well, what would you have done if you had been President after 9/11? One of the psychological consequences was that Bush who had never been particularly sympathetic to the neo-cons, who didn't really recognise this kind of labelling in foreign policy, but after 9/11 he became very open to their arguments, and to the notion that although it was not possible to come up with conclusive proof that Saddam was involved in 9/11, nonetheless he was too dangerous to be left in office.[57]

Jack Straw believes the big question for Tony Blair and for the country at the time was whether we stay close to the Americans. Conceding, that 'it is easy enough to be wise a decade after the event but things felt very differently at that time'.[58]

For the Prime Minister, standing by America was not in question. He believed that 9/11 went beyond simply an attack on America, but an attack on the West as a whole. Blair firmly believed that tackling the menace of terror was not only in Britain's national interest, but if we wanted any influence in shaping the conduct of the US response we had to offer our unequivocal and clear support.[59] The days that followed were not only a test of US strength but of Blair's belief in his ability to be a bridge between Europe and the USA.

He would be one of the first world leaders to make a public statement on the 9/11 attacks, including before Bush. Stating that, 'We, therefore, here in Britain stand shoulder to shoulder with our American friends in this hour of tragedy, and we, like them, will not rest until this evil is driven from our world.' David Manning witnessed first-hand the activism of Blair in the days that followed 9/11: 'He really threw himself into trying to ensure that there was a united response in dealing with the threat from terrorism, and in support of the United States, not least because he wanted to encourage the US to work through international institutions. He saw this as absolutely critical.'[60]

The Prime Minister rallied support, hosting the Italian Prime Minister Silvio Berlusconi and visiting France and Germany to meet with their respective leaders. Domestically, he recalled Parliament and made a formal statement which received universal support from opposition leaders. Blair saw an opportunity to carve out a role as an advocate for the US, as an informal representative, someone who could build a coalition against Al Qaeda and further terror attacks. Sir Nigel Sheinwald, a foreign policy adviser to Blair and later the British Ambassador to the USA recalls: 'I think he seized it. He realised there was an important role for a key ally of the US internationally for garnering support for what we were doing in Afghanistan and dealing with the aftermath of 9/11 but also in giving voice to the agreed policy he put together with President Bush because he was an articulate voice in support of that.'[61]

On 20 September, Blair was the first world leader to visit the USA since the attack. He flew to New York and then on to Washington DC, where he watched George W. Bush give a rare address to a joint session of Congress, laying out his strategy for responding to the attacks. There was a consensus early on between Blair and Bush that the Taliban would be given an opportunity to hand over Al Qaeda members and Bin Laden, as David Manning believes:

> After 9/11 Tony Blair and Jack Straw, and the Cabinet as a whole, were clear that something had to be done to deal with the Al Qaeda leadership. The Taliban should be given the chance to hand them over. If they didn't, all bets were off. That was a proposition that Blair made early on to Bush and to which Bush agreed. But it is not the case that Bush was itching to retaliate on Day 1, so one should not exaggerate the impact of Blair's arguing for a measured response. I remember Bush saying that he had no intention of firing missiles off into the sand for the hell of it. Throughout this period Blair was in a rather extraordinary position where he had a very good relationship with the United States and also with European leaders.[62]

In his address to Congress, Bush was quick to state that the USA had 'no truer friend than Great Britain', acknowledging Blair in the audience. The praise solidified a view held by many that Blair had signed up straight away to the American War on Terror.

The President laid out three demands directly to the Taliban: (1) 'Deliver to United States authorities all of the leaders of Al Qaeda who hide in your land'; (2) 'Release all foreign nationals, including American citizens you have unjustly imprisoned. Protect foreign journalists, diplomats and aid workers in your country. Close immediately and permanently every terrorist training camp in Afghanistan. And hand over every terrorist and every person and their support structure to appropriate authorities'; and (3) 'Give the United States full access to terrorist training camps, so we can make sure they are no longer operating.'[63]

Bush would go on to say that the War on Terror begins with Al Qaeda but will not end until 'every terrorist group of global reach has been found, stopped and defeated'.[64] For allies and enemies alike the President laid down a choice: 'every nation in every region now has a decision to make: either you are with us or you are with the terrorists'.[65] The goal was a global coalition of states united behind the USA and against international terrorism.

Blair would be on the front line pushing for countries to sign up. After his visit to the USA, Blair went on a whirlwind global tour, attending coalition building meetings in Europe, Russia, Pakistan, India, Oman, the UAE and Egypt. While Blair's new Foreign Secretary, Jack Straw was dispatched to Jordan, Iran and Israel in the hope of gaining their support.[66]

Many countries were forthcoming in answering the President's call including Russia and China, who pledged to help with anti-terror operations domestically and share intelligence. The Arab world was divided on the issue, with only four Arab leaders expressing an interest in the international campaign against terrorism. They were the Egyptian president, Hosni Mubarak; the Palestinian leader, Yasser Arafat; the Libyan leader, Muammar al-Gaddafi; and Jordan's King Abdullah II.

Pakistan offered to mediate between the Taliban and the USA, on the issue of handing over Bin Laden. Talks were held throughout the latter half of September, the Taliban position gradually shifted from initial refusal to conceding that if the US produced evidence they would try him in an Afghan court. This was rejected by the White House and instead it accused the Taliban of stalling and escalating military preparations.

On 4 October, the Prime Minister recalled Parliament to brief members on the intelligence linking Al Qaeda and Bin Laden to the 9/11 attacks. In his statement he laid out the case for intervention in Afghanistan, covering a broad history of Bin Laden's involvement in a number of terrorist attacks spanning the last decade. Although Blair conceded that much of the evidence the

Government had was 'highly sensitive' and was therefore not 'possible to release precise details without compromising people or security'.[67]

The Prime Minister laid out two clear objectives to the House of Commons: 'We must bring Bin Laden and other Al Qaeda leaders to justice and eliminate the terrorist threat they pose. And we must ensure that Afghanistan ceases to harbour and sustain international terrorism'.[68] This was the first time that Blair stated openly that he was undertaking military planning discussions with the USA.

The legal basis

Congress authorised Bush to respond to the attacks through the passing of the Authorization for use of Military Force Against Terrorists Act, which gave him the power to use all 'necessary and appropriate' force against those who perpetrated the acts.[69]

The Bush Administration argued that the 9/11 attacks though undertaken by an international terrorist organisation entitled the USA to the same right to self-defence as if attacked by another state, and therefore argued its right to self-defence under Article 51 of the UN Charter. Supporters would make the case that a UN Security Council Resolution would not be needed under Article 51. The other case advocated was that Afghanistan was a failed state and therefore intervention could be argued on humanitarian grounds. It also meant that the Taliban and Al Qaeda were considered terrorists and not soldiers, placing them outside the remit of the Geneva Conventions.[70]

For the first time in its history on 1 October NATO invoked Article 5 of the NATO Charter 'stating an attack on one is an attack on all' in response to the 9/11 attacks. International support for intervention and bringing those responsible to justice was unanimous. As Geoff Hoon, Secretary of State for Defence at the time recounts:

> When the Twin Towers were attacked in September 2001, 90 per cent of the population of this country, of virtually every country, wanted action to be taken. There was massive support, and if the Government hadn't had taken action, there would have been a huge controversy stirred up no doubt by the media. Indeed when I organised, over Christmas of 2001, the ISAF [The International Security Assistance Force], the first international force to go into Afghanistan to stabilise the situation, my phone was ringing off the hook with offers of support from around the world, because defence ministers around the world

had been told by their prime ministers to shore up public opinion, that they had to be seen to be doing something.[71]

On 7 October 2001, the USA, supported by Britain, launched airstrikes and cruise missiles from naval ships against Taliban facilities and suspected Al Qaeda training camps in Kabul, Kandahar and Herat. US and British Special Forces on the ground were deployed and joined up with the Northern Alliance in the Badakhshan Province, with the aim of pushing west to Mazar-e-Sharif and then south towards Kabul.

That evening at 9.20 p.m. Tony Blair gave a televised address to the British public making the case for UK intervention in a foreign country once again. During the address, Blair acknowledged that the American request for UK participation in Afghanistan had been made the week before: 'As to the precise British involvement, I can confirm that last Wednesday the US government made a specific request that a number of UK military assets be used in the operation which has now begun, and that I gave the authority for these assets to be deployed'.[72]

In his statement the Prime Minister made the case that British interests were at the heart of the intervention:

> The murder of British citizens, whether it happened overseas or not, is an attack upon Britain. But even if no British citizen had died, we would be right to act. This atrocity was an attack on us all, on people of all faiths and people of none. We know the al-Qaida network threaten Europe, including Britain, and indeed any nation throughout the world that does not share their fanatical views. So we have a direct interest in acting in *our self defence to protect British lives* [added emphasis].[73]

Although a few paragraphs later he would state that there was 'at present no specific credible threat to the United Kingdom'.[74]

A key British interest and something Blair highlighted as a reason to join US intervention, was the War on Drugs. Blair argued that, 'We act also because the al-Qaida network and the Taliban regime are funded in large part on the drugs trade. Ninety per cent of all heroin sold in Britain originates from Afghanistan. Stopping that trade is, again, directly in our interests.'[75] This would be the first time that a case would be made made that the War on Terror could help fight the War on Drugs.

The initial military bombardment had a limited impact on the Taliban's fighting capabilities. The US army argued this was due to the time it was taking to train and arm the Northern Alliance, who had a small number of men, estimated at between 12,000–15,000 troops in comparison to the Taliban's 40,000–45,000.[76] At the beginning of November the first UK troops were deployed forming a 1,700-strong battle group and securing the airfield at Bagram.[77]

It would not be until 9 November, over a month since the bombing began, that the Northern Alliance supported by US/UK Special Forces would fight their first strategic battle for the western city of Mazari Sharif. Twenty-four hours after the battle began the city fell to the Northern Alliance creating a momentum that would see Kabul abandoned two days later by the disheartened Taliban and an uprising in the south-western city of Herat. Northern Alliance fighters officially took over Kabul on 14 November and by doing so took virtual control of all Northern Afghanistan. Kunduz, the last Taliban stronghold in the north, fell on 25 November with the Taliban controlling less than 25 per cent of the country, mainly in the southern province of Kandahar.[78]

On 6 December, less than two months since US/UK forces began their intervention in Afghanistan, Kandahar, the last Taliban-controlled province would fall to the Northern Alliance who would now control all of Afghanistan. The International Security Assistance Force, which aimed to assist the Afghanistan Transitional Authority in creating a stable Afghanistan, was created in December 2001 in negotiations led by Britain and authorised by the UN Security Council Resolutions UNSCR 1386 and successive resolutions afterwards.[79]

The centralisation of power in No. 10

In the aftermath of 9/11, No. 10 naturally took the lead in driving policy forward. When foreign policy is the number one issue of the day the media and the public will turn to the Prime Minister to take the lead. What 9/11 changed, Jack Straw argues, is that 'foreign policy took centre stage in a way it never had done before, not just on the front page of newspapers for a few days but with the high level of troop deployment, it dominated the agenda in a way never seen in modern times before. It involved the whole country.'[80]

This put immense pressure on No. 10 and the Prime Minister to take the lead but it also appealed to Blair's personal preference and desire to have a prominent role in the War on Terror. Like all second-term prime ministers, he now had his own personalised way of running Government, and understood what worked and did not work, as well as two electoral landslides and foreign policy successes under his belt in Sierra Leone, East Timor and Kosovo. Nigel

Sheinwald attributes these factors as part of the reason why in the wake of 9/11 the initiative fell to No. 10, stating that:

> If you think back to that period, Blair had been in power over four years; he'd had two landslide victories; he's had a series of foreign policy successes. He was confident of his views on foreign policy and in a very powerful position politically. As I was saying before, where you have a Prime Minister who has been in power for a while, has been dealing with different world issues inevitably they build up a way of developing things with their colleagues in government, with people around the Cabinet table, and that gives a certain momentum to foreign policy. So I think the framework was set very quickly after 9/11 to the path we were going to be on for the years ahead. The Prime Minister had a very strong view on that. He had a new foreign secretary, so Jack Straw was foreign secretary throughout that period he started in June 2001. I think it would be fair to say that with a new foreign policy adviser in David Manning, that in the immediate aftermath of 9/11 a lot of the initiative seemed to fall to No 10 at that point.[81]

For the US administration dealing with the aftermath of 9/11 was their first priority. Therefore it was natural that the White House would develop links with No. 10. However in the following weeks some argue that Government departments, including the Foreign Office, were struggling to keep up with No. 10. As one senior adviser put it, 'I don't think the Foreign Office in the immediate aftermath of 9/11 occupied the field; they didn't put together the team, the policies, the enervative approaches, which by themselves were going to command Whitehall agreement and attention. Most government departments were struggling after 9/11 to keep up and the FCO did its very best in those circumstances but it did feel like a lot of the initiative had moved to No. 10.'

No. 10 has always struggled in regard to its foreign executive counterparts when it comes to the inaction of policy, mainly due to its size. As former Cabinet Secretary Lord Gus O'Donnell points out when comparing Government departments to No. 10: 'The power departments... have most of the resources and can go into greater detail than No 10. What No 10 has on its side is that it is small, it is nimble, very short lines of communication, clear lines up to the ultimate decision maker.'[82]

Blair had decided before the 2001 election that he wanted to reform the structure of Government by strengthening the centre. As Nigel Sheinwald recalls, this decision had come out of his past experience with Kosovo and Sierra Leone: 'I think one of his conclusions from dealing with the Balkans and Sierra Leone was that there wasn't enough grip at the centre to manage an ambitious foreign and defence policy and of course that change coincided with 9/11.'[83]

The main reform Blair enacted was the creation of a permanent foreign policy adviser, as well as a European policy adviser. Both roles would be directly appointed and answerable to the Prime Minister. The foreign policy adviser would be put in charge of the Overseas and Defence Secretariat within the Cabinet Office. Both Blair's appointments to these roles were experienced individuals who had come up through the Foreign Office. Sir Stephen Wall was brought back from Brussels where he had been Britain's European Representative to run European Affairs. Prior to this Wall had been Private Secretary to John Major, when Prime Minister, and Private Secretary to a number of foreign secretaries from 1988–91. Sir David Manning was chosen to be the new foreign policy adviser, previously serving in Brussels like Wall and in Tel Aviv as Britain's Ambassador to Israel, where he first met Blair.

Both Manning and Sheinwald would argue that what Blair undertook was merely modernising a model that already existed. Prime Ministers had always had a certain number of private secretaries that had at times taken over the mantle of a de facto foreign affairs adviser. This was certainly the case with Charles Powell under Margaret Thatcher. Manning describes these reforms as reinforcing a system already in place and designed to speed up the decision-making process: 'The purpose of the new No. 10/Cabinet Office arrangement was to give the Prime Minister additional resources to draw upon, some extra in-house capacity. He could now go direct to the OD Secretariat in the Cabinet Office to get a specific piece of work done. But in parallel No. 10 would of course also be consulting the FCO, DfID and other departments.'[84]

The reorganisation of the OD Secretariat created a vehicle for Blair to push forward foreign policy from No. 10 without having to include the Foreign Office, something which no Prime Minister had been able to do before. Sir Stephen Wall reflects:

> Douglas Hurd has argued, which I think is right, that in previous eras the Prime Minister might want to do something but had no vehicle to do it other than the Foreign Office. Now Blair had his own team who could actually execute his orders. It was more a matter of whether they wanted to involve the Foreign Office rather than whether they absolutely had to, and I think there is something in that, though again I think it's possible to overstate how significant a change that was.[85]

This reorganisation was not necessarily aimed at cutting the Foreign Office out or a reflection of a personal dislike Blair had for the Foreign Office as an institution, but more about targeting the bureaucracy of Government, Nigel Sheinwald argues: 'He wasn't a knocker of the Foreign Office as an institution but I think the reason he set up the role of the foreign policy and defence adviser, that has now become the national security adviser, the reason he set it up was because he felt at the centre of government there wasn't enough serious quality considered advice.'[86]

It would be pure coincidence that these reforms happened around the same time as 9/11, making Manning's new job pivotal. As No. 10 began to float closer to the gravitational pull of the White House, Blair forged a closer relationship with the President and Manning forged a close relationship with Condoleezza Rice, Bush's National Security Advisor.

Iraq

Richard Clarke's book shows, along with countless first-hand accounts, that discussions took place over the removal of Saddam Hussein early in Bush's presidency.[87] Defence Secretary, Donald Rumsfeld, and Bush's Vice-President, Dick Cheney, were said to have an obsession with Iraq and Saddam. There was a concern that the western policy of containment based on sanctions and inspections simply was not working.

This was a view that Blair supported in his testimony to the Chilcot Inquiry. In 2000 and early 2001 he discussed the fact that the no-fly zones were coming under increasing strain and that there were 'already moves afoot to change the blanket sanctions'.[88] Clarke writes vividly in his book that throughout early 2001 Rumsfeld and Cheney continuously brought up the threat of Saddam and wanted to know what intelligence there was on his nuclear weapons program and Iraqi-sponsored terrorism, prioritising this over Al Qaeda.[89]

Did 9/11 change the preoccupation with Iraq and Saddam? If anything it exacerbated it. Blair describes the 'calculus of risk changing'[90] that the USA would not tolerate Saddam Hussein's regime in Iraq any longer. In the aftermath of 9/11 there were accusations of Iraq funding terrorism. Cheney would ask Clarke to check and check again that Saddam was not involved with Al Qaeda and 9/11. The intelligence simply did not point to such a conclusion and the US administration would later backtrack, focusing instead on Saddam's nuclear weapons programme.

Bush's 2002 State of the Union address to Congress

The focus of Bush's State of the Union address on 27 January 2002 would be on the link between so called 'rogue' states working with terrorists. The President stated that his administration's second objective would be preventing 'terrorists and regimes who seek chemical, biological, or nuclear weapons from threatening the United States and the world.'[91] His speech would mark a change in the national discussion from terror organisations like Al Qaeda to 'rogue states'. In it, he argued that North Korea, Iran and Iraq constituted an 'axis of evil' and that by seeking weapons of mass destruction (WMDs), these regimes could provide arms to terrorists.[92] Putting particular emphasis on Iraq, Bush said:

> Iraq continues to flaunt its hostility toward America and to support terror. The Iraqi regime has plotted to develop anthrax, and nerve gas, and nuclear weapons for over a decade. This is a regime that has already used poison gas to murder thousands of its own citizens, leaving the bodies of mothers huddled over their dead children. This is a regime that agreed to international inspections, then kicked out the inspectors. This is a regime that has something to hide from the civilised world.[93]

The message was clear – with Afghanistan under control the Bush Administration would turn its full focus to Iraq and Saddam. His State of the Union speech was a message to the world that American foreign policy had now shifted and the War on Terror would encompass regime change elsewhere. It was no secret that Bush and members of his administration favoured regime change in Iraq. Their defence was that they were simply continuing the policy of the Clinton Administration with the Iraq Liberation Act of 1998 and the various UN resolutions. Blair came to the view that Saddam should be removed long before President Bush ever did, as Sir Christopher Meyer attests:

> He was given intelligence on Saddam at the end of 1997 by the Foreign Office, and I think that persuaded him that Saddam ought to be removed. There is a very illuminating speech that Blair gave in March of 1998 to a party gathering in which he basically said that we have got to get rid of Saddam Hussein preferably through diplomatic means, if not by diplomacy backed by the credible threat of force. So Blair had arrived at that position long before Bush became President.[94]

In his memoirs, Blair writes that the removal of Saddam was underpinned by the issue of weapons of mass destruction and it was not linked to the moral case against his dictatorship. He did, however, believe like Bush, that there was an alliance taking shape between rogue states and terrorist groups.[95] Where he differed from the President was the use of partisan language, which he perceived to be 'neo con' in Bush's State of the Union address. This language presented difficulties for the Prime Minister within the Labour Party, with many of his backbenchers considering the rhetoric to be unreservedly right wing. Blair also believed that the resolution of the Palestinian issue was essential to resolving this wider struggle with the Arab and Muslim world.[96]

Crawford

The Prime Minister flew out to Crawford, Texas on 7 April 2002 for a meeting with Bush to discuss a mutual strategy in dealing with Saddam. Many believe that at this meeting, Blair made a secret agreement with the President whereby the UK would join the US in a military invasion of Iraq to overthrow Saddam's regime with or without a UN mandate. No notes were taken from this meeting and no other officials were present. This secrecy ultimately fed into the speculation of a deal being cut. The contention comes down to conditionality and whether Blair gave an undertaking to Bush with conditions attached or gave him a 'blank check' as it were. Sir Christopher Meyer, an opponent of the war, contends that, 'You have to make up your mind whether Blair took a decision very early in 2002 or whether he waited until very late in the day. I happen to believe that Bush didn't take a final decision to go to war until pretty late in the day, and Tony Blair had essentially subcontracted that decision to the Americans.'[97]

What was certainly raised as part of the price for UK support was an American commitment to the Israel–Palestine peace process. In fact, Blair contends that at Crawford this was a major part of his strategy. He believed that this was the soft power component which gave equilibrium to the prospect of hard military power removing Saddam.[98] Blair's deputy, John Prescott, writes that there was a real belief in a quid pro quo: if Blair backed Bush over Iraq, then Bush might lean on Israel to get a settlement in Palestine.[99]

The second topic discussed at Crawford in relation to the UK supporting military intervention was the role of the UN and the need to gain a resolution. The Prime Minister deduced that the removal of Saddam under the responsibility to protect would be impossible, therefore the conclusion was that any military intervention would need to be under the basis of Saddam's noncompliance with pre-existing resolutions.[100]

On 14 May the UN Security Council would revamp the eleven-year-old sanctions against Iraq, this time with the aim of targeting military equipment or dual use imports. Blair called them 'smart sanctions'.[101] The hope was that these new sanctions would force Saddam into allowing nuclear weapons inspectors back into Iraq. This seemed rather unlikely with talks breaking down on 5 July in Vienna between the UN and Iraq. However on 1 August Saddam agreed to invite Hans Blix, head of the United Nations Monitoring, Verification and Inspection to Baghdad. Over a month later Iraq accepted the unconditional return of UN inspectors.

On 24 September 2002, No. 10 took the unprecedented step of publishing a dossier from the Joint Intelligence Committee outlying the threat posed by Iraq. The intelligence report claimed that there was credible evidence to suggest Saddam had nuclear weapons that could be used within forty-five minutes of him giving an order. Another claim made was that Saddam had tried to acquire materials to make a nuclear weapon from Niger.[102] In his memoirs Blair argues that the dossier contained no new evidence.[103]

The Prime Minister was forced to call an emergency debate in Parliament to discuss the dossier, in face of a threat from Labour backbenchers that they would meet as a rebel parliament. In the parliamentary debate more than fifty Labour MPs rebelled against the whip to register their opposition to Blair's stance, although the Conservative Opposition led by Iain Duncan Smith were in agreement with the Government.[104]

The United Nations

The Prime Minister was keen to stress that the USA should be patient with the UN route and try and gain a resolution, giving Saddam every opportunity to comply. This was not only to legitimise any action legally but also to appease domestic opponents at home. A commonly held view is that Blair was a moderating influence on Bush, convincing him to pursue the UN.[105] However some argue that Bush did this of his own volition after being lobbied heavily in August by Colin Powell and Condoleezza Rice.[106]

The diplomatic route seemed to pay off, when on 8 November, the UN Security Council approved the US/UK Resolution 1441. The Resolution gave Iraq 'one final opportunity to comply with disarmament regulations'.[107] It also stated that, 'false statements or omissions in the declarations submitted by Iraq pursuant to this resolution and failure by Iraq at any time to comply with, and cooperate fully in the implementation of, this resolution shall constitute a further material breach of Iraq's obligations'.[108]

The Iraqi Government accepted the resolution and Hans Blix and his team began inspections on 27 November. For many in the Bush Administration the bare minimum had been done, the Resolution constituted an international nicety that would lay the legal framework for an invasion. Rumsfeld and Cheney simply did not believe that Saddam would give up his weapons and for them talk was cheap. They wanted to start invasion preparations and were later deeply opposed to a second UN resolution.[109]

On 2 December the Foreign Office under the direction of No. 10 released a second dossier documenting Saddam's human rights abuses.[110] The document's aim was to reinforce the case for regime change in Iraq, detailing historical human rights abuses, the use of torture, rape and mass killings, the lack of rights for women in Iraq, and the wider persecution of the Kurds and Shia community under Saddam. Much of the document compiled evidence of the regime's brutality that had been collected through the 1980s (the period of time Britain was allied with Iraq) and 1990s, offering little new information. The dossier shifted the debate back to a discussion about ethical foreign policy appealing to Blair's liberal interventionism. It made the case for removing Saddam on moral grounds as a bloody dictator, quoting in its cover page a section of the speech Blair gave to the TUC conference in September that 'our quarrel is with Saddam and not the Iraqi people'.[111] Some critics of the dossier argue that it provided a failsafe in case inspectors found no WMDs. The dossier made a separate case to remove Saddam.

Five days later, Iraq, in compliance with UN Resolution 1441 handed over a 12,000-page weapons declaration, outlining a complete account of its chemical, biological and nuclear missile programmes. After analysis of the declaration, Hans Blix, however, stated that the declaration contained little new information about Iraq's weapons capability.

In January 2003 the inspectors made a significant discovery, finding twelve warheads designed to carry chemical weapons, believing the warheads were not accounted for in the declaration. The White House described the warheads as a 'smoldering, not smoking gun',[112] arguing that the missiles reinforced their belief that Saddam had WMDs. The weapons inspectors update to the UN at the end of the month reported that Saddam was cooperating but that the declaration showed that there was still no resolution to the outstanding issues.[113]

Both the UK and USA seized on the weapons inspectors' update as an admission that the Iraqi Government had no intention of disarming, despite Hans

Blix asking for more time for his team. Blair in his memoirs argues that while Iraq had opened up, the resolution said that Saddam's cooperation should be 'immediate, unconditional and active'.[114] In his mind Iraq was therefore in breach. The question then was whether the USA and Britain needed a second resolution to agree that he was in breach and support military intervention or whether the first covered it.

A second resolution

In a meeting in Washington at the end of January 2003, the Prime Minister discussed with President Bush his growing concern about a lack of evidence of Saddam's nuclear weapons programme. A leaked memo of the meeting shows that the Americans were considering painting a U2 spy reconnaissance plane with UN colours and flying it over Iraq in the hope of the Iraqis shooting it down, precipitating a war.[115] It is clear that in this meeting the President had moved to focus on invasion plans, stating that 'the diplomatic strategy had to be arranged around the military planning'.[116] This gives the impression that by this point Bush was set on war irrespective of the outcome of the inspections. Both leaders also agreed in the meeting that it was unlikely that there would be internecine warfare between the different religious and ethnic groups after the fall of Saddam.[117]

The Prime Minister was a keen advocate for a second resolution. For him it would put to rest the many sceptics in the Cabinet and within the Labour Party. He raised the issue in the meeting as an insurance policy against the unexpected. Bush offered his full support in getting a second resolution but told the Prime Minister that if they failed military action would follow anyway.

On 14 February Hans Blix reported to the UN that Saddam would still need to do more to prove that no weapons programme existed, but ultimately inspectors needed more time. The following day a million people would march in the streets of London against a war with Iraq, mirroring over 300 anti-war protests in cities all over the world.

The USA, Great Britain and Spain on 24 February submitted a proposed resolution to the UN Security Council, stating that the Council should decide that Iraq was not complying with Resolution 1441. Two days later the Government faced another parliamentary rebellion in the Commons, when an amendment to a Government motion supporting giving Saddam a final warning saw 199 MPs vote for a motion saying that the case for war with Iraq had not yet been proven. Out of the 199 MPs, 122 Labour MPs voted for the motion. Jack

Straw as Foreign Secretary was keen to stress that the vote was not an endorsement of military action in Iraq and that 'No decision to deploy British forces has yet been taken.'[118]

The proposed second UN resolution split the EU down the middle. Thirteen of the twenty-five were in favour including the ten new accession countries. France and the French President Jacques Chirac was the leading critic, allying himself with Russia and Germany who were also wary of military action in Iraq. Blair believes that this split reflected the importance varying countries put on the American alliance being a fundamental part of their foreign policy.[119] The problem, as Lord Malloch-Brown, Deputy UN Secretary General at the time recalls, was that once the US/UK reached that point of military mobilisation they could not afford to allow the Russians and the French to play them long in the Council.[120]

At the UN the resolution was amended to encompass a timetable for Saddam to disarm, and a final warning. This was an attempt to address concerns, but it was not enough to shake President Chirac who vowed that France would veto any resolution that offered a short timetable or ultimatum leading to invasion. His vow was the final nail in the coffin of the diplomatic process in the eyes of the White House, despite a US/UK deadline of Monday 17 March for the UN to back the resolution.

For Kofi Annan and his Deputy Mark Malloch-Brown the logic was obvious, which was to let the process run longer. 'While the inspectors' reports blew a bit hot and cold about the likelihood of what would or wouldn't be found; the basic point was access, was improving our discovery of incriminating evidence, which was close to zero.'[121]

Domestic opposition to the war

Domestically the Prime Minister found his Cabinet, Parliament, the Labour Party and the country split on the question of military action in Iraq. Those sceptical of the war included his foreign secretary, Jack Straw who wanted to avoid military action.

Blair and Straw had a relatively good working relationship, particularly when compared to the tensions that existed between his predecessor and the Prime Minister. This was despite the fact, as Charles Clarke puts it, that the Prime Minister and Robin Cook were 'closer ideologically and politically then he and Jack were.'[122]

Their relationship was based on a mutual respect with Straw seen as a professional. One special adviser to a Cabinet Minister at the time believes that Blair saw Straw as a big figure in the party and therefore did not want to be in difficulties with him. Jack Straw describes his relationship with Blair as complementary: 'I think it was about competence. He wouldn't have given me the job if we didn't have a close personal relationship and we also complemented each other on the stuff like the EU. He did the sort of big picture stuff and I did the detail. We were good as a pair in the European Council meetings and on Iraq he set the strategy.'[123]

Some argue that with Straw, Blair had a more malleable figure, someone who had not expected to be foreign secretary, and who was totally dominated by the Downing Street machine. The Foreign Office in the months leading up to the Iraq war found itself continuously shut out, as the Butler Report concludes; and as one former Ambassador to the USA puts it, 'they were effectively relegated to a kind of secretariat to Downing Street to do all the staff work'.

Much of the reason for that may have been that much of the initiative fell to No. 10 but also it is a reflection on Blair's closeness to Bush. The other factor was that Jack Straw built up a close relationship with Colin Powell on the basis of stopping the war, through pushing for a second UN resolution. Both were of the opinion that Saddam would comply, preventing any need for military intervention.

This view found him on the wrong side of the Prime Minister, who was convinced, like Bush, that there was no scenario where Saddam could stay in power, and therefore the Foreign Secretary and the Foreign Office were outside the tent looking in. Straw was speaking for that Foreign Office caution.

Sofa government

Jack Straw was not alone in this position. The common perception of this period of time was that Iraq was not discussed much in Cabinet, with a number of ministers feeling shut out from discussions. Instead Blair established an informal meeting of Cabinet with a number of key individuals. This form of so called 'sofa government' seemed to be where the real decisions and discussions were made. As Mike Boyce, Chief of the Defence Staff at the time of Iraq describes, the sofa government consisted of:

> Myself, the Foreign Secretary, the Defence Secretary, and the agency chiefs just sitting on the sofa, literally and chatting about what was going on, and no one else involved at all. Blair then dumping that in front of the Cabinet when it was 'Fait d'accompli', so there was no executive committee of the Cabinet if you like that involved DIFD [the Department for International Development] or the

Home Secretary, or even the Cabinet Secretary. Therefore there was I think incoherence.[124]

This form of running government reflected Blair's personal preference. One Cabinet Minister believes 'Tony only bothered with people he wanted to bother with or had to bother with'. Lord Falconer, Lord Chancellor at the time and a long-standing ally of Blair argues that sofa government was the Prime Minister's way of getting to the heart of an issue: 'Tony would quite frequently go straight to the heart of an issue and would have all the players around, they might be sitting on sofas, and there might not be a paper.'[125]

The perception that Iraq was never discussed in Cabinet is wrong. Ministers attribute for the period running up to the war little else was discussed. Margaret Beckett recalls that 'the Cabinet discussed Iraq endlessly, nearly every meeting'.[126] Charles Clarke believes it was discussed substantially, stating that:

> I think there was a civil service ran brand that has been supported by others that argues somehow that the Cabinet was usurped by the Prime Minister of the day on these questions. I just don't think it's true. During the time I was in Cabinet, including the run up to Iraq there were very substantive discussions every week on the position of the Iraq War. We were able to raise whatever points we wanted at specific points for example on the weapons of mass destruction; we specifically talked to the leadership of the intelligence services to make our own judgment of the credibility of what they said and so on.[127]

The contention surrounding the discussions the Cabinet held lies in what one distinguishes as substantial; Lord Robin Butler former Cabinet Secretary and Chair of the Butler Inquiry reviewing the intelligence before the Iraq War believes:

> When Tony Blair became prime minister, he in general used Cabinet a lot less, particularly in his early period as prime minister which was the bit I witnessed. Later on of course it was said that he used Cabinet more as time went on. Because of the review of intelligence leading up to the Iraq War, that I chaired, I saw how he treated the Cabinet in the lead up to the Iraq War, and he made a great deal of the fact that the Cabinet discussed Iraq 45 times but these discussions – and this was a point that I made in my review – were based not on papers that were provided by officials but on oral or slide presentations by himself or the Foreign Secretary or the Defence Secretary. These were very much, on my interpretation, selling the line that he wanted, and he and his colleagues wanted to sell to the Cabinet, rather than an objective discussion based on official papers.[128]

The emphasis, he contends, was to focus on presentation rather than any depth when it came to the discussions. The author put this case to Lord Falconer who was quick to state that none in the Cabinet were under any illusion about the counter-argument:

> The question to what extent did that mean arguments get overlooked; I don't think in relation to the Iraq War anybody was in any doubt about the arguments against the war. They were expressed well by Jack, well by the Foreign Office, well by Robin Cook, well by the Department of International Development, well by the Ministry of Defence; they weren't necessarily against it but the idea that there wasn't proper consideration was wrong. So yes he did do 'sofa government' by which I mean the process was pretty streamlined, he was running it on the basis that he was constantly trying to get to the heart of the issue.[129]

Jonathan Powell contends that the argument surrounding the role of Cabinet Government is the British obsession with form rather than substance, which ignores how modern government operates:

> An awful lot of rubbish has been talked about Cabinet Government. Cabinet in modern times certainly hasn't been the body where you make policy decisions, it's not the right place, you don't have the right people at it. You're making decisions on defence issues, you don't have any of the defence chiefs, the intelligence chiefs, the foreign policy experts, you have a bunch of people who don't know what you're talking about because their department is not engaged.[130]

Reasoning for sofa government: leaking

This was a view shared by Blair and that is why early on in his premiership a 'sofa government' operated for important decisions; the reasoning was to prevent leaking as a number of people have reported. One Cabinet Minister recalls that Cabinet meetings were very short and sometimes little more than half an hour. The brevity flowed from a sense that what was discussed was quickly on the one o'clock news.

The Prime Minister's defence was therefore that he could not trust his Cabinet who were shirking their Cabinet responsibility. This is a view that Charles Guthrie supports: 'What doesn't really come out about the sofa government was one of the reasons Blair set it up was because there was quite a lot of people he couldn't trust. It's very difficult if their loyalty is not completely with the Prime Minister of the day once a decision is made.'[131]

In the case of Iraq the alleged hindrance to proper Cabinet discussion was Clare Short, the Secretary of State for International Development. The fear was that she would leak any information about Iraq to the media. This was an obstacle to full Cabinet disclosure, Charles Clarke argues: 'There was a serious problem which was that Clare Short when she was in Cabinet routinely leaked to the media. I think the fact that none of us could trust Clare Short in the room was a serious inhibition to the discussion.'[132]

Reasoning for sofa government: Freedom of Information Act

The other reasoning often used in defence of Blair's sofa government was the concern that notes from discussion could be disclosed under the Freedom of Information Act. Blair describes its creation as one of his greatest regrets, arguing that it hinders frank discussion in government.[133] Lord Gus O'Donnell certainly believes that the emergence of a somewhat informal government was a consequence in large part of the Act, which made politicians particularly nervous about what kind of conversations they have when they were recorded.[134]

The counter argument is that Cabinet Ministers broke with Cabinet responsibility in retaliation for Blair's lack of trust in Cabinet and not vice versa. Any excuse detracts from what many consider a harsh truth, that Blair refused to take things to Cabinet because he was afraid of Cabinet disagreeing with him. This is certainly what many Conservatives believe as Sir Malcolm Rifkind points out: 'Even Tony Blair, one reason he didn't take things to Cabinet was to avoid that risk I assume, he just didn't want to be bothered by that kind of restraint.'[135]

What is certainly clear is that the two most important areas of the basis of military intervention, the intelligence about WMDs and the legality of intervention were not discussed substantially in Cabinet. Blair's defence to such claims was that the Cabinet was more interested in the politics rather than the practicality.

Legality of intervention

The wider concern throughout discussion over the invasion of Iraq was the question of legality. Bush was under the belief, as were most in his administration, that a single UN Resolution would be enough legal authority for the removal of Saddam, working off the back of pre-existing resolutions and following Clinton's Iraq Liberation Act. The only person in his Administration who disagreed was Colin Powell who often found himself isolated.

After Chirac's veto, Blair too was under the assumption that one UN resolution would be enough; however he found himself consistently under pressure from his backbench MPs and Cabinet ministers to push for a second. Jack Straw particularly put emphasis on the need for a second resolution after speaking with the Attorney General, Lord Peter Goldsmith QC. Straw contended in private that regime change would be unlawful.[136]

We now know thanks to the Chilcot Inquiry that on the same day as Bush's State of the Union address, Peter Goldsmith wrote to the Prime Minister providing the Government with legal advice. He cautioned of the need for a second UN Resolution. At the end of July he wrote a note to the Prime Minister. In it he said, 'my view therefore is that in the absence of a fresh resolution by the Security Council which would at least involve a new determination of a material, and flagrant breach military action would be unlawful'.[137] Blair would write in the margins of his note 'I just don't understand this.'[138]

The Attorney General would later reverse his advice, after meeting with the Bush Administration's lawyers on 7 March, stating to the Chilcot inquiry that after he had reflected 'on the position...and concluded that the better view was that there was a lawful basis for the use of force without a further [UN] resolution'.[139] Goldsmith would write this new position on a note which would be circulated to the Cabinet, who did not see his prior advice.

The concern many have is that the Attorney General was leaned on to change his position although he claims otherwise. The complete U-turn is evident for all now to see but at the time was kept from the Cabinet. Through his testimony to Chilcot we are told that after his original advice Goldsmith found himself kept out of the loop with senior advisers and that he was not being sufficiently involved in the meetings and discussions about the UN resolution and the policy behind it that were taking place at ministerial level.[140]

Indeed, Admiral Sir Mike Boyce, Chief of the Defence Staff at the time was so concerned about the legality of intervention that he sought out the Attorney General for further clarification of his position.[141] One has to take the view that No. 10 was clearly wary of the steep odds of getting a second UN resolution through and therefore anticipated its failure, making sure that if needs be the legal advice was in line with the Prime Minister's policy. Tony Blair was a qualified barrister and one cannot help but get the impression that with his experience he would second-guess any advice offered by the Attorney General.

Lord Malloch-Brown believes the difficulty Blair found himself in was the perception that he was deemed to be moving the goal posts. In fact Malloch-Brown contends that initially they may not have needed a UN Resolution. He points to countless examples of peacekeeping missions that did not have a UN resolution until after an invasion. This was the case in Kosovo.[142] 'For us the real danger was the trap Blair had gotten himself into which is going down the path of a resolution and when he realised he couldn't win it trying to move the goal posts. Suddenly a resolution wasn't necessary.'[143]

The Cabinet

Cabinet divisions over Iraq were no secret and were well reported in the press. The real question was whether all Cabinet ministers would accept collective Cabinet responsibility for the decision to invade Iraq. In this instance every minister had an opportunity to evaluate his or her conscience about whether they could support such a decision. A factor that may have swung many in Cabinet was the commitment Bush had now made to the roadmap for a Palestinian State. John Prescott writes in his book that this did indeed play a factor in swinging some in favour.[144]

Clare Short was one of the most outspoken critics in the lead-up to the war. She threatened to resign if the Government did not secure a second UN resolution, yet when the time came these threats amounted to little.

Robin Cook on the other hand offered his resignation on 17 March, stating in a letter to the Prime Minister, that 'I can't accept collective responsibility for the decision to commit Britain now to military action in Iraq without international agreement or domestic support.'[145] Resigning from his role of Leader of the House he stated that 'At Cabinet for some weeks I have been frank about my concern over embarking on military action in the absence of multilateral support.'[146] His resignation was a blow to Blair but not so significant as to change the course of direction. Cook's resignation speech in the House of Commons would be the most notable parliamentary speech in opposition to the war, giving a voice to the concerns of many about both the legality and conduct of an invasion of Iraq.

Jack Straw in his book writes that he too considered resigning over Iraq, stating that he believed his opposition to it would have stopped the war. However he chose not to, citing a powerful sense of loyalty to the Prime Minister and obligation as the country's foreign secretary.[147] Jonathan Powell supports Straw's account and believes his opposition was the right way of doing it: 'Jack did take a different stance on the Iraq war. He did write those memos and he didn't reveal that in public and stuck to a supportive public line, which in my view is the right way to do it. Robin actually didn't really contest anything in substantive terms, he almost never argued back.'[148]

Gordon Brown from all accounts rarely attended Cabinet discussions on Iraq or discussions outside of Cabinet on Iraq, his position perhaps ambiguous or indifferent. On 4 March he did make his support clear by saying he was prepared to 'spend what it takes' to disarm Iraq.[149] Yet in much of the discussion he seemed absent, with many questioning what his position was. Charles Clarke recalls a discussion he had with the Chancellor at the time: 'He was absolutely driven, as he was of all things in that era on political advantage in the Labour Party. In terms he talked to me about being against the Iraq War, we should all come out against it and stop it, I believe he said other things to other people.'[150]

What strikes many is that for a man obsessed with usurping Blair's place as Prime Minister and taking over No. 10, the Iraq war presented him with the perfect opportunity. All he would have to do is resign and it would no doubt force a change of policy in Iraq and most likely a change in leader of the Labour Party. However this simply did not happen.

The Labour Party

Iraq was the most divisive foreign policy issue for a sitting Labour Government since the war in Vietnam, with staunch backbench opposition from the beginning. On two occasions Labour MPs had defied the government whip to vote for motions against military action in Iraq (on 24 September 2002, fifty Labour MPs and on 26 February 2003, 121 Labour MPs defied the whip). There was increasing pressure from backbenchers to bring the issue of going to war to a vote, something Blair ultimately agreed to.

The hope was that the vote would unite Parliament, the Party, and the country behind the invasion of Iraq. It would also in some regards legitimise the decision to invade, tying MPs collectively to the decision and actually limiting their ability to scrutinise the executive. This is an argument that James Gray MP puts forward in his book *Who Takes Britain to War?*[151]

Relinquishing the royal prerogative, the right of the Prime Minister to take the country to war, was a historic moment, whether done with political calculation in mind or not. The risks were high for Blair. He told his close advisers many times as well as the President that if he lost the vote he would resign.[152] This message was carried to any Labour MP thinking of voting against the Government's motion, as rumours swept Westminster that he had written his letter of resignation. His threat of resignation allowed Labour whips to use the line 'do you support regime change in Baghdad or Downing Street?'[153]

Public opinion

Despite significant protests and vocal opposition to UK involvement in military intervention in Iraq, YouGov polling on the days following the parliamentary vote (21–22 March 2003) showed the British public favouring military action. Some 56 per cent of the British public when asked thought it was right that the USA and UK should take military action against Iraq, with 36 per cent thinking it was wrong and 8 per cent not sure.[154]

The Americans

The White House was becoming increasingly worried that Blair might not survive a vote in Parliament. In the days before the vote the White House, the Pentagon and the State Department had a number of telephone calls with their opposite numbers to discuss the situation. Geoff Hoon believes the vote reflected Britain's independence from American foreign policy:

> I think the United Kingdom ultimately takes its own decisions. It depends how far you want to go back. We didn't go to Vietnam. The United States was desperate for us to go. The pressure that was put on Harold Wilson to send even a fig leaf force to show we were part of it. He refused even to do that. I do not believe that the United States has a decisive influence...I called Donald Rumsfeld...I got ticked off for it...to explain that if the vote went the wrong way we would not be there and we would not be able to participate. So I recognise whatever the United States wanted...if Parliament had voted a different way...we wouldn't be involved. This is a country with strong institutions and a very independent view of the world, so the United States is an influence but it is not a decisive influence on our foreign policy.[155]

Before the vote President Bush spoke with Blair and said that if Blair lost the vote he would understand that British forces could not join the invasion. This effectively was an offer of an opt-out. The Prime Minister rebuffed the US President, telling him he was with him regardless.[156]

Bush's concern was so great that during the vote Mike Boyce the Chief of the Defence Staff sat on the phone with the Pentagon, updating them and explaining the parliamentary process as well as passing on the result.[157]

Parliament

On 18 March, the Prime Minister laid out the case to the Commons for going to war with Iraq. In his opening statement the Prime Minister set out a timeline of the many opportunities Saddam had been given from March 1992 to the day of the debate to declare his WMD programme. In each instance the Iraqi Government had provided a final declaration that had later been proven to be false. The problem, Blair stated, is that 'we are asked to believe that after seven years of obstruction and non-compliance, finally resulting in the inspectors leaving in 1998 – seven years in which he hid his programme and built it up, even whilst inspection teams were in Iraq – when they had left, he then voluntarily decided to do what he had consistently refused to do under coercion.'[158]

Blair went on to argue that Iraq continued to deny the existence of a WMD programme 'though no serious intelligence service anywhere in the world believes them'. The UN inspectors report on 7 March was in the Government's view clear evidence 'that Saddam is playing the same old games in the same old way. Yes there are concessions. But no fundamental change of heart or mind.'[159] The only reason Saddam had cooperated was because of 'The threat of force. From December to January and then from January through to February, concessions were made.'[160] Blair wrapped up his statement with a view shared by the Bush Administration that Saddam was simply too dangerous to be kept in power, that the loose link between terrorists and rogue states possessing WMDs was too dangerous, 'the possibility of the two coming together – of terrorist groups in possession of WMD, even of a so-called dirty radiological bomb is now, in my judgment, a real and present danger.'[161]

In his statement, the Prime Minister drew the comparison between Saddam and Hitler, and British appeasement of the rise of fascism in its failure to act.[162] In hindsight, Blair writes that while a direct comparison between Saddam and Hitler was perhaps a mistake, he maintains the link between a western reluctance to deal with Islamic extremism and the same reluctance to deal with the rising Nazi fascism.[163]

The Conservatives

The Conservatives under the leadership of Iain Duncan Smith had already given their assurance to the Prime Minister before the debate that he could count on the support of the Tory front bench. In his speech, Duncan Smith stated that he believed the issue too important for party politics, saying 'it is the duty of the Government to act in the national interest, and it is the duty of the Opposition to support them when they do so. The Prime Minister is acting in the national interest today. That is why he is entitled to our support in doing the right thing.'[164] He, like Blair, had come to the position long before that Saddam needed to be removed, arguing that 'Saddam Hussein is a threat to our national interest and that, if decisive action had been taken earlier, we would not now stand on the verge of war, but all that lies in the past, for we are entering the final phase of a 12-year history in relation to Iraq.'[165]

Conservative support for the Government motion would cushion the Prime Minister from Labour backbenchers rebelling against the whip, yet it raised the worrying prospect of a sitting Prime Minister passing a motion to go to war without carrying the majority of his own MPs.

The Liberal Democrats

Early on the Liberal Democrats made their opposition to any war with Iraq known. In both prior debates they raised concerns. The Liberal Democrat Leader, Charles Kennedy, and Foreign Affairs spokesman Sir Menzies Campbell spoke frequently at anti-war protests.

In his speech Charles Kennedy reiterated his party's concerns about outstanding questions regarding British involvement such as 'the supply and suitability of equipment, the eventual war aims, the participation of British forces and the bombs that might be used'.[166] As well as 'the longer term role that we hope British forces will play, if the war ensues, in the humanitarian and reconstruction roles on which they have such a distinguished track record'.[167]

Kennedy warned that any action would undermine the UN as an institution and leave Britain isolated from her allies. For his opposition to Government plans to invade Iraq, Kennedy would recall that MPs heckled him, calling him

'Chamberlain Charlie' throughout his speech in the Chamber and in the Division Lobby.[168]

Intelligence

The larger bulk of the intelligence on Saddam's weapons programme came from British intelligence sources, which became the backbone of the case for intervention in Iraq. This was evident in the numerous citations of British intelligence reports made by the American administration at the UN and by Bush in his State of the Union speech. This put enormous pressure on one intelligence dossier and its credibility.

The disclosure of the dossier on Iraq's weapons of mass destruction programme represented the first time a Joint Intelligence Committee report would be made public. Blair defended his decision to do so in the foreword of the document stating that 'in light of the debate about Iraq and Weapons of Mass Destruction, I wanted to share with the British public reasons why I believe this issue to be a current and serious threat to the UK national interest'.[169] Many however have since seen the publishing of the report as the politicisation of the intelligence services.

The report itself states that it could not be specific about its sources because 'gathering intelligence inside Iraq is not easy. Saddam's is one of the most secretive and dictatorial regimes in the world'.[170] In the Executive Summary it is also quick to point out that much of the information on his weapons programme was a rehash of information gathered in 1991 after the first Gulf War, intelligence that was twelve years old. The defence of using old intelligence is that it pointed to Saddam's intention in 1991 and the report argues that there is little reason to believe that this intention to build WMDs changed.

The most memorable parts of the report and those often quoted is the British intelligence that points to Saddam seeking to buy large quantities of uranium in Africa and a claim that Iraq could fire weapons of mass destruction forty-five minutes after the order. Each of these claims would later be discredited, but both were used by Blair and Bush to make the case to Congress and Parliament respectively that Saddam had a WMD programme. *The Sun*, the most read daily paper in Britain would carry the headline in response to the intelligence report 'Brits 45mins from doom'.

It would later turn out that much of the report was based on a plagiarised doctoral thesis. Jack Straw in his book claims that neither he nor the Foreign Office saw the report before it was published, effectively being shut out.[171]

It was this unusual step taken by No. 10 to publish the intelligence reports that convinced many MPs to back the Prime Minister. It would also become the foundation of many members' claims that they were deceived by the Government and the faulty intelligence.

The result

The Government's motion to go to war with Iraq was passed comfortably with 412 MPs voting for the amendment against 149. A rebel amendment opposing the war received 217 votes with 396 opposing the motion; of the 217 only 139 were Labour MPs. Graham Allen, a Labour MP and the leader of the rebellion, called it the largest backbench rebellion against a Labour Government.[172] Despite this, the number of Labour MPs who rebelled against the whip was much lower than Blair expected. This was most likely due to his threat of resignation and his approach of personally meeting with wavering MPs.

Preparation for war

On 17 March 2003 President Bush gave Saddam Hussein and his sons forty-eight hours to leave Iraq or face war. Military planning and preparation for invasion had been going on both in the USA and Britain from as early 2002. After returning from Crawford, in April Blair met with the military chiefs to discuss plans for intervention. The Prime Minister's thinking was that if you wanted to be part of the USA's military planning you had to be open to being a part of the action.[173]

Mike Boyce, Chief of the Defence Staff at the time, was pretty certain in a meeting in July 2002 that the USA had already decided on military action. Blair disputes this and believes that Bush had yet to make a decision. He believed that there was no doubt that Saddam only let the inspectors back in because of the build-up of military forces and the threat of military action,[174] although once assembled it seems highly unlikely that military forces would then be demobilised.

The parliamentary vote and polarising nature of the war meant that Britain's preparations were further behind than those of the USA. Sir Christopher Meyer believes that the Ministry of Defence did not get its marching orders in any serious way until late in the day. It is one of the reasons why they advanced with a lack of equipment and a lack of preparedness for the war itself. 'Geoff Hoon,

Defence Secretary wasn't given the green light until very late in the day because if the Government was seen to be making serious preparations before the Commons vote there would have been a political shit storm.'[175]

The other hindrance to early preparation was that the USA had refused to offer a date for their plans to invade. Despite a close working relationship, No. 10 continuously lacked the full picture as Meyer recounts: 'You see you had Manning talking to Rice. You had Blair from time to time talking to George W., but it never provided them with a full picture. So David Manning was being told stuff by Condi, and it took us a while to realise that what Condi told us wouldn't always stick in the administration, because Rumsfeld might not agree or Cheney might not agree.'[176]

The date of the invasion was only found out by a member of the Ambassador's staff going to the Pentagon. Even Colin Powell did not know the date and in fact was deliberately given the wrong one.[177]

The main outstanding issue of preparation was the choice of UK force contribution, something that Blair dealt with in his discussion with his Chief of the Defence Staff Mike Boyce. The belief at the time, which was advocated by the military and by No. 10, was that a higher military contribution would give Britain more sway over the overall military operation, and as Boyce puts it 'the thinking of the time'.[178] In political terms it would show the USA that Britain was a serious partner and not 'just flying a flag over a platoon to say we're there'.[179]

Jock Stirrup, Deputy Chief of the Defence Staff at the time, describes the reasoning in terms of command structure. 'It wasn't about being in Basra, because we thought we were going in the North. It was rather the need to have a sufficient contribution to allow Britain to have a slice of the command pie. A division that could operate autonomously but essentially within those divisional boundaries, operating under American command, under the American army and the core command but the division would be self-contained.'[180]

Another factor which affected the preparation for military intervention was the last minute decision by the Turkish Government to refuse British forces passage through Turkey to invade Iraq from the North (the initial plan). Instead UK forces would use bases in Kuwait to invade Iraq from the South. This change presented difficulties as Jock Strirrup recalls: 'That presented us with a great deal of challenge in terms of equipment. I remember since I was in charge of the equipment programme at the time, the terrain in the North is completely different from the south.'[181]

Invasion and insurgency

The invasion of Iraq was a great military success, with the Iraqi Republican Guard defeated and coalition forces greeted by jubilant crowds within a matter of weeks. Bush was so brave as to declare on 7 May that the war was won, while military inspectors continued to search for Saddam's WMD programme. They would come up short and instead find nothing, except the remnants and shells of a programme that had been shut down since the early 1990s. This revelation infuriated and fractured public opinion on the war and many people believed it to be a ruse.

Instead much of the line about the war began to spin about the removal of a dictator and the humanitarian side of their mission. Those closest to the Prime Minister offered the defence that this was another part of his liberal interventionism; that Saddam was a bad man and the world would be a better place without him. The failure to find an active WMD program was merely a small point. Iraq was liberated.

On 23 May, after the passing of UN Resolution 1483 which gave the USA legal authority as the governing force in Iraq, Paul Bremer, the Head of the Coalition Provisional Authority issued Coalition Provisional Authority Order Number 2.[182] This order officially dissolved the Iraqi army, police force and other entities of Saddam's Baathist state. Bremer did not consult the experts in Baghdad and instead ignored the concerns of the CIA station chief in Baghdad that he was sending 30,000 to 50,000 Baathists underground. Geoff Hoon argued with Rumsfeld about the dismissal of Iraq's army and police force but conceded that it 'was one of those judgement calls' and it wasn't his to take.[183]

This order contravened a directive given by Mike Boyce to his commanders in the field to negotiate with senior Iraqi officers. The idea was for senior officers in the Iraqi army with the Republican Guard to help maintain law and order under the supervision of British officers. Boyce argues that the plan was based on the assumption backed up by intelligence reports that many Iraqi commanders would switch sides immediately when coalition forces entered the country.[184] Instead the Iraqi army crumbled and commanders fled before the invading troops arrived. The Coalition Provisional Authority Order undermined any chance of this directive having any effect. Bremer, in his written testimony to the Chilcot Inquiry, insists that the decision to demobilise the Iraqi army was not a unilateral American ruling and that consultation was taken with Tony Blair.[185] This was clearly not relayed to the military commanders on the ground.

The effect of this order would not be fully realised until visible unrest came to the forefront in August with car bombings at the Jordanian Embassy and the UN Headquarters. In October the Ramadan Offensive marked the beginning of a bloody insurgency, often compared to the Tet Offensive, since it was believed that there would be minimal violence in the month of Ramadan; instead the opposite was true.

By early 2004, it was clear that western forces were facing a full-on insurgency from Iraqi Sunnis, many of whom were members of the now outlawed Baathist party. As a minority they feared a Shia-dominated Iraqi Government. These former Baathists, many of whom had served in the army or police force were reinforced by elements of Al Qaeda and foreign insurgents. Throughout the rest of Blair's time in office the fighting in Iraq would intensify with each year bloodier than the next, as Iraq effectively fell into a civil war between the Shia majority and the Sunni minority, with western coalition forces in the middle.

A decision to reinforce?

Blair was however shortly to be given a stark warning on troop numbers by his newly appointed envoy, John Sawers. On 11 May 2003 Sawers wrote a memo to the Prime Minister entitled 'Iraq: What's Going Wrong'. In it he outlined a number of concerns, including a summary of the US aftermath team under General Jay Garner: 'no leadership, no strategy, no coordination, no structure and inaccessible to ordinary Iraqis'.[186]

Sawers' view was that more troops were needed and he suggested that an 'operational UK presence in Baghdad is worth considering; despite the obvious political problem...one battalion with a mandate to deploy into the streets could still make an impact'. This view was supported by Major General Albert Whitley, the most senior British officer with the US land forces and later by Jeremy Greenstock when he was reassigned to Baghdad. His view was that the British 16 Air Assault Brigade due to return home should instead be brought into Baghdad.[187]

The Prime Minister and Chief of the Defence Staff, Michael Walker, ignored Sawers' plea and no extra troops were sent. The request flew in the face of the current US/UK plan. Sawers in his testimony to the Iraq Inquiry points out that both the USA and UK had plans for a rapid draw down of forces, since the Americans were aiming for a reduction to 60 per cent of their force levels and

British forces were planning to be down to 40 per cent of their maximum forces.[188]

Lord Owen considers this to be a fatal mistake and a missed opportunity to prevent the bloodshed that followed. The significance of the decision is that had Blair responded with more troops, it would have been impossible for Bush to refuse to do so as well. Rumsfeld would certainly not have been allowed to 'offramp' the 16,000 soldiers of 1st Cavalry Division.[189] It was perhaps a unique opportunity for Britain to directly affect the outcome of the military campaign and aftermath on the ground, and influence American policy.

Military planning and a lack of equipment

The insurgency highlighted two fatal flaws in military planning: a lack of equipment and inadequate troop numbers. The Pentagon had planned the invasion on the basis that they would be welcomed as liberators. In fact Donald Rumsfeld had argued weeks before the invasion that the ground force needed to be reduced. He thought America's military technical edge would make the difference.

For British forces it was a lack of equipment, specifically a lack of basic body armour and adequate numbers of helicopters. The reason for this said Jock Stirrup, as reported at Chilcot, was the timing. The rush to war did not offer enough time for forces to be adequately prepared. They were given four months to prepare.

The key current factor in the shortage of troop equipment in Iraq, and later Afghanistan, was the funding gap in the Strategic Defence Review, put together in 1998. Lord Richard Dannatt was the Director of the Defence Programme at the time. He says that once the Treasury put a 3 per cent saving on the budget the Government knew it was going to be underfunded.[190] 'It didn't matter at the beginning, in Kosovo it didn't matter; in 2001/02 it didn't matter; but when the Government began thinking about Iraq and Afghanistan big time the pips were squeaking.'[191] The military chiefs universally agree that Gordon Brown's stringent control of defence spending created many of the problems in Iraq and in Afghanistan.

The failure to plan effectively for a post-Saddam Iraq ultimately lies with the executive. Throughout the period up to the invasion the Foreign Office was frozen out, despite having a high level of expertise on the issue; as was the

Department for International Development, led by Clare Short. Her criticism of the war saw her effectively isolated from meaningful discussion.

After threatening to resign, Short was brought back in by Blair. In a meeting with UN officials and the British ambassadors, Malloch-Brown recalls that she said 'I am in charge now and I am going to coordinate the reconstruction of this country and make up for this bad war.' He continues, 'When she realised these were false promises she resigned. She realised that Blair had no control over the Americans who would really shape the reconstruction effort and even the British bit of it would be military led in the early stages.'[192]

Across the Atlantic, the State Department found themselves in a similar situation, with military planning being focused in the Pentagon. The strategic decisions were made in No. 10 with the Prime Minister taking personal oversight. The truth of the matter is simple. The Prime Minister and President did not believe that sectarian violence would occur after the fall of Saddam and ultimately did not prepare for it.

A resurgent Taliban

The western preoccupation with Iraq from 2002 onwards essentially allowed the Taliban to regroup and left the US-led mission in Afghanistan, in Richard Dannatt's eyes, to meander and tick over.[193] The USA's opposition to nation-building saw the focus in Afghanistan post-2002 largely spent on counter-terrorism. This allowed the Taliban to regain their strength in southern and eastern Afghanistan and by 2006 they were willing once again to take on the western coalition forces. Suddenly a mission that had been focused on reconstruction turned into counter-insurgency overnight.

The problem was that when the new operation was announced by the Prime Minister in 2004 and launched in early 2006, it was done so on the assumption that by the summer of 2006 British forces in Iraq would be reduced by 1,000 to 1,500. Troop levels were in fact still at around 8,000 to 9,000. Dannatt recalls that we had an army being asked to launch a new operation in Afghanistan on the basis that we had virtually finished in Iraq.[194] This false assumption created huge tension between the military chiefs and the Prime Minister over shortfalls in equipment and manpower.

These tensions were not helped by domestic politics at home. Blair and New Labour's waning popularity saw instability at the Ministry of Defence. After the

2005 General Election, Geoff Hoon was moved from his post and replaced by John Reid. He would last a year before being moved in a second reshuffle after poor local election results. Reid was replaced by Des Browne who would last the rest of Blair's tenure up until October 2008. Under Gordon Brown, Browne would occupy the positions of both Scottish and Defence Secretary. Later he would be replaced by John Hutton and after him Bob Ainsworth. In five years there were five different occupants as Secretary of State. Dannatt believes that this rapid change sent the wrong message about defence.[195] It is clear that in the regular changing of guard at the Ministry of Defence things on the ground were missed.

As Blair left office on a summer's day in June 2007, it was clear that British forces continued to face difficulties in Iraq and were about to face even further difficulties in Afghanistan. Neither country was stable.

Blair's legacy

In the end the decision to invade Iraq was fatal not only to Blair and his premiership but to British foreign policy as we know it. This single decision undermined much of his prior achievements in Kosovo and Sierra Leone and the case for a liberal interventionist philosophy.

The sadness of it all is that Blair was perhaps one of the most capable people to have sat in No. 10. He understood the importance of personality and personal relationships in pushing forward a foreign policy agenda. He had an unshakable self-belief that propelled both himself and Britain to a renewed place on the world stage.

However the tragedy was that somewhere along the way he got lost and believed in the myth that he had created. He believed in his ability to persuade and convince anyone of anything, whether that was George Bush to commit to a roadmap for Palestine, the UN to vote for a second resolution, Labour MPs and his Cabinet to commit to war and the British people of the need to remove Saddam.

In his second term he centralised foreign policy power in No. 10, enacting some common-sense reforms. The problems came largely from the growth of an informal government, a clique of advisers and ministers who mainly formed the policy. This would later be brought to Cabinet as a foregone conclusion. Domestically he dominated the foreign policy agenda but chose to contract out the decision to invade Iraq and the outcome of reconstruction and the war to the Americans. His belief in the righteousness of the cause led him to ignore the larger problems and fail to ask the right questions. In short, he had an unshakable belief that he and Bush were right.

There were however plenty of enablers around him, ironically many of whom have since disavowed his actions or their previous support for them. In 2002 he had some of the highest approval ratings of any post-war Prime Minister. He led the Labour Party out of the wilderness to two landslide elections. Therefore it is no surprise that many supported him and believed that he could do no wrong. Even to this day there is a loyal clique who believe that the decision to invade Iraq was right irrespective of its legality or the outcome. One senior Cabinet minister and close ally of Blair says that his premiership is judged largely by the quality of the one decision on Iraq. 'The middle class in the UK said it was the wrong decision and that is the defining thing. He was thrown out because of it and that is the primary lense through which the body politic look at him'.

Blair's premiership was imperial in his domestic dominance of the foreign policy agenda and the larger fact that he succumbed to an imperialist philosophy. In his memoirs he speaks of the need for more interventions. He writes that,

> beating this radicalised form of Islam and the threat posed by Islamic terrorism paired with rogue states requires a whole new geopolitical framework. It requires nation-building. It requires a myriad of interventions deep into the affairs of other nations. It requires above all a willingness to see the battle as existential and to see it through, to take the time, to spend the treasure, to shed the blood, believing that not to do so is only to postpone the day of reckoning, when the expenditure of time, treasure and blood will be so much greater.[196]

As Prime Minister he took the country to war six times in ten years making him the longest serving wartime Prime Minister since Churchill. At the heart of it, central to his belief, as Charles Guthrie puts it 'he really did believe that if good men do nothing evil prospers'.[197]

Notes

1 J. Powell, interview with S. Goodman, 14 September 2012, private offices.
2 D. Manning, interview with S. Goodman, 13 July 2012, private offices.
3 J. Powell, interview with S. Goodman, 14 September 2012, private offices.

4   T. Blair, *A Journey* (London: Hutchinson, 2010), p. 222.
5   J. Powell, interview with S. Goodman, 14 September 2012, private offices.
6   G. Ball, 'Operation Desert Fox Factsheet', Air Force Historical Studies Office, Joint Base Anacostia Bolling, Washington DC, 17 September 2014, accessed 1 August 2015: www.afhso.af.mil/topics/factsheets/factsheet.asp?id=18632.
7   Blair, *A Journey*, p. 222.
8   C. Guthrie, interview with S. Goodman, 7 March 2013, private offices.
9   C. Meyer, interview with S. Goodman, 7 February 2014, private offices.
10 R. Cook, 'Speech on the Government's Ethical Foreign Policy', *The Guardian*, Monday 12 May 1997, accessed 1 August 2015: www.theguardian.com/world/1997/may/12/indonesia.ethicalforeignpolicy.
11 C. Clarke, interview with S. Goodman, 31 October 2013, private offices.
12 S. Wall, interview with S. Goodman, 7 June 2012, private offices.
13 Blair, *A Journey*, p. 226.
14 *Ibid.*, p. 226.
15 D. Manning, interview with S. Goodman, 13 July 2012, private offices.
16 Blair, *A Journey*, p. 227.
17 *Ibid.*
18 *Ibid.*, p. 228.
19 T. Blair, *Hansard* (HC Deb, 23 March 1999, col. 165).
20 Blair, *A Journey*, p. 230.
21 B. Mason, 'Tony Blair: Kosovo Crusader', BBC News, 22 April 1999, accessed 1 August 2015: http://news.bbc.co.uk/1/hi/325989.stm.
22 W. Hague, *Hansard* (HC Deb, 23 March 1999, col. 163).
23 P. Bowers and T. Youngs, 'Kosovo: NATO and military action', House of Commons Research Paper 99/34, 24 March 1999, accessed 1 August 2015: http://researchbriefings.parliament.uk/ResearchBriefing/Summary/RP99-34#fullreport.
24 *Ibid.*
25 *Ibid.*
26 Blair, *A Journey*, p. 237.
27 Clinton, *My Life*, p. 852.
28 Blair, *A Journey*, p. 235.
29 T. Blair, Speech to the Chicago Economic Club, 22 April 1999, PBS Online, accessed 1 August 2015: www.pbs.org/newshour/bb/international-jan-june99-blair_doctrine4-23/
30 *Ibid.*
31 C. Falconer, interview with S. Goodman, 12 July 2012, private offices.
32 D. Manning, interview with S. Goodman, 13 July 2012, private offices.
33 T. Blair, Speech to the Chicago Economic Club, 22 April 1999, PBS Online, accessed 1 August 2015: www.pbs.org/newshour/bb/international-jan-june99-blair_doctrine4-23/.

34 *Ibid.*
35 J. Powell, *The New Machiavelli: How to Wield Power in the Modern World* (London: Vintage Books, 2010), p. 292.
36 Blair, *A Journey,* pp. 238–9.
37 Clinton, *My Life,* p. 855.
38 Blair, *A Journey,* p. 240.
39 M. Rifkind, interview with S. Goodman, 18 April 2012, House of Commons.
40 C. Short, *An Honourable Deception?: New Labour, Iraq, and the Misuse of Power* (London: Free Press, 2004), p. 93.
41 Blair, *A Journey,* p. 246.
42 A. Dorman, *Blair's Successful War: British Military Intervention in Sierra Leone* (Farnham: Ashgate Publishing, 2009), p. 68.
43 M. Campbell, *Hansard* (HC Deb, 8 May 2000, vol. 349, cols 518–29).
44 F. Maude, *Hansard* (HC Deb, 8 May 2000, vol. 349, cols 518–29).
45 Dorman, *Blair's Successful War,* p. 96.
46 D. Manning, interview with S. Goodman, 13 July 2012, private offices.
47 C. Guthrie, interview with S. Goodman, 7 March 2013, private offices.
48 Blair, *A Journey,* p. 229.
49 M. Dugher, interview with S. Goodman, 10 July 2012, House of Commons.
50 D. Manning, interview with S. Goodman, 13 July 2012, private offices.
51 J. Powell, interview with S. Goodman, 14 September 2012, private offices.
52 J. Straw, interview with S. Goodman, 3 July 2012, House of Commons.
53 R. Clarke, *Against All Enemies: Inside America's War on Terror* (New York: Free Press, 2004).
54 *Ibid.,* p. 225.
55 *Ibid.,* pp. 227–37.
56 C. Guthrie, interview with S. Goodman, 7 March 2013, private offices.
57 C. Meyer, interview with S. Goodman, 7 February 2014, private offices.
58 J. Straw, interview with S. Goodman, 3 July 2012, House of Commons.
59 Blair, *A Journey,* p. 352.
60 D. Manning, interview with S. Goodman, 13 July 2012, private offices.
61 N. Sheinwald, interview with S. Goodman, 3 July 2012, House of Commons.
62 D. Manning, interview with S. Goodman, 13 July 2012, private offices.
63 G.W. Bush, Transcript of Speech to a Special Joint Session of the United States Congress, 20 September 2001, accessed 1 August 2015: www.washingtonpost.com/wpsrv/nation/specials/attacked/transcripts/bushaddress_092001.html.
64 *Ibid.*
65 *Ibid.*
66 Blair, *A Journey,* p. 352.
67 T. Blair, *Hansard* (HC Deb, 4 October 2001, col. 672).
68 *Ibid.*

69 The United States Congress, Authorization for Use of Military Force Bill, S.J.Res. 23 (107th Congress), 18 September 2001, accessed 1 August 2015: www.govtrack.us/congress/bills/107/sjres23.
70 House of Commons Library, Research Paper: Operation Enduring Freedom and the Conflict in Afghanistan: an update, 31 October 2001, accessed 1 August 2015: http://researchbriefings.files.parliament.uk/documents/RP01-81/RP01-81.pdf.
71 G. Hoon, interview with S. Goodman, 9 January 2014, private offices.
72 T. Blair, 'Tony Blair's Statement', *The Guardian*, 7 October 2001, accessed 1 August 2015: www.theguardian.com/world/2001/oct/07/afghanistan.terrorism11.
73 *Ibid.*
74 *Ibid.*
75 *Ibid.*
76 House of Commons Library, 'Research Paper: Operation Enduring Freedom and the Conflict in Afghanistan: an Update', 31 October 2001, accessed 1 August 2015: http://researchbriefings.files.parliament.uk/documents/RP01-81/RP01-81.pdf
77 Blair, *A Journey*, p. 361.
78 *Ibid.*
79 *Ibid.*
80 J. Straw, interview with S. Goodman, 3 July 2012, House of Commons.
81 N. Sheinwald, interview with S. Goodman, 3 July 2012, House of Commons.
82 G. O'Donnell, interview with S. Goodman, 4 September 2012, private offices.
83 N. Sheinwald, interview with S. Goodman, 3 July 2012, House of Commons.
84 D. Manning, interview with S. Goodman, 13 July 2012, private offices.
85 S. Wall, interview with S. Goodman, 7 June 2012, private offices.
86 N. Sheinwald, interview with S. Goodman, 3 July 2012, House of Commons.
87 Clarke, *Against All Enemies*, p. 30.
88 T. Blair, Tony Blair's Statement to the Iraq Inquiry, Iraq Inquiry, 14 January 2011, accessed 1 August 2015: www.iraqinquiry.org.uk/media/50743/Blair-statement.pdf.
89 Clarke, *Against All Enemies*, pp. 264–8.
90 *Ibid.*
91 G.W. Bush, 2002 State of the Union Address to the United States Congress, 29 January 2002, accessed 1 August 2015: http://georgewbush-whitehouse.archives.gov/news/releases/2002/01/20020129-11.html.
92 *Ibid.*
93 Bush, 2002 State of the Union Address.
94 C. Meyer, interview with S. Goodman, 7 February 2014, private offices.
95 Blair, *A Journey*, p. 386.
96 *Ibid.*, p. 388.

97 C. Meyer, interview with S. Goodman, 7 February 2014, private offices.
98 Blair, *A Journey*, p. 401.
99 J. Prescott, *Prezza Pulling No Punches: John Prescott with Hunter Davies* (London: Headline Publishing Group, 2008), p. 288.
100 Blair, *A Journey*, p. 400.
101 Blair, Tony Blair's Statement to the Iraq Inquiry.
102 Her Majesty's British Government, 'Iraq's Weapons Of Mass Destruction: The Assessment of the British Government', BBC News, 24 September 2002, accessed 1 August 2015: http://news.bbc.co.uk/nol/shared/spl/hi/middle_east/02/uk_dossier_on_iraq/pdf/iraqdossier.pdf.
103 Blair, *A Journey*, p. 406.
104 A. Blick, *How To Go To War: A Handbook For Democratic Leaders* (London: Politicos, 2005), p. 60.
105 Blair, *A Journey*, p. 407.
106 C. Rice, *No Higher Honour* (London: Simon & Schuster, 2011), pp. 179–80.
107 The United Nations Security Council, Resolution 1441, 8 November 2002, accessed 1 August 2015: www.un.org/Depts/unmovic/documents/1441.pdf
108 *Ibid.*
109 D. Cheney, *In My Time* (New York: Simon & Schuster, 2011), p. 397; D. Rumsfeld, *Known and Unknown* (New York: Sentinel, 2011), p. 442.
110 Foreign & Commonwealth Office, 'Saddam Hussein: Crimes and Human Rights Abuses – A Report on the Human Cost of Saddam's Policies by the Foreign & Commonwealth Office', BBC News, 2 December 2002, accessed 1 August 2015: http://news.bbc.co.uk/nol/shared/spl/hi/middle_east/02/uk_human_rights_dossier_on_iraq/pdf/iraq_human_rights.pdf.
111 *Ibid.*
112 D. Orin, 'Iraq's Chem arms found by U.N', *New York Post*, 17 January 2003, accessed 1 August 2015: http://nypost.com/2003/01/17/iraqs-chem-arms-found-by-u-n/.
113 Blair, *A Journey*, p. 415; Cheney, *In My Time*, p. 394.
114 Blair, *A Journey*, p. 415.
115 R. Norton-Taylor, 'Blair-Bush Deal Before Iraq War Revealed in Secret Memo', *The Guardian*, 3 February 2006, accessed 1 August 2015: www.theguardian.com/world/2006/feb/03/iraq.usa.
116 *Ibid.*
117 *Ibid.*
118 J. Straw, *Hansard* (HC Deb, 26 February 2003, col. 265).
119 Blair, *A Journey*, p. 423.
120 M. Malloch-Brown, interview with S. Goodman, 21 August 2014, private offices.
121 *Ibid.*
122 C. Clarke, interview with S. Goodman, 31 October 2013, private offices.

123 J. Straw, interview with S. Goodman, 3 July 2012, House of Commons.
124 M. Boyce, interview with S. Goodman, 23 March 2014, House of Lords.
125 C. Falconer, interview with S. Goodman, 12 July 2012, private offices.
126 M. Beckett, interview with S. Goodman, 22 May 2012, House of Commons.
127 C. Clarke, interview with S. Goodman, 31 October 2013, private offices.
128 R. Butler, interview with S. Goodman, 29 October 2013, private residence.
129 C. Falconer, interview with S. Goodman, 12 July 2012, private offices.
130 J. Powell, interview with S. Goodman, 14 September 2012, private offices.
131 C. Guthrie, interview with S. Goodman, 7 March 2013, private offices.
132 Clarke, C., interview with S. Goodman, 31 October 2013, private offices.
133 'Blair criticised by Freedom of Information Inquiry MPs', BBC News, 26 July 2012, accessed 1 August 2015: www.bbc.co.uk/news/uk-politics-18987496.
134 G. O'Donnell, interview with S. Goodman, 4 September 2012, private offices.
135 M. Rifkind, interview with S. Goodman, 18 April 2012, House of Commons.
136 J. Straw, *Last Man Standing* (London: Macmillan, 2012), p. 372.
137 Office of Attorney General, Goldsmith note to the Prime Minister, Iraq Inquiry, 30 July 2002, accessed 1 August 2015: www.iraqinquiry.org.uk/media/46499/Goldsmith-note-to-PM-30July2002.pdf.
138 R. Norton-Taylor, 'Chilcot Inquiry: Blair Shut Me Out, Says Former Legal Chief Lord Goldsmith', *The Guardian*, 17 January 2011, accessed 1 August 2015: www.theguardian.com/uk/2011/jan/17/blair-ignored-goldsmith-chilcot-inquiry.
139 P. Goldsmith, Oral Evidence Transcript, Iraq Inquiry, 27 January 2010, p. 183, accessed 1 August 2015: www.iraqinquiry.org.uk/media/45317/20100127goldsmith-final.pdf.
140 *Ibid.*
141 M. Boyce, interview with S. Goodman, 23 March 2014, House of Lords.
142 M. Malloch-Brown, interview with S. Goodman, 21 August 2014, private offices.
143 *Ibid.*
144 Prescott, *Prezza Pulling No Punches*, p. 284.
145 R. Cook, 'Cook Resignation: The Letters', BBC News, 17 March 2003, accessed 1 August 2015: http://news.bbc.co.uk/1/hi/uk_politics/2858475.stm.
146 *Ibid.*
147 Straw, *The Last Man Standing*, p. 371.
148 J. Powell, interview with S. Goodman, 14 September 2012, private offices.
149 'Brown Will "Spend What it Takes" on Iraq', *The Guardian*, 4 March 2003, accessed 1 August 2015: www.theguardian.com/politics/2003/mar/04/foreignpolicy.uk.
150 C. Clarke, interview with S. Goodman, 31 October 2013, private offices.
151 J. Gray and M. Lomas, *Who Takes Britain to War?* (London: The History Press, 2014).

152 G.W. Bush, *Decision Points* (London: Virgin Books, 2010), p. 252.
153 P. Cowley, *The Rebels* (London: Politicos, 2005), p. 125.
154 YouGov Survey Results, 'The War In Iraq', YouGov, 23 March 2003, accessed 24 March 2016: https://d25d2506sfb94s.cloudfront.net/today_uk_import/YG-Archives-Ira-sTimes-WarIraq-030324.pdf.
155 G. Hoon, interview with S. Goodman, 9 January 2014, private offices.
156 Blair, *A Journey*, p. 412.
157 M. Boyce, interview with S. Goodman, 23 March 2014, House of Lords.
158 T. Blair, *Hansard* (HC, Deb, 18 March 2003, col. 762).
159 *Ibid.*, col. 763.
160 *Ibid.*, col. 764.
161 *Ibid.*, col. 768.
162 *Ibid.*
163 Blair, *A Journey*, p. 436.
164 I. Duncan Smith, *Hansard* (HC, Deb, 18 March 2003, col. 779).
165 *Ibid.*, col. 778).
166 C. Kennedy, *Hansard* (HC Deb, 18 March 2003, cols 784–5).
167 *Ibid.*
168 C. Kennedy, 'Charles Kennedy: They had the cheek to call me "Charlie Chamberlain"', *The Independent*, 21 May 2004, accessed 1 August 2015: www.independent.co.uk/voices/commentators/charles-kennedy-they-had-the-cheek-to-call-me-charlie-chamberlain-61385.html.
169 The British Government, 'Iraq's Weapons of Mass Destruction: the Assessment of the British Government', 24 September 2002, BBC News, accessed 1 August 2015: http://news.bbc.co.uk/nol/shared/spl/hi/middle_east/02/uk_dossier_on_iraq/pdf/iraqdossier.pdf.
170 *Ibid.*
171 Straw, *The Last Man Standing*, p. 376.
172 'Blair Wins War Backing Amid Revolt', BBC News, 19 March 2003, accessed 1 August 2015: http://news.bbc.co.uk/1/hi/uk_politics/2862325.stm.
173 Blair, *A Journey*, p. 402.
174 *Ibid.*, p. 405.
175 C. Meyer, interview with S. Goodman, 7 February 2014, private offices.
176 *Ibid.*
177 *Ibid.*
178 M. Boyce, interview with S. Goodman, 23 March 2014, House of Lords.
179 *Ibid.*
180 J. Stirrup, interview with S. Goodman, 11 February 2014, House of Lords.
181 *Ibid.*
182 Iraq Coalition Provisional Authority, Iraq Coalition Provisional Authority Order Number Two: Dissolution of Entities, Council on Foreign Relations, 23 August

2003, accessed 1 August 2015: www.cfr.org/iraq/iraq-coalition-provisional-authority-order-number-two-dissolution-entities/p30236.
183 D. Owen, *Hubris Syndrome: Bush, Blair and the Intoxication of Power* (London: Methuen Press, 2012), p. 126.
184 M. Boyce, interview with S. Goodman, 23 March 2014, House of Lords.
185 P. Bremer, Statement by Ambassador Bremer to the Iraq Inquiry, Iraq Inquiry, 18 May 2010, accessed 1 August 2015: www.iraqinquiry.org.uk/background/statement-bremer.aspx.
186 Owen, *Hubris Syndrome*, p. 124.
187 *Ibid*, p. 125.
188 *Ibid*, p. 129.
189 *Ibid.*, pp. 135–6; D. Owen, interview with S. Goodman, 11 May 2012, private offices.
190 R. Dannatt, interview with S. Goodman, 21 October 2014, House of Lords.
191 *Ibid*.
192 M. Malloch-Brown, interview with S. Goodman, 21 August 2014, private offices.
193 R. Dannatt, interview with S. Goodman, 21 October 2014, House of Lords.
194 *Ibid*.
195 *Ibid*.
196 Blair, *A Journey*, p. 349.
197 C. Guthrie, interview with S. Goodman, 7 March 2013, private offices.

8

Gordon Brown, 2007–10

On 27 June 2007 Gordon Brown fulfilled his lifelong ambition and ascended to the premiership. After ten years of coveting the job and at least five spent actively pursuing his predecessor to step down, he had reached the threshold of No. 10. Effectively elected unopposed as Labour Party leader he was at the height of power.

As Andrew Rawnsley in his book *The End of the Party: the Rise and Fall of New Labour*[1] rightly points out, on paper no Prime Minister in modern times entered No. 10 better qualified or prepared for the role. Brown had had a decade to think about what he wanted to do as Prime Minister, nearly a year's notice that there would be a vacancy with Tony Blair's departure, and six weeks of a formal transition to plan for his arrival. He would be the first person since Anthony Eden to become prime minister without any competition.[2]

This was ultimately down to the belief amongst many backbenchers, who were strong supporters of Brown, and even Blair himself, that Brown was somehow owed the premiership. Blair still held a level of guilt over the perception that in 1994 when he ran for the leadership he supplanted Brown, his senior partner. This belief among supporters of Brown's claim was matched by a sense of inevitability about a Brown premiership. Many of those floated as potential rivals ruled themselves out, fearing that to run against Brown would surely end in failure and be political suicide.

Brown's new dominance was not confined to the Labour Party. As Prime Minister he quickly set about culling the Cabinet he inherited from his predecessor. No less than nine members of Blair's final Cabinet resigned or were sacked or demoted.[3] In their place he promoted loyalists with relatively little Cabinet experience. Jack Straw and Alistair Darling were the only 1997 veterans, who like Brown, had served in Cabinet for ten years. As a whole, few ministers in Cabinet had the stature and personal base within the Parliamentary Labour

Party to challenge Brown. No prime minister since Ted Heath had the potential to dominate Cabinet in such a way.

Contradiction and courage

Brown's personality is one of gaping contradictions. One former Cabinet Minister serving under him believes he would make a good subject for a Shakespearean tragedy. 'He's brilliantly clever, has a powerful intellect, very hard working but a man not particularly comfortable with himself.'

These contradictions and insecurities were evident in his approach to foreign policy, between his aspirations, his writings and rhetoric, and his actions. In 2007, Brown wrote a book called *Courage: Eight Portraits*. In it he discussed the great statesmen and women he admired, who showed courage in the face of adversity.[4] The list included Nelson Mandela, Robert F. Kennedy, Dr Martin Luther King Jnr and Aung San Suu Kyi. In his mind he aspired to be on the same standing as them, arguing that courage was the greatest quality a leader could have. Contrast this to 2003 and the build-up to Iraq where Brown was nowhere to be seen.

To this day no one can offer certainty on Brown's private and personal position on the decision to invade Iraq. It is telling that the number two in government at the time, who held so much sway in domestic policy, was absent from the picture. The press at the time spoke endlessly about Robin Cook's opposition, the cautions of Jack Straw and the concerns of Clare Short but in all of this the Chancellor was missing in action.

For a man who believed in courage and coveted the job of Blair it presented him with the opportune moment to strike. To band together with the more sceptical members of the Cabinet, to rally his supporters and other Labour MPs against the war and challenge Blair to either stop preparations for war or face the resignation of his Chancellor and the very likely prospect of the majority of the Parliamentary Labour Party voting against war. This would effectively have ended Blair's premiership and catapulted Brown into it. He would be offered the accolades and titles that so many of his heroes had and his name would become synonymous with the attribute he so heavily admired.

Instead Brown was seemingly absent, later testifying to the Chilcot Inquiry on the Iraq War that the war was not his department, 'I was not Foreign Secretary or the Prime Minister.'[5] For a man who believed himself to be effectively a co-premier these explanations ring untrue. Whether he knew it at the time or not, the decision to go to war in Iraq was as much a foreign policy decision that reflected Brown's personal failings as it did Blair's.

A former Labour minister close to Brown concedes that aides around him did believe that he ducked the issue but not for the reasons the author might imply:

> He did after all believe that he had a power sharing agreement with Blair, that he did domestic and Blair did abroad with foreign policy. I honestly believe that what Gordon was up to was saying my Prime Minister has completely checked out of running NHS reform, education reform, welfare reform, the economy. So I'm becoming the domestic Prime Minister and people tell me he was enormously quiet in Cabinet on this as if though he hadn't really given it much attention to have a view. That it kind of crept up on him. That he just saw it as an opportunity to consolidate and expand his domestic empire.

The Anti-Blair

The Prime Minister's early occupation was spent in defining himself as different from his predecessor. This was the conclusion that both Charles Clarke and Margaret Beckett came to. Brown chose to remove Beckett from the Foreign Office, instead appointing his rival and another Blairite, David Miliband. In doing this Beckett recalls that Brown told her that the Government needed to look new to some degree. She could see this argument but she sometimes wondered whether he wanted to send a signal that he was not the same as Blair, even if it was more a question of perception over substance.[6] Clarke similarly argues that Brown was fixated by defining himself more as not Tony Blair than any real vision of how the country should be run.[7]

In foreign policy terms this generalised wish of not being Blair saw a drive away from classical foreign policy in favour of international development. Part of this, Jack Straw, who was at that point Lord Chancellor and Secretary of State for Justice, suggests was down to Brown's lack of any natural feel for foreign policy outside of the economic field.[8] There was simply a lack of interest in that area. This might be understandable for a new Prime Minister with a long list of manifesto pledges in domestic policy to deliver, but in Brown's case the last six years of government had been dominated by the foreign policy agenda.

Brown's immediate plans to distance himself from Blair after his Cabinet reshuffle involved putting constitutional reform front and centre. In a statement to the House of Commons on 3 July 2007, six days after taking office, Brown pushed for a radical constitutional reform agenda including the setting up of a National Security Council, giving the House of Commons the formal power to ratify treaties and formalising the role of Parliament in sanctioning decisions to go to war.[9] The last concessions particularly contrasted with the perception that Blair had bounced the House of Commons into sanctioning the war in Iraq. Other possible suggestions in his speech included a possible bill of rights and the lowering of the voting age to include sixteen or seventeen year-olds.[10] Damien McBride, a former press adviser to Brown, in his memoirs writes that the Prime Minister considered adding an annual 'State of the Union'-style address from the Prime Minister to Parliament, however it did not make the final cut.[11]

Much was made of this 'ground-breaking' speech on constitutional reform. The Prime Minister was setting out a big stall for constitutional change. Yet little came of it. Many of the possible concessions floated were either half-heartedly enacted or forgotten about altogether.

Another break from the past was the Prime Minister's decision to build a 'Government of All the Talents'. Brown wanted to recruit experts and specialists in their fields to be ministers in his Government, appointing Admiral Alan West as a minister overseeing counter-terrorism in the Home Office, along with business entrepreneur Digby Jones at the Department of Business and Enterprise, Ali Darzi at the Department of Health, Paul Myners at the Treasury and Paul Drayson in a cross-department digital role. The Prime Minister approached Mark Malloch-Brown, Deputy UN Secretary General to come and be his man in the Foreign Office.

Cabinet discussion under Brown seemed to be longer and more substantial than his predecessor. Peter Mandelson, Secretary of State for Business, Innovation and Skill under Brown and effectively the Deputy Prime Minister, believes this made Cabinet far stronger than under Tony Blair. He writes in his memoirs that the long discussions did not always please Gordon Brown, 'Still, he listened to everyone who wanted to speak, even if the impatience I sometimes detected, suggested he would rather be somewhere else.'[12] Jack Straw contended that Cabinet was now more collegial and Harriet Harman, Deputy Labour Leader also found that Cabinet discussions took much longer under Brown as everyone had their say on every issue.[13] Lord David Owen believes that Brown did genuinely try and restore Cabinet Government in the beginning.[14]

The news room

The biggest change from his predecessor came in the layout of his workspace in No. 10. Blair had been somewhat technophobic. He did not own a mobile phone and rarely used a computer, instead favouring making notes using a fountain pen. Brown, on the other hand, was wedded to his keyboard and placed two computer screens in his den, a large one on the table and an even larger one so others could join in with the drafting.[15]

Brown's premiership was more news driven then most. On the advice of Michael Bloomberg, the Mayor of New York, when he visited, the Prime Minister created an open plan 'war room' in the old press office in No. 12. 'This is the way newsrooms work,' Bloomberg told the Prime Minister, 'because of the pace of events, it creates better decision making, and better team working.' One former aide describing the changes to the workspace concedes that there is an element of truth in the argument that Brown's Government was news driven. 'Gordon's style of premiership was driven by 24 hour news, literally on a big screen permanently on in the office. His aides would sometimes change the channel because it'd be distracting him or he'd be getting annoyed when they needed him to think strategically about something else.'

Peter Mandelson in his memoirs agrees that the new layout served to magnify Brown's tendency to react to events as he had done in opposition, rather than standing back, reflecting and providing the considered judgement of a prime minister.[16] Although as soon as he became prime minister, Brown had time to do little else but react.

On Saturday 30 June, three days after taking office, a jeep filled with propane canisters was driven into the glass doors of the Glasgow International Airport terminal and set ablaze. This terrorist attack was linked to a further incident involving two car bombs that were discovered in central London on 29 June where police carried out controlled explosions disabling the bombs before they could be detonated. The Prime Minister kept his composure and set up a crisis response committee in the Cabinet Office Briefing Room. Finding and arresting those responsible, Brown then had to deal with the Government's response to a series of destructive floods in June and July, as well as an outbreak of foot and mouth disease in August.

In all of these crises the Prime Minister would chair a crisis response committee in the Cabinet Office Briefing Room (COBRA). No. 10 soon realised that the Prime Minister announcing he would chair COBRA weaved a certain spell on the media, as it conveyed the impression he was getting to grips with a crisis.

What started as a rarity soon became a compulsion, that every crisis should be met with the headline 'The PM chairs COBRA'.[17] Its over-use became more about form than substance.

By September he was seen largely in a positive light. Philip Gould, Labour's chief pollster recalls that Brown found himself 9 per cent ahead in the polls before many weeks of his premiership was out.[18] Many around him began to discuss calling a snap autumn election. The Prime Minister considered his options, choosing not to rule out the possibility despite his own timetable being for an election in the summer of 2008. Instead talk of an election began to fester. Brown did not rule it out until the last minute, in his Labour Party conference speech on 5 October. However by then the damage was done. Brown was seen as indecisive and a ditherer. He claimed he had never entertained the thought of an early election, instead blaming Douglas Alexander and Ed Miliband who he put in charge of his election campaign.[19]

The failure to call an early election would haunt his premiership. His inability to do so reinforced much of the public view that he was 'illegitimate'. Gould writes that he lost count of the number of times voters said in focus groups that he was unelected, and that he did not have a right to the job.[20] Towards the end of 2007, Brown's lead in the poll dropped and from then on Labour trailed the Conservatives. This mistake hung over him and he kicked himself for the missed opportunity. It similarly created much discord within the Labour Party. As his popularity in the polls fell so did his support within the party.

The Foreign Office

While Brown had made the decision to appoint David Miliband as Foreign Secretary it was done so to isolate him rather than bring him into the Prime Minister's tent. He was considered a potential leadership rival and in private many had urged him to run against Brown. Instead he chose to sit back, citing his relative inexperience having been only in Cabinet for two years.[21] This perception of Miliband as a rival clouded his relationship with the Prime Minister. Lord David Owen believes that it was a mistake for Miliband not to run for the Labour leadership, stating: 'The trouble with Brown was that David Miliband should have stood against Brown, he would have lost but he still would have had to be appointed Foreign Secretary and he would have been his own Foreign Secretary with his own powerbase'.[22]

Instead his decision to obfuscate merely reinforced the mistrust of those around the Prime Minister; as Jack Straw recalls there was a higher level of suspicion in respect to the Foreign Secretary.[23] Michael Dugher, Press Secretary to Brown similarly agrees that it was clear the two did not get on: 'David was considered to be the threat or his successor and in the end there was a sort of armistice, a sort of pact of not stepping on each other's toes. David stayed out of the Prime Minister's way and the Prime Minister left his foreign secretary largely to it.'[24]

Lord Malloch-Brown, the Minister of State in the Foreign Office argues that it was also the case that Miliband did not know much about foreign policy before being appointed to the position. It was a similar situation to that of Churchill and Eden:

> You started with a Prime Minister who scrabbled up old Labour, left Scottish politics, was determined to end life as a statesman and he had appointed a young foreign secretary, his sort of Anthony Eden in a way. I think he always anticipated that even if he was as close to him as Churchill was to Eden that probably he would succeed him in due course and time. A little bit like Churchill, he was willing to allow David some space to kind of run the place but he did think that the big foreign policy thinking came from him.[25]

The Foreign Office was a way to isolate Miliband and cut him off from domestic policy but it also offered him breathing space and a rare opportunity to get on with the brief. Jack Straw reflects that Miliband had slightly more autonomy in the post then he did.[26] The young Foreign Secretary struck a particularly close relationship with US Secretary of State, Hillary Clinton who described their views on how the world was changing as remarkably similar.[27]

However Miliband, in the author's discussion with him, was keen to stress that he served as a representative of Gordon's central vision; and that a line was often established between the two of them and Miliband would follow the Prime Minister's lead.[28]

When foreign policy crises emerged Brown did not call his foreign secretary: instead he called the number two, and his trusted friend Lord Malloch-Brown. The Foreign Office Minister recalls that the Prime Minister was excited by aid and its power to solve conflicts:

> (He) got very excited about conflicts like Sudan or the Kivus in the Congo or Afghanistan or Sri Lanka, or Zimbabwe, or Burma. Those were the ones that kept me up because there were always calls that came to me but not to Miliband. The thrust of the call was you've got to do something about it every time, which

you do... you can't allow the mandarins to take the energy out of foreign policy. You do have to do something if you see Tamils being killed en masse in Sri Lanka or genocide of a similar kind in Sudan or Darfur. It's not a matter of a foreign policy, a Foreign Office indolence verses a No. 10 activism – it is somehow marrying activism to knowledge and judgment and understanding of the context.[29]

As Prime Minister Brown inherited two military campaigns in Iraq and Afghanistan with a total of 12,000 UK troops deployed: 4,000 in Iraq and 8,000 in Afghanistan.[30] Brown already had long-standing tense relationships with the military chiefs going back to his days as Chancellor. Many in the military still had memories of the 1997 defence review where Brown had capped the defence budget with a 3 per cent saving that later left the military heavily underfunded.

Lord Richard Dannatt, Chief of the General Staff, believes that Gordon's spell as Prime Minister saw a continuation of the attitude that he had as Chancellor to the armed forces and to defence spending as a whole.[31] The consensus amongst the chiefs was that over a five-year period there was an overdrawing by the Ministry of Defence so that by the end of 2010 there was a £35 billion black hole in the defence budget in relation to the allocation of resources.[32]

Iraq

The Prime Minister was keen to draw a line under Iraq and, as one former aide put it, was very conscious of its negative legacy. Early on he made the decision to wind down Britain's involvement in Iraq, pledging in October 2007 that at least half of the troops deployed would be home by the spring of 2008.[33]

Another component in drawing a line under Iraq was his handling of relations with the USA and more so with the Bush Administration. The Prime Minister was keen to distance himself and move away from the friendly relations of the Bush/Blair era, as David Manning, former US Ambassador and Foreign Policy Adviser notes: 'Quite clearly Brown wanted to lower the temperature in relations with the United States. Not surprising though, he actually has enormous networks in the United States himself within the Democratic Party. As you expect he's very well plugged in and very much likes the United States. Although he was never ever going to flip over into some kind of anti-American stance, he's much too intelligent.'[34]

The closeness of communications between the White House and No. 10 continued. Sir Nigel Sheinwald, US Ambassador under Brown recalls that the video conferences between the Prime Minister and US President continued although they were less regular.[35]

In Iraq, British foreign policy and American foreign policy were passing each other by. As Brown was set on withdrawing the number of troops, Bush was set to follow through with General David Petraeus's plan and increase troop numbers for a surge. The Prime Minister had not consulted with the President about plans for the UK withdrawal, some seeing this as a direct snub.

In a visit to the troops in Iraq Brown announced that 1,000 of them would be home for Christmas.[36] This grabbed the UK headlines and brought criticism from the Leader of the Opposition, David Cameron and former Prime Minister John Major for not announcing the proposal in the House of Commons beforehand.[37] In December 2007 the UK returned control of Basra, the last of the four provinces under British control, to the Iraqi army, concentrating its forces at the city's airport.

However by March 2008 violent insurgency had broken out in Basra once again. The Iraqi army was overwhelmed and required US and UK forces to help retake control of the city. The Battle of Basra led to the suspension of the UK's withdrawal timetable. The Defence Secretary, Des Browne told Parliament in April that no further troops would be withdrawn until the region was stabilised,[38] although the Prime Minster was keen to emphasise that the UK forces mission would be over at the latest by the autumn of 2009.

When President Obama assumed office he did so with a mandate to bring the troops home from Iraq. US Defence Secretary Robert Gates, who served both Bush and Obama, describes his approach as simply wanting to end the 'bad war' in Iraq and limit the US role and scope of the 'good war' in Afghanistan.[39]

Afghanistan

While Iraq was considered a matter of drawing forces down, Afghanistan presented a far more complex problem. As Lord Malloch-Brown describes it, Afghanistan was a classic Whitehall problem, of a war which is not quite big enough to be front of mind every day as it should have been by then. This was a war that started big and died away.[40]

The decision to redeploy British forces into the Helmand province in January 2006 saw the resurgence of the Taliban and insurgent violence. Some 3,300 servicemen were sent in as part of the International Security Assistance Force expansion, at the behest of the Governor to help maintain order. The problem however was that the forces were largely under-resourced and this left them open to assault.

At home there seemed to be a lack of a coherent strategy for dealing with the UK's expanded role in Afghanistan. As one former aide to the Prime Minister describes it, Brown was happy in the early stages of his premiership to take a 'Chairman of the board approach'. He would be briefed by the Chief of the Defence Staff and largely let his Defence Secretary deal with it.

Sherard Cowper-Coles, Britain's Ambassador to Afghanistan described there being an alphabet soup of committees supposedly coordinating Britain's effort. The problem he found was the disorganised structure fed into two illusions, first that Britain could somehow have an independent strategy towards Afghanistan and secondly that British ministers could direct the military campaign from Whitehall, when in reality the military took their orders from the NATO command chain.[41]

In July 2008, the situation began being monitored and co-run by the secretaries of state for the Foreign Office, International Development and Defence. The three of them would meet regularly in what would become dubbed as 'triumvirate meetings'. Jock Stirrup, Chief of the Defence Staff would attend at times as would the Prime Minister. Lord Stirrup points out that this was before the formal establishment of a National Security Council but it was the equivalent.[42]

This approach was considered by one Government minister as a ridiculous bureaucratic compromise. The meetings were dominated by the three ministers' egos. A senior member of the Foreign Office describes the meetings as consisting of the three secretaries of state falling all over each other and fighting endless Whitehall battles. There was nobody grasping and dealing with the situation on the ground, which was a serious strategy of pacification and institution building and expanding the reach of the Kabul Government. It was, as another minister describes it, amateur hour despite some brilliant work by officials in Afghanistan.

By the summer of 2007, when Brown took the helm, the lingering problem with Afghanistan, like Iraq, was the growing public scepticism. Much of the public simply did not understand why UK armed forces were still in Afghanistan and as an extension why they were in Helmand. These questions would be asked continuously throughout Brown's premiership.

Lord Stirrup argues that the objective of military operations in Afghanistan had always been clear, even if politicians have not always been able to communicate it well. To ensure that Afghanistan does not become again a haven for global terror organisations like Al Qaeda, the way to achieve that was to spread responsible governance.[43]

The confusion over British involvement came over the cascade of the Government's sub-objectives to establishing governance, from the promotion of women's rights to the eradication of the heroin trade. Stirrup points out that the reasons for ISAF expansion had nothing to do with the military but he believes were driven by the Foreign Office and others around Whitehall, who had been trying for some time to get British forces to go to the south of the country where the poppy fields were.[44] The argument being purported was that destroying Afghanistan's poppy fields would destroy the source of the UK heroin trade. Another argument put forward was that Afghan farmers who grew poppies were reliant upon criminal activity and corruption through the trade spread through the system. In tackling the growing of poppies they were tackling corruption.

Afghanistan become a huge occupation for the Prime Minister in March 2008 when the *Sun* reported that the British Government planned to hire 'broken-down' helicopters from foreign countries and repair them for under-equipped British troops.[45] The newspaper launched a campaign supported by the Conservatives, calling for more money to be spent on helicopters. Michael Dugher, Press Secretary at the time recalls that suddenly Afghanistan became a major domestic problem as well as a policy issue for the Prime Minister:

> Suddenly Afghanistan was a major domestic problem for us, particularly when you're thinking about an election – all the campaigning the *Sun* was doing. Gordon took over all the sort of, not the day to day management but the regular management because it became a big priority that he would have to manage as Prime Minister. Suddenly there was a foreign policy issue going from having a limited amount of involvement to having a lot of involvement because the war was seeing to be going badly and it was causing huge domestic problems here with the *Sun* and Cameron using it against us.[46]

What this reflected was the reactive nature of Brown's premiership, largely news driven. Afghanistan became his personal concern only when it became the central focus of the media, although Malloch-Brown is keen to stress that the whole international system and not just the Prime Minister were slow to react to the resurgence of violence and the need for more equipment and troop numbers.[47] One Labour figure believes that when Afghanistan became a problem for the Prime Minister, 'he did a classic Gordon thing, which was to appoint Bob Ainsworth but would not let him get on with the job or did not rate him in the job. He basically appointed him but did not have confidence in him at the same time, which was impossibly unfair but a classic Gordon personnel thing.'

A lack of confidence in the Ministry of Defence may explain why Ainsworth in June 2009 became the fourth holder of the post of Defence Secretary in just three years. The job insecurity in the Ministry of Defence did impact on strategy in Afghanistan. As one former Chief of the Defence Staff put it, having four defence secretaries in three years cannot be a good thing, 'But politicians don't think about those kinds of things in Cabinet reshuffles.'

What is clear is that Brown was continuously under pressure to do more. Troop numbers were often a hot topic discussed between military chiefs and Government ministers. The belief that ministers like Douglas Alexander had was that the military continuously asked for more and more forces. Stirrup argues that he only asked for what the army could generate at a specific time. Due to the late draw down in Iraq, the British Government was limited to what it could deploy in Helmand.[48] This in part affected the British campaign in Afghanistan.

However Cowper-Coles argues that often the military would suggest military expansion to ministers and each time troops moved into an area they seemed to find they did not have enough numbers or equipment to hold it in an acceptable fashion. It was then that criticism of ministers would start, at first indirectly and then openly.[49] This criticism led to more and more issues being settled in private meetings between the Prime Minister and his senior military advisers rather than through the Cabinet Office machinery.[50]

In 2009 the British joined the American summer offensive in Helmand with the aim to clear out the Taliban. Between the beginning of May and early September more than fifty servicemen lost their lives and sixty-four were seriously injured.[51] 2009 was the deadliest year for British forces since 2001. Each casualty brought with it growing demands for withdrawal. Instead the Prime Minister agreed to commit a further 500 British troops, however he imposed conditions on their role delaying their departure.[52]

The re-election of Afghan President Mohammad Karzai in November 2009 was dogged with allegations of vote rigging. This reinforced the view held by many critics of the war that the idea of promoting good governance was flawed from the outset, with corruption at the heart of the regime in Kabul. The Prime Minister responded to the election results in a speech to the Royal College of Defence Studies. He said that in his conversations with Karzai he had argued for him to set out a positive agenda for a second term and establish a contract with the Afghan people by which the people of Afghanistan and the international community could judge his success.[53]

Karzai and Brown got on well throughout his tenure, to the point where ministers would ask Brown to raise issues on their behalf as he was one of the few people who could get straight answers out of the Afghan President.[54] The problem with Karzai was, like many of his fellow countrymen, he was convinced that the source of Afghanistan's problems were Pakistan and its Inter-Services Intelligence Directorate in particular. Karzai saw Pakistani hands in almost everything. He believed that Britain was in league with Pakistan. Time and again he would accuse the British Ambassador of colluding secretly with Pakistan to control Afghanistan.[55]

Early on in Brown's premiership the triumvirate of Alexander, Miliband and Brown considered the question of whether the mission in Afghanistan was 'doable' with the eccentric and paranoid President Karzai. Jock Stirrup put forward the case that if the conclusion was that it could not be achieved with the current Afghan President then 'we need to change it now and get our people out of there and do something different'.[56] Miliband took his views away and came back in a subsequent meeting with the conclusion that the mission with Karzai would be pretty uncomfortable and difficult, but doable. Stirrup is keen to stress that the decision to maintain support for Karzai's Government was a political and not a military decision decided largely by the Foreign Office.[57]

Brown defended the continued UK commitment to Afghanistan as part of an international effort, stressing that Britain was not alone. Forty-three governments across the world understood the importance of defeating Al-Qaeda. The USA with 60,000 and Britain with 9,000 troops may have been the biggest contributors but the rest of the international coalition had increased its numbers from 16,000 in January to over 27,000 by November 2009.[58] The Prime Minister was certain that they would be prepared to step in and do more. He fully supported the new President, Barack Obama's plan to commit an extra 30,000 troops in a strategy similar to the troop surge in Iraq, which saw President Bush in 2007 deploy an extra 20,000 troops.

However such justification seemed to fall largely on the deaf ears of a public who believed that in Afghanistan too much blood and treasure had been spilt. The total bill to the taxpayer in 2009 was approaching £12 billion; the death toll of British servicemen rose to over 300.[59] British public opinion was firmly of the view that UK involvement in stabilising Afghanistan did little to improve British security. In a BBC *Newsnight* and *Guardian* poll in July 2009, 47 per cent now said they opposed the war, while in an *Independent* poll in the same month

52 per cent of people asked said they favoured immediate withdrawal.[60] The Prime Minister was left to offer a vague commitment that troops would be home within two years but offered little in terms of an exit strategy.

Global multilateralism

Where Gordon Brown broke from his predecessors was in his view of international relations. While he had little interest for a classic foreign policy embroiled in the relations of individual nation states, he was passionate about establishing global solutions to global problems. In a speech at the John F. Kennedy Presidential Library in Boston on 18 April 2008, he declared that 'we urgently need to step out of the mindset of competing interests and instead find common interests, summoning up the best instincts and efforts of humanity in a cooperative endeavour to build new international rules and institutions for the new global era'.[61]

In private he believed that he could personally help create a new international system of governance, and in doing so be a global statesman. At the heart of this system would be a new World Bank, a new International Monetary Fund, a reformed and renewed United Nations and strong regional organisations, all built around a new global society with shared values.[62] He believed his own rhetoric. In part this view had been formed many years prior to his entering No. 10. Brown had always believed in the power of international aid and institutions. However the backdrop of the economic global crisis only reinforced his view that there urgently needed to be a new international economic consensus.

The special relationship (Brown and Obama)

Despite his belief in multilateral cooperation, the Prime Minister could not break from the political realities that underpin British foreign policy. Despite cool relations with President Bush, he was starstruck when it came to the ascendency of Barack Obama. Brown was keen to be the first leader to visit the new President and re-establish 'the special relationship'. Heading to Washington on 2 March 2009, the Prime Minister's aides were keen to put to rest anxieties that the new administration would consider them as 'part of the Bush baggage' because of Iraq.[63] They found that the President treated the Prime Minister with respect as a serious player.

Brown felt that he and Obama were cut from the similar cloth and went to great lengths to stress their closeness, informally calling him Barack. Peter Mandelson in his memoirs writes that Brown really did believe they were political soulmates, so much so that in the run-up to the 2010 election he argued that Labour's campaign needed to be like 'Obama vs. McCain'. His aides attempted to explain why such a model would not work. Douglas Alexander summed it up – that Gordon is McCain even though he wants to be Obama.[64]

Over his time in office, the UK press often viewed Brown's behaviour as sycophantic and rather undignified. One former US Ambassador, in discussing the history of the so-called 'special relationship', shakes his head when he thinks of the way Brown acted with Obama. 'The Americans always used to say to me, "You know if we forget to mention the special relationship when any of your politicians visit, or when we go to the UK, you go ape shit."' This behaviour culminated in what the press reported as the Prime Minister's humiliating efforts to secure a one-on-one meeting with the President at the UN in September 2009.[65] Damien McBride argues that some of Obama's people had already written Gordon off and were talking to David Cameron instead.[66]

The Lisbon Treaty

As Prime Minister he inherited the final preparations of the European Union's Lisbon Treaty negotiated largely in part by his predecessor. In the climate of growing euroscepticism in Britain, the Prime Minister was conflicted about attending the grand signing ceremony in December 2007. He feared that it would play badly in the press domestically. David Miliband was instead put front and centre to defend the treaty, only for No. 10 to brief that the Prime Minister had ordered him to cut the most pro-European passages.[67] In doing so he undermined the credibility of his foreign secretary.

In the end the Prime Minister chose to arrive late for the ceremony in Lisbon, missing the official signing and the celebratory leaders' lunch.[68] This halfway house between attending and not attending was seen as a snub by European leaders and his attendance still garnered critical headlines back at home. In the end it pleased no one and only drew criticism. One former Cabinet Minister reflects that they were not sure how much Brown really tried with European leaders. Whether it was a personal inability or a dislike of the grandiose back-rubbing that came with international diplomacy, the Prime Minister was not necessarily at ease.

The global financial crisis

That being said, the global financial crisis for a time changed that perception. Margaret Beckett is keen to point out that Brown was invited to brief the Eurozone Finance Ministers which is 'unbelievable' as they are 'incredibly touchy'.[69] Peter Mandelson recalls that when he went abroad with the Prime Minister to the Gulf States or to South America, foreign ministers and heads of government looked on him as a kind of Moses figure, who was going to deliver them out of this crisis into the Promised Land.[70]

The Prime Minister had come to the conclusion in the autumn of 2008 that the only solution to the mounting crisis was to rescue the markets by injecting vast sums of public money. Rescuing the financial services that had created the mess was of course not a politically popular idea. He found few allies internationally; the Americans were not recapitalising their markets and both French President Nicolas Sarkozy and German Chancellor Angela Merkel were opposed to pumping taxpayers' money into banks.[71]

As part of a minority in the face of international opinion that argued the banks should be left to reap what they had sowed, the Prime Minister embarked on a global campaign to convince world leaders otherwise. He started in the USA by attempting to convince then President Bush to push for more intervention in addition to the $700 billion Troubled Asset Recovery Plan. Bush was sympathetic, but between a Democrat-dominated Congress hostile to him personally and a Republican Party hostile to bailouts, his hands were largely tied. Brown then crossed over to European capitals carrying the same message of the need for greater intervention.

Domestically he committed the Government to taking stakes in HBOS, Lloyds, TSB and RBS in return for a £37 billion injection of capital. Barclays Bank chose to be recapitalised from private sources. The state now became the majority shareholder of RBS and owned 40 per cent of the newly created bank which saw the merging of HBOS and Lloyds. The Prime Minister created a new National Economic Council which was described by ministers as the 'War Cabinet' meeting in COBRA.[72]

The election of Barack Obama to the presidency brought with it a welcome change in policy, as the new President's first act was to pass a $787 billion financial stimulus. Both men were broadly on the same wavelength about the crisis.

The G20

Brown saw a perfect opportunity, with Britain's chairmanship of the G20, to enact the kind of multilateral cooperation he aspired to forge. Originally the event was for finance ministers and central bankers to meet but the Prime Minister instead planned to invite the heads of government of twenty countries. The twenty combined accounted for more than 80 per cent of the world's output, and to Brown it made sense for them to come together to deal with the global economic crisis. In promoting the G20 the Prime Minister saw it also as an acknowledgement of the importance of China and the other BRIC countries [Brazil, Russia, India and China].

Obama's acceptance in attending the summit was key. After the President confirmed he would be going, every other leader accepted; some even gatecrashed, including the Spanish, Dutch and Ethiopians. The Prime Minister stated that a 'grand bargain' would be struck in London leading to a 'global new deal'. In another speech months before the summit he said that it had the potential to be a 'new Bretton Woods' as significant as the 1944 conference that established the post-war financial order. John Cunliffe, the Prime Minister's senior adviser on international finance was in charge of preparing the summit while Miliband and the Foreign Office were marginalised.[73]

A week before the summit Brown embarked on a worldwide tour which marked the pre-summit process. In the space of five days he visited three continents, travelling 17,500 miles. The British media drew comparisons between Brown's globetrotting and that of his predecessor's post-9/11 tour.[74]

On 2 April the summit began as all twenty leaders assembled in London. A stark divide was reflected by Merkel and Sarkozy who were opposed to the Brown/Obama view that the world needed another round of fiscal stimulus. They formed a coalition to push for more international action against tax havens. Both Russia and China argued for a new reserve currency to replace the dollar.

The impasse to a joint agreement came in the form of a dispute between France and China over tax havens. Their differing opinions appeared to jeopardise the possibility of all twenty leaders signing a joint communiqué. In the end President Obama brought the two warring parties together and offered a compromise that they would 'take note' of an OECD list which named and shamed offshore rogue tax havens rather than the French preference of endorsing a blacklist. China did not belong to the OECD therefore the compromise allowed both parties to save face.[75]

The final deal saw the world leaders collectively pledge to inject $1.1 trillion into the global economy. The IMF's resources would be tripled to $750 billion, developing nations would be given access to $250 billion of currency reserves and another $250 billion was promised in credit for trade finance.[76] The Summit was seen as a huge success and Brown garnered praise from his fellow world leaders for his chairmanship and from the media.[77]

To him the agreement validated his belief that multilateral global engagement was the foreign policy of the future and that countries could finally move past the interests of the single nation state. The G20 represented the pinnacle of Brown's journey as an international statesman. He had staked his reputation on a positive outcome and felt its success came with his acceptance as a world leader in his own right. He had won the international debate and persuaded his peers of the merits of stimulus. The Prime Minister took particular pride at the agreement on debt relief for developing nations, a policy close to his heart. However the domestic political strain he was under was beginning to show.[78]

The Copenhagen Summit

Riding high, the Prime Minister now switched his attention to the United Nations Climate Change Summit in Copenhagen. In his address to the UN General Assembly on 23 September, the Prime Minister declared that an agreement on climate change at Copenhagen was the next great test of global cooperation.[79] As in April, Brown planned to be at the centre of any deal forged between the world leaders. He had been the first leader to declare his attendance to an event more reserved for government ministers and in doing so other leaders signalled their intention to attend. The Prime Minister had once again pioneered the advancement of multilateral summits at a head of state level.

The Foreign Office was once again sidelined. Ed Miliband, as Climate Change Secretary was chosen by the Prime Minister to head the UK negotiating team over his brother.

The summit lasted a week but many of the leaders of the richer nations would only arrive later in the week. Brown decided to attend for the whole week, his strategy being that if he could get the leaders of the developing nations to make concessions on the first few days of the summit, then on the last he could convince the richer counties to do the same. They would have to show willing. This theory was dubbed by No. 10 as the Prime Minister's 'domino theory'.[80]

However before the summit had even begun it was in disarray, when a draft copy of the Danish provisional agreement was leaked to the press. The leaders of the developing countries reacted furiously, interpreting the text as a departure from the Kyoto Protocols and the principle that richer nations which have emitted the bulk of CO_2 emissions should take on firm commitments to reduce greenhouse gases while poorer nations were not compelled to act. The leaders of developing countries were particularly outraged about the establishment of a disproportionate cap, which would allow developing countries to emit 1.44 tonnes of carbon per person by 2050 while allowing richer countries to emit 2.67 tonnes.[81] In response the Danish were keen to stress that it was a working framework and not the final document.

From the outset of the discussion, the leak created a level of distrust between the developing and the developed nations, since the latter already believed that negotiations were being taken behind closed doors and feared a 'stitch up'. As the hours of the summit passed little progress was made in terms of establishing a plan that suited everyone.

Instead the USA, South Africa and China, along with the developing nations of Brazil and India held their own discussions, shutting out both the European and developing countries. The Prime Minister was snubbed.[82]

In all fairness as the two biggest chief carbon emitters, if China and the USA could reach an agreement then the summit could be a great success. However in terms of influence it was clear that the Prime Minister of Britain had little to none. While he and French President Sarkozy worked tirelessly to salvage an accord, it was far less than the Prime Minister had hoped for.[83]

The accord took note and supported the continuation of the Kyoto Protocols for a cut in carbon emissions but did not offer any new specific targets. While there was agreement for the creation of a $100 billion fund by 2020 to help developing nations deal with the effects of climate change there were no details of where the money would come from.[84]

Ed Miliband accused China of 'hijacking' the summit, arguing that Bejing had vetoed moves to give legal force to the accord and prevented agreement on 50 per cent global reductions in greenhouse emissions – 80 per cent in most developed counties by 2050.[85] Brown conceded that he feared the talks would collapse and called for a new international body to take charge of future negotiations.[86] If the success of the G20 showed the possibilities of multilateral diplomacy then the frustrations and failure of Copenhagen showed its shortcomings.

EU President and High Representative for Foreign Affairs

The passing of the Lisbon Treaty created with it the posts of President of the European Commission, President of the European Parliament, and President of the European Council, changing the common practice of the presidency rotating between members, and the new position of High Representative of the European Union for Foreign Affairs and Security Policy. These positions would have to be filled and demanded prime ministerial involvement. Michael Dugher recalls that it was entirely run by Gordon Brown, not because he was particularly interested but because it was a big decision and the institutions demanded it.[87]

No sooner had the treaty been signed than there was speculation about who would get the top job of EU President. Tony Blair's name was continuously brought up. Since leaving No. 10 he made no secret of his desire for the job. He had the private backing of French President Nicolas Sarkozy and many considered it a job suited to a high-profile statesman. While Brown still had deep animosity towards his predecessor he pushed strongly for Blair in private.[88]

However calls for Blair to get the job faced a backlash from Martin Schulz, the Leader of the Socialist group in the European Parliament, and other critics of the war in Iraq. Blair was considered toxic. Sarkozy in private proposed that Brown take the job, which he quickly rejected. Instead European leaders settled on the former Belgian Prime Minister Herman Van Rompuy, favouring a more reserved character.

The question then came back to what position a Brit should fill. Both the Foreign Office and Brown's aides pushed the Prime Minister to pursue the High Representative job, as they believed it to be prestigious. Brown offered his longstanding rival David Miliband the job. To him it made natural sense to put up the British Foreign Secretary for the role, however it is hard not to be cynical about Brown having the perfect opportunity to dispatch a rival off to Brussels once and for all. Miliband was torn between the opportunity of being a huge figure on the European stage and his desire to one day be prime minister.[89]

In the end Miliband passed, and Peter Mandelson suddenly thrust himself into contention, unilaterally ringing around European capitals to garner support. The Prime Minister interceded and told Mandelson that the socialist grouping in the European Parliament wanted a woman for the position.[90] In the end Brown appointed Baroness Cathy Ashton, the UK's EU Trade Commissioner to the role, despite her being relatively unknown in British and European political circles. Run directly from No. 10, Mandelson in his memoirs describes the appointment process as a 'slapdash approach to filling an important role'.[91] It confirmed to many of Brown's critics his indecisiveness and disorganised approach to decision-making.

The bunker

A by-product of Brown's premiership being media led and crisis driven was the mentality and make-up of the people around him. A criticism often levelled at him was that he surrounded himself with spin doctors whose preoccupation before coming to No. 10 was the removal of Tony Blair – the likes of Damian McBride and Charlie Whelan. These men were used to briefing the press and working in opposition, first against the Tories and secondly against Blair.

Alistair Darling writes in his memoirs that they sought fresh enemies and he personally, throughout his time as Chancellor, was in their crosshairs.[92] While Jack Straw never fell out of favour, he concedes that the people Brown surrounded himself with, the disreputable conspirators at court who fed his suspicious tendencies and gradually separated him from the senior people in his Cabinet, always made things worse.[93]

There was a clear distrust between No. 10 and other government departments. Damien McBride in his book writes that he would routinely place moles on the ministerial teams of suspect Cabinet ministers and cultivate contacts within their camps, to keep abreast of any new conspiracy.[94]

Lord David Owen believes that as things for Brown became worse and worse, his premiership came down into more and more of a bunker mentality. 'His is the premiership of the bunker.'[95]

The decision to not call an early election and Brown's fall in the polls from early 2008 onwards created growing discontent within the party. As the public deemed his premiership illegitimate, members of the parliamentary party and Government began to question his leadership and the prospects of a pending General Election. There was not one but three plots to remove him from the premiership. At the heart of these conspiracies was always the name of David Miliband. This created huge distrust between the Foreign Secretary and the Prime Minister and by default the Foreign Office and No. 10 the likes of which had not been seen since Thatcher and Howe.

The first plot took place in September 2008 when twelve Labour backbenchers signed a letter demanding a leadership contest. The second and most serious came after the 2009 local elections. James Purnell, the Secretary of State for Work and Pensions tendered his resignation; the plan was for other ministers to join him, reaching a crescendo, until David Miliband would finally tender his resignation urging Brown to step down or face a leadership challenge.[96]

In the end Caroline Flint the second minster planning to resign delayed her resignation, Miliband got cold feet and Purnell was left high and dry. Both Miliband and Darling in fact managed to use Purnell's resignation to get out of the Prime Minister a promise that he would not move either of them from their current posts.[97]

The third one came in the form of a joint letter in January 2010, from former Cabinet ministers Geoff Hoon and Patricia Hewitt encouraging Brown to step down and urging others to join their cause. In the end nothing came of that letter either. In all three of the plots Government whips told rebels that if they moved against Brown they would face a general election and defeat.[98] The fear of the electorate, as some might call it, kept the Prime Minister afloat. However the continued attempts throughout his premiership to remove him from the post meant that too much of his attention was focused on the internal divisions within his party and government, then on foreign policy at large.

Distrust festered as each Cabinet minister became weary of the cadres surrounding the Prime Minister and the methods they were enacting to deal with anyone they deemed disloyal. Rhodes argues that a prime minister's influence and authority comes from those with whom they surround themselves; if this is the case then Brown's influence was seriously undermined by his advisers.

Prime ministerial debates

Prime ministerial debates as part of the general election campaign had been floated as early as 1964 when Wilson challenged Douglas-Home. Margaret Thatcher was similarly challenged by Callaghan in 1979, though she dismissed the idea as alien to Britain. The question of presidential-style debates was raised again by Kinnock against Major and Thatcher and Hague against Blair.[99] In 2009 similar calls were made by David Cameron and Nick Clegg. This time the request fell on sympathetic ears. Brown was trailing in the polls and his advisers believed that he had nothing to lose in debating Cameron and the inclusion of Clegg.

ITV, Sky and the BBC would each hold a debate with the first half dedicated to a particular segment. Sky's debate focused on international affairs and was the first time that the leaders of the main parties debated foreign policy live on TV. A record 2.1 million people tuned in to watch.[100] The hope was that it would allow the audience to analyse each candidate in the role as the de facto Commander and Chief, as well as Britain's representative on the world stage.

Instead they received a rather lacklustre half an hour of questioning. Topics varied from British membership of the European Union and the military campaign in Afghanistan, to the rather off topic discussion of what the individual leaders were doing to be more environmentally friendly and discussion surrounding the Pope's visit to Britain and the Catholic Church. The strongest exchanges concerned the European Union and discussion of Britain's membership, with both Clegg and Cameron favouring referendums. Brown argued that it would be damaging to discuss repatriation of powers while he was negotiating with European leaders on a response to the global financial crisis and tackling climate change. He declared that Cameron was anti-European while Nick Clegg was anti-American when Britain needed to work with both the USA and Europe.[101]

On Afghanistan both Clegg and Cameron criticised the Prime Minister for the lack of equipment and helicopters for troops. Cameron launched a particular attack on the failure to find a political solution, arguing that the Afghan army and Government were not representative of the Afghan people as a whole.[102] The public were split on the winner of the debate between Nick Clegg and David Cameron, although the debate marked a comeback for Brown who had seriously underperformed in the first. In foreign policy terms it represented the first of its kind but the varied issues, limited time and political barbs from all three leaders gave the impression that there was little projection of their own foreign policy vision.

The debate presented a great opportunity to redefine how the public scrutinises a prime minister's foreign policy yet it fell short. It focused more on form then substance. Brown's earlier trumpeting of global solutions to global problems seemed to fall flat and his performance largely gave the audience the impression that like his opponents he had little interest or knowledge of foreign policy at large.

A Brownite foreign policy?

It seems fair to argue that much of Brown's time as prime minister was occupied by the 2008 international economic crisis which one may argue is not in itself a classic foreign policy, although it clearly had global dimensions. Jack Straw certainly believes that once the Northern Rock crisis happened, Brown's preoccupation was with the financial crisis. If he ever thought he could do something for example about peace in the Middle East, it was not going to happen after that.[103] David Miliband also agrees that the global financial crisis 'consumed Gordon's attention in a way that Tony's was by the post 9/11 conflicts. Gordon also had a difficult election to fight'.[104]

Brown's other occupation, as Miliband rightly points out, was the election and with it the internal political divisions within the Labour Party as already discussed. Aside from that, Brown believed in multilateralism, that the best way to make change was to get as many world leaders in a room as possible and get an agreement. For that to happen the Prime Minister and his trusted advisers had to remain at the helm of foreign policy. The Foreign Office was largely treated with suspicion and subordinated both when it came to the G20 Summit and to the Copenhagen UN Summit.

Overall Brown lacked much of a foreign policy vision and seemed to react to crises as and when they arose. As one senior figure in the Foreign Office at the time said 'Gordon hadn't given much thought to a broader foreign policy vision aside from the belief that if you threw money and debt relief at things they somehow self-healed'. It meant that Miliband had a greater hand in dealing with the day-to-day foreign policy management but the Prime Minister was quick to sweep up any foreign policy success or priority. While given space Miliband was also constantly kept under surveillance from a suspicious No. 10.

Brown's greatest inheritance was that of Iraq and Afghanistan; in both he failed to leave any credible mark. In Iraq he followed through on a pre-agreed timetable and in Afghanistan he left the policy largely to the Triumvirate, intervening only when criticised and following the USA's lead when it came to the surge.

While he went to great lengths to distance himself from Blair by setting up the Iraq Inquiry and proposing the enshrinement of Parliament's right to vote on war, these actions were born out of personal animosity to his predecessor and were not a real recognition of how damaging these military ventures had become to British foreign policy. Both the Iraq Inquiry and the enshrinement of Parliament's right to vote were done on a lacklustre basis. Initially the inquiry would be held behind closed doors and the witness list was short. Under public pressure this changed quickly to be held publicly and with everyone, including himself expected to attend. However the greatest failure was to set a clear timetable and at the time of writing the Inquiry has yet to publish its findings, six years after its establishment. Similarly, like much of his push for constitutional reform, the Prime Minister failed to enshrine in law Parliament's right to vote on military intervention and it still remains a convention.

As prime minister Brown maintained a tight control on foreign policy and while he may have restored discussion in Cabinet and allowed Miliband to serve out his time in the Foreign Office in isolation, he did little to dismiss the claims of a dominate premiership. The problem was that while he had all the power he did not or could not wield it into a coherent foreign policy. Whether that was through a lack of interest or other distractions is very much for others to decide. What one can certainly see is that throughout his time in office UK foreign policy was reactive and news driven.

Notes

1 A. Rawnsley, *The End of the Party: The Rise and Fall of New Labour* (London: Penguin Books, 2010).
2 *Ibid.*, p. 460.
3 N. Allen and H. Ward, '"Moves on a Chess Board": a Spatial Model of British Prime Ministers' Powers over Cabinet Formation', *British Journal of Politics and International Relations*, May 2009, 11:2, 238–58.
4 G. Brown, *Courage: Eight Portraits* (London: Bloomsbury, 2007).
5 G. Brown, Transcript of Oral Evidence to Iraq Inquiry, Iraq Inquiry, 5 March 2010, p. 60, accessed 1 August 2015: www.iraqinquiry.org.uk/media/45558/100305-brown-final.pdf.
6 M. Beckett, interview with S. Goodman, 22 May 2012, House of Commons.
7 C. Clarke, interview with S Goodman, 31 October 2013, private offices.
8 J. Straw, interview with S. Goodman, 3 July 2012, House of Commons.
9 G. Brown, *Hansard* (HC Deb, 3 July 2007, col. 815).
10 *Ibid.*
11 D. McBride, *Power Trip: A Decade of Policy, Plots and Spin* (London: Biteback Publishing, 2013), p. 285.
12 P. Mandelson, *The Third Man: Life at the Heart of New Labour* (London: Harper Press, 2010), pp. 442–3.
13 Rawnsley, *The End of the Party*, p. 463.

14 D. Owen, interview with S. Goodman, 11 May 2012, private offices.
15 Mandelson, *The Third Man*, p. 449.
16 *Ibid.*, p. 451.
17 Rawnsley, *The End of the Party*, p. 467.
18 P. Gould, *The Unfinished Revolution: How New Labour Changed British Politics Forever* (London: Abacus, 2011), p. 503.
19 Rawnsley, *The End of the Party*, p. 510.
20 Gould, *The Unfinished Revolution*, p. 501.
21 Rawnsley, *The End of the Party*, p. 435.
22 D. Owen, interview with S. Goodman, 11 May 2012, private offices.
23 J. Straw, interview with S. Goodman, 3 July 2012, House of Commons.
24 M. Dugher, interview with S. Goodman, 10 July 2012, House of Commons.
25 M. Malloch-Brown, interview with S. Goodman, 21 August 2014, private offices.
26 J. Straw, interview with S. Goodman, 3 July 2012, House of Commons.
27 H. Clinton, *Hard Choices* (London: Simon Schuster, 2014), p. 207.
28 D. Miliband, interview with S. Goodman, 20 March 2012, House of Commons.
29 M. Malloch-Brown, interview with S. Goodman, 21 August 2014, private offices.
30 'Where are British troops and why?', BBC News, 29 April 2008, accessed 1 August 2015: http://news.bbc.co.uk/1/hi/uk/4094818.stm.
31 R. Dannatt, interview with S. Goodman, 21 October 2014, House of Lords.
32 *Ibid.*
33 H. Mullholland and D. Summers, 'UK Iraq troops to be cut to 2,500', *The Guardian*, 8 October 2007, accessed 1 August 2015: www.theguardian.com/politics/2007/oct/08/iraq.iraq.
34 D. Manning, interview with S. Goodman, 13 July 2012, private offices.
35 N. Sheinwald, interview with S. Goodman, 3 July 2012, House of Commons.
36 T. Harding and A. Porter, 'Gordon Brown's Basra pullout "is a stunt"', *Telegraph*, 3 October 2007, accessed 1 August 2015: www.telegraph.co.uk/news/uknews/1564934/Gordon-Browns-Basra-pullout-is-a-stunt.html.
37 'Brown Pledges to Bring Half Our Troops Home by Next Spring', *Evening Standard*, 7 October 2007, accessed 1 August 2015: www.standard.co.uk/news/brown-pledges-to-bring-half-our-troops-home-by-next-spring-7278952.html; N. Robinson, *Live from Downing Street: the Inside Story of Politics, Power and the Media* (London: Bantham Press, 2012), pp. 327–8.
38 D. Browne, *Hansard* (Citation HC Deb, 1 April 2008, col. 628).
39 R. Gates, *Duty: Memoirs of a Secretary At War* (London: W.H. Allen, 2014), p. 569.
40 M. Malloch-Brown, interview with S. Goodman, 21 August 2014, private offices.
41 S. Cowper-Coles, *Cables from Kabul: the Inside Story of the West's Afghanistan Campaign* (London: Harper Press, 2011), p. 93.

42 J. Stirrup, interview with S. Goodman, 11 February 2014, House of Lords; Cowper-Coles, *Cables from Kabul*, p. 177; A. Seldon and G. Lodge, *Brown At 10* (London: Biteback, 2010), p. 300.
43 J. Stirrup, interview with S. Goodman, 11 February 2014, House of Lords.
44 *Ibid.*
45 Seldon and Lodge, *Brown At 10*, p. 302.
46 M. Dugher, interview with S. Goodman, 10 July 2012, House of Commons.
47 M. Malloch-Brown, interview with S. Goodman, 21 August 2014, private offices.
48 J. Stirrup, interview with S. Goodman, 11 February 2014, House of Lords.
49 Cowper-Coles, *Cables from Kabul*, p. 177.
50 *Ibid.*, p. 178.
51 Rawnsley, *The End of the Party*, p. 667.
52 *Ibid.*, p. 668.
53 G. Brown, 'Speech to the Royal College of Defence Studies – London 6th November 2009', in Brown, *The Change We Choose: Speeches 2007–09* (London: Mainstream Publishing, 2010), p. 101.
54 Seldon and Lodge, *Brown At 10*, p. 304.
55 Cowper-Coles, *Cables from Kabul*, pp. 68 and 158.
56 J. Stirrup, interview with S. Goodman, 11 February 2014, House of Lords.
57 *Ibid.*; Cowper-Coles, *Cables from Kabul*, p. 157.
58 G. Brown, 'Speech to the Lord Mayor's Banquet – Guildhall London 16th November 2009', in Brown, *The Change We Choose*, p. 55.
59 Rawnsley, *The End of the Party*, p. 667.
60 CM Poll for the BBC/*Guardian*, 10–11 July 2009, accessed 1 August 2015: www.icmunlimited.com/pdfs/2009_july_guardiian_bbc_afghanistan_poll.pdf; N. Morris and K. Sengupta, 'Voters Turn Against War in Afghanistan', *Independent*, 28 July 2009, accessed 1 August 2015: www.independent.co.uk/news/uk/politics/voters-turn-against-war-in-afghanistan-1763227.html.
61 G. Brown, 'Kennedy Memorial Lecture – Kennedy Presidential Library and Museum Boston 18th April 2008', in Brown, *The Change We Choose*, p. 18.
62 *Ibid.*, p. 27.
63 Rawnsley, *The End of the Party*, p. 617.
64 Mandelson, *The Third Man*, p. 502.
65 Robinson, *Live from Downing Street*, p. 355.
66 McBride, *Power Trip*, p. 297.
67 D. Summers, 'No. 10 Admits PM Changed Miliband Speech', *The Guardian*, 16 November 2007, accessed 1 August 2015: www.theguardian.com/uk/2007/nov/16/eu.gordonbrown.
68 Seldon and Lodge, *Brown At 10*, p. 68.
69 M. Beckett, interview with S. Goodman, 22 May 2012, House of Commons.
70 Mandelson, *The Third Man*, pp. 450–1.

71 Rawnsley, *The End of the Party*, p. 579.
72 *Ibid.*, p. 596.
73 *Ibid.*, pp. 621–2.
74 *Ibid.*, pp. 622–3; Seldon and Lodge, *Brown At 10*, pp. 223 and 231.
75 Rawnsley, *The End of the Party*, p. 631; Seldon and Lodge, *Brown At 10*, p. 240.
76 The International Monetary Fund, 'London Summit Leaders' Statement', 2 April 2009, accessed 1 August 2015: www.imf.org/external/np/sec/pr/2009/pdf/g20_040209.pdf.
77 Robinson, *Live from Downing Street*, p. 345.
78 Clinton, *Hard Choices*, pp. 207–8.
79 G. Brown, 'Speech to the UN General Assembly – New York 23rd September 2009', in Brown, *The Change We Choose*, p. 44.
80 A. Stratton, 'Gordon Brown Basks in Limelight of Copenhagen Climate Change Summit', *The Guardian*, 18 December 2009, accessed 1 August 2015: www.theguardian.com/environment/2009/dec/18/gordon-brown-copenhagen-summit.
81 J. Vidal, 'Copenhagen Climate Summit in Disarray After "Danish Text" Leak', *The Guardian*, 8 December 2009, accessed 1 August 2015: www.theguardian.com/environment/2009/dec/08/copenhagen-climate-summit-disarray-danish-text; Seldon and Lodge, *Brown At 10*, p. 355.
82 G. Hewitt, 'Europe Snubbed in Copenhagen?', BBC News, 22 December 2009, accessed 1 August 2015: www.bbc.co.uk/blogs/legacy/thereporters/gavinhewitt/2009/12/s_5.html; Seldon and Lodge, *Brown At 10*, p. 357.
83 Hewitt, 'Europe Snubbed in Copenhagen?'
84 'Copenhagen Climate Summit: Talks "Held to Ransom", Gordon Brown Says', *Telegraph*, 21 December 2009, accessed 1 August 2015: www.telegraph.co.uk/news/earth/copenhagen-climate-change-confe/6857072/Copenhagen-climate-summit-talks-held-to-ransom-Gordon-Brown-says.html.
85 *Ibid.*
86 *Ibid.*
87 M. Dugher, interview with S. Goodman, 10 July 2012, House of Commons.
88 Rawnsley, *The End of the Party*, p. 675; S. Brown, *Behind the Black Door* (London: Ebury Press, 2011), pp. 362–3; Seldon and Lodge, *Brown At 10*, p. 346.
89 Rawnsley, *The End of the Party*, pp. 677–8; Seldon and Lodge, *Brown At 10*, p. 348.
90 Rawnsley, *The End of the Party*, p. 677; Mandelson, *The Third Man*, p. 494.
91 *Ibid.*, p. 497.
92 A. Darling, *Back from the Brink: 1,000 Days at Number 11* (London: Atlantic Books, 2011), p. 323.
93 Straw, *The Last Man Standing*, p. 518.
94 McBride, *Power Trip*, p. 246.

95 D. Owen, interview with S. Goodman, 11 May 2012, private offices.
96 McBride, *Power Trip*, p. 247.
97 Rawnsley, *The End of the Party*, p. 657.
98 *Ibid.*, p. 658.
99 M. Cockrell, 'Why 2010 Will See the First TV Leaders Election Debate', BBC News, 10 April 2010, accessed 1 August 2015: http://news.bbc.co.uk/1/hi/uk_politics/election_2010/8612153.stm.
100 'TV Debate: Clegg and Cameron Neck and Neck', British Sky Broadcasting, 23 April 2010, accessed 1 August 2015: http://news.sky.com/skynews/Home/Politics/Leaders-Debate-Nick-Clegg-And-David-Cameron-Joint-Winners-In-Sky-News-Poll-Of Polls/Article/201004415613588?lpos=Politics_Carousel_Region_0&lid=ARTICLE_15613588_Leaders_Debate%3A_Nick_Clegg_And_David_Cameron_Joint_Winners_In_Sky_News_Poll_Of_Polls.
101 'Election 2010: Gloves Off in Second Leaders' Debate', BBC News, 23 April 2010, accessed 1 August 2015: http://news.bbc.co.uk/1/hi/uk_politics/election_2010/8638738.stm.
102 *Ibid.*
103 J. Straw, interview with S. Goodman, 3 July 2012, House of Commons.
104 D. Miliband, interview with S. Goodman, 20 March 2012, House of Commons.

9

David Cameron, 2010–15

Whether David Cameron would become prime minister was uncertain right until he walked through the door of No. 10. The 2010 General Election was only the second time since the Second World War that a hung parliament was returned, with the Conservatives falling twenty seats short of a parliamentary majority, despite a largely unpopular Labour Government, who seemed spent after thirteen years of Government, and Cameron himself having a strong lead in approval ratings.

Coalition

Cameron was left with a choice between a minority Conservative Government, which probably would not last out the year, or a coalition. He chose the latter, entering into talks with Nick Clegg and the Liberal Democrats. Over five days in May the first coalition government in seventy years was formed, culminating in David Cameron and his new Deputy Prime Minister holding a press conference in the garden of No. 10. They produced the coalition agreement, a document merging parts of the Conservative and Liberal Democrat manifesto. Between them the Government would have a majority of seventy-six.

The agreement stipulated that the Liberal Democrats would be given five Cabinet posts including Clegg's role as Deputy Prime Minister. In the instance of a Cabinet reshuffle a minister would be changed like for like by party. Every Cabinet committee would have a chair and co-chair from the respective parties. A Coalition Committee was set up to deal with any Coalition issues.[1]

In terms of foreign policy the agreement offered little departure from the outgoing Labour Government. The Coalition would continue to support British deployment and the international coalition efforts in Afghanistan and the continued pressure put on Iran over its nuclear programme. On Europe, where the two parties differed the most, there was a pledge that in the event of another European treaty change transferring powers, there would be a referendum. This 'referendum lock' would ensure British sovereignty and was a compromise between Tory backbenchers who wished for an in/out referendum and recognition from both parties of failed pledges to offer a referendum on the Lisbon Treaty.[2]

David Cameron

At the age of forty-three, David Cameron became the youngest prime minister since Lord Liverpool in 1812. He came to No. 10 with no experience in foreign policy. He had only been an MP for nine years, five of which were as Leader of the Opposition. Prior to that he was the Shadow Education spokesman. Like his contemporaries he came up through the ranks as a special adviser to Norman Lamont as Chancellor and Michael Howard as Home Secretary.

Like all prime ministers his first priority was the Coalition's domestic agenda and the pressing issue of tackling Britain's deficit. This meant that his early role in foreign policy was limited, instead delegating much of it to the Foreign Office and his foreign secretary William Hague. This decision reflected Cameron's personal style as a natural manager, taking a hands-off approach or as one Labour Shadow Minister calls it the 'Chairman of the Board Approach'. William Hague is keen to point out that as Prime Minister Cameron does tend to let a minister who he has confidence in, get on with the job and that is his natural instinct. That is why Cameron's tenure in No. 10 has seen such a small turnover of ministers in Cabinet reshuffles.[3]

The Foreign Office

William Hague as a former Leader of the Conservative Party and Government minister under John Major was both experienced and had his own political base within the party. As a Tory grandee he forged a close relationship with Cameron in opposition and the trust between the two men filtered into government. Hague recalls that he had four and half years as Shadow Foreign Secretary, working together with Cameron and developing some of the things they would do in government.[4]

Aside from Afghanistan, on which Cameron had strong views due to its prominence in the media and having visited a number of times as Leader of the Opposition, and the personal responsibility he held as a prime minister responsible for their safety and continued deployment of British troops, he had not thought much about foreign policy. This gave Hague largely a free hand in conducting it: 'He came into office with well-developed views about Afghanistan but I felt as Foreign Secretary in his administration, I had a great deal of freedom to propose what I wanted about much of the rest of foreign policy.'[5]

The Foreign Secretary's freedom he attributes to the ease of personal access and trust between the two men.[6] For the first time since perhaps Major's Government, the Foreign Secretary was a member of the Prime Minister's inner circle. Hague would regularly attend the Prime Minister's own internal meetings at No. 10 at the start of every day. This would prevent problems between the Premier and Foreign Secretary arising later on, because 'you've always discussed it first thing in the morning'.[7] Alistair Burt, a former Foreign Office minister under Hague, believes that their trusting relationship came from the fact that there was a situation where the Prime Minister had a Foreign Secretary who was not a rival for his job and did not seek to be.[8]

The Hague–Cameron relationship offers a stark comparison to that of Carrington and Thatcher, where a relatively seasoned statesman and party grandee offered a strong foreign policy counterbalance to an inexperienced Prime Minister. Sir Malcolm Rifkind believes that the Foreign Office is back to being the centre of foreign policy deliberation, with the Prime Minister seeing the Foreign Office as an asset rather than a liability.[9] This is certainly something that Hague found during his tenure, that the Foreign Office was able to recover some of its lost role in defining the foreign policy agenda and proposing the way forward. This, he explains, is partly down to the creation of the National Security Council which has formalised the Foreign Office role.[10]

National Security Council

The creation of a National Security Council by the Coalition Government was a step towards breaking from past allegations of foreign policy being run by a small clique of people in informal settings, often referred to as 'Sofa Government'. The National Security Council meets three times a week and the Prime Minister invariably chairs it. The Council sees the combined attendance of the relevant government ministers, the heads of the security and intelligence agencies and the Chief of the Defence Staff. These reforms saw the creation of a permanent secretary level National Security Adviser whose job was coordinating preparation for the meetings across Whitehall. A National Security Secretariat was created to support the adviser's role, incorporating a number of officials across departments.

As a body the National Security Council stands independently from other Whitehall departments, including No. 10. In the past prime ministers would have their own foreign policy advisers and a foreign policy unit. These were now replaced by the National Security Adviser and the Council itself. Its creation took foreign policy deliberation physically out of the confines of No. 10 and a prime minister's close group of advisers. Foreign policy would be formalised through the Council and not in the informal manner for which so many had criticised Cameron's predecessors.

However has the Council changed the growing trend of prime ministerial dominance in foreign policy?

Gus O'Donnell, former Cabinet Secretary believes that the National Security Council has become a very important tool in bringing ministers into things earlier.[11] Its creation naturally suited the nature of Coalition Government, as William Hague points out:

> The Liberal Democrats have always played a full role in the National Security Council, and indeed one of the reasons the National Security Council gained life in a coalition government, is that it was necessary...of course it's the only way to bring all these things to discussion in the full between the parties. You can't have a discussion...the sofa style discussions of the past; there are two parties in the Coalition. They've always played their full part in the NSC. In terms of what we're talking about, I think that it has strengthened the more collective nature of foreign policy in government, rather than prime ministerial decision making alone in foreign policy.[12]

This does not mean however that the Council is immune to party politics. Lord David Richards, former Chief of the Defence Staff under Cameron, recalls that before a National Security Council meeting the Prime Minister would often meet with Conservative ministers and advisers to establish a consensus of opinion:

> The war cabinet as such today, is the National Security Council. Given at the time that I was on the Council there were a number of Liberal Democrats on it who could instinctively have a contrary view to their Tory colleagues the latter

would tend to hold a pre-meeting or 'small group' to discuss options. Then with a sort of powerful quorum, having agreed a particular outcome and having rehearsed the arguments together, they would then have a proper NSC meeting. Sometimes I was in on these small groups and others I suspect I was not. There were small groups on other issues like Syria, on which I had a clear view and where I wasn't always in agreement, privately, with the Government's line. There were probably meetings that did not involve me that should have done.[13]

Dr Liam Fox, former Defence Secretary under Cameron, agrees that the Council brings a wider range of views. However he embodies the partisan stance that many Conservative ministers took in relation to their Liberal Democrat counterparts. He believes that 'if you are confident in your own policy making ability' their participation should not present problems, citing the example of the renewal of Trident, which the Liberal Democrats opposed.[14] As Defence Secretary, Fox conducted an internal investigation to verify the cost and numbers and after convincing himself the numbers were correct he then took the issue to the Council. 'I was then happy for the NSC with the Lib Dems. They could conduct any investigation they wanted.'[15] He sees the creation of the NSC as nothing but an advantage.

Lord Richards is keen however to draw the distinction between these private meetings and that of Blair's 'sofa government'. While he concedes that under Cameron there has been a bit of 'sofa government', he would take it formally to the NSC and COBRA where the decision was made, the distinction being that the formal decision was made in the NSC rather than the internal meetings beforehand.[16] It does however reinforce the established view that Cameron will seek to gain a consensus beforehand to get the outcome he wishes, closing out those who might offer alternative advice.

Afghanistan

Like his predecessor, Cameron had the hefty inheritance of Afghanistan with 10,000 British troops in the south of the country. He had taken a close interest in it as Leader of the Opposition and continued that interest as Prime Minister. Liam Fox believes the reason for this was simple, in that the Prime Minister has to write to the families of those who have lost their lives and that this makes his interest far more than an academic exercise but a personal one.[17]

Cameron supported the original intervention in 2001, believing it had been just and necessary; but he felt that after nine years there were severe practical limits to what could be achieved in the country. He backed the US surge, supported talks with moderate elements of the Taliban and, like the USA, wanted to leave Afghanistan in a relative state of stability.[18]

As prime minister he was keen to begin to see the withdrawal of combat troops from the country and the returning of control to the Afghan army. It was not a question of whether to withdraw or when but how to achieve a dignified and secure exit. At the NATO Summit in Lisbon in November 2010 the assembled leaders agreed on a timetable for the phased withdrawal of troops towards the end of 2014. Cameron agreed that British troops would continue in their role of training and advising the Afghan National Army and at home pledged that troops would be out by 2015.

The withdrawal of British forces as part of the NATO mission would be based on a number of conditions: the capability of the Afghan National Army to shoulder security tasks without assistance, the level of security allowing the population to resume routine daily activities, the degree of development of local government and whether the ISAF mission was properly placed to phase itself out while maintaining the level of security for the Afghan people.[19]

Events on the ground in Afghanistan continued to influence the widely held scepticism of the British public. Parliamentary polls in the country in September had been marred by violence and allegations of fraud. The Dutch had pulled out their armed forces in the summer and the remaining European nations were also considering doing the same.

In the House of Commons on 9 September 2010, MPs voted for the first time since 2001 on the continued deployment of British troops through the newly created Backbench Business Committee. The motion passed 310 votes to 14. It reinforced the strange situation that in nine years, while there had been ministerial statements and general debates on the military campaign in Afghanistan, there had never been a specific vote, unlike Iraq. The vast majority of MPs supported the Government's position but prominent Conservative backbenchers criticised Cameron's setting of an artificial deadline arguing that it would give succour to the enemy.[20]

The other criticism levelled at the Prime Minister from members of Parliament was that the timetable for withdrawal was influenced by the recent Government defence review which enacted deep cuts to the armed forces.[21] The Coalition Government saw Afghanistan as costly in economic terms and the sooner the campaign was over the sooner it could cut back on defence spending.

In this Britain stood toe to toe with the USA, and the newly elected Prime Minister with President Obama. Sir Nigel Sheinwald, former British

Ambassador to the USA recalls that both men continued to have regular video conferences to discuss the situation on the ground as their predecessors had done.[22] The Prime Minister would continue to accept the USA's lead in strategy on the ground with the US surge now in full swing. His aides argued that when it came to the Afghan campaign 'the weather was made in Washington'.[23] This was demonstrated by the handing over of control of all 8,000 British troops in Helmand to a US General as part of a reorganisation of the command structure in June 2010 as the death toll of British troops reached 300.

2011 proved to be one of the bloodiest years of the conflict with the United Nations recording the number of civilian deaths reaching over 3,000, an 8 per cent increase from 2010. This marked the fifth year in a row that the number of civilian deaths had significantly risen. The number of suicide bombings rose to 450 ,an 80 per cent increase from 2011.[24] Incidents of Afghan soldiers attacking the ISAF troops training them had now become a prominent feature of the conflict. The Ministry of Defence recorded twenty-one attacks by purported Afghan soldiers on UK forces in 2011, leaving thirty-five dead, a huge increase from the six attacks the year before.[25] The use of high-profile political assassinations by the Taliban came to the forefront with the assassination of President Karzai's half-brother in July.[26]

Against this background of growing instability, President Karzai gained the backing of tribal elders to begin talks with the USA to secure a US–Afghan Strategic Partnership, which would create the framework for Afghanistan's security after NATO's withdrawal. These talks dragged on throughout 2012 and 2013, as Karzai eventually refused to sign the treaty, citing the insufficient provision of security by the USA in the post-NATO phase. These frustrations created a tense setting for all those still committed to the ISAF mission. The question for Cameron throughout this period was whether Britain should consider staying with American forces after the NATO withdrawal.

The NATO summit in May 2012 confirmed the timetable for pulling forces out of Afghanistan by the end of 2014. However the newly elected French President, François Hollande chose to bring forward the date of removal of French forces to the end of 2012. This decision led to calls for British forces to do the same. The Prime Minister was keen however to stick to the timetable and dismissed them.

In February 2013, Cameron held talks between Afghan President Karzai and Pakistan's President Asif Ali Zardari in which both sides agreed to work for a peace deal and back the opening of an Afghan office in Doha, asking the Taliban to do the same. These talks were largely seen as an important step in normalising relations between the two countries, for which Cameron's chairmanship was praised. However the sticking point over whether Afghanistan or the USA should directly talk to the Taliban would later lead to Karzai refusing to sign the defensive partnership.

Both NATO forces and the USA began to look towards a post-Karzai Afghanistan. The constitution limited his role to two terms. He had already announced that he would not seek a third term, although many still believed he might consider amending the constitution or using the insecurity to extend his stay. The Presidential election held in April 2014 between Ashraf Ghani and Abdullah Abdullah produced inconclusive results, heading to a second round in July. The results declared Ghani the victor but Abdullah refused to concede, citing fraud. The country was in deadlock for months until both sides agreed to a US-led audit.

Completed in September 2013 the audit verified the result. Both men agreed to serve in a National Unity Government with Ghani as President and Abdullah as Chief Executive with powers similar to that of a prime minister. Ghani swiftly signed the defensive partnership which would allow for Obama to stick to the plan of keeping 9,800 US troops in Afghanistan after NATO's pull-out. On the issue of leaving troops behind there was not a word out of Europe, says Lord David Richards. In discussing British influence on the USA, he believes 'for want of a bit of effort we could have said we'll be there with you America… Afghanistan take note… the aim is to give you a couple more years to get your act together'.[27]

The Prime Minister ultimately thought the idea of Britain staying as a nation building power for the decades it would take to construct a fully functioning democracy was ludicrous.[28] Instead Cameron made the decision to stick with NATO's timetable and in October 2014 the last of British troops left Helmand. The Prime Minister, visiting troops, was keen to tell them that the mission centred on establishing domestic security had been a success.[29] These comments came despite criticism that the mission had been a failure, most notably from former President Karzai, who bizarrely claimed that the war had been forced on the Afghan population and was not an Afghan war.[30] Cameron's aim from day one of taking office was clear and that was to bring British troops home; in that sense it was achieved. The wider success of our time in Afghanistan is more debatable. 2014 marked the bloodiest year for Afghan Security Forces, with 4,600 of them being killed. The USA has responded by shifting their timetable for the remaining US troops to stay longer to ensure security.[31]

Libya

David Cameron, not even a year into the job as Prime Minister was given a ringside seat to what looked like the disintegration of the old order in North Africa and the Middle East. What has now been dubbed the 'Arab Spring' started in Tunisia with a market trader's self-immolation. This sparked mass protests nationwide leading to the fall of the dictatorial regime of Zine El Abidine Ben Ali. Similar movements quickly spread like wildfire across the Arab world. Mass street protests, with the aim of regime change, appeared in Egypt, Libya, Yemen, Bahrain and Syria, as well as minor protests in Saudi Arabia, Oman, Jordan, Algeria, Sudan, Iraq, Kuwait, Morocco, Lebanon, Iran and the Palestinian territories.

Regimes that had existed for decades were overthrown in a matter of weeks. Like uprooted trees blown over by a strong wind of change, the regimes of Ben Ali in Tunisia and Hosni Mubarak in Egypt crumbled. Other Arab regimes responded in a mixture of ways, some favoured buying off the protestors with welfare entitlement and pledges of government spending while others chose to supress the protestors violently.

Colonel Muammar-al Gaddafi chose the latter. Having ruled Libya since 1969 when he led a coup to overthrow an unpopular king, he saw the initial protests in Benghazi as a few troublemakers and sought to crush them. However by 17 February 2011 the protests had spread to the cities of Ajdabiya, Darnah and Zintan. Three days later the protests had turned into a full on armed rebellion as rebel forces took control of Benghazi, Tobruk and Baida. The country was now in a state of civil war.

It is understandable why the Prime Minister initially approached Libya with caution. The consensus in Britain was now solidly behind the view that the 2003 Iraq War was a disaster and that achievements in Afghanistan were few and far, and beginning to fade. The FCO also predicted early on that Gaddafi would not face a significant threat.

Cameron was kept abreast of the situation on the ground with intelligence reports and briefings from his Chief of Staff Ed Llewellyn, who worked for Paddy Ashdown when he was the High Representative for Bosnia Herzegovina at the height of the Balkans conflict.

The turning point was a speech Gaddafi made on 22 February 2011 addressing the protests. He said that they represented 1 per cent of the total population and were on drink and drugs supplied by the West.[32] He urged his supporters to attack the 'cockroaches' opposing his rule, vowing that he would 'cleanse

Libya house by house'.³³ The fear was that Gaddafi's forces were set to massacre the inhabitants of rebel-held Benghazi. For both Llewellyn and the Prime Minister it looked like it could be Srebrenica all over again.

At a meeting of the National Security Council, the Prime Minister put to those in attendance the question, 'Is it in our national interest or not to get involved?'³⁴ He felt the question answered itself. If the situation was not addressed Libya would become a source of instability on Europe's doorstep, a refugee crisis waiting to happen. The country was already responsible for 2 per cent of global oil production with much greater potential for reserves. Libya was a central part of Britain's strategic and commercial interests in the region.³⁵

Cameron was swayed by the keen advocacy of French President Nicolas Sarkozy for intervention. Sarkozy was quick to call for sanctions against Gaddafi and called for targeted airstrikes against Gaddafi's regime if his forces used chemical weapons or targeted civilians. In a speech he said, 'the strikes would be solely of a defensive nature if Mr Gaddafi makes use of chemical weapons or airstrikes against non-violent protesters'.³⁶ Many believe that France's enthusiastic desire for intervention rested not just on humanitarian concerns but the substantial French oil and business contracts in Libya.³⁷

From 1 March 2011 the Cabinet had been discussing the possibility of intervention in Libya. There were a broad range of opinions amongst ministers, from the passionate argument for military intervention made by Education Secretary, Michael Gove renowned for his neo-conservative views to the cautious concerns from the Secretary of State for Defence Liam Fox.³⁸

The idea of a no-fly zone was first advocated by the Australian Prime Minister Kevin Rudd. *The Economist* that month pointed out that control of the Libyan air zone was critical for Gaddafi to retain power; whoever had the air power could in effect control the 1000 km road from Tripoli to Benghazi.³⁹ No serious discussion about the adoption of a no-fly zone in No. 10 happened until the second week of March and even then the Foreign Office felt that the idea would not work.⁴⁰ Caroline Ashton, the EU Foreign Minister expressed similar concerns that a no-fly zone would be highly risky and could end up killing large numbers of civilians.⁴¹

However on 7 March at a special regional meeting of the Cabinet in Derby, the Prime Minister told ministers that he now believed a no-fly zone was absolutely essential, and that all political and diplomatic forces must be deployed to achieve an international agreement.⁴² Deputy Prime Minister Nick Clegg agreed, stating that 'we must be doing this. It is the right thing to be doing.'⁴³ The Cabinet was now solidly behind the Prime Minister's position.

In a joint letter issued on the eve of the 11 March EU summit, Sarkozy and Cameron called for immediate action to end the violence in Libya, for EU countries to enact an arms embargo of Libya and plans to be put into place for military action including a no-fly zone. The letter warned that Gaddafi might be guilty of crimes against humanity; this in effect would give France and Britain the legal cover under the Geneva conventions to intervene and offer a case for a UN resolution under the auspices of the Responsibility to Protect.[44]

International support

The passionate Anglo-French rhetoric for intervention was met with deep scepticism across the EU, splitting NATO down the middle. Germany was particularly sceptical, warning that it was dangerous and ill-advised.[45] The USA, war weary from Iraq and Afghanistan, was also unenthusiastic about the possibility of a third military intervention. President Obama remained unattached. Cameron relentlessly lobbied Washington, sometimes speaking with the President daily as the moment of decision drew near. Meanwhile Hague spoke to Secretary of State Hillary Clinton, and Llewellyn spoke to Elizabeth Sherwood Randall, Senior Director for European Affairs on the US National Security Council.[46]

Cameron was under no illusions. He understood that the absolute maximum he could expect was a time-limited commitment to give strictly defined support to the Anglo-French initiative. With this President, in these circumstances, some in No. 10 thought even that was a lot to ask.[47] The Obama Administration was split. Samantha Power and Susan Rice the President's National Security Advisers and Hillary Clinton were in favour of intervention. Defence Secretary, Robert Gates argued against, citing that what was happening in Libya was not a vital national interest of the USA. He stated that he was worried how overstretched and tired the US military was, and the possibility of a protracted conflict.[48]

In the end Gaddafi's rhetoric paired with British and French pressure, as well as clear signs of Arab League support won over a reluctant President. Obama agreed to support the NATO campaign on two conditions, first that a UN Resolution would encompass support for further military action other than just a no fly-zone and secondly that US involvement would be limited with NATO allies shouldering much of the burden.[49]

US support was crucial in uniting NATO but what was more important was the backing of the Arab League. Its support gave the UN resolution credibility and dispelled any claims of another Iraq-like western coalition. The League's backing however had as much to do with the numerous scores individual members had to settle with Gaddafi than genuine concerns for the Libyan civilian populace.

Britain played a lead role in drafting Resolution 1973 which was passed on 17 March 2011, with Russia, China, Brazil, India and Germany abstaining. The resolution condemned the actions of Gaddafi and the systematic attacks on civilians, which it said could be considered crimes against humanity. Member states were authorised 'to take all necessary measures to protect civilian populated areas under threat of attack in the Libyan Arab Jamahiriya, including Benghazi, while excluding a foreign occupation force of any form on any part of Libyan territory'.[50] The specific prohibition of forces on the ground was designed to reassure countries in the region that there would not be a repeat of an Iraq-like occupation.

The Commons case for intervention

The passing of the UN resolution made the argument for intervention in Libya far easier to sell when Cameron advocated his case in the House of Commons debate on military action on 22 March 2011. The Commons voted overwhelmingly in favour of intervention with 557 MPs voting in favour and 13 against, with the Labour Opposition front bench under the leadership of Ed Miliband supporting the Government. Only one Conservative MP voted against the motion, John Baron.

Hague recalls that this was the moment when the Government took the decision. It was done because the situation in Libya 'was so catastrophic, and life was at stake so dramatically, and in such large numbers that we had to do something about it.'[51]

This decision came despite polling from the ITV Network and ComRes showing that 53 per cent of British people polled thought it was unacceptable for British personnel to lose their lives in action against the Gaddafi regime. Just one in three people agreed with the decision to take military action.[52] Journalists would later remark that the unequivocal support of Miliband gave Cameron political cover from any damage that intervention might produce.

NATO divisions

The NATO campaign in Libya did not start out smoothly. Early on there were disputes over who should lead it. French President Nicolas Sarkozy felt that

France should naturally lead and organised an emergency summit on 19 March in Paris for NATO allies and Arab nations to discuss coordinating military action. At the summit he took David Cameron and Hillary Clinton to one side and confided that French planes were already en-route to Libya. When the larger group found out about this secret it caused uproar. Silvio Berlusconi, the Italian Prime Minister, threatened to walk out and deny NATO access to Italian military airbases. He was upset that Sarkozy had not consulted him and felt that because Libya was a former colony of Italy, it should take the lead.[53]

President Obama had already outlined that the USA would lead the first part of the air campaign which would involve destroying Libya's air defence systems; US forces would then hand over to NATO.[54] Sarkozy objected to this proposal, arguing that France should lead the rest of the campaign. In the end he settled for British and French planes patrolling the more aggressive part of the no-fly zone.[55]

The other tension in the NATO coalition was between Turkey's Prime Minister Recep Erdogan and Sarkozy. Edrogan felt that Turkey had been deliberately shut out of NATO planning and sought to narrow the parameters of NATO operations in Libya. The Turkish Prime Minister only relented after President Obama assured him that there would be no ground troops involved in the mission.[56]

The campaign at home

The National Security Council met three times a week throughout the Libya crisis with the Prime Minister in the chair. Nick Clegg and the Liberal Democrats were on board with both parties seeing eye to eye on NATO's campaign. Where the difference of opinion came, says one former foreign secretary, was between Liam Fox and the Ministry of Defence, and the rest of the Government. After the recent cuts to the defence budget and armed forces they were considered to be 'inherently hostile to it'. Despite this Cameron was able to convince Fox to support the overall strategy.

This did not stop there being tensions between the Defence Secretary and Prime Minister. Cameron was particularly upset with Fox's decision to rule the collateral damage estimation at 0 without consulting him. This effectively ruled out targets where there was the slightest risk of civilian casualty. Fox defended the decision in an interview with the *Guardian*, arguing that the country needed to exorcise the ghost of Iraq and part of that was by showing a higher regard for human life.[57]

NATO's bombing campaign was swift. With superior air power the rebels were able to capture Tripoli in a matter of months. Richards recalls that, given the advance along the coast was proving sluggish and taking too long, the quick resolution of the campaign was a direct result of a decision to shift effort to support an attack on Tripoli from the south by a different and more capable group; this was effectively his decision.[58]

The Libya intervention marked the first time that the Alliance was under Anglo-French leadership and not American, a precondition set by Obama for US support.[59] NATO statistics found that it destroyed more than 5,900 military targets in around 9,700 strike sorties, with France, Britain and the USA conducting 70 per cent of the raids.[60] The Prime Minister in his statement to the House of Commons on 11 September 2011 estimated that the UK had made 2,400 sorties, a fifth of all NATO airstrikes, against some 900 targets. At its peak 2,300 British servicemen were deployed with thirty-six aircraft and eight warships conducting operations.[61]

Despite the Anglo-Franco leadership, Liam Fox is keen to argue that the mission would not have been possible without the Americans. 'Britain simply didn't have the military capabilities, in terms of air to air refuelling...a lot of the logistics and a lot of the intelligence reconnaissance was all American. They weren't providing upfront leadership but they were none the less providing the military hardware which we wouldn't have managed without.'[62] US Defence Secretary, Robert Gates supports this claim, writing in his memoirs that of the twenty-eight NATO allies who voted to support the military mission in Libya, just half provided some kind of contribution, and only eight actually provided aircraft for the strike mission.[63]

On 15 September 2011, Cameron and Sarkozy landed in Tripoli as victors. They were mobbed wherever they went, cheered with elation, with scenes reminiscent of Tony Blair visiting Kosovo after the war in 1998. Like Blair, Cameron's experience in Libya shaped him, as he took on his newfound status as an international statesman. The Prime Minister pledged that Britain would stand by Libya and that the NATO campaign would continue until all of Gaddafi's forces were defeated.[64]

Post-war reconstruction

When the USA handed control of the mission over to NATO it did so on the basis that the reconstruction would be undertaken largely by their European partners. This was despite warnings from notable Senators that NATO would not be able to finish the job on its own. Defence Secretary Robert Gates's response was that the last thing the USA needed was another enterprise in nation-building; it was up to other countries to shoulder the burden.[65]

For Britain, the post-war phase was run by the Department for International Development using the newly formed stabilisation unit largely made up of contractors. Cameron was keen that the lessons were learned from Iraq and early on directed Andrew Mitchell, Secretary of State for International Development to assemble the team to liaise with the Libyan National Transitional Council.[66]

Lord Richards remembers the Ministry of Defence had little involvement in the reconstruction effort. He believes they should have done, as most of those with experience in post-conflict reconstruction were still in the military and not in DIFD. The problem was that Whitehall and the Government knew what was required and put together a mechanism of delivery, but the detail was not sufficient. 'It was bound to fail', he said, 'because there were no Libyans you could talk to.' This he argues was a structural problem.[67]

The other issue was that of political will. This was clearly lacking. Richards believes that Cameron, along with the rest of those in attendance at the National Security Council understandably just did not want to get heavily involved on the ground, even in the post-war phase. In their eyes we had done our bit and won the war.[68] Cameron's statement in the House in early September 2011 certainly reflected that tone, when he stated that Libya was fully capable of funding its own reconstruction. 'Of course there was a role for foreign advice, help and support but we didn't want to see an army of foreign consultants driving around in four by fours giving the impression that this is something being done to the Libyans, rather than done by them.'[69]

On 23 October 2011 the National Transition Council, the main opposition group, declared Libya liberated and laid out a timetable to hold elections. In January 2012 violence began to erupt between rival rebel groups frustrated with the slow pace of reforms. The violence was precipitated by underlying questions of regional autonomy for the oil-rich east centred in Benghazi. Libya was largely divided along tribal lines with a weak central government in Tripoli.

The Libyan Government's failure to disarm the populace saw the rise of rival militia groups and outbreaks of further violence. A weak army and police force led to the Government employing and funding some of these militias for protection, like the Al-Qaqa Brigade and the 17 February Martyrs Brigade. While the sole aim of other militias such as the Ansar al-Sharia Brigade was to create an Islamic Libyan state and ally themselves with Al Qaeda and Islamic State.

The growing instability was marked by the September 2012 attack on the US Consulate in Benghazi which killed the US Ambassador. In response to the attack the USA along with Britain and other European countries closed their embassies in Libya. The lack of political stability and Government authority was highlighted by the brief kidnapping of the Libyan Prime Minister Ali Zeidan in October 2013.

It was clear by 2014 that the country was on the verge of civil war. Protests erupted outside the General National Congress over its refusal to disband after its mandate expired. A former General of the Libyan National Army, Khalifa Haftar launched an attack on Islamists in Benghazi and attacked the parliament building, accusing the Government of being in thrall to Islamists. In July the Ansar al-Sharia Brigade took control of Benghazi and in October took the key port of Dehra. The Libyan Army managed by the end of the year to recapture Benghazi but Derna still remains in the hands of the brigade at the time of writing, and this despite the army launching an offensive in March and Egypt launching airstrikes against the militants.

The collapse of the Libyan state and the civil war has been a key factor in the current migrant crisis in the Mediterranean. Thousands of migrants from North Africa fleeing conflicts are making the dangerous crossing with the help of people smugglers. Ed Miliband in his only foreign policy speech of the 2015 General Election argued that the crisis in the Mediterranean was linked to the failure of post-conflict planning in Libya. He said that David Cameron was wrong to assume that Libya was a country whose institutions could simply be left to evolve and transform themselves.[70]

As Prime Minister, Cameron set out to use the NATO campaign in Libya to exorcise the ghosts of Iraq except now with its collapse he has only reinforced them. As with Iraq, the failure in Libya was a lack of coherent planning for reconstruction. None of the NATO powers of France, Britain or the USA were interested in nation-building and it is therefore no surprise that the Libyan state, as with Iraq, has fragmented along tribal lines.

Mission creep and right to protect

The other consequence of the Libyan intervention would not be felt until late in 2013, when Cameron once again went to the United Nations, this time asking for a resolution to protect the people of Syria from chemical weapons. Russia has vetoed a number of UN Resolutions related to Syria, citing Libya as an example of 'mission creep'. They felt that NATO had overstepped its mandate from protecting civilians to regime change. The Russians and Chinese were particularly angry, feeling that in the UN Security Council they had been deliberately misled.[71]

Lord Malloch-Brown, former UN Deputy Secretary General, believes there was an absolute cast iron responsibility to protect case, for saving the civilians of Benghazi from 'a genocidal bloodletting by Gaddafi'.[72] There was not, however, a case in international law for going past that to a regime change strategy. Brown believes that by showing himself willing to go beyond what he sought as a mandate from the UN, in the case of Libya, Cameron exposed himself to the rejection of the Syria vote.[73]

Syria

Like Libya, Syria was not immune to the shifting winds in the Middle East, however much Bashar al-Assad claimed in interviews otherwise. In Dera'a, a medium-sized town in southern Syria in the province of the same name, a group of fifteen boys wrote 'the people want to bring down the regime' on the walls of their school. They were arrested, beaten and tortured while in prison. On Friday 18 March the local people in Dera'a marched in protest about the boys' treatment. The regime quickly cracked down on the protestors killing five demonstrators.[74]

The protests spread to the capital, Damascus, as well as to the cities of Homs and Baniyas as protestors demanded the release of political prisoners. By May the army had been fully deployed in Homs, Daraa and areas of Damascus, with hundreds reported to have been killed.[75] In response the EU and USA tightened sanctions on Syria.

During these crackdowns soldiers were ordered to shoot at protestors or warned that they themselves would be shot.[76] This led to wide defections across the Syrian army, taking with them military hardware. The defections quickly turned a civilian protest movement into a rebel army, with the Free Syrian Army being officially formed in the summer of 2011. The rebel army saw the merging of defecting military officers, all from the Alawite sect like Assad himself, with the protestors who encompassed Shiite, Sunni, Kurdish and Christians.

Similarly at this time a number of jihadi rebel groups sprang up in Syria, their stated aim to create an Islamic state in Syria. The biggest of these was the Islamic State of Iraq and the Levant (ISIS), which had risen to prominence a few years earlier in the Iraqi civil war. The groups are composed of a mixture of local and foreign jihadists.

In defence of the growing possibility of civil war, Assad argued that he was fighting Al Qaeda and that any foreign intervention to topple him would leave Al Qaeda affiliates in positions of power. In 2011 at the start of the uprisings, Assad, like Saddam Hussein in 2003, emptied his jails of many of these extremists. In an interview with *Newsweek* magazine Mohammed Al Saud, a Syrian dissident with the National Coalition for Syrian Revolutionary and Opposition Forces said that the majority of the current ISIS leadership was released from jail by Assad. He did this under the belief that 'if you do not have an enemy, you create an enemy'.[77]

Following the first anniversary of the uprising in March 2012, the UN estimated that more than 8,000 people had been killed.[78] The uprising and violence had now spread to more areas of the capital Damascus and to the city of Aleppo.

A political solution

In the same month, former UN Secretary-General Kofi Annan supported by the Arab League, proposed a six-point peace plan that would create a ceasefire and begin a political solution to the conflict. As the UN Envoy he headed with a team of observers to Syria to broker a deal.[79] By August he would resign from his role as UN–Arab League mediator citing that disunity in the Security Council, the rising violence and the Syrian Government's unwillingness to cooperate made a political solution at that time impossible.[80]

Lord Malloch-Brown who was Deputy Secretary General under Annan believes there were moments where a political solution was possible, and goes further to say that Kofi Annan was much closer to a solution than people realise. The sticking point was the language of such an agreement. Annan believed that the international community could not ask Assad to step down as a precondition to a conference. The language painfully agreed was that a transitional government would be formed to run the country until elections and that all members of the new government had to be acceptable to both sides. This was viewed by all the negotiators, the leaders of the State Department and the Foreign Office as a clear unambiguous code that Assad would have to step down because he would never be acceptable to the rebels.[81]

However the White House, coming to a presidential election, thought the wording was unacceptable. Brown believes Britain and France could have pressed the White House and made the case that it was a reasonable concession to save the haemorrhaging of life. There was however, no such demand or pressure.[82]

Assad was not Gaddafi and Syria was not Libya. This reality is what dominated much of the debate. Politically, Assad's regime has close ties with China, Russia and Iran and unlike Gaddafi he has had a far less antagonistic relationship with the Arab League. These relationships paired with the raw feelings both China and Russia had over the Libyan intervention meant that any move in the UN Security Council to pass a resolution condemning the violence, calling for a ceasefire or a right to protect the civilians was vetoed. On the issue of Syria there was diplomatic deadlock at the UN.

Militarily, Assad was in a stronger position then Gaddafi. While Gaddafi's army was nothing more than a tribal militia, the Syrian Army is a well trained professional army funded and armed by Russia. Syria is one of Russia's largest arms importers, providing its sole naval base in the Mediterranean. They have access to heavy weaponry, helicopters and chemical weapons, with clearly a military superiority over the rebels.[83]

Arming the rebels

With a political solution looking near to impossible and the rebels outgunned, the question of whether the UK should arm the moderate rebel forces in Syria was hotly debated throughout 2012. The view from the Foreign Office early on was that putting more arms into the situation would not necessarily help. Alistair Burt, a Foreign Office minister at the time says that this view held for many months.[84] Both the EU and the USA put an arms ban on Syria along with other sanctions.

The Richards Plan

In the summer of 2012 before stepping down as Chief of the Defence Staff, General Sir David Richards drew up a plan to train and equip a 100,000-strong Syrian rebel army at bases in Turkey and Jordan and provide air cover in ending the conflict. In discussing his plan, he explains that a key part of it would have been a carefully choreographed information operation building up the image in the mind of Assad's soldiers that their defeat was inevitable. The training would have been swift in transforming the opposition from not knowing one side of the gun from another to in three months being introduced to smart tanks and artillery; overall the training would have taken a year. Concurrently a Government in waiting would be prepared and they would know in advance what their policies and structures would be. 'You would only offer this plan and certain victory', he cautions, 'if the other Arab States and Opposition groups got behind it. You would do this by telling them that if they did not, Assad would be allowed to win.' In terms of legality under the Right to Protect Doctrine, Richards advocated that the plan would have to work effectively as the result otherwise would be a deterioration of the situation which would undermine the humanitarian rationale and there would reach a point where it was not legal any more.[85]

His plan was sent to the National Security Council Secretariat. It never got a formal acknowledgement. He never found out why. He followed it formally by sending two letters over the next nine months, and also verbally.[86]

Did the Prime Minister see the plan? Richards could not say definitely but is confident that he knew about it.[87] Whitehall sources told BBC *Newsnight* that the plans had been considered by the Attorney General and Prime Minister.[88]

The plan was known about in Washington, because Richards briefed his counterpart, the Chairman of the Joint Chiefs about it. It is believed that when Cameron headed across to Washington he was asked not to bring up Richards' plan when discussing Syria with President Obama. In the end Richards was told that it was more than the market could bear.[89]

Lord Dannatt, former Chief of the General Staff, believes that ultimately there was no political appetite for it in No. 10 so it did not happen. 'It was almost thought to be frowned upon that the Chief of the Defence Staff had even gone so far as to propose a plan like that, without merely trying to put military context substance into a policy aspiration that ministers had arrived at.' Dannatt believes it is a debate about 'what's chicken and what's egg, after all ministers can't know what the military can do without the military showing them'.[90] In essence Richards' plan built a clear picture of logistically what a plan for intervention would look like.

No. 10's silence on the plan reflected poor leadership on Cameron's part. Whether it was a lack of interest or a lack of American will it is still hard to determine why it was rejected or ignored and will continue to be a subject of speculation.

The debate continues

At that time in August 2012, a similar debate was taking place in the USA. The President was presented with a similar plan to arm moderate rebels by David

Petraeus, now Director of the Central Intelligence Agency. Secretary of State Hillary Clinton supported the plan but the President raised concerns about the vetting process of the rebels and whether arming them would be enough to drive Assad from power. Obama asked those assembled for examples of instances when the USA had backed an insurgency that could be considered a success. Few could think of any. In the end the President's inclination was to stay the current course and only provide non-lethal support to moderate rebels.

In the UK, the topic of arming the rebels continued to be debated. William Hague advocated a change in policy in early 2013. Burt recalls that the Foreign Office's position changed when it became obvious that the regime was using very heavy weaponry, barrel bombs and attacks from the air. Hague became active amongst his European colleagues in getting a partial lifting of the EU arms embargo. Backed up by the French, the Foreign Secretary argued that by supplying arms to moderate forces there would be less killing.[91] This move was widely opposed by twenty-five of the twenty-seven other EU countries but they wanted to maintain a unified policy.[92] Hague was a driving force behind UK foreign policy in a way that many of his predecessors were not, attempting to bring Cameron around to the idea.

Lord Malloch-Brown believes that there were good arguments being deployed on either side. The first argued that the only way to get the moderate voice heard, not just by Assad, but by the more radical rebel elements, was to arm the centre. This was the argument the British and French were making. The counter-argument offered by other members of the EU was that 'we've got a conflict that already has a runaway loss of life, just shoving more arms into the region is pouring paraffin onto the conflict'.[93]

The Cabinet was deeply divided on the issue of arming moderate Syrian rebels with Nick Clegg, Justice Minister Christopher Grayling, International Development Secretary Justin Greening, Minister without Portfolio Ken Clarke, and Foreign Affairs Spokesman Baroness Warsi alleged to be opposed.[94] So were many Conservative backbenchers and other parliamentarians, recalls Liam Fox: 'I think one of the problems with Syria was that you had the Prime Minister and Foreign Secretary set on helping some of the rebels in Syria. I think a lot of MPs felt that they might be dragged into it by the back door as it were.'[95]

Without a Cabinet agreement and under parliamentary pressure including a letter signed by eighty-one Conservative MPs, Hague conceded on 18 June, that any decision to arm Syrian moderate rebels would be subject to a debate and vote in Parliament. This unprecedented concession Hague defends, stating, 'I have said if we took that step, it should be discussed in Parliament because it is a major foreign policy step, and Parliament needed reassurance about that, because some people felt it would be a way around Parliament, and that it was a way of intervening while claiming we were not intervening. I did always say we would come back to Parliament if we want to send arms to the Syrians.'[96]

This decision has spurned much criticism from a number of former chiefs of the defence staff, who all believe that the concession to the House of Commons now restricts the Prime Minister's role in foreign policy. It reflects the weakening of his foreign policy prerogative. One former Chief believes it means now that the Prime Minister and Foreign Secretary and the advice, decisions and relationships they strike with their counterparts, can never be trusted again because they will now always be subject to Parliament second-guessing them. It has created a convention that may well hinder any future decisions to arm rebel groups and hinder the Prime Minister's ability to command foreign policy.

The rise of ISIS and the fall of moderate opposition

The origins of the Islamic State of Iraq and Levant go back to the 2003 Iraq war. Many of their leadership fought as part of the Sunni insurgency against the perceived western occupation and were imprisoned in Abu Ghraib and Camp Bucca. They originally fought as part of Al Qaeda's network in Iraq and pledged their support to Osama Bin Laden but as time went on the group were considered too radical even for them.[97]

In Syria in 2011 ISIS emerged as one of a number of Muslim rebel groups which hoped to overthrow Assad's regime along with Jahbat Al Nusra, an Al Qaeda affiliate. It is widely believed that Assad, like Saddam Hussein in 2003, emptied his jails in the summer of 2011 of many of these extremists including the majority of ISIS's leadership.[98] He called it a 'general amnesty'. He did this so he could create the narrative that was the choice was between him, a secular dictator and Al Qaeda and Muslim fundamentalists – that the uprisings were sponsored by radical, anti-western islamists.

Some suggest that he went further than just releasing their leadership from jail but indirectly financed and trained them. This was done by the Syrian Government covertly buying oil directly from the oil rich Eastern Province of Deir al-Zour under Al Nusra control. This financing allowed these organisations to buy arms, train and grow.[99]

The second allegation lodged against the Assad regime is that it by and large ignored ISIS and other jihadi groups from 2011 to mid-2014. Instead the regime focused its attention on fighting the moderate Free Syrian Army. ISIS was given time to recruit and train, as well as consolidate its status amongst other jihadi groups, as 2012 saw much infighting amongst them.

Hague asserts that Britain knew Assad was breeding extremism in various ways: 'this was absolutely discussed over a long period, particularly when the conflict in Syria began. That has been one of the arguments we have made to Russia and Iran that it wasn't in their interest to let this conflict go on, but Assad through oppression and through then trying to divide the opposition in the way described, has fed the extremism.'[100]

A consequence of the failure of the Syrian vote in the House of Commons and the decision of the international community not to intervene was the demoralisation of the moderate Free Syrian Army. They were a strong fighting force throughout 2012 and at the beginning of 2013 they had been making gains in the capital of Damascus. By the end of the year they were in retreat.

Lord Richards believes that there is an argument to be made that by putting in a minimal amount of effort, no lethal support and not doing it properly, western policy has aggravated the humanitarian situation and contributed to the creation of ISIS on the ground.[101] Out of sheer frustration that led to the creation of ISIS. Of the so-called 'good' opponents some chose to give up, others carried on hopelessly ill-coordinated and with no command structure, while others turned to ISIS saying 'We don't like them but they are getting things done.'

Since the chemical weapon attacks and the vote in September 2013 there have been record levels of defections to ISIS reported by the Free Syrian Army.[102] Many of them have been young fighters who have grown disillusioned with the lack of international support.

This problem was exacerbated as the Geneva peace talks in London in January 2014 between the Assad Government and the official Syrian opposition stalled. Neither side would agree on a transitional government. The Syrian Deputy Foreign Minister dismissed any talk of Assad stepping down as 'a dream' and used the conference to condemn what he called foreign-sponsored terrorism.[103] Neither the Kurdish rebels and the Islamic rebel groups were invited and nor was Iran. The Foreign Office confirmed in April that a third round of peace talks had not been planned as the process had effectively stalled.

William Hague is however keen to point out that the Syrian opposition thought it was worth taking a serious part in.

> There are many hopeless looking peace deals that have worked out successfully over time, but it did need Russia and Iran to play that role. You're right in some senses so say the Assad Regime has looked at it from a position of strength, in

the sense that they have not so far been militarily defeated. Looked at from a different perspective, they're not really in a position of strength, they've lost control over large parts of their country, are unlikely to recover that, they can't return Syria to what it was and therefore in the end are going to need some sort of agreement with other people in Syria.[104]

Assad's defiance was reinforced by the announcement that he planned to stand for re-election despite only controlling just over half of the country. The vote held on 4 June 2014 in Government-controlled areas of Syria saw him win 88.7 per cent of the vote against two approved Government challengers.[105] To the West it was considered largely a sham with much of Eastern and Northern Syria not voting. However once again it struck a blow to the morale of moderate opposition, as Assad used the result to maintain his legitimacy.

ISIS surge

On 10 June ISIS rebels crossed the border from Syria into Iraq and seized Mosul, Iraq's second largest city, sending shockwaves across the world. Who was this group? Where had they come from? How had no one seen this? Such were questions bouncing around Whitehall, Westminster and no doubt in No. 10. ISIS had seized the initiative and with a few thousand fighters had contributed to one of the biggest military upsets of recent times. They had taken control of parts of Fallujah in Western Iraq in January with little to no response from the West. Mosul however was a wake-up call.

Within weeks they began solidifying their gains and effectively rolled over the Iraqi army who were better equipped, better funded and had more numbers. ISIS added the Northern cities of Tal Afar and Tikrit to their territory and continued with the aim of capturing Baghdad itself.

The June surge stopped forty-seven miles north of Baghdad in Baquba and the West let out a collective sigh of relief. Stopped but not deterred, ISIS declared their new territory in Iraq and existing territory in Syria as an Islamic caliphate urging Muslims from all over the world join their struggle. In a few short weeks ISIS had created what so many in the West had feared for years, the creation of a radical Islamic state which could house terrorists and extremists alike.

The creation of the Islamic State through the ISIS military surge in Iraq was made possible by the Iraqi Prime Minister Nouri al-Maliki. Both the demoralised Iraqi army and the disillusioned Sunni populace in much of Northern Iraq made the Islamic State possible. Under his rule Maliki had done little to heal the country's clear divisions. He had turned a blind eye to Shia militias which had over the years terrorised the Sunni minority. The Iraqi army which had some estimated $25 billion worth of investment from the USA since 2003 was still plagued with allegations of cronyism and questions raised about their fighting ability.[106] In the end the Sunni populace in the North, tired of Maliki, welcomed ISIS, while the Shia-dominated army simply lacked the will to fight ISIS on the battlefront and the material support of the populace.

The Kurdish Peshmerga in the north of Iraq filled the void left by the army and clashed with ISIS forces. In the south of the country the Iraqi army fought to hold on to the capital and launch a counter-offensive. Once again Cameron found himself an onlooker to events beyond his control.

Western inaction throughout June and July continued despite the reports and images of mass executions of civilians, members of the Iraqi military and police force, along with anyone who refused to convert and pledge allegiance to the new Islamic caliphate. Instead Iran and Assad stepped in to fill the void; both increased their aid and support to Iraq. Iran deployed the Iranian Revolutionary Guard to Baghdad to bolster the Iraqi army and help fight ISIS, while the Syrian air force finally began bombing ISIS positions across the border.[107] There is an irony that all of a sudden regimes once considered to be the enemy were suddenly on the same side.

On 6 August after Kurdish forces withdrew, ISIS captured the town of Qaraqosh, often referred to as the Christian capital of Iraq. Over 100,000 Christians fled towards the autonomous Kurdish region. Thousands of Yazidis, a minority Christian religious group declared devil worshippers by ISIS, fled up Mount Sinjar. In response prominent leaders in the Church of England called on the Prime Minister to act. The UN Refugee Agency estimated that over 40,000 Iraqis faced starvation on the mountain without food, shelter or water.[108]

A call to action

Pressure was now on the international community to respond to the prospect of a humanitarian disaster and the more concerning issue of the possible defeat of the Kurdish Peshmerga. The Prime Minister weighed up his options while President Obama announced on 8 August the authorisation of limited airstrikes against ISIS in Iraq, to prevent the fall of the Kurdish capital of Erbil, where US troops and advisers were stationed, and the launching of a humanitarian effort to help the Iraqis on Mount Sinjar.

Cameron just could not escape the shadow of Iraq and found himself under pressure from a number of MPs to recall Parliament to discuss the situation in Iraq and the possibility of UK participation with its airstrikes. Conor Burns, the Conservative backbencher, wrote to the Speaker to demand the recall of Parliament to debate the UK's response to the massacre of Christians. These calls were not limited to Government MPs, and Labour MPs Tom Watson and Graham Allen, as well as Mike Gapes former Chairman of the Foreign Affairs Select Committee all called for clarification of the Government's position.[109] Tom Watson argued that the UK 'cannot abandon Iraq to the black flags of ISIS any more than we could leave Europe to the Kaiser or to his black-shirted inheritors 22 years later'.[110]

A year on from the Syria vote and another Middle Eastern conflict, a country in a state of civil war, the same Islamic rebels, an embattled regime, and fleeing civilians in the cross-fire – David Cameron found himself once more under pressure to recall Parliament. For many MPs the fear in light of the pace of events was that the Prime Minister might commit UK forces to aid the USA before Parliament was back in session. No. 10 issued a statement that the UK would join with the USA to provide humanitarian aid.

On returning from holiday and chairing COBRA, the Prime Minister reiterated that due to the basis of the humanitarian operation that Britain was involved in it was not necessary for Parliament to be recalled. This was despite criticism from members in the military including General Richard Shirreff who argued that 'what we have got is this commitment-phobic government terrified to be seen to be putting boots on the ground at a time when they are trying to extract from everything'.[111]

Cameron's position was supported by both of the other party leaders. Ed Miliband in particular, as Leader of the Opposition, welcomed the Prime Minister's humanitarian aid commitment and his cautious approach to military intervention. This was in spite of the British public being split on the issue, with a YouGov poll finding that 37 per cent of the public supported British involvement whilst 36 per cent disapproved.[112]

Lord Dannatt correctly points out the problem: 'the perceived effect of the September 2013 vote was that we're not going to get involved at all and that was probably not right and led to ISIS. ISIS having gained quite a lot of capability and strength then switched their focus of fighting the Assad Regime and roared into Iraq in June and July.'[113]

One former minister believes that Cameron throughout the summer was 'torn between his instinct, which was on show with Syria and the fact that he's not a fool. He knows that intervention in Libya broke the country. His judgment on joining the Americans will be very much for him a moral, domestic, political and an electoral one.' The real question, they believe, is whether a limited intervention can buy time for the Kurds to organise a serious counter-offensive and for Baghdad to form an inclusive government.

The Prime Minister's decision to delay such a vote and to sit and wait reflected his weakened position. Ultimately he was unwilling to act unless he was certain that he could secure the support of Parliament. While he wobbled, the USA began a series of airstrikes in Iraq and widened its focus to include Syria with the support of aircraft from Saudi Arabia and the United Arab Emirates.

The Commons case for airstrikes against ISIS in Iraq

After discussions with Nick Clegg and Ed Miliband, the Prime Minister agreed to finally hold a vote on the question of joining the US airstrikes on 26 September. The vote would come sixteen days after the President announced the expansion of US airstrikes to cover Syria as well and a month and a half after the initial American announcement of bombing in Iraq.

However to gain the Labour leader's support and avoid another loss like the year before, Cameron conceded that the motion would be limited to Iraq and not Syria. Any decision to expand airstrikes into Syria would require a further Commons vote. In the seven-hour debate, he argued that the British Government was responding to a request from the Government of Iraq for military support which gave it legal cover for its participation.[114]

Cameron made the case that the threat of ISIS, like Al Qaeda before it, risked breeding extremism at home and increasing the possibility of domestic acts of terrorism.[115] Additionally the threat the ISIS advance posed to regional neighbours, including Turkey, made it a NATO priority. In the debate he reiterated that the situation would not change the Government's policy on arming the Free Syrian Army despite the USA committing to do just that.[116]

There is a case for intervention in Syria which is not restricted by a legal barrier, but the Prime Minister argued that it was better to proceed on the basis of consensus. Leader of the Opposition Ed Miliband's speech, like those in the Syria and Libya debates focused on drawing distinctions between his position and the Iraq War in 2003.[117] He was also keen to explain the distinction between supporting airstrikes in Iraq but not Syria. This argument is founded on the notion that his opposition to military intervention in Syria the year before was still the correct decision.

Miliband argued that without an invitation from a democratic state, in the case of Syria, it would be better to seek a UN Security Council resolution. The other distinction he made was the question of ground forces. He said that while Iraq had the Iraqi Army and Peshmerga, there was no force in Syria that could fight on the ground against ISIS. His final distinction was that there was no understanding of what overall outcome the Government should seek in Syria. The basis for his support, he argued, was multilateral agreement.[118]

However this argument is fatally flawed. It firstly assumes there are different legal criteria for airstrikes in Iraq then in Syria; if this is so, the insinuation is that the USA and her coalition partner's airstrikes are illegal. Miliband is also well aware that Russia would not allow any UN Resolution on Syria and therefore such a decision would not happen. Thirdly he does not even acknowledge the Free Syrian Army, which while dramatically reduced still exist in some form in Syria.

In the end 523 MPs voted for military action while 43 opposed. Both Labour and Government MPs were whipped. William Hague is keen to point out that the decision of the Commons to back Cameron over the issue of airstrikes in Iraq is proof that he is no longer a 'back-broken' foreign policy Prime Minister as Lord Ashdown once said, as Britain is now the second biggest contributor to a different military strategy in the Middle East.[119]

Such claims however fall short, especially when we look at the actual size of Britain's deployment to Iraq. The total force accounts for a few hundred military advisers in Baghdad and six Tornado jets. As one backbench Labour MP put it to the author, 'what was all the fuss for? Britain's role in the contribution is seen as an irrelevance.' The international community waited two months to react to ISIS and Britain waited a further month before signing up to join the USA. However when it did, it did so only in Iraq and not Syria. The dithering over the possibility of gaining parliamentary support and the confusing concession to the Labour opposition demonstrate only further the weakness of Cameron in foreign policy.

It reinforced the Prime Minister's inability to act without the prior consent of Parliament and in offering a motion which MPs would find hard to oppose. The return of British forces to a military role in Iraq only reinforces its shadow over British foreign policy and its consequence of the weakened role of the Prime Minister under Cameron.

Nearly a year on and the tide has not been turned against ISIS. The airstrikes have been largely ineffectual with ISIS making gains in Iraq and Syria, capturing the Iraqi city of Ramadi and the Syrian city of Palmyra. Once again a superior Iraqi army in experience and equipment was in retreat with some in the West questioning their will to fight the ISIS threat. The West is faced once again with the question of western ground troops, while Saudi Arabia, the Gulf States and other countries of the Arab League involved in the coalition campaign have become preoccupied instead with a military intervention in Yemen. Victory against ISIS does not seem to be within sight.

Hague's departure

The greatest casualty in British foreign policy towards Syria has been William Hague, who tended his resignation and left Government on 15 July 2014. At the time he cited his desire to leave Parliament at the next election but one cannot help wondering whether the failure to end the Syrian civil war factored in his decision. As Foreign Secretary he had taken a lead role in advocating for intervention and had persuaded the Prime Minister to get on board. Where Cameron was absent, Hague was visible, shuttling between countries attempting to forge a diplomatic agreement, as well as pushing for the arming of moderate Syrian rebels and intervention on a broader scale.

After the vote on intervention in Syria was rejected there were rumours circulating around Westminster that Hague had tendered his resignation but it was rejected by the Prime Minister. Alistair Burt cannot confirm whether it was the case but does recall that Hague was very depressed after the vote.[120] The former Foreign Secretary himself is quick to reject such claims, and offers the assurance that it was planned well in advance and had little to do with government policy on Syria,[121] but one cannot help but see the disappointment and frustration that he must feel. As one former Foreign Secretary said to the author: 'William Hague will never put the knife into Cameron, he'll go. The day you see a resignation from Hague, it will be that he is unhappy with the policy but he can see that he's heading for a confrontation but he's not going to have one.'

His departure came at a crucial time as ISIS surged through Iraq. Many experts in the region had warned of this possibility for some time and it came as a by-product of first failing to create a legitimate and inclusive Government in Iraq and secondly failing to intervene effectively in Syria.

The loss of Hague will no doubt be felt in our foreign policy. In his second term Cameron, now having gained experience, will take a more hands-on approach to foreign affairs. The appointment of Philip Hammond, the former

Defence Secretary to replace Hague, will see Cameron with a far more malleable Foreign Secretary who will be on less of an equal footing than his predecessor. Some argue that a shift back to No. 10 taking more of a role in foreign policy leadership has already begun, as Baroness Warsi, a former Minister of State for the Foreign Office wrote in her resignation letter: 'There is however great unease across the Foreign Office, amongst both Ministers and senior officials, in the way recent decisions are being made.'[122]

The impact of the Coalition

The Coalition and Liberal Democrats seem to have had a limited impact on David Cameron's foreign policy. Hague points out that on Libya and Syria the two parties have seen eye to eye. He believes it has not made a difference in terms of the specific policy decisions. In fact the Liberal Democrats, who vehemently opposed the Iraq War in 2003, loyally backed Cameron on intervention in Libya, Syria and now with Iraq.[123]

Liam Fox agrees with Hague that foreign policy has not been something that the Liberals had particularly focused on. For much of the Government they did not have ministers in the Ministry of Defence or the Foreign Office.[124] Sir Menzies Campbell, former Liberal Democrat Foreign Policy Spokesman says he was surprised the leadership gave up the two junior posts because the debates and decisions are made in the departments as well as the National Security Council.[125]

The NSC as discussed earlier has built in a structure of consensus in foreign policy which was perhaps made possible by the Coalition. Lord O'Donnell certainly believes that by virtue of being in a Coalition with the Liberal Democrats there has been a broad consensus in foreign policy.[126] The only issue that has been problematic is that of the European Union and Cameron's desire to renegotiate Britain's membership. This is an issue which Nick Clegg and the Liberal Democrats have been largely left out of.

A look towards Europe and renegotiation

One former Foreign Secretary believes that Nick Clegg was shut out when Cameron flew to Brussels in December 2011 and used Britain's veto on a new EU Treaty, which would have given budgetary powers over individual member states to the European Commission. Cameron decided to do this beforehand with Chancellor George Osborne and did not tell his Deputy Prime Minister, choosing instead 'to deal with Nick when we need to'.

The greatest sticking point between the two parties has been over Cameron's decision to hold an in/out referendum on the question of Britain's membership of the European Union on 23 June 2016, which he failed to get through in the last Parliament. This pledge is a clear concession to many of his Eurosceptic backbenchers who have regularly rebelled against the Government, as well as an attempt to placate the growing popularity of the United Kingdom Independence Party which favours leaving the European Union and received 3.9 million votes in the 2015 General Election.

The issue of Europe has been particularly divisive amongst Conservative colleagues in the Cabinet as well. Hague as Foreign Secretary has been notably absent from much of the debate over Europe and the referendum. Lord Heseltine in an advisory role in the Department for Business, Skills and Enterprise offers his scepticism on Cameron's position, believing that 'the Europeans will go on and Britain will hover on the brink but you'll find that in the end we come around'.[127]

A Cabinet reshuffle in July 2014 saw the bolstering of Eurosceptic ministers. Ken Clarke, the Shadow Minister without Portfolio and prominent Europhile announced his retirement, while Dominic Grieves, the Attorney General notably in favour of the European Human Rights Act was sacked. His replacement, Jeremy Wright is a relative unknown in the legal community but supports the Prime Minister's position on scrapping the Human Rights Act. Both Michael Fallon, the new Defence Secretary and Philip Hammond the new Foreign Secretary have said in the past that they would vote to leave the European Union. Fallon described the Cabinet as certainly 'Eurosceptic' leaning, with the crucial ministries held by Eurosceptic ministers.[128]

Britain's membership and the referendum have dominated the headlines since Cameron's re-election in May 2015. The result was considered a huge upset with the polls predicting a hung parliament but instead the Conservatives gained a parliamentary majority of fifteen.

While this has been considered a great Conservative victory it still does not secure Cameron's position. Alistair Burt believes that he would need a majority of thirty or forty to cover him from the people who have an animus against him.[129] Another Conservative backbencher supports Burt's claim saying that 'they can think of fifteen bastards who would mess that up. We could certainly be in for a re-run of the early 1990s when a different Conservative Prime

Minister with a similar sized majority fought his Eurosceptic backbenchers over Britain's role in Europe.'

Cameron understands this prospect, and that is why the Friday after his re-election he met with the Chairman of the backbench 1922 Committee, which is comprised of many notable Eurosceptics, and met with its members on the Monday. He no doubt has an informal or formal arrangement with his backbenchers about the renegotiations and his future leadership of the party. Setting out on a tour of European capitals reminiscent of Macmillan, Heath and Wilson before, Cameron met with German Chancellor Angela Merkel, French Prime Minister Manuel Valls, Dutch Prime Minister Mark Rutte and Polish Prime Minister Ewa Kopacz. His aim, like Wilson and Callaghan before him is to pave the way for friendly negotiations rather than hostile demands.

The problem is that the debate around EU membership has the possibility to distract the Prime Minister from other foreign policy issues, consuming the parliamentary agenda and the Prime Minister's foreign policy agenda, in terms of the time spent discussing membership with other leaders, rather than Syria or Iraq. It raises the question of Britain's relevance in foreign affairs, the criticism that Britain is turning inwards and not focusing outwards.

Some believe that under Cameron, Britain has gone over the brink and is now completely irrelevant. One former Downing Street adviser under Blair believes,

> we've really talked ourselves out of the game in Europe, no one is coming to us and trying to make deals because why would they? They don't need the British vote. If you look at the United States we've had the pivot to Asia and Obama isn't interested in what Cameron has to say. So I think we have teetered over the edge. Not totally. We're still a medium sized power and still have as much significance as Spain

A resurgent Russia

Another prominent issue of British foreign policy under David Cameron has been Britain's increasingly complex and tense relationship with Russia. Much was made after President Obama's election in 2008 of a major resetting of relations between Russia and the West; this was helped with the stepping down of Vladimir Putin from the presidency to be replaced by his loyal supporter Dmitry Medvedev.

However Putin's resumption of the presidency, after the lifting of constitutional limits in March 2012, saw with it the resumption of tensions between

Russia and the West. The greatest factor in the reestablishment of old suspicions and strained relations has come in the differing opinions and interests over the Syrian uprisings and civil war. Assad, a long-standing ally of Russia, has been the benefactor of Russian arms and financial and political support, which has been the difference at times between his regime's impending collapse and its survival at the time of writing.

Where the current civil war in Syria has become a metaphor for the chronic paralysis of western foreign policy in the realms of meaningful intervention it has had the opposite effect on Russia's foreign policy, emboldening it. The decision not to intervene in Syria in 2013 after the use of chemical weapons by the Syrian army, despite western guarantees to the opposition force in Syria of it being a 'red line', had the direct consequence of empowering Russia to reassert its influence in Eastern Europe without fear of consequences. This was epitomised by the Russian annexation of Crimea and the civil war taking place in Ukraine.

Ukraine and Crimea

Russia has long viewed the expansion of membership of NATO and the EU with great concern. This is in part down to the generally held belief that historically Russia has been invaded when encircled. The enlargement of the European Union in 2004 to include many of its former Eastern European satellites was not welcomed by Putin or Russia, but was accepted on the basis that they would accept it as long as there was a buffer between them. This buffer took the form of Ukraine, Belarus and Georgia.

The question of NATO membership was the primary cause of the 2008 war between Georgia and Russia, which ended with NATO quietly abandoning Georgia's proposed membership. Similarly Russia viewed the proposed EU Association Agreement that Ukraine was poised to sign at the EU Summit in Vilnius on 28 November 2013 with hostility, seeing it as a precursor to full membership.

The Ukrainian President Viktor Yanukovych, despite being elected on a platform of stronger ties with the EU, came under increasing pressure from Moscow. He refused to sign the agreement, a decision which sparked mass protests in Kiev and across the whole of Ukraine calling for his removal. The issue reflected what many felt was the Yanukovych's Government's long-standing corruption. On 22 February 2014 after at least 100 protestors had lost their lives in clashes with the riot police and army, Yanukovych fled to Russia.[130]

In early March reports began to surface in Crimea of pro-Russian separatists wearing unmarked military uniforms seizing government buildings and communication hubs. At the same time Putin ordered military exercises on Ukraine's border involving around 8,500 troops, stating that Russian troops at Sevastopol naval base were being put on high alert to protect 'Russian citizens' in Crimea.[131]

The Crimean Prime Minister along with the Crimean Parliament called for Russian assistance and issued their desire to join the Russian Federation. Putin answered these calls by supporting a referendum at 'the point of a gun'. On 16 March Crimeans voted by 96.7 per cent to join Russia, declaring their independence from Ukraine.[132]

In response to the referendum Britain, the European Union and the USA imposed sanctions on Russia which included travel bans for Government officials and the freezing of their assets abroad.

Following the annexation of Crimea similar instances of pro-Russian separatists seizing government buildings and calling for independence from Ukraine occurred in the Eastern cities of Luhansk, Kramatorsk, Donetsk, Slavyansk, Yenakiyeve, Mariupol, Kharkiv and Druzhkivk. In response the Ukrainian Government conducted anti-terrorism missions against the rebels in a bid to take back the eastern part of the country. Ukrainian troops struggled in their mission finding the rebels to be well armed and well trained, rumoured to be supported by Russian Special Forces and Russian veterans.[133]

While the annexation of Crimea and the separatist rebel uprisings in Eastern Ukraine received condemnation from the European Union collectively and the USA it did not spur the international community to find a solution. Europe was particularly divided over the issue, with Britain and France pushing for more to be done but a hesitant German Chancellor, who was conscious of Germany's heavy reliance on Russia for gas.[134]

On 17 July Malaysian Airlines Flight MH17 from Amsterdam was shot down over rebel-held territory in Eastern Ukraine, killing 298 passengers and crew. The shooting down of MH17 represented a turning point in the West's view of the Ukrainian conflict and led quickly to international condemnation of Russia. David Cameron led calls for further joint sanctions amongst European leaders with the USA against Russia.[135] These sanctions targeted the Russian banking industry, trade with the Russian energy and defence sector as well as Russian assets abroad.

Meeting at the NATO Summit in Wales on 4 September, the Prime Minister gave the first commitment from European NATO countries to spend 2 per cent of GDP on defence, something which he had resisted pledging in the past. The summit also saw the creation of a NATO High Readiness Joint Task Force and a commitment for NATO troop deployments to Eastern European countries threatened by Russia including Poland, Lithuania, Latvia and Estonia.[136]

At the same time as the NATO Summit, talks in Minsk between the Ukrainian Government and leaders of the self-proclaimed rebels reached a shaky ceasefire with the help of officials from Russia and the Organisation for Security and Cooperation in Europe (OSCE).

Over the next few months the ceasefire was broken a number of times. In February 2015 German Chancellor Angela Merkel and French President François Hollande took it upon themselves to meet with Putin and try to hammer out a new peace plan. This move was seen by the UK press as a particular snub to David Cameron, with General Sir Richard Shirreff, former NATO commander, arguing that over Ukraine it reinforced the view that Cameron was a 'foreign policy irrelevance'.[137]

The agreement reached between Putin, Merkel, Hollande and new Ukrainian President Petro Poroshenko would see a new ceasefire, withdrawal of foreign militias and the decentralisation of power to the rebel regions.[138] However since the summit the agreement has not been fully enforced, the ceasefire continues to remain shaky and the future of Ukraine remains unresolved. It is a frozen conflict.

April 2015 saw the Russian economy contract by 2 per cent for the first time since 2009.[139] The slowing of Russia's economy has been seen as a validation of the US and European policy of sanctions however it also has been influenced by low oil prices. Oil prices dropped by 35 per cent in 2014[140] and at the time of writing on 28 November 2015 stands at $41.71 a barrel, a new low from $110 a year earlier.[141] This is largely down to Saudi Arabia who through OPEC has increased the production level of oil to drive down prices; this has had devastating consequences for Russian exports with oil and gas accounting for 70 per cent.[142] Sanctions paired with low oil prices have seen the Russian ruble lose half its value in 2014 and fall by 20 per cent in the summer of 2015 putting further pressure on Putin.[143]

The Cold War once again

Despite Russia's economic trouble, Putin has pushed forward with increased military spending and stepped up the projection of military power abroad. The reason for this, says Sergei Pugachev a former adviser to Putin, is that after returning to the Kremlin the President had a stark choice between liberalising the country's economy or to engineer something that would distract hard-pressed citizens from their economic woes.[144] Putin chose the latter and has used the annexation of Crimea and the rising tensions with the West as that distraction.

In 2014 Russia increased its military budget by 26 per cent in nominal terms with the aim to reach the same spending per GDP as the USA.[145] This includes putting more than forty intercontinental ballistic missiles into service, the first time it has increased its nuclear arsenal in years.[146] In response the USA has pledged to resurrect the idea of constructing an anti-ballistic missile shield in Poland.

Another factor in Russia's posturing has been the increasing number of incursions into UK airspace by Russian jets, which has become a regular occurrence since Putin's return to the Kremlin. In 2015 there were four such instances where Russian jets had to be escorted out of UK airspace.[147] Many see it as Russia attempting to test Britain's response times. Similarly in November 2015 a Russian nuclear submarine was spotted off the coast of Scotland. With the increase in military spending, Russia's nuclear arsenal, and posturing in UK airspace and territorial waters, one could be forgiven for believing that we are back in the days of the Cold War.

Russia's expanding role in Syria

The primary reason for Assad's regime's survival has been the material and political support of Russia; without it his fate would no doubt have been similar to that of Gaddafi. Prior to the Syrian civil war, Russia provided Syria with 71 per cent of its military needs;[148] this figure has no doubt risen as the country has descended further into violence and destruction.

However Assad's position has grown more unstable through 2014 and into 2015. At the end of September 2015, it was estimated that the Syrian Government controlled as little as 20 per cent of the whole of Syria.[149] ISIS and the other rebel groups seemed to have the upper hand, as ISIS made gains in a key suburb of Damascus. This concerned Russia so much that it sped up shipments of military supplies, sending tanks, new anti-aircraft missile launchers and deployed military advisers on the ground.

Assad's forces were coming close to losing control of the key road link between Damascus and Tartus, south of Homs, which connected the capital with supply lines in the coastal mountains where much of the Government's support remained. If ISIS captured and held the road it would cut off Assad from his supplies and support, destabilising the regime in a way it would not recover.[150]

In response to the threat, on 30 September 2015 Russia launched airstrikes in Syria against rebel groups designed to back up and support Assad's regime. This is the first time Russian forces had undertaken a military campaign outside of Europe since the end of the Cold War. In response to Russia's air campaign on 2 October the governments of France, Germany, Qatar, Saudi Arabia, Turkey, the USA and the UK in a joint statement criticised Russia for largely targeting moderate rebel groups and for ignoring ISIS. According to the The Royal United Services Institute, approximately 80 per cent of Russian airstrikes in the first month targeted armed opposition groups fighting the Assad regime rather than ISIS.[151]

Many analysts concluded that Russia's intervention in Syria only further complicated the situation making the establishment of a no-fly zone impossible. In the UK it had the effect of frustrating David Cameron's plans to hold a vote after summer recess on the expansion of UK airstrikes in Iraq to Syria, as well as adding weight to MPs opposed to military intervention, with the Foreign Affairs Select Committee arguing in a report that the civil war is no longer an internal war but a 'multi-layered conflict' with many now considering it a proxy war.[152]

Cameron's foreign policy

As Prime Minister, David Cameron spends more time on foreign policy than any of his predecessors. Yet his accomplishments have been few and far between. He does not have a natural interest in foreign policy. Instead he has been happy to largely take decisions in consultation with advisers and other ministers. This may be understandable given the economic recession the country was in when he assumed office and the pressing domestic commitments of a first-term premier.

The Coalition Government saw a formalisation of the way foreign policy is conducted, with the creation of the National Security Council and a permanent National Security Adviser and secretariat. This has progressed and streamlined the process of decision-making but has not prevented the Prime Minister taking informal soundings before meetings to establish a majority opinion within them. Some may argue that this was reflective of distrust between the two parties rather than Cameron's own personal dominance, yet it reinforces the image of a prime ministerial foreign policy agenda.

Since 2010 there has been huge global instability and conflict, the most notable being the Arab Spring which has fundamentally undermined stability in the Middle East and parts of North Africa. Libya, Iraq and Syria are now states in civil war, with a number of countries in the region fighting Islamic insurgencies. The international community has collectively failed to support the democratic movements in these countries, instead favouring the old order. The Arab Spring has dominated Cameron's foreign policy agenda and is in the author's mind the primary lens through which his premiership will be viewed.

While Cameron was one of the first to join intervention in Libya, he had no interest in its reconstruction and that failure has tainted much of his foreign policy. Similarly British policy on Syria has been wholly inadequate. Along with the USA, Britain failed to support a pre-existing group of moderate rebels who would have provided a credible alternative to the Assad Regime. Paired with the failure to intervene to destroy all of Assad's chemical weapons, this policy has led to the dispersal and defeat of moderate rebel forces in Syria, who, losing heart and ground, chose to defect to the stronger Islamic rebel groups or to flee.

This failure effectively to end the Syrian Civil War through force of arms or a diplomatic process has fuelled the rise of the Islamic State, and a new threat of global terrorism. Cameron's inaction paired with those of his international colleagues has had far-reaching consequences for North Africa, the Middle East and now for Europe, as it tries to deal with the wave of refugees largely fleeing Libya, Syria, Iraq and Afghanistan.

A key factor in his premiership has been the informal concession to Parliament of a vote on military action. Cameron does deserve credit for encouraging legislative oversight of foreign policy. Parliament since 2010 has voted to approve NATO airstrikes in Libya, airstrikes in Iraq as part of a US-led coalition and has voted against airstrikes in Syria. This has given the Commons a greater say in foreign policy than at any other time but it has also provided the Prime Minister with political cover over charges of indecision and inaction. It has allowed him to put off tough foreign policy decisions blaming parliamentary scepticism and a lack of a democratic mandate. It has ultimately masked weak leadership and indecisiveness.

The War in Iraq continues to hang heavily over British foreign policy, as the British public continue to maintain scepticism over military intervention particularly in the Middle East. This has certainly constrained Cameron's ability to dominate foreign policy. The negative legacy has been used to cite limited involvement in the reconstruction of Libya and of involvement in Syria. Yet it is a self-fulfilling prophecy; in trying to avoid the negative legacy of Iraq, Cameron has managed to extend it. The failed reconstruction in Libya has led the country to fall into a sectarian civil war, failure to intervene in Syria has led to the rise of ISIS and an Iraq once again divided along ethnic lines, and British planes patrolling Iraqi airspace once again.

In David Cameron, we have a Prime Minister who like his predecessor does not have a natural interest or ideological approach to foreign policy. His foreign policy is largely underpinned by Conservative pragmatism, a sense of what is both politically and technically doable. This view offers an abundance of opportunities to limit a wider role for Britain on the world stage, beyond international business and global trade. Yet it is reflective of a man who does not have a vision of Britain's role in the world and much of an interest in the trappings of international diplomacy, despite maintaining No. 10's ability to command the foreign policy agenda.

Notes

1 HM Government, 'The Coalition: Our Programme of Government', May 2010, accessed 1 August 2015: www.gov.uk/government/uploads/system/uploads/attachment_data/file/78977/coalition_programme_for_government.pdf.
2 *Ibid.*
3 W. Hague, interview with S. Goodman, 2 March 2015, House of Commons.
4 *Ibid.*
5 *Ibid.*
6 *Ibid.*
7 *Ibid.*
8 A. Burt, interview with S. Goodman, 30 January 2014, House of Commons.
9 M. Rifkind, interview with S. Goodman, 18 April 2012, House of Commons.
10 W. Hague, interview with S. Goodman, 2 March 2015, House of Commons.
11 G. O'Donnell, interview with S. Goodman, 4 September 2012, private offices.
12 W. Hague, interview with S. Goodman, 2 March 2015, House of Commons.
13 Richards, D., interview with S. Goodman, 2 December 2014, private offices.
14 L. Fox, interview with S. Goodman, 31 January 2014, House of Commons.
15 *Ibid.*
16 D. Richards, interview with S. Goodman, 2 December 2014, private offices.
17 L. Fox, interview with S. Goodman, 31 January 2014, House of Commons.

18 M. D'Ancona, *In It Together: The Inside Story of the Coalition Government* (London: Viking, 2013), p. 161.
19 B. Smith, House of Commons Library Research Paper, 'Prospects for Afghanistan as ISAF Withdrawal Approaches', Research paper 14/18 19, March 2014, P. 7, accessed 1 August 2015: http://researchbriefings.parliament.uk/ResearchBriefing/Summary/RP14-18.
20 R. Norton-Taylor, 'Commons Vote Backs Afghanistan Deployment', *Guardian*, 9 September 2010, accessed 1 August 2015: www.theguardian.com/politics/2010/sep/09/commons-backs-afghanistan-deployment.
21 *Ibid*.
22 N. Sheinwald, interview with S. Goodman, 3 July 2012, House of Commons.
23 D'Ancona, *In It Together*, p. 161.
24 D. Pearse, Afghan Civilian Death Toll Reaches Record High', *Guardian*, 4 February 2012, accessed 1 August 2015: www.theguardian.com/world/2012/feb/04/afghan-civilian-death-toll-record.
25 L. Evans, P. McClean and A. Sedghi, 'UK Soldiers Killed in "Insider" Attacks In Afghanistan – The Full List', *Guardian*, 18 September 2012, accessed 1 August 2015: www.theguardian.com/news/datablog/2012/sep/18/nato-afghanistan-insider-attacks-soldiers.
26 J. Partlow and K. Sieff, 'Ahmed Wali Karzai, Half-Brother of Afghan President, Killed by Trusted Confidant', *Washington Post*, 12 July 2011, accessed 1 August 2015: www.washingtonpost.com/world/karzais-brother-killed-by-guard-in-kandahar-home/2011/07/12/gIQAgI3FAI_story.html.
27 D. Richards, interview with S. Goodman, 2 December 2014, private offices.
28 D'Ancona, *In It Together*, p. 161.
29 P. Wintour, 'David Cameron Tells UK Troops Their Work in Afghanistan "Will Live Forever"', *Guardian*, 3 October 2014, accessed 1 August 2015: www.theguardian.com/world/2014/oct/03/david-cameron-uk-troops-afghanistan-camp-bastion.
30 T. Craig, 'Afghan President Hamid Karzai Slams U.S. Government Policy in Afghanistan', *Washington Post*, 23 September 2014, accessed 1 August 2015: www.washingtonpost.com/world/afghan-president-hamid-karzai-slams-us-government-policy-in-afghanistan/2014/09/23/a3b58cf4-4342-11e4-b47c-f5889e061e5f_story.html.
31 P. Stewart, 'U.S. to Keep More Troops in Afghanistan as Violence Spikes', Reuters, 6 December 2014, accessed 1 August 2015: http://www.reuters.com/article/2014/12/06/us-usa-afghanistan-military-idUSKBN0JK0GH20141206.
32 'Libya Protests: Defiant Gaddafi Refuses to Quit', BBC News, 22 February 2011, accessed 1 August 2015: www.bbc.co.uk/news/world-middle-east-12544624.
33 'Libya Protests: Defiant Gaddafi Refuses to Quit', BBC News, 22 February 2011, accessed 1 August 2015: www.bbc.co.uk/news/world-middle-east-12544624.

34 D'Ancona, *In It Together*, p. 165.
35 *Ibid.*, p. 165.
36 N. Watt, 'Nicolas Sarkozy Calls for Air Strikes on Libya if Gaddafi Attacks Civilians', *Guardian*, 11 March 2011, accessed 1 August 2015: www.theguardian.com/world/2011/mar/11/nicolas-sarkozy-libya-air-strikes.
37 S. Tisdall, 'Lessons From Libya: How Cameron And Sarkozy Got Lucky', *Guardian*, 13 October 2011, accessed 1 August 2015: www.theguardian.com/commentisfree/2011/oct/13/lessons-from-libya-obama-cameron-sarkozy.
38 D'Ancona, *In It Together*, p. 166.
39 'Libya's No Fly Zone: the Military Balance, Muammar Qaddafi Has Enough Military Power at his Disposal to Make Dislodging him a Bloody and Uncertain Business', *The Economist*, 3 March 2011, accessed 1 August 2015: www.economist.com/node/18291539.
40 Jeremy Bowen, *The Arab Uprisings: The People Want the Fall of the Regime* (London: Simon & Schuster, 2013), p. 140.
41 N. Watt, 'Nicolas Sarkozy Calls for Air Strikes on Libya if Gaddafi Attacks Civilians', *Guardian*, 11 March 2011, accessed 1 August 2015: www.theguardian.com/world/2011/mar/11/nicolas-sarkozy-libya-air-strikes.
42 D'Ancona, *In It Together*, pp. 165 and 167.
43 *Ibid.*, p. 168.
44 'Letter from David Cameron and Nicolas Sarkozy to Herman Van Rompuy', *Guardian*, 10 March 2011, accessed 1 August 2015: www.theguardian.com/world/2011/mar/10/libya-middleeast.
45 Tisdall, 'Lessons from Libya'.
46 D'Ancona, *In It Together*, p. 170.
47 *Ibid.*, p. 170.
48 R. Gates, *Duty*, p. 511.
49 Clinton, *Hard Choices*, pp. 370–1.
50 The United Nations Security Council, United Nations Resolution 1973, 17 March 2011, accessed 1 August 2015: www.un.org/en/ga/search/view_doc.asp?symbol=S/RES/1973(2011).
51 W. Hague, interview with S. Goodman, 2 March 2015, House of Commons.
52 'Poll: UK Divided on Combat Mission in Libya', Sky News, 22 March 2011, accessed 1 August 2015: http://news.sky.com/story/843756/poll-uk-divided-on-combat-mission-in-libya.
53 Clinton, *Hard Choices*, pp. 373–4.
54 Gates, *Duty*, p. 521.
55 Clinton, *Hard Choices*, p. 375.
56 *Ibid.*, p. 375.
57 D'Ancona, *In It Together*, p. 177.
58 D. Richards, interview with S. Goodman, 2 December 2014, private offices.

59 J. Bowen, *The Arab Uprisings: the People Want the Fall of the Regime* (London: Simon Schuster, 2013), p. 310.
60 *Ibid.*, p. 160; Clinton, *Hard Choices,* p. 212.
61 D. Cameron, 'David Cameron Libya Statement in Full', politics.co.uk, 5 September 2011, accessed 1 August 2015: www.politics.co.uk/comment-analysis/2011/09/05/david-cameron-libya-statement-in-full.
62 L. Fox, interview with S. Goodman, 31 January 2014, House of Commons.
63 Gates, *Duty*, p. 522.
64 R. Gladstone and R. Nordland, 'Cameron of Britain and Sarkozy of France Visit Libya', *New York Times*, 15 September 2011, accessed 1 August 2015: www.nytimes.com/2011/09/16/world/africa/cameron-and-sarkozy-in-tripoli-libya-to-meet-new-leaders.html?_r=0.
65 Gates, *Duty*, p. 521.
66 D'Ancona, *In It Together,* p. 171.
67 D. Richards, interview with S. Goodman, 2 December 2014, private offices.
68 *Ibid.*
69 D. Cameron, *Hansard* (HC Deb, 5 September 2011, col. 24).
70 'Full text of Ed Miliband's Foreign Policy Speech at Chatham House', Labourlist, 24 April 2014, accessed 1 August 2015: http://labourlist.org/2015/04/full-text-of-ed-milibands-foreign-policy-speech-at-chatham-house/.
71 Gates, *Duty,* p. 530.
72 M. Malloch-Brown, interview with S. Goodman, 21 August 2014, private offices.
73 *Ibid.*
74 Bowen, *The Arab Uprisings*, p. 120.
75 L. Fadel, 'Protesters Shot as Demonstrations Expand Across Syria', *Washington Post*, 25 March 2011, accessed 1 August 2015: www.washingtonpost.com/world/protesters-shot-as-demonstrations-expand-across-syria/2011/03/25/AFTnewWB_story.html.
76 Bowen, *The Arab Uprisings*, p. 121.
77 S. Speakman-Cordall, 'How Syria's Assad Helped Forge ISIS', *Newsweek*, 21 June 2014, accessed 1 August 2015: www.newsweek.com/how-syrias-assad-helped-forge-isis-255631.
78 'Syria Unrest: Fierce Firefight Erupts in Damascus', BBC News, 19 March 2012, accessed 1 August 2015: www.bbc.co.uk/news/world-middle-east-17425062.
79 The United Nations, 'Six-Point Proposal of the Joint Special Envoy of the United Nations and the League of Arab States', 14 April 2012, accessed 1 August 2015: www.un.org/en/peacekeeping/documents/six_point_proposal.pdf.
80 I. Black, 'Kofi Annan Resigns as Syria Envoy', *Guardian*, 2 August 2012, accessed 1 August 2015: www.theguardian.com/world/2012/aug/02/kofi-annan-resigns-syria-envoy.
81 M. Malloch-Brown, interview with S. Goodman, 21 August 2014, private offices.

82 Ibid.
83 D. Lesch, *Syria: The Fall of the House of Assad* (London: Yale University Press, 2013), p. 136.
84 A. Burt, interview with S. Goodman, 30 January 2014, House of Commons.
85 D. Richards, interview with S. Goodman, 2 December 2014, private offices; N. Hopkins, 'Syria Conflict: UK Planned to Train and Equip 100,000 Rebels', BBC News, 3 July 2014, accessed 1 August 2015: http://www.bbc.co.uk/news/uk-28148943.
86 D. Richards, interview with S. Goodman, 2 December 2014, private offices.
87 Ibid.
88 R. Akkoc, 'Britain Planned to Train and Equip 100,000 Syrian Rebels', *Telegraph*, 4 July 2012, accessed 1 August 2015: www.telegraph.co.uk/news/worldnews/middleeast/syria/10945457/Britain-planned-to-train-and-equip-100000-Syrian-rebels.html.
89 D. Richards, interview with S. Goodman, 2 December 2014, private offices; Seldon and Snowden, *Cameron At 10*, pp. 327–8.
90 R. Dannatt, interview with S. Goodman, 21 October 2014, House of Lords.
91 A. Burt, interview with S. Goodman, 30 January 2014, House of Commons.
92 I. Traynor, 'UK Forces EU to Lift Embargo on Syria Rebel Arms', *Guardian*, 28 May 2013, accessed 1 August 2015: www.theguardian.com/world/2013/may/28/uk-forced-eu-embargo-syria-rebel-arms; Seldon and Snowden, *Cameron at 10*, p. 329.
93 M. Malloch-Brown, interview with S. Goodman, 21 August 2014, private offices.
94 M. Chorley and T. Shipman, 'Cabinet Split Over Plans to Arm Syrian Rebels: Cameron Under Pressure Amid Claims Peace Talks Are "Doomed to Fail"', *Daily Mail*, 6 June 2013, accessed 1 August 2015: www.dailymail.co.uk/news/article-2336720/Cabinet-split-plans-arm-Syrian-rebels-Cameron-pressure-claims-peace-talks-doomed-fail.html#ixzz3lRTfWiPF.
95 L. Fox, interview with S. Goodman, 31 January 2014, House of Commons.
96 W. Hague, interview with S. Goodman, 2 March 2015, House of Commons.
97 M. Chulov, 'Isis: the Inside Story', *Guardian*, 11 December 2014, accessed 1 August 2015: www.theguardian.com/world/2014/dec/11/-sp-isis-the-inside-story.
98 Speakman-Cordall, 'How Syria's Assad Helped Forge ISIS'.
99 R. Sherlock and R. Spencer, 'Syria's Assad Accused of Boosting Al-Qaeda With Secret Oil Deals', *Telegraph*, 20 January 2014, accessed 1 August 2015: www.telegraph.co.uk/news/worldnews/middleeast/syria/10585391/Syrias-Assad-accused-of-boosting-al-Qaeda-with-secret-oil-deals.html.
100 W. Hague, interview with S. Goodman, 2 March 2015, House of Commons.
101 D. Richards, interview with S. Goodman, 2 December 2014, private offices.
102 K. Sengupta, 'Syrian Rebels Consider Joining Forces With Regime Troops to Fight Al-Qa'ida', *Independent*, 3 December 2013, accessed 1 August 2015:

www.independent.co.uk/news/world/middle-east/syrian-rebels-consider-joining-forces-with-regime-troops-to-fight-alqaida-8981081.html.
103 'Syrian Government and Opposition Trade Accusations at Geneva II Talks', *Guardian*, 10 February 2014, accessed 1 August 2015: www.theguardian.com/world/2014/feb/10/syrian-government-opposition-trade-accusations-geneva-ii.
104 W. Hague, interview with S. Goodman, 2 March 2015, House of Commons.
105 'Bashar al-Assad Wins Re-Election in Syria as Uprising Against Him Rages on', *Guardian*, 4 June 2014 accessed 1 August 2015: www.theguardian.com/world/2014/jun/04/bashar-al-assad-winds-reelection-in-landslide-victory.
106 D. Kirkpatrick, 'Graft Hobbles Iraq's Military in Fighting ISIS', *New York Times*, 23 November 2014, accessed 1 August 2015: www.nytimes.com/2014/11/24/world/middleeast/graft-hobbles-iraqs-military-in-fighting-isis.html?emc=edit_th_20141124&nl=todaysheadlines&nlid=68502098&_r=0.
107 'Maliki Confirms Syrian Planes Have Bombed Isis Positions', *Guardian*, 26 June 2014, accessed 1 August 2015: www.theguardian.com/world/2014/jun/26/maliki-syrian-planes-bomb-iraq-isis-us.
108 R. Jalabi, 'Who Are the Yazidis and Why is Isis Hunting Them?", *Guardian*, 11 August 2014, accessed 1 August 2015: www.theguardian.com/world/2014/aug/07/who-yazidi-isis-iraq-religion-ethnicity-mountains.
109 R. Syal, 'Iraq Crisis: David Cameron Under Pressure to Recall Parliament', *Guardian*, 11 August 2014, accessed 1 August 2015: www.theguardian.com/world/2014/aug/11/iraq-crisis-david-cameron-pressure-recall-parliament.
110 T. Watson, 'We Cannot Abandon Iraq to the Black Flag of ISIS – Parliament Must Be Recalled', Labourlist, 8 August 2014, accessed 1 August 2015: http://labourlist.org/2014/08/we-cannot-abandon-iraq-to-the-black-flag-of-isis-parliament-must-be-recalled/.
111 'Iraq Crisis: General Says UK "Commitment-Phobic"', BBC News, 12 August 2014, accessed 1 August 2015: http://www.bbc.co.uk/news/uk-28750491.
112 W. Jordan, 'Majority Now Support RAF Air Strikes', YouGov, 8 September 2014, accessed 1 August 2015: https://yougov.co.uk/news/2014/09/08/majority-now-support-raf-air-strikes-iraq-and-syri/.
113 R. Dannatt, interview with S. Goodman, 21 October 2014, House of Lords.
114 D. Cameron, *Hansard* (HC Deb, 26 September 2014, col. 1263).
115 *Ibid.*, col. 1262.
116 *Ibid.*, col. 1259.
117 E. Miliband, *Hansard* (HC Deb, 26 September 2014 col. 1274).
118 *Ibid.*, col. 1270.
119 W. Hague, interview with S. Goodman, 2 March 2015, House of Commons.
120 A. Burt, interview with S. Goodman, 30 January 2014, House of Commons.
121 W. Hague, interview with S. Goodman, 2 March 2015, House of Commons.

122 'In Full: Warsi's Resignation Letter and PM's Response', BBC News, 5 August 2014, accessed 1 August 2015: www.bbc.co.uk/news/uk-politics-28657623.
123 W. Hague, interview with S. Goodman, 2 March 2015, House of Commons.
124 L. Fox, interview with S. Goodman, 31 January 2014, House of Commons.
125 M. Campbell, interview with S. Goodman, 9 September 2013, House of Commons.
126 G. O'Donnell, interview with S. Goodman, 4 September 2012, private offices.
127 M. Heseltine, interview with S. Goodman, 30 May 2012, Department for Business, Innovation and Skill.
128 'Cabinet "Certainly Eurosceptic", Says Michael Fallon', BBC News, 16 July 2014, accessed 1 August 2015: www.bbc.co.uk/news/uk-politics-28324237.
129 A. Burt, interview with S. Goodman, 30 January 2014, House of Commons.
130 Human Rights Watch, World Report 2015 Chapter Ukraine, January 2015 accessed 7 February 2015: www.hrw.org/sites/default/files/related_material/ukraine_3.pdf.
131 Y. Kravtsova, 'Russia Heightens Tension With Military Exercises Near Ukrainian Border", *Telegraph*, 13 March 2014, accessed 28 November 2015: www.telegraph.co.uk/news/worldnews/europe/ukraine/10695077/Russia-heightens-tension-with-military-exercises-near-Ukrainian-border.html.
132 S. Smith, 'Why Should the Crimean Referendum Not Be Recognised?', Foreign & Commonwealth Office Blog, 17 March 2014, accessed 28 November 2015: http://webarchive.nationalarchives.gov.uk/20141204000047/http://blogs.fco.gov.uk/simonsmith/2014/03/17/why-should-the-crimean-referendum-not-be-recognised/.
133 M. Hendrick, 'The Ukrainian Crisis: Russia's Relationship With Former Soviet States Post EU/NATO Enlargement', *EP Today*, 9 May 2014, accessed 28 November 2015: http://eptoday.com/ukrainian-crisis-russias-relationship-soviet-states-post-eunato-enlargement/.
134 S. Meichtry and N. Winning, 'European Rifts Emerge Over Sanctions for Russia', *Wall Street Journal*, 19 March 2014, accessed 28 November 2015: http://www.wsj.com/articles/SB10001424052702303287804579447513076140776.
135 A. Chakelian, 'David Cameron Calls For More Sanctions on Russia After the MH17 Crash', *New Statesman*, 21 July 2014, accessed 28 November 2015: www.newstatesman.com/politics/2014/07/david-cameron-calls-more-sanctions-russia-after-mh17-crash.
136 L. Brooke-Holland and C. Mills, 'NATO Wales Summit 2014: Outcomes', House of Commons Research Library, 12 September 2014, accessed 28 November 2015: http://researchbriefings.parliament.uk/ResearchBriefing/Summary/SN06981.
137 B. Riley-Smith, 'David Cameron a "Foreign Policy Irrelevance" Over Russia, Says Britain's Former Top Commander in Nato', *Telegraph*, 6 February 2015,

accessed 28 November 2015: www.telegraph.co.uk/news/politics/
liberaldemocrats/11394788/David-Cameron-a-foreign-policy-irrelevance-over
-Russia-says-Britains-former-top-commander-in-Nato.html.

138 A. Luhn and M. Weaver, 'Ukraine Ceasefire Agreed at Belarus Talks', *Guardian*, 12 February 2015, accessed 28 November 2015: www.theguardian.com/world/2015/feb/12/ukraine-crisis-reports-emerge-of-agreement-in-minsk-talks.

139 'Russian Economy Shrinks 2% as Sanctions Bite – Medvedev', BBC News, 21 April 2015, accessed 28 November 2015: www.bbc.co.uk/news/world-europe-32396792.

140 M. Stephens, 'Why is Saudi Arabia Using Oil as a Weapon?', BBC News, 3 December 2014, accessed 28 November 2015: www.bbc.co.uk/news/world-middle-east-30289546.

141 Oil Price Net, Crude Oil and Commodity Prices, 29 November 2015, accessed 29 November 2015: www.oil-price.net/.

142 L. Elliot, 'Stakes Are High as US Plays the Oil Card Against Iran and Russia', *Guardian*, 9 November 2014, accessed 28 November 2015: www.theguardian.com/business/economics-blog/2014/nov/09/us-iran-russia-oil-prices-shale.

143 S. Forbes, 'Why Russia is Wrecking the Ruble', *Forbes Magazine*, 16 December 2014, accessed 28 November 2015: www.forbes.com/sites/steveforbes/2014/12/16/why-russia-is-wrecking-the-ruble/; L. Ragozin, 'Russia's Ruble Falls to All Time Low on China's "Black Monday"', UAToday, 24 August 2015, accessed 28 November 2015: http://uatoday.tv/business/russia-s-ruble-falls-to-all-time-low-on-china-s-quot-black-monday-quot-480641.html.

144 L. Harding, 'Sergei Pugachev: "Putin's Banker" Now Lives In Fear Of Man He Put Into Power', *Guardian*, 28 July 2015, accessed 28 November 2015: www.theguardian.com/world/2015/jul/28/sergei-pugachev-putins-banker-interview-lives-in-fear.

145 M. Adomanis, 'Russian Military Spending: Drawing Blood From a Stone', *Forbes Magazine*, 19 May 2015, accessed 28 November 2015: www.forbes.com/sites/markadomanis/2015/05/19/russian-military-spending-drawing-blood-from-a-stone/.

146 A. Withnall, 'Vladimir Putin Announces Russia Will Add More Than 40 Intercontinental Ballistic Missiles to Nuclear Arsenal in 2015', *Independent*, 17 June 2015, accessed 28 November 2015: www.independent.co.uk/news/world/europe/vladimir-putin-announces-russia-will-add-40-new-ballistic-missiles-to-nuclear-arsenal-in-2015-10323304.html.

147 D. Lidington, Written Answer, Foreign & Commonwealth Office, 6 July 2015, *Hansard*, accessed 28 November 2015: www.theyworkforyou.com/wrans/?id=2015-07-01.5072.h&s=russian+jets#g5072.q0.

148 'Obama: Russia's Strategy in Syria "Doomed to Fail"', Al Jazeera, 11 September 2015, accessed 28 November 2015: www.aljazeera.com/news/2015/09/russia-continue-supply-arms-syria-assad-150911100637986.html.
149 'Why Russia is an Ally of Assad', *The Economist*, 30 September 2015, accessed 28 November 2015: www.economist.com/blogs/economist-explains/2015/09/economist-explains-22.
150 *Ibid.*
151 L. Brooke-Holland, C. Mills and B. Smith, 'ISIS/Daesh: the military Response in Iraq and Syria', House of Commons Research Library Paper, 3 November 2015, accessed 28 November 2015: http://researchbriefings.parliament.uk/ResearchBriefing/Summary/SN06995.
152 House of Commons Foreign Affairs Committee, 'The Extension of Offensive British Military Operations to Syria', 29 October 2015, accessed 28 November 2015: www.publications.parliament.uk/pa/cm201516/cmselect/cmfaff/457/457.pdf.

Conclusion

This book has chronicled the increasingly personalised and dominant role of the Prime Minster in foreign policy. It is hard to dispute the impact that a Prime Minister's personality and personal inclinations have on shaping foreign policy decision making both in the process of how decisions are reached but also over their implementation. The individual occupant's choices affect everything.

Foreign policy choices reflect a premier's personal strengths as well as their shortcomings. Sometimes these strengths can also become great weaknesses; for Margaret Thatcher her tendency to divide the world between those who were with her and those who were against her was a great advantage in fighting the 'conviction'-fuelled Cold War but became increasingly problematic when she dealt with other European leaders.

A Prime Minister's experience or personal interest in international relations is often a key factor on wider decisions and their impact. Jim Callaghan was shaped by his time at the Foreign Office since when he assumed the premiership he already had long-standing relations with all of the world leaders which he could put to good use. Tony Blair had a natural interest in the history of conflicts and conflict prevention before entering No. 10.

Similarly even a less active Prime Minister indirectly influences foreign policy by the prime ministerial appointment of Cabinet ministers (particularly who they choose as Foreign Secretary), foreign policy advisers and those they invite into their 'inner circle'. Gordon Brown's decision to appoint rival David Miliband as Foreign Secretary and to isolate him from his inner circle did have an impact on the foreign policy decision-making process. Similarly David Cameron's decision to appoint William Hague, a seasoned politician, to Foreign Secretary and to have him as a close adviser had an equal impact on the way foreign policy decisions in the Coalition Government were made.

The Prime Minister now spends more time on foreign affairs and international relations than at any time in the past, and certainly more time than on any other issue. Even if a prime minister has no endearing interest in foreign policy, and seeks to delegate or focus their attention elsewhere, it does not change the fact that the nature of modern diplomacy requires a prime minister's active cooperation and personal input far more so than ever before. President

Obama or President Putin wants to deal with the prime minister personally, not their foreign ministers or any advisers, no matter how able they are.

Yet discussion of foreign policy in our public life is severely deficient in comparison to domestic concerns. In the 2015 General Election campaign, foreign policy was rarely mentioned. The Labour Leader of the Opposition and candidate for Prime Minister, Ed Miliband gave only one speech on foreign policy. Aside from Europe, which was focused on domestic concerns, it was rarely mentioned in the prime ministerial debates. In Jeremy Paxman's BBC in-depth interviews with the leaders he asked only two questions on foreign policy, one to David Cameron about the collapse of the state of Libya and another to Ed Miliband on the situation in Syria.

It is incumbent on both the national media through its reporting and ordinary citizens to recognise the shift of the Prime Minister's role in foreign policy and to move the debate accordingly. So much of the job is now foreign policy based, as every domestic issue increasingly needs international or European support. The devolution of power to regional assemblies, parliaments and to cities and mayors also means that more public services, taxes and local decisions are now the responsibility of other bodies, freeing the premier to focus on international responsibilities.

We need a societal change towards vetting those who seek the premiership against their ability to conduct foreign policy and the personal qualities needed as an international diplomat and de facto commander-in-chief. In both France and the USA a significant factor in the electing of their Executive is the consideration of how they would conduct themselves on the world stage with other leaders and their ability to deal with foreign policy crises. Such a process should be replicated in the United Kingdom.

Over the last few years we have seen the emergence of an informal convention that Parliament should be consulted and able to vote on military action, as well as the creation of a formal National Security Council. Both of these evolutions offer clear oversight against prime ministerial overreach in foreign policy but parliamentary involvement in particular has allowed for paralysis in our foreign policy. It has allowed for the politicisation of foreign policy issues, which at times has undermined the traditional bipartisan approach that foreign policy has often engendered. Ironically the national interest may have suffered as a consequence. There is a need for formal parameters establishing Parliament's role and a mechanism for the Prime Minister to react rapidly to world events, without having to wait for prior approval, in certain circumstances. Essentially we need a Parliamentary War Powers Act.

Most members of parliament do not have an interest or expertise in foreign affairs. Instead they are focused largely on domestic issues and the interests of their electoral constituents. Some see foreign policy largely through an ideological position. A formal role for Parliament may encourage members to expand their knowledge on foreign policy and garner an interest, which would see real legislative scrutiny of a premier's foreign policy as well as real debate.

These reforms should include the strengthening and updating of the role of the Foreign Affairs Select Committee, to scrutinise not just the work of the Foreign Office but the work of No. 10 and the Prime Minister in foreign policy. The Prime Minister should be compelled to testify as he does to the Joint Select Committee. A secret vote in the Committee on possible military intervention could be an effective sounding board prior to a vote in the full Commons, indicating to a Prime Minister the opinion of the legislative branch without biasing other members' opinions.

There needs to be a wider understanding of the fluidity of foreign policy. International crises are not static and do not operate in a vacuum. Often there are short windows of opportunity to act and intervene or face a worse situation later on. This is particularly evident in Syria at the time of writing. From 2011 to the end of 2013 the international community had a chance to offer assistance to moderate opposition, composed of those who had initially revolted against the Assad regime. The Free Syrian Army, made up of soldiers who had defected from the Government and moderate civilians, was estimated at its height in July 2012 to be anywhere between 30,000 to 100,000-strong.[1] It was calculated at the time of the vote in the House of Commons that rebel forces effectively controlled 60 per cent of the country; of that 60 per cent at least 30 per cent was controlled by the Free Syrian Army (this included Aleppo, Syria's second largest city, and parts of Damascus).[2] The Syrian National Council was set up in 2011 to create an alternative political structure for all minorities opposed to the Syrian Government, composed of Kurds, Shias, Sunnis and Christians. It was designed to deliberately avoid sectarian conflict at the point of Assad being overthrown, as seen in Libya and Iraq.

Since the parliamentary vote the situation in Syria has drastically changed, with the Islamic State of Iraq and the Levant (ISIL) and the other Islamist rebels making headway, the moderate rebels have largely stagnated, fled or defected. This is reflected by the revelation that since 2014 the USA has only trained four or five rebels, well below its target of 5,000.[3] Since the parliamentary vote the composition of the rebels has dramatically changed from a more or less 50–50 moderate to extremist element to an almost exclusively extremist element in

2015. It is a topic of great debate to consider how that composition might have been affected if the vote had gone the other way and the moderates were supported instead of abandoned.

The stark choice is now between the embattled dictatorial Assad regime and Islamic extremists and there is no end in sight for the conflict. Commentators predict the Syrian Civil War could go on as long as the fifteen-year civil war neighbouring Lebanon faced. There was a small window to act and force a clear outcome. That window is now closed.

In Libya in 2011 the West faced the opposite problem. Both French President Nicolas Sarkozy and David Cameron identified the short window to act after Gaddafi threatened a bloodletting in Benghazi and they moved quickly to establish consensus for intervention within NATO, the Arab League and the UN, convincing even the sceptical US President. The window was identified and action was taken. However that enthusiasm and momentum to intervene was not matched by such similar efforts in the post-war reconstruction. The hopes of forging a stable post-Gaddafi state slipped away as the days and months passed with Libya joining Syria in open civil conflict.

The other part of understanding the fluidity of foreign policy is recognising the butterfly effect of decision making. Inaction is still a decision and can have just as far-reaching consequences as the choice to act. A foreign policy of deferral is dangerous. What, with the benefit of hindsight, would our political leaders in Parliament now say about the far-reaching implications of the House of Commons vote on 29 August 2013; would they consider voting in a different way had they the chance? There can certainly be no doubt that this vote has had lasting damage on David Cameron's premiership even if not discussed frequently. It ruled out any possibility of western intervention against the Assad Regime, undermined any moderate opposition but more so it empowered Russia. It is no coincidence that within months of the West backing down over its 'red line' to intervene if chemical weapons were used on civilians by the Assad Regime, Russia annexed Crimea and is continuing to destabilise Eastern Ukraine.

In international diplomacy, as in life, your word is your bond and a Prime Minister breaks it at his or her peril. Whether establishing a red line of intervention over the use of chemical weapons was a realistic or well thought out policy, is a side point. Once President Obama set out this 'red line' and Cameron backed it they needed to follow through. The decision to back down sent a clear signal to other world leaders that there was no appetite in the western world for military intervention irrespective of the circumstances and that

Cameron and Obama personally should not be taken at their word. To Russian President Vladimir Putin in particular it meant that when the Ukrainian President Viktor Yanukovych was ousted by pro-democracy protestors in February 2014, Putin could choose to destabilise Ukraine militarily and annex Crimea without any significant concern of a military response from NATO or his British counterpart.

Some may argue that the rise of the so-called Islamic State and the decision to deploy the Royal Air Force to join a US-led coalition conducting airstrikes against ISIS in Iraq invalidates this view. However, nearly a year after the beginning of the bombing campaign Martin Dempsey, the chairman of the US Joint Chiefs of Staff has called the fight against ISIS 'tactically stalemated'.[4] ISIS has largely held onto the size of territory under its control. While its presence around Baghdad, the Iraqi city of Tikrit and along the north-western border with Turkey has receded, it has expanded in central Syria near Palmyra and in Iraq near Ramdi (rebel groups now control 5/6ths of Syria).[5] Airpower has had a limited impact and many British and American military commanders believe that only ground troops will defeat ISIS.[6] Yet there is little public and parliamentary appetite for such a decision.

The final point is one that arises in every foreign policy book. It addresses the ongoing role of Britain in the world. This has been a recurring theme throughout this book. Looking at the remarkable role Britain has played in international events throughout the last fifty years, it is clear that it continues to have a pivotal role to play on the world stage.

A popular view is that Britain's role in the world is diminished and irrelevant, that it should turn inwardly or limit its world view to Europe. This argument is deeply misguided. While in military and hard power terms it is certainly true that Britain is smaller, in soft power terms it is still one of the most important players in the world. Not only is the international aid budget as a percentage of GDP the sixth largest in the world but Britain has some of the oldest and strongest relations with countries across the world. Its influence and relationships stretch globally and are matched by one of the most competent and effective diplomatic corps. Britain still engenders great respect – when it talks others listen.

What remains a truth regardless is that diplomacy is and has always been a matter of personal relationships and individual character and every modern analysis shows this trend shows no signs of abating. Soft power is limited only by the vision and characteristics of the occupant of No. 10, who ultimately decides how we utilise our history and international relationships and to what end. Perhaps idealistically, it should be said that if this power is mastered by a capable premier, it can be used for the betterment of the whole world.

Notes

1 'Over 100,000 Defected from Syrian Army, Arab League Monitor Report', Ya Libnan, 10 July 2012, accessed 1 August 2015: http://yalibnan.com/2012/07/10/over-100000-defected-from-syrian-army-report/; M. Kelley, 'A Full Extremist-To-Moderate Spectrum Of The 100,000 Syrian Rebels', Business Insider, 19 September 2013, accessed 1 August 2015: www.businessinsider.com.au/graphic-the-most-accurate-breakdown-of-the-syrian-rebels-2013–9.
2 B. Hubbard, 'Momentum Shifts in Syria, Bolstering Assad's Position', New York Times, 17 July 2012, accessed 1 August 2015: www.nytimes.com/2013/07/18/world/middleeast/momentum-shifts-in-syria-bolstering-assads-position.html?_r=1.
3 'Syria Crisis: "Only Four or Five" US-Trained Syrian Rebels Are Still Fighting', BBC News, 17 September 2015, accessed 14 November 2015: www.bbc.co.uk/news/world-middle-east–34278233.
4 K. Gilsinan, 'How ISIS Territory Has Changed Since the U.S. Bombing Campaign Began', The Atlantic, 11 September 2015, accessed 14 November 2015: www.theatlantic.com/international/archive/2015/09/isis-territory-map-us-campaign/404776/.
5 T. Dzimwasha, 'Isis in Syria: Islamic State and Other Rebels Now Control Most of the Country', International Business Times, 22 August 2015, accessed 14 November 2015: www.ibtimes.co.uk/isis-syria-islamic-state-other-rebels-now-control-most-country-1516616; K. Gilsinan, 'How ISIS Territory Has Changed'.
6 J. Halliday, 'Ex-Army Chief Urges PM to Consider "Boots on the Ground" To Fight Isis', Guardian, 24 May 2015, accessed 1 August 2015: www.theguardian.com/world/2015/may/24/ex-army-chief-urges-pm-to-consider-boots-on-the-ground-to-fight-isis.

Epilogue

This book opened with a vote on intervention in Syria, it now closes with a vote on intervention in Syria. On 2 December 2015, two years and three months since the last vote, MPs assembled to debate extending airstrikes from Iraq into Syria.

A number of events in the weeks before had pushed the Government to first delay and then speed up its timetable for a vote in the House of Commons. Initially, David Cameron hoped to put a vote on expanding airstrikes to Syria in October 2015, but his plans were thwarted by the Foreign Affairs Select Committee which argued that he had not met the requirements of a legal basis for intervention, consideration of the military challenges, the political situation, other international actors and the capacity for diplomacy.[1]

However the bombing of Russian airliner KGL9268 on 31 October over Egypt, which killed 224 people, and the terrorist attacks on Paris on the evening of 13 November which killed 130 people, drastically changed the public mood. A similar attack happened the day before in Beirut killing 42 people and a week before that in Ankara killing 300. The attacks in Paris, like 7/7 and 9/11, shook the public conscience. All over the world there was an outpouring of sympathy. Many on social media posted the French flag and iconic buildings across the world were lit up with French colours.

In response to the attacks, French President François Hollande declared a state of emergency, ordered domestic counter-terrorist raids, placed restrictions on France's borders, and stepped up airstrikes in Syria against ISIS. Addressing the French Assembly, he said France was at war and encouraged his allies to join him in tackling ISIS.[2]

The attacks reignited ongoing peace talks in Vienna, which had already moved in a positive direction, with the inclusion of Iran and a more cooperative Russian approach, since Russia's widening involvement in Syria. All participants agreed to readopt the 2012 Geneva Communiqué and to designate the UN to restart direct talks between the Syrian Government and moderate Syrian rebel groups over a transitional government[3] leading to monitored elections.

On 20 November 2015, the United Nations Security Council unanimously passed UN Resolution 2249 condemning the recent attacks and calling member states to: 'to take all necessary measures, in compliance with international law, in particular with the United Nations Charter…to redouble and coordinate their efforts to prevent and suppress terrorist acts committed specifically by ISIL…and to eradicate the safe haven they have established over significant parts of Iraq and Syria.'[4] The Resolution reflects the first time that there has been unity in the Council on the Syrian Civil War, breaking four years of deadlock. Many consider it offered clear legal precedent and UN authorisation for military action against ISIS by all member states.

For David Cameron the Paris attacks and the downing of the Russian airliner only reinforced his view that Britain needed to expand UK airstrikes into Syria and attack ISIS in the heartland of its territory. However despite the public outpouring of support for France, he knew this would not be an easy task.

The UK had been in a precarious position since Parliament voted in August 2014 to launch airstrikes in Iraq but not in Syria, a decision which had put British foreign policy largely out of sync with their close allies France and the USA, who were already launching airstrikes in both countries. Still reeling from the Commons rejection of intervention in 2013, Cameron had accepted its decision on the basis that expanding the bombing in Syria would become a natural precursor to be debated at a later date.

The combination of a number of sceptical Tory backbenchers and a new leader of the Labour Party with a reputation for being openly anti-war, meant that any vote would be close. Another loss in the Commons would be fatal not only to his own premiership but to the future prestige of the office, as well as wider UK foreign policy.

Paris had brought the Syrian Civil War and the question of defeating ISIS to the forefront of public consciousness on the issue, which while beneficial also looked to complicate things. Despite the Syrian Civil War being in its fifth year, many members of the public had not paid much attention to its growing developments. The sudden surge in public debate after Paris brought with it a cloud of misinformation which overwhelmed any meaningful debate on the subject. High emotions on the issue of war seemed to polarise and divide opinions on extending airstrikes into Syria.

Nowhere was this division of opinion more evident than within the Parliamentary Labour Party. Labour's position on expanding airstrikes was complicated and confused by conflicting opinions between Labour leader, Jeremy Corbyn and his Shadow Cabinet, in particular Shadow Foreign

Secretary Hilary Benn. The decisive factor in the outcome of the vote would be the decision by Corbyn whether to whip Labour MPs into opposing airstrikes.

Initially he had hinted that there would be a free vote but a few days later Corbyn stated that the party would come to a common position, implying that he would whip the vote. The problem the Labour leader found himself in was that as someone who had rebelled against the whip in past votes on military intervention, any attempt to whip the vote would be met with claims of hypocrisy and consequently, open defiance.

Consequently Corbyn was under conflicting pressure from many in the Parliamentary Labour Party for a free vote and from many Labour activists to whip the vote against. Elected by a large majority and under a new system allowing non-members to make a one-off payment to vote, he believed he had a clear mandate from Labour Party members to push for a whipped vote.[5] However in a Shadow Cabinet meeting on Friday 27 November, a number of Shadow ministers made it clear that if there was not a free vote they would resign. The meeting ended with a decision to be confirmed on the Monday of the week of the vote.[6] Corbyn used the weekend to reach out directly to party members to survey their views and directing them and members of the grass-roots organisation 'Momentum' to lobby Labour MPs directly.[7]

Over the weekend MPs returned to their constituencies to consult members, constituents and their consciences. After a Shadow Cabinet meeting it was agreed that Labour MPs would have a free vote. In response some on the left of the party argued that Corbyn had just handed the Prime Minister victory.[8] However Cameron still estimated that he would need at least thirty to forty Labour MPs to vote with the Government to offset rebels on his own side.

This would not be an easy feat. Public opinion on the matter intensified and polarised further. Those against airstrikes compared the vote to the 2003 decision to invade Iraq and held mass demonstrations in large numbers in London and around the rest of the country, while those who favoured airstrikes accused opponents of being pacifists and appeasers.

Ordinary MPs, some only a few months in the job, found themselves under great pressure, being bombarded by phone calls and inundated with emails to oppose. Some had their offices and homes picketed by protestors and some even received death threats. The situation had largely got out of control.

Falsehoods existed on both sides of the argument. Those opposed made assertions that ISIS was funded and armed by the governments of Turkey and the Gulf States and that the best way to stop ISIS, like any ordinary state, would be to cut off its funding and arms. In truth, much of the organisation's funding comes from individual donors, taxes levied, towns looted and their lucrative ransom and slave trade, while they inherited the vast cache of their arms from the Iraqi and Syrian army as well as other rebel groups they had defeated or captured in battle.

The Prime Minister asserted that there were 70,000 moderate rebels who could fight ISIS and be supported as troops on the ground, a clear alternative to supporting Assad's forces, which had been the most contentious subject when discussing intervention. This statement first emerged in Cameron's briefing to the House on 26 November and he repeated it again on the day of the debate, although it was not backed up by credible figures.[9] In fact No. 10 was warned by a senior Ministry of Defence official that this figure was misleading.[10] As further inspection shows, the 70,000 are comprised of at least 400 different groups, many of whom are local fighters, who while not as extreme as ISIS are by no means a coherent fighting force with democratic ideals.

On the day of the vote, there was a tense atmosphere around the Palace of Westminster, made worse by comments of David Cameron in a closed meeting with the 1922 Committee coming to light, warning Tory backbench MPs against voting alongside 'a bunch of terrorist sympathisers'.[11]

His comments brought a poisonous atmosphere to the Chamber, as he was asked a number of times by opposition MPs to apologise and 'to clear the air' for the slur which they argued was unbecoming of the office of Prime Minister.[12] He refused but looked increasingly sheepish as MPs were distracted from the important and complicated arguments and counter-arguments for intervention and delayed the substantive debate.

Cameron's remarks reflected the increasingly partisan nature of the debate. It had become about the personal differences between himself and Corbyn, which paralleled the differences between an increasingly right-leaning Conservative Party and an increasingly left-leaning Labour Party. Intervention in Syria was just one of many issues over which the two sides fervently disagreed. The tension in the remarks also showed how close the vote might be.

Despite Tory MPs being whipped to support the Government, many were still uncertain about airstrikes. The Liberal Democrats, all eight of them, were whipped to vote in favour, the Northern Irish Democratic Unionist Party similarly offered the Government the support of its MPs. While all 54 Scottish Nationalist MPs pledged to vote against, who would be joined by a large portion of Labour MPs, many Labour MPs had still not made their minds up.

The Labour Party was in the unique and curious position of having the unofficial Prime Minister in waiting take a position against intervention and the Foreign Secretary in waiting taking a position supporting it. In normal circumstances such a peculiar disagreement would not be allowed to exist, but on this most particular day it did. An Opposition is a shadow government. The way it conducts itself is representative of how it would conduct itself in government. In government, a prime minister and his foreign secretary would never be allowed to disagree publicly. It would be catastrophic in terms of foreign policy.

Labour MPs received two separate party briefings, one from Corbyn arguing that the Prime Minister had not made the case for expanding the airstrikes and one from Hilary Benn saying the contrary. Both referred to a resolution passed at the September Labour Party Conference which listed a number of requirements that would have to be met before the Party could support the Government. These included the clear and unambiguous authorisation from the United Nations, an EU-wide plan to provide humanitarian assistance to the refugees bombing might create, assurances that such bombing would be exclusively directed at military targets associated with ISIS and that any military action be subordinated to international diplomatic efforts.[13] Ultimately Benn believed the Government's resolution met these requirements, while Corbyn did not.

Initially the Labour Party petitioned for a two-day debate arguing that the complexity of the issues justified more time. This the Government rejected, instead calling a ten-hour debate on Wednesday 2 December 2015. At 11.40am the Prime Minister put forward the Government's motion:

> That this House notes that ISIL poses a direct threat to the United Kingdom; welcomes United Nations Security Council Resolution 2249 which determines that ISIL constitutes an 'unprecedented threat to international peace and security' and calls on states to take 'all necessary measures' to prevent terrorist acts by ISIL and to 'eradicate the safe haven they have established over significant parts of Iraq and Syria'; further notes the clear legal basis to defend the UK and our allies in accordance with the UN Charter; notes that military action against ISIL is only one component of a broader strategy to bring peace and stability to Syria; welcomes the renewed impetus behind the Vienna talks on a ceasefire and political settlement; welcomes the Government's continuing commitment to providing humanitarian support to Syrian refugees; underlines the importance of planning for post-conflict stabilisation and reconstruction in Syria; welcomes the Government's continued determination to cut ISIL's sources of finance, fighters and weapons; notes the requests from France, the US and regional allies for UK military assistance; acknowledges the importance of

seeking to avoid civilian casualties, using the UK's particular capabilities; notes the Government will not deploy UK troops in ground combat operations; welcomes the Government's commitment to provide quarterly progress reports to the House; and accordingly supports Her Majesty's Government in taking military action, specifically airstrikes, exclusively against ISIL in Syria; and offers its wholehearted support to Her Majesty's Armed Forces.[14]

Despite some strong contributions from a number of senior and prominent MPs, many watching the debate within the confines of the Palace of Westminster commented on its poor quality. One Labour MP described it as 'a contest to see who could describe ISIS in the worst terms'. To someone well versed in the Syrian Civil War it was clear that many MPs had little prior knowledge of its developments outside the talking points of the current news cycle. Nor had many of the parliamentary researchers tasked with writing their MP's speeches.

Once again the shadow of Iraq loomed large, with many members making comparisons between the 2003 vote and the current one. MPs questioned the strategy, legality and necessity of expanding the bombing or as some euphemistically described it 'taking the country to war'. Many asked how the Prime Minister who asked the House only two years ago to bomb Assad could now ask them to authorise airstrikes against those he is fighting. Much was made of the UK's hellfire missiles and their 'unique' laser targeting capability which could limit collateral damage. One would be forgiven for thinking that this missile capability was the crux of the Government's argument.

The most memorable speech of the night came in the form of Hilary Benn's closing remarks. In his impassioned plea to members he argued that 'we are faced here by fascists... and what we know about fascists is that they need to be defeated' and that is why 'socialists and trade unionists and others joined the International Brigade in the 1930s to fight against Franco'.[15]

His speech received a standing ovation from the Government benches and some of the Opposition benches too. It would later be described as one of the best speeches of the Parliament so far and a speech reflective of a leader in waiting. It persuaded many of his colleagues to join him in walking with the Government through the division lobby.

At 10.15pm the Government's motion was carried by 397 to 223, a majority of 174. Some 66 Labour MPs, a third of the Parliamentary Labour Party, voted in favour of airstrikes, including 11 members of the Shadow Cabinet most notably Hilary Benn (Foreign), Angela Eagle (First Secretary), Heidi Alexander (Business), Lucy Powell (Health), Michael Dugher (Culture) and even the Deputy Leader Tom Watson. Only 7 Conservative MPs defied the Government whip and voted against airstrikes. In the end the Government received a comfortable majority over a divided opposition.

At the time of writing the debate over Syria's future and how best to defeat ISIS and end the civil war continues. Two days after the vote the Secretary of State for Defence, Michael Fallon said that the campaign to defeat ISIS may take at least two years and that is only supported by the notion of a successful negotiated peace process.[16] There is discussion of de-selection and recriminations from party activists against Labour MPs who voted with the Government.

On the same day German MPs voted 445 votes to 146 to deploy Tornado reconnaissance jets, a naval frigate and 1,200 soldiers to the region to help tackle ISIS in a non-combat role, making it Germany's biggest current military operation abroad.[17]

The idea of a transitional government in Damascus is still far from a reality. No Syrian will soon forget that it was Assad, rather than ISIS, who plunged the country into civil war when his regime ordered soldiers to fire upon unarmed protesters and then ordered officers to shoot disobedient soldiers. His regime's desperate brutality created the sectarian and fertile conditions for ISIS to take root and grow. As long as he is the ruler of Syria any universal political reconciliation will be virtually impossible.

Conclusions

The events leading up to and the House of Commons vote on extending airstrikes from Iraq to include Syria only reinforce many of this book's recommendations going forward.

The Foreign Affairs Select Committee played an important role in offering oversight of the Government's proposed policy of expanding bombing into Syria. Its report was useful and actually influenced the Prime Minister to revise his strategy. It brought with it a need to pause and gave ordinary MPs much to consider.

The Paris attacks brought the realities of the Syrian Civil War and ISIS's brutal methods to many ordinary members of the public. It sparked an intense and continuing public debate about how best to end the Syrian Civil War, how best to tackle and defeat ISIS and also how to deal with radicalisation and terrorism here in the UK. Public responses and opinions varied, from those who were well informed to a sizeable portion who argued strongly on either side of the debate but with insufficient understanding to back it up. It reinforces the need for all of us in society to do more to engage with foreign affairs not just reactively in times of crises directly involving the issue of war and intervention but also to conflicts as they develop.

The Syrian civil war did not start when refugees started pouring through Eastern Europe. ISIS was not founded when Paris was attacked. The war has been happening for a long time, and the reasons for the civil war were brewing for decades before that. Failure to be sufficiently informed leads to dogmatic and polarised opinions influenced by emotion, innuendo and intuition which makes consensus – and effective decision making – impossible. Foreign policy making does not happen in a vacuum. A prime minister must take into account the public mood. The public mood – and by extension their parliamentary representatives – drastically affected the last Syrian vote in 2013 and did so again in 2015.

Similarly the quality of contributions by MPs to the debate, with a few notable exceptions, reinforce the need for MPs to engage with foreign policy themselves and pay attention to developing conflicts long before they are asked to speak and vote on the matter. The Commons has now had four debates on the subject within four years and there clearly needs to be a mechanism set up to regularly brief MPs on important developments and unfolding events abroad in case they need to vote on them.

The Prime Minister now spends more than 80 per cent of his time on foreign policy. In an increasingly interconnected world that proportion will only grow further. The importance of international relations and foreign policy cannot be overstated, and whether the public can see a prospective candidate for the job as de facto Commander in Chief is definitely an important factor in elections. That is why if the Labour Party is to win the next General Election it must have a realistic, coherent foreign policy that people – and other world leaders – can trust.

The legacy of Iraq lies at the heart of the upset and division over airstrikes in Syria. This shadow will not be shaken until the Chilcot Inquiry's final report is published. Its delay continues to paralyse prime ministerial authority over foreign policy. The British public will not be able to trust another prime minister on the issue of war until they are assured that there is recourse for what they consider to be malicious or falsely crafted policy. For trust to be rebuilt, the balance between prime ministerial power and accountability must be re-established. Those who make the difficult decisions must be willing to accept ultimate responsibility and, in some cases, punishment if they abuse that covenant. Trust between actors is the heart of diplomacy and foreign policy making, and trust between the governors and the governed is the heart of effective political and democratic leadership.

Notes

1. House of Commons Foreign Affairs Committee, 'The Extension of Offensive British Military Operations to Syria', House of Commons, 29 October 2015, pp. 4–5.
2. H. Samuel, 'Francois Hollande: France at War Against "Cowards"', *Telegraph*, 16 November 2015, accessed 5 December 2015: www.telegraph.co.uk/news/worldnews/europe/france/11999097/Francois-Hollande-says-France-at-war-against-cowards.html.
3. European Union External Action, 'Joint Statement: Final Declaration on the Results of the Syria Talks in Vienna as Agreed by Participants', 30 October 2015, accessed 5 December 2015: http://eeas.europa.eu/statements-eeas/2015/151030_06.htm.
4. United Nations Security Council, UN Resolution 2249, 20 November 2015, accessed 5 December 2015: www.un.org/en/ga/search/view_doc.asp?symbol=S/RES/2249%282015%29.
5. S. Whale, 'Diane Abbott Calls for Labour MPs to be Whipped Against Bombing in Syria', Politics Home, 30 November 2015, accessed 5 December 2015: www.politicshome.com/foreign-and-defence/articles/story/diane-abbott-calls-labour-mps-be-whipped-against-bombing-syria.
6. 'Jeremy Corbyn Faces Threat of Shadow Cabinet Resignations', BBC News, 27 November 2015, accessed 5 December 2015: www.bbc.co.uk/news/uk-politics-34940728.
7. R. Mason, 'Jeremy Corbyn Seeks Grassroots Labour Support For Stance Against Bombing Syria', *Guardian*, 27 November 2015, accessed 5 December 2015: www.theguardian.com/politics/2015/nov/27/jeremy-corbyn-labour-bombing-syria-isis-airstrikes.
8. Whale, 'Diane Abbott Calls for Labour MPs to be Whipped'.
9. D. Cameron, Speech in the House of Commons, 'Syria Statement', *Hansard* (HC Deb, 26 November 2015, col. 1491); D. Cameron, Speech in the House of Commons, 'Syria Debate', *Hansard* (HC Deb, 2 December 2015, col. 333).
10. V. Ward, 'David Cameron "Warned by Military Chiefs Not To Claim There Were 70,000 Friendly Syrian Troops"', *Telegraph*, 4 December 2015, accessed 5 December 2015: www.telegraph.co.uk/news/uknews/defence/12032691/David-Cameron-warned-by-military-chiefs-not-to-claim-there-were-70000-friendly-Syrian-troops.html.

11 A. Withnall, 'David Cameron Brands Jeremy Corbyn a "Terrorist Sympathiser" For Opposing Syria Air Strikes', *Independent*, 2 December 2015, accessed 5 December 2015: www.independent.co.uk/news/uk/politics/david-cameron-calls-jeremy-corbyn-a-terrorist-sympathiser-for-opposing-syria-air-strikes-a6756731.html.

12 A. McDonald, Speech in the House of Commons, 'Syria Debate', *Hansard* (HC Deb, 2 December 2015, col. 340).

13 R. Syal, 'Labour Conference Sets Terms For Supporting UK Military Action in Syria', *Guardian*, 30 September 2015, accessed 5 December: www.theguardian.com/politics/2015/sep/30/labour-conference-conditions-support-military-action-syria.

14 D. Cameron, Speech in the House of Commons, 'Syria Debate', *Hansard* (HC Deb, 2 December 2015, c323).

15 H. Benn, Speech in the House of Commons, 'Syria Debate', *Hansard* (HC Deb, 2 December 2015, col. 486).

16 P. Wintour, 'David Cameron Warns of Lengthy Syria Campaign', *Guardian*, 3 December 2015, accessed 5 December 2015: www.theguardian.com/world/2015/dec/03/first-uk-airstrikes-syria-deal-real-blow-isis-michael-fallon.

17 'Syria Conflict: German MPs Vote For Anti-IS Military Mission', BBC, 4 December 2015, accessed 5 December 2015: www.bbc.co.uk/news/world-europe-35002733.

Bibliography

Books

Andrew, Christopher, *Defence of the Realm: The Authorised History of MI5* (London, Penguin Books, 2010).
Ashdown, Paddy, *A Fortunate Life* (London: Aurum Press, 2009).
Barber, Anthony, *Taking the Tide: A Memoir* (Norwich: Michael Russell, 1996).
Barber, James, *Who Makes British Foreign Policy?* (Mliton Keynes: Open University Press, 1976).
Benn, Tony, *Against the Tide: Diaries 1973–1977* (London: Hutchinson, 1989).
Blair, Tony, *A Journey* (London: Hutchinson, 2010).
Blick, Andrew, *How To Go To War: A Handbook For Democratic Leaders* (London: Politicos, 2005).
Bowen, Jeremy, *The Arab Uprisings: The People Want the Fall of the Regime* (London: Simon & Schuster, 2013).
Brown, George, *In My Way: The Political Memoirs of Lord George-Brown* (London: Victor Gollancz, 1971).
Brown, Gordon, *Courage: Eight Portraits* (London: Bloomsbury, 2007).
Brown, Gordon, 'Kennedy Memorial Lecture – Kennedy Presidential Library and Museum Boston 18th April 2008', in Brown, *The Change We Choose*.
Brown, Gordon, 'Speech to the UN General Assembly- New York 23rd September 2009', in Brown, *The Change We Choose*.
Brown, Gordon, 'Speech to the Royal College of Defence Studies – London 6th November 2009', in Brown, *The Change We Choose: Speeches 2007–09* (London: Mainstream Publishing, 2010).
Brown, Gordon, 'Speech to the Lord Mayor's Banquet – Guildhall London 16th November 2009', in Brown, *The Change We Choose*.
Brown, Sarah, *Behind the Black Door* (London: Ebury Press, 2011).
Bush, George H. and Brent Scowcroft, *A World Transformed* (New York: Alfred A Knopf, 1998).
Bush, George W., *Decision Points* (London: Virgin Books, 2010).
Callaghan, James, *Time and Chance* (London: Politicos, 2006).
Campbell, John, *Margaret Thatcher Volume Two: The Iron Lady* (London: Jonathan Cape, 2003).

Carrington, Peter, *Reflect on Things Past: Memoirs of Lord Carrington* (London: Collins, 1988).
Castle, Barbara, *The Castle Diaries: 1964–70* (London: Weidenfeld & Nicolson, 1984).
Cheney, Richard, *In My Time* (New York: Simon & Schuster, 2011).
Clarke, Richard, *Against All Enemies: Inside America's War on Terror* (New York: Free Press, 2004).
Clinton, Bill, *My Life* (London: Arrow Books, 2005).
Clinton, Hillary, *Hard Choices* (London: Simon Schuster, 2014).
Connor, Ken, *Ghost Force: The Secret History of the SAS* (London: Cassell, 1998).
Cooper, Chester, L., *The Lost Crusade: America in Vietnam* (New York: Dodd, Mead & Company, 1970).
Cowley, Phillip, *The Rebels* (London: Politicos, 2005).
Cowper-Coles, Sherard, *Cables from Kabul: The Inside Story of the West's Afghanistan Campaign* (London: Harper Press, 2011).
Craddock, Percy, *In Pursuit of British Interests* (London: John Murray, 1997).
Crossman, Richard, *The Diaries of a Cabinet Minister, vol. 1, Minister of House 1964–66* (London: Hamish Hamilton & Jonathan Cape, 1975).
Crossman, Richard, *The Diaries of a Cabinet Minister, vol. 2, 1966–1968* (London: Holt, Rinehart & Winston, 1977)
D'Ancona, Matthew, *In It Together: The Inside Story of the Coalition Government* (London: Viking, 2013).
Darling, Alistair, *Back From the Brink: 1,000 Days At Number 11* (London: Atlantic Books, 2011).
Dickie, John, *Inside the Foreign Office* (London: Chapmans, 2000).
Dorman, Andrew, *Blair's Successful War: British Military Intervention in Sierra Leone* (Farnham: Ashgate Publishing, 2009).
Dorril, Stephen, *MI6: Fifty Years of Special Operations* (London: Harper Collins, 2000).
Douglas-Home, Alec, *The Way The Wind Blows* (London: Collins, 1976).
Dunleavy, Patrick, *Prime Minister, Cabinet and the Core Executive*, ed. R.A.W. Rhodes (Basingstoke: Macmillan Press, 1995).
Foot, Paul, *The Politics of Harold Wilson* (Harmondsworth: Penguin, 1968).
Gates, Robert, *Duty: Memoirs of a Secretary At War* (London: W.H. Allen, 2014).
Gordon Walker, Patrick, *Patrick Gordon-Walker: Political Diaries 1932–1971*, ed. Robert Pearce (London: Historians Press, 1991).
Gordon Walker, Patrick, *The Cabinet* (London: Jonathan Cape, 1972).
Gorman, Teresa (with Helen Kirby), *The Bastards, Dirty Tricks and the Challenge to Europe* (London: Pan Books, 1993).
Gould, Philip, *The Unfinished Revolution: How New Labour Changed British Politics Forever* (London: Abacus, 2011).

Gray, James and Mark Lomas, *Who Takes Britain to War?* (London: The History Press, 2014).

Healey, Denis, *Time of My Life* (London: Politicos, 2003).

Heath, Edward, *The Course of My Life* (London: Hodder & Soughton, 1998).

Hennessey, Peter, *The Prime Minister: The Office and Its Holders Since 1945* (London: Penguin Books, 2000).

Hill, Jonathan and Sarah Hogg, *Too Close to Call: Power and Politics John Major in No. 10* (London: Warner Books, 1995).

Hurd, Douglas, *Memoirs* (London: Abacus, 2003).

Jenkins, Roy, *Life at the Centre* (London: Politicos, 2006).

Johnson, Lyndon, *The Vantage Point: Perspectives of the Presidency 1963–1969* (New York, Chicago and San Francisco: Holt, Rinehart & Winston, 1971).

Kissinger, Henry, *White House Years* (London: Weidenfeld & Nicolson/Michael Joseph, 1979).

Lamont, Norman, *In Office* (London: Little Brown and Company, 1998).

Lawson, Nigel, *Memoirs of a Tory Radical* (London: Biteback Publishing, 2010).

Lesch, David, *Syria: The Fall of the House of Assad* (London: Yale University Press, 2013).

Major, John, *The Autobiography* (London: Harper Collins, 1999).

Mandelson, Peter, *The Third Man: Life at the Heart of New Labour* (London: Harper Press, 2010).

Mason, Roy, *Paying the Price* (London: Robert Hale, 1999).

McBride, Damian, *Power Trip: A Decade of Policy, Plots and Spin* (London: Biteback Publishing, 2013).

Mockli, Daniel, *European Foreign Policy During the Cold War: Heath, Brandt, Pompidou and the Dream of Political Unity* (London: I.B. Tauris, 2008).

Moore, Charles, *Margaret Thatcher: The Authorised Biography Volume 1: Not for Turning* (London: Allen Lane, 2013).

Morgan, Kenneth, *Callaghan: A Life* (Oxford: Oxford University Press, 1997).

Nott, John, *Here Today Gone Tomorrow: Recollections of an Errant Politician* (London: Politicos, 2002).

Owen, David, *The Hidden Perspective: The Military Conversations 1906–1914* (London: Haus Publishing, 2014).

Owen, David, *Hubris Syndrome: Bush, Blair and the Intoxication of Power* (London: Methuen Press, 2012).

Owen, David, *In Sickness and In Power: Illness in Heads of Government, Military and Business since 1900* (London: Methuen, 2016).

Pimlott, Ben, *Harold Wilson* (London: Harper Collins, 1992).

Powell, Colin, *My American Journey* (New York: Random House, 1995).

Powell, Jonathan, *The New Machiavelli: How to Wield Power in the Modern World* (London: Vintage Books, 2010).

Prescott, John, *Prezza Pulling No Punches: John Prescott with Hunter Davies* (London: Headline Publishing Group, 2008).

Pym, Francis, *The Politics of Consent* (London: Hamish Hamilton Publishers, 1984).

Rawnsley, Andrew, *The End of the Party: The Rise and Fall of New Labour* (London: Penguin Books, 2010).

Reagan, Ronald, *An American Life* (London: Hutchinson, 1990).

Rice, Condoleezza, *No Higher Honour* (London: Simon Schuster, 2011).

Riddell, Peter, *Hug Them Close: Blair, Clinton, Bush and The Special Relationship* (London: Politicos, 2004).

Ridley, Nicholas, *My Style of Government* (London: Hutchinson, 1991).

Robinson, Nick, *Live from Downing Street: The Inside Story of Politics, Power and the Media* (London: Bantham Press, 2012).

Rumsfeld, Donald, *Known and Unknown* (New York: Sentinel, 2011).

Schwarzkopf, Norman (with Peter Petre), *The Autobiography: It Doesn't Take A Hero* (London: Bantam Press, 1992).

Seldon, Anthony, *Major: a Political Life* (London: Phoenix, 1998).

Seldon, Anthony and Guy Lodge, *Brown at 10* (London: Biteback, 2010).

Seldon, Anthony and Peter Snowdon, *Cameron at 10: Inside the Coalition 2010-2015* (London: William Collins, 2015).

Short, Clare, *An Honourable deception?: New Labour, Iraq, and the Misuse of Power* (London: Free Press, 2004).

Smith, Ian, *Bitter Harvest: The Great Betrayal* (London: Black Zed, 2001).

Stewart, Michael, *Life and Labour* (Sussex: Sidgwick & Jackson, 1980).

Straw, Jack, *Last Man Standing: Memoirs of a Political Survivor* (London: Macmillan, 2012).

Thatcher, Margaret, *The Autobiography* (London: Harper Collins, 1995).

Theakston, Kevin (ed.), *British Foreign Secretaries Since 1974* (London: Routledge, 2004).

Whitelaw, Willie, *The Whitelaw Memoirs* (London: Aurum Press, 1991).

Wilson, Harold, *The Final Term: The Labour Government 1974-76* (London: Wiedenfeld & Nicolson/Michael Joseph, 1979).

Wilson, Harold, *The Labour Government 1964-70: a Personal Record* (London: Weidenfeld, Nicolson/Michael Joseph, 1971).

Wood, J.R.T, *A Matter of Weeks Rather Than Months: The Impasse Between Harold Wilson and Ian Smith: Sanctions, Aborted Settlements and War 1965-1969* (British Columbia, Canada: Trafford Publishing, 2008).

Wood, J.R.T, *So Far and No Further! Rhodesia's Bid For Independence During the Retreat From Empire 1959-1965* (British Columbia, Canada: Trafford Publishing, 2005).

Ziegler, Philip, *Heath: The Authorised Biography* (London: Harper Press, 1993).

Articles

Adomanis, Mark, 'Russian Military Spending: Drawing Blood From A Stone', *Forbes Magazine*, 19 May 2015, accessed 28 November 2015: www.forbes.com/sites/markadomanis/2015/05/19/russian-military-spending-drawing-blood-from-a-stone.

Akkoc, Raziye, 'Britain Planned To Train and Equip 100,000 Syrian Rebels', *Telegraph*, 4 July 2012, accessed 1 August 2015: www.telegraph.co.uk/news/worldnews/middleeast/syria/10945457/Britain-planned-to-train-and-equip–100000-Syrian-rebels.html.

Al Jazeera, 'Obama: Russia's Strategy in Syria "Doomed to Fail"', 11 September 2015, accessed 28 November 2015: www.aljazeera.com/news/2015/09/russia-continue-supply-arms-syria-assad-150911100637986.html

Alexander, Douglas, 'Douglas Alexander: Syria – What's Next?', *Telegraph*, 30 August 2013, accessed 1 August 2015: www.telegraph.co.uk/news/worldnews/middleeast/syria/10277675/Douglas-Alexander-Syria-what-next.html?mobile=basic.

Allen, Nicholas and Anthony King, 'Off With Their Heads: British Prime Ministers and the Power to Dismiss', *British Journal of Political Science*, 40:2 (2010), 249–78.

Allen, Nicholas and Hugh Ward, '"Moves on a Chess Board": A Spatial Model of British Prime Ministers' Powers over Cabinet Formation', *British Journal of Politics and International Relations*, 11:2 (2009), 238–58.

Baker, David, Andrew Gamble and Steve Ludlam, 'The Parliamentary Siege of Maastricht 1993 Conservative Divisions and British Ratification', *Parliamentary Affairs*, 47:1 (1994), 37–60.

Ball, Gregory, 'Operation Desert Fox Factsheet', Air Force Historical Studies Office, Joint Base Anacostia Bolling, Washington DC, 17 September 2014 accessed 1 August 2015: www.afhso.af.mil/topics/factsheets/factsheet.asp?id=18632.

BBC News, 'Blair Criticised by Freedom of Information Inquiry MPs', 26 July 2012, accessed 1 August 2015: www.bbc.co.uk/news/uk-politics-18987496.

BBC News, 'Blair Wins War Backing Amid Revolt', 19 March 2003, accessed 1 August 2015: http://news.bbc.co.uk/1/hi/uk_politics/2862325.stm.

BBC News, 'Cabinet "Certainly Eurosceptic", says Michael Fallon', 16 July 2014, accessed 1 August 2015: www.bbc.co.uk/news/uk-politics-28324237.

BBC News, 'Crispin Blunt: UK "Didn't Need To Put Hand on Dagger"', 30 August 2013, accessed 1 August 2015: www.bbc.co.uk/news/uk-23895544.

BBC News, 'Election 2010: Gloves Off in Second Leaders' Debate', 23 April 2010, accessed 1 August 2015: http://news.bbc.co.uk/1/hi/uk_politics/election_2010/8638738.stm.

BBC News, 'In Full: Warsi's Resignation Letter and PM's Response', 5 August 2014, accessed 1 August 2015: www.bbc.co.uk/news/uk-politics-28657623.

BBC News, 'Iraq Crisis: General Says UK "Commitment-Phobic"', 12 August 2014, accessed 1 August 2015: www.bbc.co.uk/news/uk-28750491.

BBC News, 'Jeremy Corbyn Faces Threat of Shadow Cabinet Resignations', 27 November 2015, accessed 5 December 2015: www.bbc.co.uk/news/uk-politics-34940728.

BBC News, 'Libya Protests: Defiant Gaddafi Refuses To Quit', 22 February 2011, accessed 1 August 2015: www.bbc.co.uk/news/world-middle-east-12544624.

BBC News, 'Obama: US Cannot Ignore Syria Chemical Weapons', 7 September 2013, accessed 1 August 2015: www.bbc.co.uk/news/world-us-canada-23999066.

BBC News, 'Reagan's Apology to Thatcher Over Grenada Revealed', 10 November 2014, accessed 1 August 2015: www.bbc.co.uk/news/uk-29986729.

BBC News, 'Russian Economy Shrinks 2 Per Cent As Sanctions Bite – Medvedev', 21 April 2015, accessed 28 November 2015: www.bbc.co.uk/news/world-europe-32396792.

BBC, 'Syria Conflict: German Mps Vote For Anti-IS Military Mission', 4 December 2015, accessed 5 December 2015: www.bbc.co.uk/news/world-europe-35002733.

BBC News, 'Syria Crisis: Cameron Loses Commons Vote on Syria Action', 30 August 2013, accessed 1 August 2015: www.bbc.co.uk/news/uk-politics-23892783.

BBC News, 'Syria Crisis: "Only Four Or Five" US-Trained Syrian Rebels Are Still Fighting', 17 September 2015, accessed 1 August 2015: www.bbc.co.uk/news/world-middle-east-34278233.

BBC News, 'Syria Crisis: Russia and China Step Up Warning Over Syria', 27 August 2013, accessed 1 August 2015: www.bbc.co.uk/news/world-us-canada-23845800.

BBC News, 'Syria Unrest: Fierce Firefight Erupts In Damascus', 19 March 2012, accessed 1 August 2015: www.bbc.co.uk/news/world-middle-east-17425062.

BBC News, 'Where Are British Troops and Why?', 29 April 2008, accessed 1 August 2015: http://news.bbc.co.uk/1/hi/uk/4094818.stm.

Black, Ian, 'Kofi Annan Resigns As Syria Envoy', *Guardian*, 2 August 2012, accessed 1 August 2015: www.theguardian.com/world/2012/aug/02/kofi-annan-resigns-syria-envoy.

Bowers, Paul and Tim Youngs, 'Kosovo: NATO and Military Action', House of Commons Research Paper 99/34, 24 March 1999, accessed 1 August 2015: http://researchbriefings.parliament.uk/ResearchBriefing/Summary/RP99-34#fullreport.

British Sky Broadcasting, 'TV Debate: Clegg and Cameron Neck and Neck', 23 April 2010, accessed 1 August 2015: http://news.sky.com/skynews/Home/Politics/Leaders-Debate-Nick-Clegg-And-David-Cameron-Joint-Winners-In-Sky-News-Poll-Of-Polls/Article/201004415613588?lpos=Politics_Carousel_Region_0&lid=ARTICLE_15613588_Leaders_Debate percent3A_Nick_Clegg_And_David_Cameron_Joint_Winners_In_Sky_News_Poll_Of_Polls.

Brooke-Holland, Louisa and Claire Mills, 'NATO Wales Summit 2014: Outcomes', House of Commons Research Library Paper, 12 September 2014, accessed 28 November 2015: http://researchbriefings.parliament.uk/ResearchBriefing/Summary/SN06981.

Brooke-Holland, Louisa, Claire Mills and Ben Smith, 'ISIS/Daesh: The Military Response in Iraq and Syria', House of Commons Research Library Paper, 3 November 2015, accessed 28 November 2015: http://researchbriefings.parliament.uk/ResearchBriefing/Summary/SN06995.

Carswell, Douglas, 'Be Happy! The Defeat of the Government Will Send a Powerful Message to Whitehall', *Telegraph*, 29 August 2013, accessed 1 August 2015: http://blogs.telegraph.co.uk/news/douglascarswellmp/100233338/be-happy-the-defeat-of-the-government-will-send-a-powerful-message-to-whitehall.

Castle, Stephen and Steven Erlanger, 'Britain's Rejection of Syrian Response Reflects Fear of Rushing to Act', *New York Times*, 29 August 2013, accessed 1 August 2015: www.nytimes.com/2013/08/30/world/middleeast/syria.html?_r=0.

Chakelian, Anoosh, 'David Cameron Calls For More Sanctions on Russia After the MH17 Crash', *New Statesman*, 21 July 2014, accessed 28 November 2015: www.newstatesman.com/politics/2014/07/david-cameron-calls-more-sanctions-russia-after-mh17-crash.

Charbonneau, Louis and Michelle Nichols, 'UN Security Council Powers Meet Again on Syria: No Outcome', Reuters, 29 August 2013, accessed 1 August 2015: www.reuters.com/article/2013/08/29/us-syria-crisis-un-idUSBRE97S17R20130829.

Chorley, Matt and Tim Shipman, 'Cabinet Split Over Plans To Arm Syrian Rebels: Cameron Under Pressure Amid Claims Peace Talks Are "Doomed To Fail"', *Daily Mail*, 6 June 2013, accessed 1 August 2015: www.dailymail.co.uk/news/article-2336720/Cabinet-split-plans-arm-Syrian-rebels-Cameron-pressure-claims-peace-talks-doomed-fail.html#ixzz3lRTfWiPF.

Chulov, Martin, 'Isis: The Inside Story', *Guardian*, 11 December 2014, accessed 1 August 2015: www.theguardian.com/world/2014/dec/11/-sp-isis-the-inside-story.

Cockrell, Michael, 'Why 2010 Will See the First TV Leaders Election Debate', BBC News, 10 April 2010, accessed 1 August 2015: http://news.bbc.co.uk/1/hi/uk_politics/election_2010/8612153.stm.

Cohen, Tom and Laura Smith-Spark, 'US, Russia Agree To Framework On Syria Chemical Weapons', CNN, 15 September 2013, accessed 1 August 2015: http://edition.cnn.com/2013/09/14/politics/us-syria.

Cooper, Kristiina, 'William Hague on Humour – and His Worst Moment as Foreign Secretary', BBC News, 18 July 2014, accessed 1 August 2015: www.bbc.co.uk/news/uk-politics-28377955.

CM Poll for the BBC/The Guardian, 10–11 July 2009, accessed 1 August 2015: www.icmunlimited.com/pdfs/2009_july_guardiian_bbc_afghanistan_poll.pdf.

Cowley, Philip and Mark Stuart, 'This Parliament Remains On Course To Be the Most Rebellious Parliament Since 1945', Conservative Home, 14 May 2013, accessed 1 August 2015: www.conservativehome.com/platform/2013/05/philip-cowley-and-mark-stuart-for-1000am-tuesday.html.

Craig, Tim, 'Afghan President Hamid Karzai Slams U.S. Government Policy in Afghanistan', *Washington Post*, 23 September 2014, accessed 1 August 2015: www.washingtonpost.com/world/afghan-president-hamid-karzai-slams-us-government-policy-in-afghanistan/2014/09/23/a3b58cf4-4342-11e4-b47c-f5889e061e5f_story.html.

Daragahi, Borzou, 'Assad Still Using Chemical Weapons, Say Syrian Rebels', *Financial Times*, 21 October 2014, accessed 1 August 2015: www.ft.com/cms/s/0/9e18f7e8-5460-11e4-84c6-00144feab7de.html.

Davies, Peter, 'Sterling & Strings', *London Review of Books*, 30:22 (2008), 17–18, accessed 1 August 2015: www.lrb.co.uk/v30/n22/peter-davies/sterling-and-strings.

Dyson, Stephen, 'Cognitive Style and Foreign Policy: Margaret Thatcher's Black-and-White', *International Political Science Review*, 30:1 (2009), 33–4.

Dzimwasha, Taku, 'Isis in Syria: Islamic State and Other Rebels Now Control Most Of the Country', *International Business Times*, 22August 2015, accessed 1 August 2015: www.ibtimes.co.uk/isis-syria-islamic-state-other-rebels-now-control-most-country-1516616.

Economist, 'Libya's No Fly Zone: The Military Balance, Muammar Qaddafi Has Enough Military Power at his Disposal To Make Dislodging Him a Bloody and Uncertain Business', 3 March 2011, accessed 1 August 2015: www.economist.com/node/18291539.

Economist, 'Why Russia is an Ally of Assad', 30 September 2015, accessed 28 November 2015: www.economist.com/blogs/economist-explains/2015/09/economist-explains-22.

Elliot, Larry, 'Stakes Are High as US Plays the Oil Card Against Iran and Russia', *Guardian*, 9 November 2014, accessed 28 November 2015: www.theguardian.com/business/economics-blog/2014/nov/09/us-iran-russia-oil-prices-shale.

Esplin, Mark, 'Syria Chemical Weapons: The Analysis That Proves Assad Launched Chlorine Gas Attacks', *Telegraph*, 29 April 2014, accessed 1 August 2015: www.telegraph.co.uk/news/worldnews/middleeast/syria/10795813/Syria-chemical-weapons-the-analysis-that-proves-Assad-launched-chlorine-gas-attacks.html.

Evans, Lisa, Paul McClean and Ami Sedghi, 'UK Soldiers Killed in "Insider" Attacks in Afghanistan – the Full List', *Guardian*, 18 September 2012, accessed 1 August 2015: www.theguardian.com/news/datablog/2012/sep/18/nato-afghanistan-insider-attacks-soldiers.

Evening Standard, 'A Turning Point for PM and UK', 30 August 2013, accessed 1 August 2015: www.standard.co.uk/comment/comment/evening-standard-comment-a-turning-point-for-the-pm-and-the-uk-8791287.html.

Evening Standard, 'Brown Pledges To Bring Half Our Troops Home By Next Spring', 7 October 2007, accessed 1 August 2015: www.standard.co.uk/news/brown-pledges-to-bring-half-our-troops-home-by-next-spring-7278952.html.

Fadel, Leila, 'Protesters Shot As Demonstrations Expand Across Syria', *Washington Post*, 25 March 2011, accessed 1 August 2015: www.washingtonpost.com/world/

protesters-shot-as-demonstrations-expand-across-syria/2011/03/25/AFTnewWB_story.html.

Fisher, Max, 'Russia Urges Syria to Give Up Chemical Weapons. Game Changer or Shrewd Bluff?', Washington Post, 9 September 2013, accessed 1 August 2015: www.washingtonpost.com/blogs/worldviews/wp/2013/09/09/russia-urges-syria-to-give-up-chemical-weapons-game-changer-or-a-shrewd-bluff.

Forbes, Steve, 'Why Russia Is Wrecking The Ruble', Forbes Magazine, 16 December 2014, accessed 28 November 2015: www.forbes.com/sites/steveforbes/2014/12/16/why-russia-is-wrecking-the-ruble.

Foreign Affairs Magazine, 'The Year of Europe?', The Council on Foreign Relations, January 1974, accessed 1 August 2015: www.foreignaffairs.com/articles/24476/z/the-year-of-europe.

Gilsinan, Kathy, 'How ISIS Territory Has Changed Since the U.S. Bombing Campaign Began', *Atlantic*, 11 September 2015, accessed 1 August 2015: www.theatlantic.com/international/archive/2015/09/isis-territory-map-us-campaign/404776.

Gladstone, Rick and Rod Nordland, 'Cameron of Britain and Sarkozy of France Visit Libya', *New York Times*, 15 September 2011, accessed 1 August 2015: www.nytimes.com/2011/09/16/world/africa/cameron-and-sarkozy-in-tripoli-libya-to-meet-new-leaders.html?_r=0.

Groves, Jason, 'Six Ministers Who Missed the Vote: Chief Whip Under Fire for Shambles in Commons is Exposed', *Daily Mail*, 30 August 2013, accessed 1 August 2015: www.dailymail.co.uk/news/article-2406731/Ministers-missed-vote-Chief-Whip-shambles-Commons-exposed.html.

Guardian, 'Bashar al-Assad wins re-election in Syria as uprising against him rages on', 4 June 2014 accessed 1 August 2015: www.theguardian.com/world/2014/jun/04/bashar-al-assad-winds-reelection-in-landslide-victory.

Guardian, 'Brown Will "Spend What It Takes" On Iraq', 4 March 2003, accessed 1 August 2015: www.theguardian.com/politics/2003/mar/04/foreignpolicy.uk.

Guardian, 'Letter from David Cameron and Nicolas Sarkozy to Herman Van Rompuy', 10 March 2011, accessed 1 August 2015: www.theguardian.com/world/2011/mar/10/libya-middleeast.

Guardian, 'Maliki Confirms Syrian Planes Have Bombed Isis Positions', 26 June 2014, accessed 1 August 2015: www.theguardian.com/world/2014/jun/26/maliki-syrian-planes-bomb-iraq-isis-us.

Guardian, 'Syrian Government and Opposition Trade Accusations at Geneva II Talks', 10 February 2014, accessed 1 August 2015: www.theguardian.com/world/2014/feb/10/syrian-government-opposition-trade-accusations-geneva-ii.

Halliday, Josh, 'Ex-Army Chief Urges PM To Consider "Boots on the Ground" To Fight Isis', *Guardian*, 24 May 2015, accessed 1 August 2015: www.theguardian.com/world/2015/may/24/ex-army-chief-urges-pm-to-consider-boots-on-the-ground-to-fight-isis.

Harding, Luke, 'Sergei Pugachev: "Putin's Banker" Now Lives In Fear of Man He Put Into Power', *Guardian*, 28 July 2015, accessed 28 November 2015: www.theguardian.com/world/2015/jul/28/sergei-pugachev-putins-banker-interview-lives-in-fear.

Harding, Thomas and Andrew Porter, 'Gordon Brown's Basra Pullout "is a Stunt"', *Telegraph*, 3 October 2007, accessed 1 August 2015: www.telegraph.co.uk/news/uknews/1564934/Gordon-Browns-Basra-pullout-is-a-stunt.html.

Harper, Tom, and Jason Lewis, 'Revealed: How MI5 bugged 10 Downing Street, the Cabinet and at least five Prime Ministers for 15 YEARS', *Mail on Sunday*, 18 April 2010, accessed 1 August 2015: www.dailymail.co.uk/news/article-1266837/Revealed-How-MI5-bugged-10-Downing-Street-Cabinet-Prime-Ministers-15-YEARS.html#ixzz3PYvFTp9N.

Hendrick, Mark, 'The Ukrainian Crisis: Russia's relationship with former Soviet States Post EU/NATO Enlargement', EP Today, 9 May 2014, accessed 28 November 2015: http://eptoday.com/ukrainian-crisis-russias-relationship-soviet-states-post-eunato-enlargement.

Hewitt, Gavin, 'Europe Snubbed in Copenhagen?', BBC News, 22 December 2009, accessed 1 August 2015: www.bbc.co.uk/blogs/legacy/thereporters/gavinhewitt/2009/12/s_5.html.

Hodges, Dan, 'The Truth About the Syria Vote: Miliband Changed His Mind', *Telegraph*, 29 August 2013, accessed 1 August 2015: http://blogs.telegraph.co.uk/news/danhodges/100233087/the-truth-about-the-syria-vote-miliband-changed-his-mind.

Hopkins, Nick, 'Syria Conflict: UK Planned To Train and Equip 100,000 Rebels', BBC News, 3 July 2014, accessed 1 August 2015: www.bbc.co.uk/news/uk-28148943.

House of Commons Library, 'Operation Enduring Freedom and the Conflict in Afghanistan: an Update', Research Paper, 31 October 2001, accessed 1 August 2015: http://researchbriefings.files.parliament.uk/documents/RP01-81/RP01-81.pdf.

Hubbard, Ben, 'Momentum Shifts in Syria, Bolstering Assad's Position', *New York Times*, 17 July 2012, accessed 1 August 2015: www.nytimes.com/2013/07/18/world/middleeast/momentum-shifts-in-syria-bolstering-assads-position.html?_r=1.

Human Rights Watch, World Report 2015 Chapter Ukraine, January 2015 accessed: www.hrw.org/sites/default/files/related_material/ukraine_3.pdf.

Hutton, Robert and Thomas Penny, 'Historic Vote Sees Cameron Defeated by Lawmakers on Syria', Bloomberg, 29 August 2013, accessed 1 August 2015: www.bloomberg.com/news/2013-08-29/historic-vote-sees-cameron-defeated-by-lawmakers-on-syria.html.

Jalabi, Raya, 'Who Are the Yazidis and Why Is Isis Hunting Them?', *Guardian*, 11 August 2014, accessed 1 August 2015: www.theguardian.com/world/2014/aug/07/who-yazidi-isis-iraq-religion-ethnicity-mountains.

Jordan, William, 'Majority Now Support RAF Airstrikes', YouGov, 8 September 2014, accessed 1 August 2015: https://yougov.co.uk/news/2014/09/08/majority-now-support-raf-air-strikes-iraq-and-syri.

Kelley, Michael, 'A Full Extremist-To-Moderate Spectrum Of The 100,000 Syrian Rebels', *Business Insider*, 19 September 2013, accessed 1 August 2015: www.businessinsider.com.au/graphic-the-most-accurate-breakdown-of-the-syrian-rebels-2013-9.

Kennedy, Charles, 'Charles Kennedy: They Had the Cheek To Call Me "Charlie Chamberlain"', *Independent*, 21 May 2004, accessed 1 August 2015: www.independent.co.uk/voices/commentators/charles-kennedy-they-had-the-cheek-to-call-me-charlie-chamberlain-61385.html.

Kirkpatrick, David, 'Graft Hobbles Iraq's Military in Fighting ISIS', *New York Times*, 23 November 2014, accessed 1 August 2015: www.nytimes.com/2014/11/24/world/middleeast/graft-hobbles-iraqs-military-in-fighting-isis.html?emc=edit_th_20141124&nl=todaysheadlines&nlid=68502098&_r=0.

Kirkup, James, 'Russia Mocks Britain, the Little Island', *Telegraph*, 5 September 2013, accessed 1 August 2015: www.telegraph.co.uk/news/worldnews/europe/russia/10290243/Russia-mocks-Britain-the-little-island.html.

Kravtsova, Yekaterina, 'Russia Heightens Tension With Military Exercises Near Ukrainian Border', *Telegraph*, 13 March 2014, accessed 28 November 2015: www.telegraph.co.uk/news/worldnews/europe/ukraine/10695077/Russia-heightens-tension-with-military-exercises-near-Ukrainian-border.html.

Libnan, Ya, 'Over 100,000 Defected from Syrian army, Arab League Monitor Report', 10 July 2012 accessed 1 August 2015: http://yalibnan.com/2012/07/10/over-100000-defected-from-syrian-army-report.

Lidington, David, Written Answer, Foreign & Commonwealth Office, 6th July 2015, *Hansard*, accessed 28th November 2015: www.theyworkforyou.com/wrans/?id=2015–07–01.5072.h&s=russian+jets#g5072.q0.

Luhn, Alec and Matthew Weaver, 'Ukraine Ceasefire Agreed At Belarus Talks', *Guardian*, 12 February 2015, accessed 28 November 2015: www.theguardian.com/world/2015/feb/12/ukraine-crisis-reports-emerge-of-agreement-in-minsk-talks.

Lynch, Kevin, 'Syria Chemical Weapons: Assad Still Using Chlorine Gas in Attacks, Claims Francois Hollande', *Independent*, 20 April 2014, accessed 1 August 2015: www.independent.co.uk/news/world/middle-east/syria-chemical-weapons-assad-still-using-chlorine-gas-in-attacks-claims-franois-hollande-9272495.html.

Mason, Barnaby, 'Tony Blair: Kosovo Crusader', BBC News, 22 April 1999, accessed 1 August 2015: http://news.bbc.co.uk/1/hi/325989.stm.

Mason, Rowena, 'Ed Miliband Restores Party Confidence in His Leadership on Syria Motion', *Guardian*, 30 August 2013, accessed 1 August 2015: www.theguardian.com/politics/2013/aug/30/syria-ed-miliband-labour-party-confidence-leadership.

Mason, Rowena, 'Jeremy Corbyn Seeks Grassroots Labour Support For Stance Against Bombing Syria', *Guardian*, 27 November 2015, accessed 5 December 2015:

www.theguardian.com/politics/2015/nov/27/jeremy-corbyn-labour-bombing-syria-isis-airstrikes.

Meichtry, Stacy and Winning, Nicholas, 'European Rifts Emerge Over Sanctions for Russia', *Wall Street Journal*, 19 March 2014, accessed 28 November 2015: www.wsj.com/articles/SB10001424052702303287804579447513076140776.

Morris, Nigel and Kim Sengupta, 'Voters Turn Against War In Afghanistan', *Independent*, 28 July 2009, accessed 1 August 2015: www.independent.co.uk/news/uk/politics/voters-turn-against-war-in-afghanistan-1763227.html.

Mullholland, Helen and Deborah Summers, 'UK Iraq Troops To Be Cut To 2,500', *Guardian*, 8 October 2007, accessed 1 August 2015: www.theguardian.com/politics/2007/oct/08/iraq.iraq.

Murphy, Jim, 'Thoughts on Syria', Jim Murphy's Blog, 1 September 2013, accessed 1 August 2015: www.jimmurphymp.com/jims-blog/blog.aspx?b=29.

Norton-Taylor, Richard, 'Blair-Bush Deal Before Iraq War Revealed In Secret Memo', *Guardian*, 3 February 2006, accessed 1 August 2015: www.theguardian.com/world/2006/feb/03/iraq.usa.

Norton-Taylor, Richard, 'Chilcot Inquiry: Blair Shut Me Out, Says Former Legal Chief Lord Goldsmith', *Guardian*, 17 January 2011, accessed 1 August 2015: www.theguardian.com/uk/2011/jan/17/blair-ignored-goldsmith-chilcot-inquiry.

Norton-Taylor, Richard, 'Commons Vote Backs Afghanistan Deployment', *Guardian*, 9 September 2010, accessed 1 August 2015: www.theguardian.com/politics/2010/sep/09/commons-backs-afghanistan-deployment.

Norton-Taylor, Richard, 'No 10 Downing Street Bugged By MI5, Claims Historian', *Guardian*, 18 April 2010, available 1 August 2015: www.theguardian.com/uk/2010/apr/18/mi5-bugged-10-downing-street.

Oil Price Net, Crude Oil and Commodity Prices, 29 November 2015, accessed 29 November 2015: www.oil-price.net.

Orin, Deborah, 'Iraq's Chem Arms Found by U.N', *New York Post*, 17 January 2003, accessed 1 August 2015: http://nypost.com/2003/01/17/iraqs-chem-arms-found-by-u-n.

Osborne, Peter, 'Lord Carrington: "I Wish David Cameron Would Stop Holding His Wife's Hand"', *Telegraph*, 19 May 2013, accessed 1 August 2015: www.telegraph.co.uk/news/politics/10065066/Lord-Carrington-I-wish-David-Cameron-would-stop-holding-his-wifes-hand.html.

Partlow, Joshua and Kevin Sieff, 'Ahmed Wali Karzai, Half-Brother of Afghan President, Killed By Trusted Confidant', *Washington Post*, 12 July 2011, accessed 1 August 2015: https://www.washingtonpost.com/world/karzais-brother-killed-by-guard-in-kandahar-home/2011/07/12/gIQAgI3FAI_story.html.

Pearse, Damian, 'Afghan Civilian Death Toll Reaches Record High', *Guardian*, 4 February 2012, accessed 1 August 2015: www.theguardian.com/world/2012/feb/04/afghan-civilian-death-toll-record.

Powell, Enoch, 'Rivers of Blood Speech', Birmingham Conservative Association Meeting, 20 April 1968, accessed 1 August 2015: www.telegraph.co.uk/comment/3643823/Enoch-Powells-Rivers-of-Blood-speech.html.

Ragozin, Leonid, 'Russia's Ruble Falls To All Time Low On China's "Black Monday"', UAToday, 24 August 2015, accessed 28th November 2015: http://uatoday.tv/business/russia-s-ruble-falls-to-all-time-low-on-china-s-quot-black-monday-quot-480641.html.

Rt. Hon. John Redwood MP, 'Some Thoughts on 5 Big Rebellions in Parliament', John Redwood's Diary, 11 September 2013, accessed 1 August 2015: http://johnredwoodsdiary.com/2013/09/11/some-thoughts-on-5-big-rebellions-in-this-parliament.

Riley-Smith, Ben, 'David Cameron A "Foreign Policy Irrelevance" Over Russia, Says Britain's Former Top Commander in Nato', *Telegraph*, 6 February 2015, accessed 28 November 2015: www.telegraph.co.uk/news/politics/liberaldemocrats/11394788/David-Cameron-a-foreign-policy-irrelevance-over-Russia-says-Britains-former-top-commander-in-Nato.html.

Robinson, Nick, 'Miliband on Israel, PM Plan And Thatcher Comparison', BBC News, 12 April 2014, accessed 1 August 2015: www.bbc.co.uk/news/uk-politics-26998207.

Robinson, Nick, 'The Politics of Bombing Syria', BBC News, 28 August 2013, accessed 1 August 2015: www.bbc.co.uk/news/uk-politics-23869303.

Robinson, Nick, 'Why the PM Buckled on the Syria Vote', BBC News, 29 August 2013, accessed 1 August 2015: www.bbc.co.uk/news/uk-politics-23880268.

Samir, Ayman and Yasmine Saleh, 'Arab League Leaders to Blame Assad for Chemical Weapons Attack', Reuters, 28 August 2013, accessed 1 August 2015: www.reuters.com/article/2013/08/28/us-syria-crisis-league-idUSBRE97R12X20130828.

Samuel, Henry, 'Francois Hollande: France at War Against "Cowards"', *Telegraph*, 16 November 2015, accessed 5 December 2015: www.telegraph.co.uk/news/worldnews/europe/france/11999097/Francois-Hollande-says-France-at-war-against-cowards.html.

Sengupta, Kim, 'Syrian Rebels Consider Joining Forces With Regime Troops To Fight Al-Qa'ida', *Independent*, 3 December 2013, accessed 1 August 2015: www.independent.co.uk/news/world/middle-east/syrian-rebels-consider-joining-forces-with-regime-troops-to-fight-alqaida-8981081.html.

Sherlock, Ruth and Richard Spencer, 'Syria's Assad Accused of Boosting Al-Qaeda With Secret Oil Deals', *Telegraph*, 20 January 2014, accessed 1 August 2015: www.telegraph.co.uk/news/worldnews/middleeast/syria/10585391/Syrias-Assad-accused-of-boosting-al-Qaeda-with-secret-oil-deals.html.

Sky News, 'Poll: UK Divided On Combat Mission In Libya', 22 March 2011, accessed 1 August 2015: http://news.sky.com/story/843756/poll-uk-divided-on-combat-mission-in-libya.

Smith, Ben, 'Prospects for Afghanistan as ISAF withdrawal approaches', Research Paper 14/18 19, March 2014, p. 7, accessed 1 August 2015: http://researchbriefings.parliament.uk/ResearchBriefing/Summary/RP14-18.

Smith, Simon, 'Why Should the Crimean Referendum Not Be Recognised?', Foreign & Commonwealth Office Blog, 17 March 2014, accessed 28 November 2015: http://webarchive.nationalarchives.gov.uk/20141204000047/http://blogs.fco.gov.uk/simonsmith/2014/03/17/why-should-the-crimean-referendum-not-be-recognised.

Speakman-Cordall, Simon, 'How Syria's Assad Helped Forge ISIS', *Newsweek*, 21 June 2014, accessed 1 August 2015: www.newsweek.com/how-syrias-assad-helped-forge-isis-255631.

Stephens, Michael, 'Why is Saudi Arabia Using Oil as a Weapon?', BBC News, 3 December 2014, accessed 28 November 2015: www.bbc.co.uk/news/world-middle-east-30289546.

Stewart, Phil, 'U.S. To Keep More Troops In Afghanistan As Violence Spikes', Reuters, 6 December 2014, accessed 1 August 2015: www.reuters.com/article/2014/12/06/us-usa-afghanistan-military-idUSKBN0JK0GH20141206.

Stratton, Allegra, 'Gordon Brown Basks In Limelight Of Copenhagen Climate Change Summit', *Guardian*, 18 December 2009, accessed 1 August 2015: www.theguardian.com/environment/2009/dec/18/gordon-brown-copenhagen-summit.

Summers, Deborah, 'No10 Admits PM Changed Miliband Speech", *Guardian*, 16 November 2007, accessed 1 August 2015: www.theguardian.com/uk/2007/nov/16/eu.gordonbrown.

Syal, Rajeev, "Iraq crisis: David Cameron under pressure to recall parliament", *Guardian*, 11 August 2014, accessed 1 August 2015: www.theguardian.com/world/2014/aug/11/iraq-crisis-david-cameron-pressure-recall-parliament.

Syal, Rajeev, 'Labour Conference Sets Terms For Supporting UK Military Action In Syria', *Guardian*, 30 September 2015, accessed 5 December: www.theguardian.com/politics/2015/sep/30/labour-conference-conditions-support-military-action-syria.

Telegraph, 'Copenhagen Climate Summit: Talks "Held To Ransom", Gordon Brown Says', 21 December 2009, accessed 1 August 2015: www.telegraph.co.uk/news/earth/copenhagen-climate-change-confe/6857072/Copenhagen-climate-summit-talks-held-to-ransom-Gordon-Brown-says.html.

Theakston, Kevin, 'Political Skills and Context In Prime Ministerial Leadership In Britain', *Politics and Policy*, 30:2 (2008), 283–323.

Tiley, Marc, 'Britain, Vietnam and the Special Relationship', *History Today*, 63:12 (2013), accessed 1 August 2015: www.historytoday.com/marc-tiley/britain-vietnam-and-special-relationship.

Tisdall, Simon, 'Lessons From Libya: How Cameron And Sarkozy Got Lucky', *Guardian*, 13 October 2011, accessed 1 August 2015: www.theguardian.com/commentisfree/2011/oct/13/lessons-from-libya-obama-cameron-sarkozy.

Traynor, Ian, 'UK Forces EU To Lift Embargo On Syria Rebel Arms', *Guardian*, 28 May 2013, accessed 1 August 2015: www.theguardian.com/world/2013/may/28/uk-forced-eu-embargo-syria-rebel-arms.

Vickers, Rhiannon, 'Harold Wilson, the British Labour Party, and the War in Vietnam', *Journal of Cold War Studies*, 10:2 (2008), 43–72.

Vidal, John, 'Copenhagen Climate Summit In Disarray After "Danish Text" Leak', *Guardian*, 8 December 2009, accessed 1 August 2015: www.theguardian.com/environment/2009/dec/08/copenhagen-climate-summit-disarray-danish-text.

Ward, Victoria, 'David Cameron "Warned By Military Chiefs Not To Claim There Were 70,000 Friendly Syrian Troops"', *Telegraph*, 4 December 2015, accessed 5 December 2015: www.telegraph.co.uk/news/uknews/defence/12032691/David-Cameron-warned-by-military-chiefs-not-to-claim-there-were-70000-friendly-Syrian-troops.html.

The Washington Post Editorial Board, 'Obama Gives Syria's Assad Another Pass on Chemical Weapons', 23 October 2014, accessed 1 August 2015: www.washingtonpost.com/opinions/obama-gives-syrias-assad-another-pass-on-chemical-weapons/2014/10/23/1fe92762-5a05-11e4-bd61-346aee66ba29_story.html.

Watson, Tom, 'We Cannot Abandon Iraq To the Black Flag Of ISIS – Parliament Must Be Recalled', Labourlist, 8 August 2014, accessed 1 August 2015: http://labourlist.org/2014/08/we-cannot-abandon-iraq-to-the-black-flag-of-isis-parliament-must-be-recalled.

Watt, Nicholas, 'Nicolas Sarkozy Calls For Airstrikes On Libya If Gaddafi Attacks Civilians', *Guardian*, 11 March 2011, accessed 1 August 2015: www.theguardian.com/world/2011/mar/11/nicolas-sarkozy-libya-air-strikes.

Whale, Sebastian, 'Diane Abbott Calls For Labour MPs To Be Whipped Against Bombing In Syria', Politics Home, 30 November 2015, accessed 5 December 2015: https://www.politicshome.com/foreign-and-defence/articles/story/diane-abbott-calls-labour-mps-be-whipped-against-bombing-syria.

Wheeler, Brian, 'Wilson "Plot": The Secret Tapes', BBC News, 9 March 2006, accessed 1 August 2015: http://news.bbc.co.uk/1/hi/uk_politics/4789060.stm.

Wintour, Patrick, 'David Cameron Tells UK Troops Their Work In Afghanistan "Will Live Forever"', *Guardian*, 3 October 2014, accessed 1 August 2015: www.theguardian.com/world/2014/oct/03/david-cameron-uk-troops-afghanistan-camp-bastion.

Wintour, Patrick, 'David Cameron Warns of Lengthy Syria Campaign', *Guardian*, 3 December 2015, accessed 5 December 2015: www.theguardian.com/world/2015/dec/03/first-uk-airstrikes-syria-deal-real-blow-isis-michael-fallon.

Wintour, Patrick, 'John Kerry Gives Syria a Week to Hand Over Chemical Weapons or Face Attack', *Guardian*, 9 September 2013, accessed 1 August 2015: www.theguardian.com/world/2013/sep/09/us-syria-chemical-weapons-attack-john-kerry.

Wintour, Patrick, 'Labour Reshuffle: A Victory for Talent or a Purge of the Blairites?', *Guardian*, 7 October 2013, accessed 1 August 2015: www.theguardian.com/politics/2013/oct/07/labour-reshuffle-victory-talent-blairites.

Withnall, Adam, 'David Cameron Brands Jeremy Corbyn a "Terrorist Sympathiser" For Opposing Syria Airstrikes', *Independent*, 2 December 2015, accessed 5 December 2015: www.independent.co.uk/news/uk/politics/david-cameron-calls-jeremy-corbyn-a-terrorist-sympathiser-for-opposing-syria-air-strikes-a6756731.html.

Withnall, Adam, 'Former Lib Dem Leader Paddy Ashdown "Ashamed" by Commons Vote Against War', *Independent*, 30 August 2013, accessed 1 August 2015: www.independent.co.uk/news/uk/politics/former-lib-dem-leader-paddy-ashdown-ashamed-by-commons-vote-against-war-8791383.html.

Withnall, Adam, 'Vladimir Putin Announces Russia Will Add More Than 40 Intercontinental Ballistic Missiles To Nuclear Arsenal In 2015', *Independent*, 17 June 2015, accessed 28 November 2015: www.independent.co.uk/news/world/europe/vladimir-putin-announces-russia-will-add–40-new-ballistic-missiles-to-nuclear-arsenal-in-2015-10323304.html.

YouGov, 'Iraq Trends Poll', 18 March 2003, accessed 1 August 2015: http://iis.yougov.co.uk/extranets/ygarchives/content/pdf/trackerIraqTrends_060403.pdf.

YouGov, 'Syria and the Shadow of Iraq', 28 August 2013, accessed 1 August 2015: https://yougov.co.uk/news/2013/08/28/syria-and-shadow-iraq.

Interviews

Armstrong, Baron Robert, interview with Sam Goodman, 18 December 2013, House of Lords.

Beckett, Rt. Hon. Dame Margaret, MP, interview with Sam Goodman, 22 May 2012, House of Commons.

Boyce, Baron Admiral Sir Michael, interview with Sam Goodman, 23 March 2014, House of Lords.

Burt, Rt. Hon. Alistair, interview with Sam Goodman, 30 January 2014, House of Commons.

Butler, Baron Robin, interview with Sam Goodman, 29 October 2013, private residence.

Campbell, Rt. Hon. Sir Menzies, MP, interview with Sam Goodman, 9 September 2013, House of Commons.

Carrington, Rt. Hon. Baron Peter, interview with Sam Goodman, 19 April 2012, House of Lords.

Clarke, Rt. Hon. Charles, interview with Sam Goodman, 31 October 2013, private offices.

Dannatt, Baron General Sir Richard, interview with Sam Goodman, 21 October 2014, House of Lords.
Donoughue, Baron Bernard, interview with Sam Goodman, 26 November 2013, House of Lords.
Dugher, Michael, MP, interview with Sam Goodman, 10 July 2012, House of Commons.
Falconer, Rt. Hon. Baron Charles, interview with Sam Goodman 12 July 2012, private offices.
Fox, Rt. Hon. Liam, MP, interview with Sam Goodman, 31 January 2014, House of Commons.
Guthrie, Baron Field Marshall Sir Charles, interview with Sam Goodman, 7 March 2013, private offices.
Hague, Rt. Hon. William, MP, interview with Sam Goodman, 2 March 2015, House of Commons.
Heseltine, Rt. Hon. Baron Michael, interview with Sam Goodman, 30 May 2012, Department for Business, Innovation and Skill.
Hoon, Rt. Hon. Geoff, interview with Sam Goodman, 9 January 2014, private offices.
Howard, Rt. Hon. Baron Michael, interview with Sam Goodman, 5 November 2013, House of Lords.
Howe, Rt. Hon. Baron Geoffrey, interview with Sam Goodman, 25 June 2012, House of Lords.
Howell, Rt. Hon. Baron David, interview with Sam Goodman, 15 May 2012, the Foreign Office.
Hurd, Rt. Hon. Baron Douglas, interview with Sam Goodman, 18 June 2012, private residence.
Kaufman, Rt. Hon. Sir Gerald, MP, interview with Sam Goodman, 11 October 2013, House of Commons.
King, Rt. Hon. Baron Tom, interview with Sam Goodman, 31 January 2014, House of Lords.
Malloch-Brown, Rt. Hon. Baron Mark, interview with Sam Goodman, 21 August 2014, private offices.
Manning, Sir David, interview with Sam Goodman, 13 July 2012, private offices.
Meyer, Sir Christopher, interview with Sam Goodman, 7 February 2014, private offices.
Miliband, Rt. Hon. David, MP, interview with Sam Goodman, 20 March 2012, House of Commons.
O'Donnell, Baron Gus, interview with Sam Goodman, 4 September 2012, private offices.
Owen, Rt. Hon. Baron David, interview with Sam Goodman, 11 May 2012, private offices.
Powell, Jonathan, interview with Sam Goodman, 14 September 2012, private offices.

Richards, Baron General Sir David, interview with Sam Goodman, 2 December 2014, private offices.
Rifkind, Rt. Hon. Malcolm, MP, interview with Sam Goodman, 18 April 2012, House of Commons.
Sheinwald, Sir Nigel, interview with Sam Goodman, 3 July 2012, House of Commons.
Stirrup, Baron Air Marshall Sir Jock, interview with Sam Goodman, 11 February 2014, House of Lords.
Straw, Rt. Hon. Jack, MP, interview with Sam Goodman, 3 July 2012, House of Commons.
Walker, Baron Field Marshall Sir Michael, interview with Sam Goodman, 3 February 2014, House of Lords.
Wall, Sir Stephen, interview with Sam Goodman, 7 June 2012, private offices.

Hansard

Benn, Rt. Hon. Hilary, MP, Speech in the House of Commons, 'Syria Debate', *Hansard* (HC Deb, 2 December 2015, col. 486).
Bennett, Fredric, MP, Point of Order House of Commons, 'Vietnam', *Hansard* (HC Deb, 4 March 1965, vol. 707, col. 1530).
Blair, Rt. Hon. Tony, MP, Speech in the House of Commons, 'Afghanistan', *Hansard* (HC Deb, 4 October 2001, col. 672).
Blair, Rt. Hon. Tony, MP, Speech in the House of Commons, 'Iraq Debate', *Hansard* (HC Deb, 18 March 2003, cols 762, 763, 764 and 768)
Blair, Rt. Hon. Tony, MP, Speech in the House of Commons, 'Kosovo', *Hansard* (HC Deb, 23 March 1999, col. 165).
Bottomley, Rt. Hon. Arthur, MP, Statement to the House of Commons, 'Rhodesia', *Hansard* (HC Deb, 8 March 1965, vol. 708, cols 35–40).
Brown, Rt. Hon. Gordon, MP, Speech in the House of Commons, 'Constitutional Reform', *Hansard* (HC Deb, 3 July 2007, col. 815).
Browne, Rt. Hon. Des, MP, Statement in the House of Commons, 'Afghanistan', *Hansard* (HC Deb, 1 April 2008, col. 628).
Butler, Lord Robin, Speech in the House of Lords, 'Iraq', *Hansard* (HL Deb, 22 February 2007, col. 1230).
Callaghan, Rt. Hon. James, MP, Speech in the House of Commons, 'European Communities Bill Debate', *Hansard* (HC Deb, 28 October 1971, vol. 823, cols 2076–217).
Cameron, Rt. Hon. David, MP, Speech in the House of Commons, 'Libya', *Hansard* (HC Deb, 5 September 2011, col. 24).
Cameron, Rt. Hon. David, MP, Speech in the House of Commons, 'Syria Debate', *Hansard* (HC Deb, 29 August 2013, cols 1437, 1428, 1425, 1436).

Cameron, Rt. Hon. David, MP, Speech in Parliament, 'Iraq Debate', *Hansard* (HC Deb, 26 September 2014, cols 1259, 1262 and 1263).

Cameron, Rt. Hon. David, MP, Speech in the House of Commons, 'Syria Statement', *Hansard* (HC Deb, 26 November 2015, col. 1491).

Cameron, Rt. Hon. David, MP, Speech in the House of Commons, 'Syria Debate', *Hansard* (HC Deb, 2 December 2015, cols 323 and 333).

Campbell, Rt. Hon. Sir Menzies, MP, Speech in the House of Commons, 'Sierra Leone', *Hansard* (HC Deb, 8 May 2000, vol. 349, cols 518–29).

Davis, Rt. Hon. David, MP, Speech in the House of Commons, 'Syria Debate', *Hansard* (HC Deb, 29 August 2013, col. 1469).

Duncan Smith, Rt. Hon. Iain, MP, Speech in the House of Commons, 'Iraq Debate', *Hansard* (HC Deb, 18 March 2003, cols 778 and 779).

Galloway, George, MP, Speech in the House of Commons, 'Syria Debate', *Hansard* (HC Deb, 29 August 2013, col. 1471).

Hague, Rt. Hon. William, MP, Speech in the House of Commons, 'Kosovo', *Hansard* (HC Deb, 23 March 1999, col. 163).

Heath, Rt. Hon. Edward, MP, Speech in the House of Commons, 'European Communities Bill', *Hansard* (HC Deb, 28 October 1971, vol. 823, cols 2076–217).

Kawczynski, Daniel, MP, Speech in the House of Commons, 'Syria Debate', *Hansard* (HC Deb, 29 August 2013, col. 1430).

Kennedy, Rt. Hon. Charles, MP, Speech in the House of Commons, 'Iraq Debate', *Hansard* (HC Deb, 18 March 2003, cols 784–5).

Llwyd, Elfyn, MP, Speech in the House of Commons, 'Syria Debate', *Hansard* (HC Deb, 29 August 2013, col. 1464).

Maude, Rt. Hon. Francis, MP, Speech in the House of Commons, 'Sierra Leone', *Hansard* (HC Deb, 8 May 2000, vol. 349, cols 518–29).

McDonald, Andy, MP, Speech in the House of Commons, 'Syria Debate', *Hansard* (HC Deb, 2 December 2015, col. 340).

McDonnell, John, MP, Speech in the House of Commons, 'Syria Debate', *Hansard* (HC Deb, 29 August 2013, col. 1462).

Miliband, Rt. Hon. Edward, MP, Speech in the House of Commons, 'Syria Debate', *Hansard* (HC Deb, 29 August 2013, cols 1443, 1440, 1142).

Miliband, Rt. Hon. Edward, MP, Speech in Parliament, 'Iraq Debate', *Hansard* (HC Deb, 26 September 2014, cols 1270 and 1274).

Owen, Albert, MP, Speech in the House of Commons, 'Syria Debate', *Hansard* (HC Deb, 29 August 2013, col. 1484).

Rifkind, Rt. Hon. Sir Malcolm, MP, Speech in the House of Commons, 'Syria Debate', *Hansard* (HC Deb, 29 August 2013, col. 1442).

Robertson, Angus, MP, Speech in the House of Commons, 'Syria Debate', *Hansard* (HC Deb, 29 August 2013, col. 1457).

Ruddock, Dame Joan, MP, Speech in the House of Commons, 'Syria Debate', *Hansard* (HC Deb, 29 August 2013, col. 1428).

Straw, Rt. Hon. Jack, MP, Speech in the House of Commons, 'Iraq', *Hansard* (HC Deb, 26 February 2003, col. 265).
Straw, Rt. Hon. Jack, MP, House of Commons Speech, 'Syria Debate', *Hansard* (HC Deb, 29 August 2013, col. 1451).
Wilson, Rt. Hon. Harold, MP, Speech in the House of Commons, 'European Communities Bill Debate', *Hansard* (HC Deb, 28 October 1971, vol. 823, cols 2076–217).
Wilson, Rt. Hon. Harold, MP, Statement to the House of Commons, 'Rhodesia', *Hansard* (HC Deb, 1 November 1965, vol. 718, cols 629–48).
Wilson, Rt. Hon. Harold, MP, Speech in the House of Commons, 'Vietnam', *Hansard* (HC Deb, 17 May 1966, vol. 728, C1119).
Wilson, Rt. Hon. Harold, MP, Speech in the House of Commons, 'Vietnam', *Hansard* (HC Deb, 29 June 1966, vol. 730, cols 1796–7).

Government and NGO documents, statements and reports (reference)

Attorney General, Office of, Goldsmith Note to the Prime Minister, Iraq Inquiry, 30 July 2002, accessed 1 August 2015: www.iraqinquiry.org.uk/media/46499/Goldsmith-note-to-PM-30July2002.pdf.
Blair, Tony, Speech to the Chicago Economic Club, 22 April 1999, PBS Online, accessed 1 August 2015: www.pbs.org/newshour/bb/international-jan-june99-blair_doctrine4–23/.
Blair, Tony, 'Tony Blair's Statement', *Guardian*, 7 October 2001, accessed 1 August 2015: www.theguardian.com/world/2001/oct/07/afghanistan.terrorism11.
Blair, Tony, 'Tony Blair's Statement to the Iraq Inquiry', Iraq Inquiry, 14 January 2011, accessed 1 August 2015: www.iraqinquiry.org.uk/media/50743/Blair-statement.pdf.
Bremer, Paul, Statement by Ambassador Bremer to the Iraq Inquiry, Iraq Inquiry, 18 May 2010, accessed 1 August 2015: www.iraqinquiry.org.uk/background/statement-bremer.aspx.
British Government, 'Iraq's Weapons Of Mass Destruction: The Assessment Of The British Government', BBC News, 24 September 2002, accessed 1 August 2015: http://news.bbc.co.uk/nol/shared/spl/hi/middle_east/02/uk_dossier_on_iraq/pdf/iraqdossier.pdf.
British Government, 'The Coalition: Our Programme of Government', May 2010, accessed 1 August 2015: https://www.gov.uk/government/uploads/system/uploads/attachment_data/file/78977/coalition_programme_for_government.pdf.
Brown, Gordon, Transcript of Oral Evidence to Iraq Inquiry, Iraq Inquiry, 5 March 2010, p. 60 accessed 1 August 2015: www.iraqinquiry.org.uk/media/45558/100305-brown-final.pdf.

Bush, George W., 2002 State of the Union Address to the United States Congress, 29 January 2002, accessed 1 August 2015: http://georgewbush-whitehouse.archives.gov/news/releases/2002/01/20020129-11.html.

Bush, George W., Transcript of Speech to a Special Joint Session of the United States Congress, 20 September 2001, accessed 1 August 2015: www.washingtonpost.com/wpsrv/nation/specials/attacked/transcripts/bushaddress_092001.html.

Cabinet Office, 'Correspondence: Syria, Reported Chemical Weapons Use, Joint Intelligence Committee Letter, 29 August 2013, accessed 1 August 2015: www.gov.uk/government/publications/syria-reported-chemical-weapons-use-joint-intelligence-committee-letter.

Cameron, David, 'David Cameron Libya Statement In Full', politics. co. uk, 5 September 2011, accessed 1 August 2015: www.politics.co.uk/comment-analysis/2011/09/05/david-cameron-libya-statement-in-full.

Cook, Robin, 'Speech on the Government's Ethical Foreign Policy', *Guardian*, Monday 12 May 1997, accessed 1 August 2015: www.theguardian.com/world/1997/may/12/indonesia.ethicalforeignpolicy.

Cook, Robin, 'Cook Resignation: The Letters', BBC News, 17 March 2003, accessed 1 August 2015: http://news.bbc.co.uk/1/hi/uk_politics/2858475.stm.

CVCE, 'Declaration of the Nine Foreign Ministers, 6th November 1973, in Brussels, on the Situation in the Middle East', Press & Information Office of the Federal Government of Germany, 1977, Bonn, Germany, accessed 1 August 2015: www.cvce.eu/content/publication/1999/1/1/a08b36bc-6d29-475c-aadb0f71c59dbc3e/publishable_en.pdf).

European Union External Action, 'Joint Statement: Final Declaration on the Results of the Syria Talks in Vienna as Agreed by Participants', 30 October 2015, accessed 5 December 2015: http://eeas.europa.eu/statements-eeas/2015/151030_06.htm

Foreign and Commonwealth Office, 'Saddam Hussein: Crimes And Human Rights Abuses- A Report On the Human Cost Of Saddam's Policies by the Foreign & Commonwealth Office', BBC News, 2 December 2002, accessed 1 August 2015: http://news.bbc.co.uk/nol/shared/spl/hi/middle_east/02/uk_human_rights_dossier_on_iraq/pdf/iraq_human_rights.pdf.

Goldsmith, Rt. Hon. Baron Peter, Oral Evidence Transcript, Iraq Inquiry, 27 January 2010, p. 183, accessed 1 August 2015: www.iraqinquiry.org.uk/media/45317/20100127goldsmith-final.pdf.

Hammond, Rt. Hon. Philip, MP, 'Press Release: Foreign Secretary Condemns Assad's Use of Chlorine in Syria', Foreign and Commonwealth Office, 10 September 2014, accessed 1 August 2015: https://www.gov.uk/government/news/foreign-secretary-condemns-assads-use-of-chlorine-in-syria.

Hague, Rt. Hon. William, MP, 'Written Statement on Historical Role of UK Companies in Supplying Dual Use Chemicals to Syria', Foreign and Commonwealth Office, 9 July 2014, accessed 1 August 2015:

www.gov.uk/government/speeches/statement-on-the-historical-role-of-uk-companies-in-supplying-dual-use-chemicals-to-syria.

House of Commons Foreign Affairs Committee, 'The Extension of Offensive British Military Operations to Syria', 29 October 2015, accessed 28 November 2015: www.publications.parliament.uk/pa/cm201516/cmselect/cmfaff/457/457.pdf.

International Monetary Fund, 'London Summit Leaders' Statement', 2 April 2009, accessed 1 August 2015: https://www.imf.org/external/np/sec/pr/2009/pdf/g20_040209.pdf .

Iraq Coalition Provisional Authority, Iraq Coalition Provisional Authority Order Number Two: Dissolution of Entities, Council on Foreign Relations, 23 August 2003, accessed 1 August 2015: www.cfr.org/iraq/iraq-coalition-provisional-authority-order-number-two-dissolution-entities/p30236.

Labour Party, '1964 Labour Manifesto', 16 October 1964, accessed 1 August 2015: www.politicsresources.net/area/uk/man/lab64.htm.

Miliband, Ed, 'Full Text of Ed Miliband's Foreign Policy Speech at Chatham House', Labourlist, 24 April 2014, accessed 1 August 2015: http://labourlist.org/2015/04/full-text-of-ed-milibands-foreign-policy-speech-at-chatham-house/.

The Organization for the Prohibition of Chemical Weapons and the United Nations, 'Ninety-six Percent of Syria's Declared Chemical Weapons Destroyed – UN-OPCW Mission Chief"', 4 September 2014, accessed 1 August 2015: http://opcw.unmissions.org/AboutOPCWUNJointMission/tabid/54/ctl/Details/mid/651/ItemID/341/Default.aspx.

Prime Minister's Office, 'Guidance: Chemical Weapon Use by Syrian Regime, UK Government Legal Position', Cabinet Office, 29 August 2013, accessed 1 August 2015: www.gov.uk/government/publications/chemical-weapon-use-by-syrian-regime-uk-government-legal-position/chemical-weapon-use-by-syrian-regime-uk-government-legal-position-html-version.

Rule 74 of the International Committee of the Red Cross, incorporating the Hague Declaration concerning Asphyxiating Gases, the Geneva Gas Protocol, the Chemical Weapons Convention and the Statute of the International Criminal Court.

Security Service Mi5, 'The Wilson Plot', accessed 1 August 2015: www.mi5.gov.uk/home/about-us/who-we-are/mi5-history/the-cold-war/the-wilson-plot.html.

The United Nations, 'Six-Point Proposal of the Joint Special Envoy of the United Nations and the League of Arab States', 14 April 2012, accessed 1 August 2015: www.un.org/en/peacekeeping/documents/six_point_proposal.pdf.

The United Nations Security Council, United Nations Resolution 216, 12 November 1965 accessed 1 August 2015: www.un.org/en/ga/search/view_doc.asp?symbol=S/RES/216(1965).

The United Nations Security Council, UN Resolution 217, 20 November 1965 accessed 1 August 2015: www.un.org/en/ga/search/view_doc.asp?symbol=S/RES/216(1965).

The United Nations Security Council, United Nations Security Council Resolution 678, passed 29 November 1990, accessed 1 August 2015: www.un.org/Docs/scres/1990/scres90.htm.

The United Nations Security Council, Resolution 1441, 8 November 2002, accessed 1 August 2015: www.un.org/Depts/unmovic/documents/1441.pdf.

The United Nations Security Council, United Nations Resolution 1973, 17 March 2011, accessed 1 August 2015: www.un.org/en/ga/search/view_doc.asp?symbol=S/RES/1973(2011).

United Nations Security Council, UN Resolution 2249, 20 November 2015, accessed 5 December 2015: www.un.org/en/ga/search/view_doc.asp?symbol=S/RES/2249 per cent282015 per cent29.

United States Congress, Authorization for Use of Military Force Bill, S.J.Res.23 (107th Congress), 18 September 2001, accessed 1 August 2015: www.govtrack.us/congress/bills/107/sjres23.

United States Congress, 'The Tonkin Gulf Resolution' (H.J. RES 1145), 4 August 1964, accessed 1 August 2015: www.ourdocuments.gov/doc.php?doc=98.

Archive material

British National Archives, London, CAB 129/158, The Prime Minister's Office, 'The European Economic Communities Memorandum', 2 August 1971.

British National Archives, London, CAB 129/182/18, The Cabinet Office, 'Memorandum: EEC White Paper – Harold Wilson', 21 March 1975.

British National Archives, London, PREM 13/104 , 'The Prime Minister's Visit to the United States and Canada', 6–10 December 1964, p. 31*Foreign Relations of the United States, 1964–1968*, See also 'Memorandum of Conversation', 8 December 1964, in , vol. I, p. 985.

British National Archives, London, UK, PREM 13/693, TNAUK, Telegram from Philip Noel-Baker, 'Telegram from Philip Noel-Baker to Michael Stewart', 22 March 1965.

British National Archives, London, PREM 15/62, Memo by William Neld, 'EEC Negotiations 1970: Memo to Prime Minister William Neld', 8 December 1970.

British National Archives, London, PREM 15/62, Memo by Willie Whitelaw, 'EEC Negotiations 1970: Memo – Willie Whitelaw, Lord President of the Council – 10 Reasons for joining EEC', 19 June 1970–30 December 1970.

British National Archives, London, PREM 15/62, The Prime Minister's Office, 'EEC Negotiations 1970: Memo Negotiating Objectives', 19 June 1970–30 December 1970.

British National Archives, London, PREM 15/62, The Prime Minister's Office, 'EEC Negotiations1970: Minutes of Meeting with Canadian Premier', 16 December 1970.

British National Archives, London, PREM 15/62, The Prime Minister's Office, 'EEC Negotiations 1970: Secret Memo 1970', 19 June 1970–30 December 1970.

British National Archives, London, PREM 15/62, The Prime Minister's Office, 'EEC Negotiations 1970: Telegram Heath to Brandt', 12 December 1970.

British National Archives, London, PREM 15/62, The Prime Minister's Office, 'EEC Negotiations 1970: Minute of meeting with Pompidou & Soames to Foreign Office', 23 November 1970.

British National Archives, London, PREM 15/370, Memo from Nicholas Barrington, 'UK EEC Application: Strategic Memo About the Meeting With Pompidou', 21 April 1971.

British National Archives, London, PREM 15/370, Memo by Anthony Barber, 'UK EEC Application: Chancellor of Duchy Memo to No. 10', 27 March 1971–21 April 1971.

British National Archives, London, PREM 15/372, The Prime Minister's Office, 'EEC Policy Memo 1971: Telegram to Downing St Copy of PM's talks with Pompidou, A M Palliser', 10 May 1971–24 May 1971.

British National Archives, London, PREM 15/1981, Telegram from Edward Heath, 'UK/US Relations Telegrams 1973: Heath to Nixon', 25 April 1973.

British National Archives, London, PREM 16/19, Cabinet Office, 'Record of Telephone Conversation between the Prime Minister and the Prime Minister of Turkey', 25 July 1974.

British National Archives, London, PREM 16/74, The Prime Minister's Office, 'Extract of Note on the Lunch Given by President of France for the Prime Minister', 18 July 1974.

British National Archives, London, PREM 16/74, The Prime Minister's Office, 'Record of Meeting Between the British Prime Minister and French President Giscard d'Estaing', 19 July 1974.

British National Archives, London, PREM 16/76, German Foreign Ministry, 'Extracts from the German Chancellor's remarks on British Membership of EEC, Bonn, Germany', 16 November 1974.

British National Archives, London, PREM 16/76, The Prime Minister's Office, 'Summary Note of Foreign Secretary meeting with French President at Elysee Palace', 19 November 1974.

British National Archives, London, PREM 19/944, The Prime Minister's Office, 'Telegram from President Reagan to the Prime Minister', 7 August 1981.

British National Archives, London, PREM 19/1656, The Prime Minister's Office, 'Record of the Meeting Between the British Prime Minister and US President Reagan at Camp David', 22 December 1984.

Lyndon Baines Johnson Presidential Library, Texas, USA, McGeorge Bundy, 'McGeorge Bundy Memo to President Johnson', 22 March 1965, in vol. 4, Memoranda to the President, NSF.

Index

9/11, 1, 189–93, 195–8, 247, 254, 315

Afghanistan 21, 128, 139, 188–9, 191–5, 199, 220–2, 237–43, 253–4, 261, 263, 265 266–9, 271, 298
Ainsworth, Bob 222, 241
Alexander, Douglas 20–1, 236, 242–3, 245
Alexander, Heidi 320
Al Qaeda 189, 191–4, 198–9, 219, 241, 243, 275, 278, 282, 287
Annan, Kofi 174, 204, 278
Arab League 6–7, 10, 271, 278–9, 289, 312
Arab Spring 5, 269, 298
Argentina 118–19, 120–4
Armstrong, Robert 74, 79, 127, 140, 141
Ashdown, Paddy 14, 24, 150, 178, 180, 269, 288
Ashton, Cathy 251, 270
Assad, Basher-Al 5–7, 13, 23, 25–7, 277–86, 293, 296–8, 311–12, 318, 320–1
Australia 38, 69, 121

Beckett, Margaret 141, 206, 233, 246
Benn, Hilary 317, 319–20
Benn, Tony 55, 92–3, 103, 107, 149, 163
Berlusconi, Silvio 191, 273
Biafra 50–1
  see also Nigeria
Bin Laden, Osama 189, 191–3, 282
  see also 9/11; Al Qaeda
Blair, Tony 23–4, 28, 109, 173, 251–2, 254, 265, 274, 292, 309
  and 2005 Cabinet re-shuffle, 222
  and 9/11, 188–9
  and the Americans/public opinion on Iraq, 212–13
  and Bill Clinton and Iraq, 174, 175, 176
  and the Cabinet on Iraq, 210–11
  and Clare Short, 221
  and Crawford, 201
  and departure, 231
  and EU Presidency, 250
  and Gordon Brown distancing himself, 234–5, 238
  and Iraq, 199–200
  and Iraq intelligence, 215
  and Iraq military preparations, 216–19
  and Jack Straw, 204–5
  and Kosovo, 179–84
  and the Labour Party on Iraq, 211–12
  and legacy, 223
  and legality of Iraq, 209
  and No. 10 Foreign Policy Unit, 196–8
  and the Parliamentary vote, 213–14
  and power sharing with Gordon Brown, 232–3
  and Robin Cook, 178
  and Sierra Leone, 185–7
  and sofa government, 206–8
  and troop deployment, 220
  and United Nations, 202–3
  and War on Terror and Afghanistan, 190–5
Blix, Hans 201–3
Bosnia Herzegovina 15, 160–8, 178–9, 184, 269
Boyce, Michael 23, 205, 209, 213, 216–18
Brandt, Willy 65, 67, 88
Brown, George 43, 49–51, 53–6, 104
Brown, Gordon 21, 29, 222, 252, 254, 255, 309
  and Afghanistan, 239–44
  and the appointment of EU High Representative for Foreign Affairs, 250–1
  and Barack Obama, 244–5
  and Cabinet re-shuffle, 233
  and constitutional reform, 234
  and the Copenhagen Summit, 248–50
  and David Miliband, 236–7
  and defence spending, 220

and an early election, 236
and the financial crisis, 246–7
G20, 247–8
and Iraq 238–9
and Iraq Cabinet attendance, 211
and No. 10 layout, 235
and Parliament's right to vote on war, 28
position on Iraq 232–3
Prime Minister, 231
and the Prime Ministerial debates, 253
Browne, Des 222, 239
Burt, Alistair 16, 18, 21, 263, 279, 281, 289, 291
Bush, George H. 99, 148–9, 151–2, 165, 189
Bush, George W. 188–93, 198–203, 205, 208–10, 212–13, 215–16, 218, 220, 222–3, 238–9, 243–4, 246
Butler, Rab 43–4
Butler, Robin 148, 206
  Butler Report 205–6

Cabinet 3, 40, 44, 46–50, 52, 54, 56, 64, 79–80, 90–2, 94, 99, 103–8, 113, 115, 120, 131, 141–2, 147–50, 154–5, 160, 163, 166, 179, 185, 191, 196–7, 203, 205–10, 231–2, 235, 242, 270, 281, 291
  Cabinet government 78, 80, 207, 234
  Cabinet Office 99, 148, 185, 197, 235, 242
  Cabinet Office Briefing Room A (COBRA) 185, 235–6, 246, 265, 286
Callaghan, James 29, 114, 115, 133, 154, 164, 252, 292, 309
  and arms to South Africa, 49
  Cabinet style, 110–11
  and the Cyprus crisis, 95–8
  and the economic crisis, 104–08
  and the European Economic Community Referendum, 91–2
  and the Falkland Islands, 119
  Foreign Secretary, 86
  and Jimmy Carter, 110
  and the Inner Cabinet, 55
  and the inquiry into MI5 surveillance of Wilson, 99
  and naval exercises with South Africa, 94
  and opposition to the European Economic Community, 69
  Prime Minister, 103
  and the renegotiation of membership of the European Economic Community, 87–91
  and the Six Day War, 51
  and summitry diplomacy, 109
Cameron, David 3, 298, 299, 309–10, 312
  and Afghanistan, 265–8
  and the Chemical Weapons Agreement with Russia, 26
  and the Coalition Government, 17, 290
  and Barack Obama, 245
  and the Foreign Office, 262–3
  and helicopters in Afghanistan, 241
  and the House of Commons vote on Airstrikes (ISIS) in Iraq, 287–8
  and the House of Commons vote on Airstrikes (ISIS) in Syria, 297, 315–18
  and the House of Commons Vote on Syria, 5 –9, 12–4, 16, 19, 22–4, 27, 29
  and the ISIS surge in Iraq, 285–6
  and Libya, 269–74, 276–7
  and the National Security Council, 263–5
  Prime Minister, 261–2
  and the Prime Ministerial debates, 253
  and the reconstruction of Libya, 274–5
  and the renegotiation of European Union Membership, 290–2
  and the right of parliament to vote on war, 28
  and Russia and the Annexation of Crimea, 292, 294–5, 313
  and Syria, 277, 280–1
  and William Hague, 289–90
  and the withdrawal of troops from Iraq, 239
Campbell, Menzies 15–16, 19, 185, 214, 290
Canada 52, 121, 163
Carrington, Peter 76–8, 114–18, 120–1, 141, 161–2, 164, 263
Carter, Jimmy 106, 108–10, 118, 128
Castle, Barbara 49, 55, 92

Central Policy Review Staff (CPRS) 79–80, 98, 127
Cheney, Richard 189–90, 198, 202, 217
China 12, 40, 74–5, 125–7, 175, 179–80, 189, 192, 247–9, 272, 279
see also Hong Kong
Chirac, Jacques 204, 209
Churchill, Winston 44, 78, 115, 147, 223, 237
Clarke, Charles 18, 176, 204, 206, 208, 211, 233
Clarke, Ken 16, 163, 281, 291
Clarke, Richard 189, 198
Clegg, Nick 6, 18–19, 253, 261, 270, 273, 281, 287, 290
Clinton, Bill 165, 173–5, 178–83, 188–9, 199, 209
Clinton, Hilary 237, 271, 273, 281
Coalition Government the, 18, 261–4, 266, 290, 297, 309
Cold War 35–6, 129, 138–9, 161, 163, 169, 295–7, 309
Commonwealth 38, 40–2, 44–5, 49, 55, 61, 65, 67, 77, 91, 93, 96, 117–18, 122, 131, 133–4
Conservative Party 18, 61–2, 76, 78, 93, 113–14, 117–18, 133, 136, 142, 147, 153–4, 156, 158, 160, 163, 262, 318
Cook, Robin 174–6, 180, 187, 204, 207, 210, 232
Craddock, Percy 127, 129, 134, 148, 162
Crimea 293–4, 296, 312–13
Croatia 161–2, 167, 177
Crosland, Anthony 104, 107
Cyprus 72, 95–8, 130

Dannatt, Richard 161, 166–7, 220–2, 238, 280, 286
De Gaulle, Charles 43, 52, 61, 63, 67
Delors Report 136, 152
Department for International Development 15, 20, 185, 205, 207, 221, 240, 275
Donoughue, Bernard 85–7, 90, 98, 111
Douglas-Home, Alec 36–7, 44, 61–2, 65, 72, 74–80, 252
Dugher, Michael 187, 237, 241, 250, 320
Duncan Smith, Iain 201, 214

Ecevit, Bulent 95–7
Eden, Anthony 28, 51–2, 56, 61–2, 78, 115, 231, 237
Egypt 5, 51–2, 72, 108–9, 192, 269, 276, 315
Elysee Place 64, 69
Erdogan, Recep 273
d'Estaing, Giscard 88–9, 108
Ethical Foreign Policy 20, 175–6, 187, 203
Eurosceptic 153–4, 158, 160, 169, 291–2
European Economic Community (EEC) 43, 54, 61–2, 64–8, 70–5, 77–8, 80, 86–93, 103, 108, 115–16, 134, 136, 139–40, 155, 158, 162
European Exchange Rate Mechanism (ERM) 136–8, 156–7
European Monetary Union (EMU) 134, 136, 154, 156
European Union (EU) 6, 24, 104, 153, 158, 164, 184, 187, 204–5, 250–1, 253, 270–1, 277, 279, 281, 290–4, 319

Falconer, Charles 181, 206–7
Falklands Islands 119–20, 123–4, 132
Falklands War 126–7, 129
Fallon, Michael 291, 321
Foot, Michael 92, 103–5
Ford, Gerald 106–7, 110
Foreign Affairs Select Committee 15, 286, 297, 311, 315, 321
Foreign Office 3, 15, 17, 21, 24, 26–7, 37, 39, 42, 53–4, 65–6, 74, 76, 80, 88, 94, 104, 107, 115–16, 119, 122, 124–7, 129, 133–42, 147, 152, 164–5, 168, 176, 184–5, 190, 196–9, 202, 205, 207, 215, 220, 233–4, 236–8, 240–1, 243, 247–8, 250, 252, 254–5, 262–3, 270, 278–9, 281, 283, 290, 309, 311
Fox, Liam 16, 265, 270, 273–4, 281, 290
France 24, 51–2, 64, 67, 88–9, 116, 132, 135, 152, 157, 163, 166, 175, 177–8, 191, 204, 247, 270–1, 273–4, 276, 278, 294, 297, 310, 315–16, 319
Free Syrian Army 277, 282–3, 287–8, 311

G20 24, 247–8, 250, 254
Gaddafi, Muammar 131–2, 192, 269–72, 274, 277, 279, 296, 312

Galtieri, Leopoldo 119, 121–2
Gates, Robert 239, 271, 274–5
General Election 39, 47, 62–3, 71, 87, 92, 108, 114, 124, 160, 222, 251–2, 261, 286, 291, 310, 322
Germany 65, 67, 88–91, 107, 110, 116, 135–6, 139–40, 157, 161–2, 164, 177, 191, 204, 271–2, 294, 297, 321
Global Financial Crisis (2008) 246, 253–4
Goldsmith, Peter 209
Gorbachev, Mikhail 138–40
Gordon Walker, Patrick 37, 40, 52–3, 55
Greece 95–7, 153
Grenada 129–31
Gulf War 147–8, 150, 152, 168, 174, 215
Guthrie, Charles 175, 183, 187, 189, 207, 223

Hague, William 5, 18, 20, 25–6, 28, 179, 252, 262–4, 271–2, 281, 283, 288–91, 309
Haig, Alexander 123
Hammond, Philip 289 291
Healey, Denis 49, 52, 55, 86, 103–5, 110, 149
Heath, Edward 29, 47, 81, 85, 110, 113–15, 121, 127, 142, 150, 232, 292
  and Alec Douglas-Home, 73–4
  and Bosnia, 163
  and the Central Policy Review Staff, 79–80, 98
  and China, 74–5
  and the Conservative Party, 61
  and the debate in the House of Commons on British membership of the European Economic Community, 67–71
  and the European Economic Community Referendum, 93
  and the Falkland Islands, 119
  and Iraq, 149
  Leader of the Opposition, 62
  and military bases East of Suez, 78
  and negotiating British membership of the European Economic Community, 63–6, 86–7
  and Richard Nixon, 63, 71
  and South Africa and South Rhodesia, 76, 77
  and the Yom Kippur War, 72–3
Heseltine, Michael 115, 141, 147, 291

Hollande, Francois 24, 267, 295, 315
Hong Kong 125–6
Hoon, Geoff 22, 193, 212, 216, 218, 222, 252
House of Commons 3, 5, 7, 16, 25, 38–9, 44, 46, 50–1, 68, 120, 210, 234, 239, 266, 272, 274, 282–3, 311–12, 321
  see also Parliament; Westminster
House of Lords 70, 173
Howard, Michael 149, 155, 262
Howe, Geoffrey 79, 114, 125–7, 131–9, 141, 252
Howell, David 78
Hurd, Douglas 15, 65, 79–80, 115, 137, 139–40, 147–9, 154–6, 159, 161–3, 167–8, 197
Hussein, Saddam 15, 148, 150–1, 174–5, 190, 198–205, 208, 213–16, 218, 220–2, 278, 282

International Law 7, 9, 11, 13, 95, 150, 179, 277, 316
International Monetary Fund (IMF) 105–7, 244, 248
The International Security Assistance Force (ISAF) 193, 241, 266–7
Iraq 1–2, 10–11, 17, 21–3, 27, 148–9, 151–2, 168, 174–5, 179, 184, 188, 198–223, 232–4, 238–40, 242–3, 245, 250, 254, 266, 269, 271–3, 275–8, 282, 284–90, 292, 298–9, 311, 313, 315–22
Islamic State of Levant and Iraq (ISIS/ISIL) 2, 27, 275, 277–8, 282–9, 296–9, 311, 313, 315–22
Israel 51–2, 72–3, 108–9, 173, 192, 197, 200
Italy 65, 89, 121, 153, 157, 177, 273

Jenkins, Roy 70, 87, 89, 93, 103–4
Johnson, Lyndon 36–42, 53, 89
Joint Intelligence Committee (JIC) 9, 22, 201, 215

Karzai, Mohammad 242–3, 267–8
Kaufman, Gerald 49, 55, 149
Kennedy, Charles 214
Kennedy, John 36, 244
Kennedy, Robert 232
Kerry, John 25
King, Martin Luther 232

King, Tom 16, 139, 148–9, 151
Kinnock, Neil 150, 158, 252
Kissinger, Henry 63, 67, 71–2, 75, 96
Kitchen Cabinet 55
Kohl, Helmut 132, 135, 139–40, 152–3, 155–7
Kosovo 177–84, 195–6, 210, 220, 222, 274
Kuanda, Kenneth 110, 134
Kuwait 15, 17, 148, 150–1, 217, 269

Labour Party 20, 35, 38–41, 44, 49–50, 53, 56, 62, 69, 76, 87–8, 92, 94, 99, 108, 141, 159, 173, 179, 200, 203–4, 211, 223, 231–2, 236, 254, 316–20, 322
Lavrov, Sergei 25
Lebanon 51, 129–31, 133, 269, 312
Liberal Democrats 6, 15, 17–9, 150, 160, 178, 185, 214, 261, 264–5, 273, 290, 318
Liberal Interventionism 20, 181, 187, 202, 218, 222
Libya 2, 5, 9, 17, 23, 131–3, 192, 269–77, 279, 287, 290, 298–9, 310–12
Lisbon Treaty 245, 250, 262

Maastricht Treaty 152, 154–62, 168–9
Macmillan, Harold 35–6, 43, 49, 61–3, 66, 76, 78, 80, 115, 122, 292
Major, John 16, 126, 138, 167, 197, 239, 262
  and Bill Clinton, 165
  and Bosnia, 160–1, 163–5
  and the Foreign Office, 168
  Foreign Secretary, 137
  and the Gulf War, 148–9
  and the Maastricht Treaty, 152–60
  Prime Minister, 147
  and the Safe Havens policy, 151–2
al-Maliki, Nouri 284–5
Malloch-Brown, Mark 17, 21, 204, 210, 221, 234, 237, 239, 241, 277–8, 281
Mandela, Nelson 134, 232
Mandelson, Peter 234–5, 245–6, 251
Manning, David 173, 178, 182, 186, 188, 191, 196–8, 217, 238
McBride, Damian 234, 245, 251
Medvedev, Dmitry 292
Merkel, Angela 246–7, 292, 295

Meyer, Christopher 175, 190, 199–200, 216–17
Miliband, David 233, 236–7, 243, 245, 247, 250–2, 254–5, 309
Miliband, Edward 6–7, 11, 13, 19–20, 22, 26, 236, 248–9, 272, 276, 286–8, 310
Milosevic, Slobodan 161, 167, 177–8, 180, 182–4
Ministry of Defence 94, 129, 151, 185–6, 207, 216, 221–2, 238, 242, 267, 273, 275, 290, 318
Mitterrand, Francois 135, 140, 152, 155–6
Mubarak, Hosni 192, 269
Mugabe, Robert 117–18, 187
multilateralism 42, 72, 131, 210, 244, 247–8, 250, 254, 288

Nasser, Gamal 51–2
National Security Council 6, 28, 234, 240, 263–5, 270–1, 273, 275, 280, 290, 297, 310
Neo-Conservatism 190, 200, 270
New Zealand 65, 67–9, 87, 121
Nigeria 50–1, 110
Nixon, Richard 63, 71–2, 74–5, 96
No. 10 Downing Street 3, 8, 12, 17, 26, 28, 35–6, 41, 44, 53, 55–6, 62, 66, 79–80, 88, 94, 98–9, 122, 125, 127, 132–5, 137, 141–2, 147, 160, 168, 176, 179, 183, 195–8, 201–2, 205, 209, 211–12, 216–17, 221–2, 231, 235, 238, 244–5, 249–52, 254, 261–4, 270–1, 280, 284, 286, 290, 292, 299, 309, 311, 313, 318
no-fly zone 22–3, 152, 164, 270, 273, 297
North Atlantic Treaty Organisation (NATO) 6, 10, 72, 96, 128, 140, 166–7, 177, 179–80, 182–4, 193, 240, 266–8, 271–4, 276, 287, 293–5, 298, 313
Northern Alliance 189, 194–5
Nott, John 116, 120, 122

Obama, Barack 5–6, 10, 24–6, 239, 243–5, 247–8, 266, 268, 271, 273–4, 280–1, 285, 292, 310, 312–13
O'Donnell, Gus 148, 196, 208, 264, 290
The Organization of the Petroleum Exporting Countries (OPEC) 52, 73, 296

Owen, David 107, 109–11, 127, 138, 164–5, 168, 220, 234, 236, 251

Parkinson, Cecil 122, 125, 137
Parliament 2, 6, 12, 14–17, 24, 26–9, 39, 44, 47, 50, 53, 56, 64–8, 70, 76, 90–2, 108, 120, 131, 149–50, 153–4, 158–60, 166, 191–2, 201, 204, 211–13, 215, 234, 239, 261, 266, 276, 281–2, 286–9, 291, 298, 310–12, 316, 320
  see also House of Commons; Westminster
Petraeus, David 239, 281
Pompidou, Georges 63, 66–7, 69, 73, 80, 88
Powell, Charles 127–8, 140, 148–9, 197
Powell, Colin 201, 205, 209, 217
Powell, Enoch 62
Powell, Jonathan 173, 175, 183, 188, 207, 210
Powell, Lucy 320
Power, Samantha 271
Prescott, John 200, 210
Putin, Vladimir 24, 292–6, 310, 313
Pym, Francis 68, 121–5

Reagan, Ronald 121–2, 128–30, 132–3, 138, 189
referendum 44, 69–70, 87, 91–2, 103–4, 114, 155–9, 177, 262, 291, 294
Reid, John 222
Responsibility to Protect 200, 271, 277
Revolutionary United Front (RUF) 184–6
Rice, Condoleezza 201, 217
Rice, Susan 271
Richards, David 264–5, 268, 274–5, 279–80, 283
Rifkind, Malcolm 19, 122, 138, 141, 153, 163, 168, 184, 208, 263
Royal Prerogative 160, 211
Rumsfeld, Donald 190, 198, 202, 212, 217–18, 220
Russia 12–14, 25–7, 35, 41–2, 50–2, 166–7, 175, 177, 179–80, 183, 189, 192, 204, 247, 272, 276–7, 279, 283, 288, 292–7, 312–13, 315–16

San Suu Kyi, Aung 232
Safe Haven (policy) 152, 166, 316, 319

Sarkozy, Nicolas 246–7, 249–50, 270–4, 312
Saudi Arabia 17, 147–8, 269, 287, 289, 295, 297
Schmidt, Helmut 88–91, 106–10
Serbia 161–2, 167, 177–8, 180, 183
Shadow Cabinet 21, 62, 74, 76, 87, 114, 316–17, 320
Sheinwald, Nigel 191, 196–8, 238, 266
Shirreff, Richard 286, 295
Short, Clare 207–8, 210, 221, 232
Sierra Leone 184–7, 195–7, 222
Smith, Ian 43–9, 56, 74, 76–7, 80, 110, 117
sofa government 205–8
South Africa 47, 49–51, 76–7, 94–5, 117–18, 133–4, 249
Southern Rhodesia 43, 46–7, 49
Soviet Union 52, 72, 75, 95, 97, 128–9, 138–9
(the) special relationship 24, 63, 71–2, 128, 245
Stewart, Michael 39, 47, 50, 53–4
Stirrup, Jock 217, 220, 240–3
Straw, Jack 22, 188, 190–2, 195–6, 204–5, 209–10, 215, 231–4, 237, 251, 254
Suez Crisis 1, 28, 51–2, 61
Summit 24, 42, 45, 52, 55, 70, 73, 87, 89–90, 98, 108–9, 116–18, 134, 136, 140–1, 152, 155, 159, 164, 178, 247–9, 254, 266–7, 271, 273, 293–5
Syria 2–3, 5–14, 17–18, 20–8, 51–2, 72, 265, 269, 276–90, 292–3, 296–9, 310–13, 315–16, 318–22

Taliban 189, 191–5, 221, 239, 242, 266–8
Thatcher, Margaret 29, 108, 147, 153, 156, 168, 179, 197, 252, 309
  and Bosnia, 164
  and the Cabinet, 141–2
  and the Cold War, 138–9
  and the European Economic Community Budget, 115–17
  and the European Economic Community Referendum, 93
  and the European Monetary Union, 136
  and the Falklands War, 119–25

and Francis Pym, 121
and Grenada, 130-1
and the Gulf War, 15, 148, 150
and Hong Kong, 125-6
and John Major, 137-8
and the Lancaster House Summit, 118
and Lebanon, 130
Leader of the Conservative Party, 113-14
and Libya, 132
and the Maastricht Treaty, 155, 158-9
and the No. 10 Foreign Policy Unit, 127
and Peter Carrington, 115, 263
and the Reunification of Germany, 139-140
and Ronald Reagan, 128-30
and South Africa, 133
and the Yom Kippur War, 72
Treasury, HM 98, 105-6, 108, 116, 127, 137, 156, 220, 234
Turkey 95-8, 151, 217, 273, 279, 287, 297, 313, 317

Ukraine 293-5, 312-13
United Nations (UN) 7-8, 11-13, 17, 19, 26, 35, 40, 47-8, 51, 73, 75-6, 95, 97-8, 121, 130, 132-3, 148-52, 161-2, 164-7, 174-5, 177-81, 183-6, 193, 195, 199-205, 208-10, 213-15, 218-19, 221-2, 234, 244-5, 248, 254, 267, 271-2, 276-9, 285, 288, 312, 315-16, 319
  United Nations Security Council 5, 7-8, 11-12, 47-8, 97-8, 121, 148, 177, 186, 193, 195, 201, 203, 277, 279, 288
United States of America (USA) 24, 36-8, 42, 51-2, 56, 63, 65, 71-3, 75, 80-1, 96, 106-9, 121, 123-4, 128-33, 139, 148, 152, 161, 165-7, 173-4, 179-80, 182-3, 190-4, 198, 201-3, 205, 212, 216-19, 238, 243, 246, 249, 253, 266-8, 271, 273-7, 279-81, 285-8, 294, 296-8, 310-11, 316

Vietnam 1, 36-42, 45, 48, 50-3, 55-6, 63, 211-12

Walker, Charles 23, 219
Wall, Stephen 115, 128, 137, 139, 147, 163, 165, 168, 176, 197
War Cabinet 122-4, 148, 264
War on Terror 1, 189, 191-2, 194-5, 199
Westminster 56, 186, 212, 284, 289, 318, 320
  see also the House of Commons; Parliament
Whitehall 28, 136, 142, 196, 239-41, 264, 275, 280, 284
Whitelaw, Willie 64, 114-15, 122
White House 17, 25, 36, 38, 41, 72, 109, 148, 165, 179, 183, 188, 192, 196, 198, 202, 204, 212, 238, 278
Wilson, Harold 3, 29, 56, 62-3, 75-6, 78, 80, 100, 104, 109, 115, 132-3, 252, 292
  and arms to Nigeria, 50-1
  and the ban on arms to South Africa, 49-50,
  and the Cyprus crisis, 95-8
  and the debate in the House of Commons on British membership of the European Economic Community, 69
  and the European Economic Community Referendum, 91-4
  and the Falkland Islands, 119
  and the Foreign Office, 53-4
  and James Callaghan, 86
  and the Kitchen Cabinet, 54-5
  and MI5 Surveillance, 99
  and negotiating British membership of the European Economic Community, 42-3
  and the No. 10 Policy Unit, 98, 127
  and opposition to selling arms to Chile, 94-5
  Prime Minister, 35, 85
  and the renegotiation of membership of the European Economic Community, 86-91, 154
  resignation, 103
  and the Six Day War, 51-3
  and Southern Rhodesia, 43-8
  and Vietnam, 36-42, 212

Yeltsin, Boris 183